PRAISE FOR *AS THEY SEE 'EM*

"Though not about home-run-hitting batters, fast-balling pitchers or pennant winning managers, this is the best baseball book of any type in years. *New York Times* reporter Bruce Weber provides a fascinating tour of the subculture of Major League umpires—how they are trained, how they live and how they think."

—*The Wall Street Journal*

"[*As They See 'Em*] is a wonderfully detailed look at the craft of umpiring. . . . I must say that reading this book has given me a new appreciation for the men in blue. . . . It seems the funniest baseball stories involve umpires."

—Jim Bouton, *The New York Times Book Review*

"[Umpiring is] a necessary, extraordinarily demanding and insufficiently appreciated craft. Now, however, comes *As They See 'Em: A Fan's Travels in the Land of Umpires* by Bruce Weber of the *New York Times*. Forests are felled to produce baseball books, about six hundred a year, most of them not worth the paper they should never have been printed on. Weber's, however, is a terrific introduction to, among much else, the rule book's Talmudic subtleties."

—George F. Will, *The Washington Post*

"A no-holds-barred insider examination of the private world of baseball umpires . . . Baseball fans will love the insightful, richly textured account. . . . [Weber's] book lifts heads-and-shoulders above other baseball tomes by putting a funny, surprising treasury of anecdotes from the sport at its entertaining core."

—*Publishers Weekly*

"[*As They See 'Em* is] a fascinating tour of what Weber calls 'umpire nation.' Here is the inside dope on what it means to perform this essential, thankless, and not especially well-paid job."

—*Boston Globe*

"The best baseball book I've read in a long time is *As They See 'Em: A Fan's Travels in the Land of Umpires* by Bruce Weber . . . So little is known about umpires, yet they live amongst us like one of those primitive societies that keep getting discovered in the jungles of Africa. The light Weber shines on them is illuminating, for their sake and for ours."

—Michael Silverman, *Boston Herald*

"Entertaining and highly informative."

—*The Christian Science Monitor*

"Bruce Weber spent three years traveling with and talking to big league umps to see what life is like for the men in blue, and his book amounts to a sociological study of an exotic tribe."

—*Sports Illustrated*

"Speaking of getting to know something about a world we know little about: I can't say enough good things about *As They See 'Em,* Bruce Weber's book about umpires and umpiring. I know I praised it last week, but I finished it the other night—terrific ending—and said to myself, 'I'd love to illuminate a darkened world the way Bruce Weber did.'"

—Peter King, SI.com

"Hugely entertaining."

—*Newsday*

"Bruce Weber's book *As They See 'Em* will not make umpires glamorous, but it may make the game as they see it finally visible. And this vivid piece of reporting comes at a time when many fans may feel that umpires, however imperfectly, have upheld the character of the game . . . while chemically infused players and disingenuous executives blighted a whole generation of baseball with suspicion."

—*The New York Times*

"A richly detailed, smart, sassy and sad account of organized baseball's itinerant—and invisible—'tribal society' of three hundred men and a couple of women . . . a feast for fans hungry for baseball lore."

—NPR.org

AS THEY SEE 'EM

A Fan's Travels
in the Land of Umpires

BRUCE WEBER

SCRIBNER

New York   London   Toronto   Sydney

SCRIBNER
A Division of Simon & Schuster, Inc.
1230 Avenue of the Americas
New York, NY 10020

Grateful acknowledgment is made for permission to reprint excerpts
from the following copyrighted works: "Yer Out!" by Charles Ghigna and test questions
from the Jim Evans Academy of Professional Umpiring by Jim Evans.

First Scribner trade paperback edition March 2010

SCRIBNER and design are registered trademarks of The Gale Group, Inc.,
used under license by Simon & Schuster, Inc., the publisher of this work.

For information about special discounts for bulk purchases,
please contact Simon & Schuster Special Sales at 1-800-456-6798
or business@simonandschuster.com.

The Simon & Schuster Speakers Bureau can bring authors to your live event.
For more information or to book an event contact the Simon & Schuster Speakers Bureau
at 1-866-248-3049 or visit our website at www.simonspeakers.com.

Manufactured in the United States of America

1   3   5   7   9   10   8   6   4   2

Library of Congress Control Number: 2008041641

ISBN 978-0-7432-9411-9
ISBN 978-0-7432-9413-3 (pbk)
ISBN 978-1-4165-4538-5 (ebook)

To the memory of my parents,
and
to Robert, Lynne, and Jake

CONTENTS

The Land of Umpires

Where do you find such a man: A man involved in a game who has the authority of a sea captain, the discretion of a judge, the strength of an athlete, the eye of a hunter, the courage of a soldier, the patience of a saint and the stoicism to withstand the abuse of the grandstand, the tension of an extra-inning game, the invective of a player and the pain of a foul tip in the throat? He must be a tough character, with endurance and the ability to keep his temper and self-control, he must be unimpeachably honest, courteous, impartial, and firm, and he must compel respect from everyone!

—Branch Rickey

Just about the first thing they teach you at umpire school is how to yank your mask off without upsetting your hat. Umpires place great stock in their appearance, and if you're trying to make a call or follow a play with your hat askew or caught in your mask straps or—the worst—spilled in the dirt, you look foolish, inept, exactly the image you don't want the ballplayers, the managers and coaches, or the fans to have of you.

Like everything else in umpiring, or at least in umpire instruction, the method for removing the mask is reasoned and precise. You keep your head straight, your eyes forward, and move your hand to your mask, not the other way around. The only reason you remove your mask in the first place is to watch a play on the field, and you never want to turn your eyes down, away from the play, even for a moment. There's no worse feeling, umpires will tell you, than looking up from an instant's distraction, seeing the ball on the ground, and not knowing how it got there.

Anyway, you grab the mask with your left hand, wrapping your thumb, forefinger, and middle finger around it at seven o'clock. You don't use your whole hand. You can't, really, because your ball-and-strike indicator is also in the left hand, held snug against the palm by the ring finger and the pinkie. So with the three available fingers, in one swift motion you pull the mask straight out from your face to clear the bill of your cap, then straight up and off. You don't toss it aside; the catcher is the only one who ever throws a mask. If you have to come out from behind the plate and run to a spot to make a call, if you have to hold up your arms to signal foul, even if you have to use your left hand and pump hard with your elbow to sell the call that a ball was touched in fair territory, you hold your mask tight.

This is all, of course, rudimentary, something a professional umpire will do with muscle memory and a shrug, the way a concertmaster will toss off a warm-up arpeggio. But the reward is real. When you do it right, with the casual adroitness that approximates instinct, it looks both graceful and aggressive, leaving you, the plate umpire, properly possessed of the authority and dignity of your office.

Naturally, for a beginner it is a harder trick to perform than it sounds, and for me, a fifty-two-year-old student umpire, it was the first of many skills that looked simple and proved annoyingly resistant to mastery. During school drills, I'd get it right a couple of times, then let my concentration slip, undoubtedly because of something else to focus on. I'd come out from behind the plate to follow the path of an outfield fly ball or to straddle the third-base line to judge a line drive fair or foul, pull off the mask, and my hat would end up on the ground—usually smack-dab on the baseline so it was marked with a telltale streak of lime—or merely jostled and tipped crooked, the bill off-center like a rapper's, or tipped forward and shading my eyes. How you can pull your mask upward and have your hat tip forward I don't know, but that it is possible I am a witness. It wasn't until school was done and I went out on the field to work an actual game and my frustration continued that I solved the problem for good (or thought I did)—by buying a hat with a narrower brim. Who knew different-size baseball-cap brims even existed?

It turns out that an ordinary baseball cap has a brim about 3¼ inches wide, with eight seams sewn into it. The brim of a base umpire's cap is a little narrower, maybe 3 inches and six seams wide, and the brim of an ordinary plate umpire's hat, which is what we were issued in school, is narrower still, 2½ inches and four seams. The gradations downward continue until you get to a kind of skullcap with a 1½-inch brim that looks like an appetizer portion of cantaloupe. Umpires call this version the beanie, and when you remove your mask, it makes you look like a refugee from the nineteenth century. But I liked the eccentricity of it and bought one.

Umpires, however, cannot afford eccentricity. Later I would discover a scene in the popular film *A League of Their Own* in which the actor Tom Hanks, playing a manager, accosts an umpire wearing the beanie. "Did anyone ever tell you you look like a penis with that little hat on?" he says. But I wasn't aware of this at the time, and the first game I wore it, I noticed the teenaged players giggling at me behind their hands. Whenever I made a call one of them didn't care for, he rolled his eyes and gave me a look—what a geek!

Immediately after the game, I went back to the store and bought a hat with a two-inch brim, and when I came back the next day to work a game in the same league, I held much more authority in the eyes of the players. Or so it seemed to me, which is really all that mattered.

At this point perhaps you are thinking, okay, taking the mask off, enough already. This is far too much detail about a mundane thing. And that's correct, except that the process I just described is a perfect analog of learning to be an umpire. You master the fundamentals, you cast them off when they don't serve, and in the end you accommodate yourself to the game and its participants. It turns out you're not alone out there. It only feels that way.

The impetus for this book was a visit I made in January 2005 to the Jim Evans Academy of Professional Umpiring in Kissimmee, Florida, in order to write a story for the *New York Times,* where I work as a reporter. I thought it would be a lark, a chance to talk baseball rules and baseball trivia—I'm the kind of baseball fan who has never gotten over his boyhood obsession, who reads the sports page before the front page and pores over box scores as though they were hieroglyphic finds—not to mention a chance to wear short sleeves in midwinter.

But what I found there in three days of observing—the whole course of instruction runs five weeks—was weird and intriguing, an amalgam of strict vocational schooling in subject matter as concrete as auto mechanics and behavioral instruction as delicate and interpretative as you'll find in any acting workshop. Moreover, virtually everything I saw was new to me.

The experience persuaded me to write two more stories for the paper that year about umpiring. For one, I went on the road with a crew of Double A umpires, three young men locked together for a season, traveling long distances in a van packed with their belongings through Texas, Missouri, Kansas, and Arkansas. For the other, I met in major league ballparks and four-star hotels with Bruce Froemming, then the senior umpire in the major leagues.

I came away from these three stories convinced that a land of umpires exists, that it has citizens, laws, and a culture, and that it is exotic enough—both in the context of baseball and the context of, well, the known world—to warrant further exploring. Indeed, the presumption of this book is that professional umpires are an unusually isolated and circumscribed group, sort of like the inhabitants of a remote country that few people have ever visited, and that I am the sociologist who was dispatched to send back word of what life is like there.

I spent just about all of 2006 and 2007 and part of 2008 in the land of umpires, beginning when I went back to the Evans academy and enrolled as a student in the five-week program. From then on I went where the tales of professional umpires took me, sort of like a ball bouncing erratically across a pebble-strewn infield. It wasn't a comprehensive investigation, but for the most part it was a lot of fun.

Among other places, my travels took me to Cocoa, Florida, where a team of former professional umpires was evaluating umpire-school graduates for jobs in the minor leagues; to Cedar City, Utah, where a former air force engineer, Grant Secrist, was keeping alive his quest to create a simulator, akin to the one used by fighter pilots, to train major league umpires in calling balls and strikes; to the exurbs of Phoenix, Arizona, and the farm country of Ohio, homes of two former umpires—Don Denkinger and Larry Barnett, respectively—who made two of the most controversial calls in World Series history; to southern Connecticut to visit with the candid ex-commissioner of baseball, Fay Vincent; and to central California, where Doug Harvey, the legendary National League umpire who narrowly missed being the ninth umpire inducted into the Hall of Fame in 2007, waxed formidable and egocentric about what it takes to make it in the major leagues.

I spent several weeks with minor league umpires in places like Boise, Idaho; Huntsville, Alabama; Omaha, Nebraska; Bowie, Maryland; Des Moines, Iowa; Fresno, California; Trenton, New Jersey; Chattanooga, Tennessee; Wilkes-Barre, Pennsylvania; and Portland, Maine, getting to know some of the young men (and one young woman) who were willing, remarkably, to put up with endless indignities—rotten pay, long road trips, mediocre hotels, cramped locker rooms, not to mention the utter thanklessness of the umpiring task—for up to a decade or more in pursuit of the unlikely possibility of a major league job opportunity.

To talk to major league umpires, I went to spring training in Florida in 2006 and Arizona in 2006 and 2007. I went to the 2006 All-Star weekend in Pittsburgh and over two seasons spent regular-season series with different big league crews in New York, Milwaukee, Chicago, San Diego, Phoenix, and St. Louis.

I spent the 2006 World Series traveling between Detroit and St. Louis with Randy Marsh, Tim McClelland, John Hirschbeck, Mike Winters, Wally Bell, and Alfonso Marquez, the six men who'd earned the privilege of officiating the games between the Tigers and the finally triumphant Cardinals; during the 2007 World Series, I went to Denver, home of the Colorado Rockies, and sat down with five of the six crew members—Mike Everitt, Ted Barrett, Ed Montague, Laz Diaz, and Chuck Meriwether—before the Red Sox completed their four-game sweep and everybody went home.

In the end, I conducted about two hundred interviews with working and retired umpires, with players and coaches in the major and minor leagues, and with baseball executives both current and former.

Both in baseball generally and in umpire-dom particularly, these were eventful years. During this time, minor league umpires, testing the power of their fledgling union (it was incorporated in 1999), went out on strike for the first time over the issue of their pitiful salaries. Ria Cortesio, the only woman umpire in professional baseball and the sixth in history, was dismissed, after nine years in the game, by minor league officials. After a flurry of miscalls in which rightful home runs were ruled foul or in play—or fly balls that should have been foul or in play were ruled home runs—the use of instant replay to help umpires on batted balls near the home run boundaries was instituted toward the end of 2008.

The revelation, in the summer of 2007, that a National Basketball Association referee, Tim Donaghy, had been providing inside information to gamblers and betting on games he himself was officiating sent a shudder not only through basketball but other professional sports. Donaghy's actions cast suspicion on all officials, who are hardly viewed with respect under the best of circumstances; the result in baseball was that the administration of the game tightened security around the hiring and monitoring of umpires, probing into their lives with investigative checks that umpires found humiliating and invasive.

And of course the issue of performance-enhancing drugs grew steadily in prominence, culminating, on December 13, 2007, with the release of former senator George Mitchell's report on his twenty-month investigation into the use of steroids, human growth hormone, and other illegal substances by major league players, and the subsequent challenge to his findings by Roger Clemens. Clemens, possibly the preeminent right-handed pitcher in baseball history, was merely the biggest name in a 409-page document that identified eighty-six players by name and concluded that the use of these substances was widespread and that it had been at best overlooked and at worst condoned by both baseball's administration and the players' union.

Umpires essentially shrugged; they had been aware for a decade or more that some players were juicing. They could tell by the players' bodies and also by their temperaments. When I asked whether they ever thought of reporting what they saw, several umpires said yes, they thought about it, but decided not to because it wasn't their responsibility.

"If I went to a manager and said, 'Hey, do you know your third baseman is so high he's foaming at the mouth?' he'd just tell me to mind my own business," one veteran umpire told me. "'You do your fuckin' job and I'll take care of my team.' That's the mind-set."

Indeed, the reaction of many umpires to the Mitchell report was with perhaps the one essential umpire emotion: indignation. As one umpire wrote to me in an e-mail, "Why don't you ask baseball about the perception for the last ten years of the umpires being the aggressors on the field when we now know that most players were on either steroids or amphetamines?"

What was most striking about all these events was what little effect they had on the way umpires do their jobs and live their lives. As a group they are remarkably unshakable and certain of themselves. It wasn't much remarked on, but anyone who was paying attention during those years could see that the criticism of umpires was steadily escalating. On talk radio and Weblogs, the excoriation was high; the disdain from the broadcast booth was regular and severe. In one extraordinary moment in September 2007, Chipper Jones, the star third baseman for the Atlanta Braves, spurred by his displeasure with home plate umpire Rick Reed, exploded in a postgame interview:

"It's a joke," Jones said to George Henry of the Associated Press, as part of a long tirade about umpiring in the big leagues. "Major League Baseball ought to be ashamed. It's abysmal. It's awful. Not all of them but some of them. It's awful."

The level of disdain began to approach that of the 1990s, when the print media, supported by substantial dissatisfaction among baseball's club owners and administrators, led a public-opinion revolt against umpires with a wave of stories complaining about their weight, their arrogance, their lack of hustle, and their missed calls, often with animosity-provoking headlines such as "The Belligerent Men in Blue," which appeared in the *Sporting News.*

But when I brought this up to umpires, suggesting they were going through another bad patch, most of them shrugged. Nah, they said. Business as usual. Indeed, what I found in the land of umpires was a society with rock-solid traditions of both thought and deed, and if current events tended to have any effect on those traditions, it was only to harden them, to make umpires more, well, umpirish.

To speak generally, umpire nation is a place buried deep in the conservative, middle-American heart, where the prevailing and not-necessarily-consistent values are similar to those you'd find on the floor of a large factory: The union is lionized, management is held in suspicion, yet the privilege and affluence that come with managerial power are nonetheless coveted.

In umpire nation, Applebee's and Chili's are high-end establishments, steak is a gourmet meal, and, for some reason, lite beer is preferable to regular beer. It's a place where the playing of the national anthem before a ball game is serious business, where women are discomforting, Jews are a novelty, homosexuals are unwanted, and liberals tend to keep their opinions to themselves.

In umpire nation travel is so relentless that it is more deadening than broadening. It's a place where outward confidence is a must, and the mistakes that erode the foundations of self-esteem are obsessed over. The denizens are proud of what they do and resentful they aren't better paid and better recognized. They are defined and held together by the powerful bond of their singular profession, but, as in a large dysfunctional family, the differences among them are varied, deep-seated, and often bitter.

Umpire nation also has its own language, or at least a patois, and it is anything but delicate. The usual four-letter imprecations are well represented in the daily umpire lexicon, but it has one especially distinguishing feature: the word "horseshit."

For some reason, "horseshit" is specifically a baseball term, having been the most popular and utilitarian curse word in the game for generations, as familiar a locution at the ballpark as "strike three."

I suppose it's a relative of "bullshit," a word many people who aren't in baseball casually use, though it doesn't mean quite the same thing. "Bullshit" is basically a noun that means "baloney," and it occasionally morphs into an adjective, e.g., a bullshit explanation. "Horseshit" is first and foremost an adjective, and though a horseshit explanation is, I suppose, the same thing as a bullshit explanation— and Webster's defines the two words more or less the same way—in baseball "horseshit" means "worthless" or "irredeemable," and it is applicable to, well, everything. A second baseman who has trouble with the double play turns a horseshit pivot; the home run hit off the lefty reliever came on a horseshit slider; the stretch of games through the middle of August that includes seventeen straight playing days and three doubleheaders is horseshit scheduling.

Far and away, however, the most frequent targets of the word are umpires. They have horseshit strike zones. They make horseshit calls. Their eyesight is horseshit. Their attitudes are horseshit. Their positioning is horseshit. At one game I attended, Alex Rodriguez, the Yankees celebrity third baseman, sauntered over to Bruce Froemming and gave him an unsolicited compliment, something about how much he appreciated all of Froemming's years of professionalism. Froemming reported this to me, and when I asked Rodriguez about it the next day, he shrugged. He said Froemming, as the longest-serving umpire, deserved it.

"After all, all we do is tell them they're horseshit," Rodriguez said.

* * *

Since the late 1970s when their union coalesced behind the aggressive leadership of a Philadelphia lawyer named Richie Phillips, major league umpires have won substantial concessions from baseball. All of them earn six-figure incomes now, around $400,000 for the most senior guys. But none of that has mitigated their belief that they are tolerated by baseball's administrators with distaste.

Major league officials, like current players and managers, don't exactly admit to this. They are generally loath to discuss umpires; among other things, the privately and widely held assumption in baseball is that the umpires are vindictive and, when slighted, will extract vengeance either on the field or at the bargaining table. When officials do talk about umpires for public consumption, it's usually to brag about what a good job they do or about how relations between baseball and the umpires have improved in the last few years.

Even so, the essential enmity does ooze into public view from time to time. During the 2007 season, for example, after the Donaghy scandal, Major League Baseball sought permission from the current union, the World Umpires Association, to conduct in-depth credit checks on its members. The union sought a concession from baseball, an added crew member for the World Series, in return. Negotiations immediately became contentious.

"The discussions broke down over one, and only one, issue, and that was the WUA's demand that we make an economic concession in return for the members being forthcoming on what we view to be an integrity issue," Rob Manfred, baseball's vice president for labor relations, told the *New York Times*. "We strongly indicated that we were offended by the effort to trade economics against integrity."

It was the tone of Manfred's rhetoric, rather than its substance, that was telling. Baseball officials would be within the limits of reasonable argument in saying major league umpires now have relatively little to complain about in terms of their compensation and benefits package, and that the integrity of the game should be everyone's concern, so baseball shouldn't have to pay the umpires any further to safeguard it.

Umpires, on the other hand, might rightfully resent Manfred's indignant seizing of the high road, since their record for integrity is the one baseball can legitimately brag about. It was the players, not the umpires, who conspired to throw the 1919 World Series. A manager,

Pete Rose, not an umpire, was banned from the game forever for betting on games. The owners, not the umpires, were caught colluding to keep player salaries from rising between 1985 and 1988.

Umpires were not surprised by Manfred's statements. They never are when anyone from Major League Baseball disparages them; the received disdain and suspicion are well ingrained in their collective psyche. They speak about it with a shrug and a sneer.

"We're a necessary evil," Larry Young, a major league veteran who would retire after 2007, said to me before a game at Shea Stadium, using the phrase that I heard often from umpires as a sardonic acknowledgment of their lower-caste status. "The trainers, they're on the same level with us. The only ones who get treated worse than us are the scouts."

Perhaps naively, I found myself surprised by this. Like most baseball fans, I think, I was under the impression that the authority that umpires are given on the field allies them naturally with baseball's management. But in fact it seems umpires have few allies in the establishment of the game.

Mike Port, who became the major league vice president in charge of umpiring for the 2006 season after working in the front offices of the Red Sox and the Angels, told me that in thirty years of going to meetings with general managers and owners, he never heard a single kind word uttered about umpires. The closest thing to a compliment he could recall, he said, was a comment about the umpire Billy Williams, who made a habit of removing his dentures before taking the field.

"And one guy said, 'With five being the best and one being the worst, I'd give him a one,'" Port said. "'But I'd make it a five if he'd put his teeth in.' And remember, that's the *nicest* thing I ever heard."

"I didn't like the umpires," Frank Cashen, the former general manager for world championship teams with the Orioles and the Mets admitted. "Nobody in my position did."

"I can tell you this," said Steve Phillips, the former ESPN analyst who spent from 1998 through 2003 as the general manager of the Mets. "Management never cared for the umpires."

"The owners basically see them like bases," Fay Vincent, the baseball commissioner from 1989 to 1992, told me. "They say, 'We need a base, we need an umpire, same thing. We've got to pay them, they're human beings, but they're basically bases.'"

*   *   *

Significantly, my foray into the land of umpires came after the tense and combative decade of the 1990s, and after the umpire cataclysm of 1999, a season that changed what it meant to be a major league umpire, humbling a group of men very unused to humility. That summer, some two decades' worth of open hostility between the umpires' union and baseball's administration finally exploded in a battle the umpires resoundingly lost.

What happened, in sum, was this: In an attempt to bring baseball to the bargaining table, the union, pushed by Richie Phillips, pursued an aggressive strategy that turned out to be folly and brought ruin on itself. Phillips urged the umpires to resign en masse, and an overwhelming majority of the union members did. But instead of being cowed, baseball simply accepted the resignations and began hiring minor league umpires to replace the resignees. In a panic, many umpires rescinded their resignations, not all of them in time. In the end, twenty-two big league umpires lost their jobs, some of them permanently; the union was decertified, and a new union, with entirely different leadership, was formed. Further, the commissioner's office established full control over umpire administration. In the aftermath, lawsuits and animosity were flying every which way. League turned against league and umpire turned against umpire.

"If you were to go to Jerry Crawford, who was president of the union back then," John Hirschbeck said to me, "he'd say it was all because that asshole Hirschbeck didn't stick with us."

Hirschbeck became the leader of the new union, and Crawford did, in fact, say something very much like that to me. And though seven years had passed before I met either Crawford or Hirschbeck or any of the other umpires who were burned by these events, certain wounds clearly remained raw.

The residual ill feelings made a group of reticent men even more so. Indeed, this is probably a good time to point out that umpires, especially in the big leagues, tend to be wary of outsiders. Even though there are divisions among them, they do share a circle-the-wagons loyalty to one another. Several major league umpires declined, politely but firmly, to talk with me. A handful of others would speak only of the weather.

No doubt there is a contrary impulse in many of them—"Hey, we're worthy of the spotlight, so why shouldn't we bask in it?"—but on the whole they're not the easiest guys for a reporter to deal with, exemplary neither at returning phone calls nor keeping appointments. In the end I managed to speak at some length with about a third of the umpires who worked in the major leagues between 2006 and 2008.

Actually, it wasn't easy getting people to talk *about* umpires, either. Current players generally veer away from the subject as if it had germs—"Oh, man, do we *have* to go there?" the catcher Paul Lo Duca, then with the Mets, said to me at the 2006 All-Star game— except to mouth platitudes, believing that umpires will hold grudges and redress them on the field. Kenny Lofton, the much traveled outfielder whom I encountered in the locker room at Dodger Stadium when he was playing for the Dodgers, looked for a moment as if he had a load to get off his mind, but then he just laughed. "I'll have a lot to say about them after I retire," he said. For their part, the umpires tended to laugh, too, whenever I told them the players are afraid to talk about them for fear of retribution. "Good, that's what we want them to think" was the usual response.

I tried to talk with several managers who are or were known as umpire baiters, but they wouldn't say much, either. Earl Weaver, the legendary former manager of the Baltimore Orioles who was famous for his tantrums, answered the phone at his home at noon one day and said he didn't have time to talk about umpires. Weaver was genuinely disliked by a lot of umpires, though in his Hall of Fame induction speech, he spoke of them with admiration. I said I'd come to see him at his convenience, but he brushed me off.

"They're my friends, but I don't have time to talk about them," he said. "I really don't."

I approached Lou Piniella, the volatile manager who took over the Chicago Cubs in 2007, at the Cubs spring training camp in Mesa, Arizona, but he said he was busy, even though he wasn't; he was just hanging around on the field about an hour and a half before a preseason game. As he walked away, he turned back to me and said, "You know, I don't think I ever want to talk to you about umpires."

Bobby Cox, the venerable manager of the Atlanta Braves, who in 2007 set the record for the most times in a career being ejected by umpires, spoke with me amiably for about ten minutes one early evening in the visitors' dugout at Shea Stadium in New York. I asked him if in the old days, when he was a player—in the 1960s, he played third base for a woeful Yankee team—the umpires would use the strike zone as a weapon to exact revenge on a player or enforce discipline.

"Years and years ago they could, sure," he said. "If they didn't like you, you know, they could get you. It is more uniform now. It's good. The umpiring's fine."

He said the general attitude of the umpires was not the way it used to be, but when I asked him how it used to be and how things had changed, he told me he thought we could write a bestseller together if he answered that question and that it was a shame for me he wasn't going to.

All of this helps explain why umpires don't get written about much. In most accounts of the development of the game, umpiring generally gets a few scant pages, usually concentrating on the early days, when professional baseball was a scoundrel's playground and the umpire plied his trade at some physical risk. The only extant volume devoted solely to the history of umpiring, *The Umpire Story*, by James M. Kahn, was published more than half a century ago, in 1953; and the last (and best) book-length reportorial look at umpires, *The Best Seat in Baseball, But You Have to Stand!*, by Lee Gutkind, who spent the 1974 season traveling with a major league crew, is now more than thirty years old.

With or without reason, the umpires felt betrayed by Gutkind— among other things, he reported on some unenlightened racial attitudes and revealed some less-than-savory nocturnal activities—and three decades later, the sting lingers. At least a dozen times the Gutkind book was offered to me as an explanation for why umpires, even those who weren't around in the 1970s, distrust reporters.

Not surprisingly, they've preferred to tell their own stories. Beginning in 1935 with *Standing the Gaff*, an amusing if unsophisticated volume of recollections by Harry "Steamboat" Johnson, a legendary minor league umpire in the first half of the twentieth century, many umpires have published autobiographies. Most of these books are ghostwritten and somewhat suspect. Anecdotes tend to recur in them from one to the next, and according to other umpires, they were written with the twin ideas that anything that happens to one umpire might as well have happened to any of them and that apocrypha is fair game. Ron Luciano, who was known for his on-field flamboyance—he liked to signal a runner out on a close play by mimicking a sharpshooter with a pistol—and who went on to a career as a broadcaster, wrote four separate anecdote-heavy memoirs, and his fellow umpires remembered his sending them letters, asking for material. (Luciano, alas, came to a sad end, taking his own life in 1995.)

Umpires in general feel free to borrow from a pool of stories. More than once, in interviews, I heard about the catcher who asked the plate umpire to get confirmation from the first-base umpire that the batter had checked his swing. Depending on who was telling the story, the plate umpire was either Art Williams or Emmett Ashford, both of whom were African-American; whoever it was did as requested, received the safe sign from his colleague at first (who in this story is never identified except as a Caucasian), then said to the catcher, "There, now you've got it in black and white."

Two different umpires told me that, once, when they were behind the plate, Carl Yastrzemski turned around angrily after a called strike and said to them, "Where was that pitch at?" Each umpire said he answered, "Carl, don't you know better than to end a sentence with a preposition?"

This is, of course, the beginning of an old joke—I've heard a variation attributed to Winston Churchill—the baseball version of which ends after the next pitch and another called strike, with Yastrzemski turning around again and saying, "Where was that pitch at, asshole?" A third umpire told me the exact same story, except that in his version the hitter was Lou Piniella.

The collective reticence of umpires is matched by a collective defiance. They consider their fraternity a bulwark against the forces of baseball corruption and chaos, even though, as a breed, they can hardly claim to be moral paragons. After all, they live on the road, which has tested a great number of umpire marriages. They have a fondness for dirty jokes, many of which disparage women or homosexuals (though it is widely known among them, and the secret is kept, that at least one major league umpire is gay).

Wired after work, they stay out late at night, and many of them drink rapaciously. "If you can't umpire hungover, you can't umpire," goes a tried-and-true umpire saying, and as Don Denkinger, who worked in the American League from 1969 to 1998, recalled, "I didn't have to drink every night when I was umpiring, but I did."

There isn't a whole lot of tell-all in the following pages, so I'll stipulate right now that I witnessed some behavior on the part of some professional umpires that they probably wouldn't want their wives or children to know about. I'll stipulate as well that within the fraternity, some of the feuds are as monumentally petty as any office spat can be: This guy is hungover so often that he forgets to make the plane reservations for his crewmates; that guy is afraid to eject anyone; this guy won't suck it up and work with an injury; this other guy is a kiss-ass to supervisors; and that crew chief is a condescending jerk, mad at the young guys because they don't fawn over him the way he fawned over older guys when he was coming up.

But I never saw any umpire do anything that made me question his on-the-field integrity. It bears acknowledging that in 130 years, only one major league umpire has ever been accused of professional dishonesty, and that was in 1882.

"The integrity of the game is the umpires," Doug Harvey said to me. "Nobody else. The entire integrity of the game is the umpires."

Harvey is an especially fervid umpiring evangelist, but he's got an argument. For one thing, the vast majority of people who think they know baseball (and that includes players, even at the major league level) aren't terribly familiar with the rulebook, an arcane and convoluted document that has more nooks and crannies than an English muffin. (If you think you're so smart, describe a situation in which the umpire is required—required!—to give a manager a choice of two different outcomes of a play resulting from a batted ball.*)

---

*Men on first and third, one out. As the hitter swings at the pitch, his bat ticks the catcher's glove, but he makes contact with the ball as well, hitting a fly to right, where the fielder makes the catch. The runner from third tags up and scores; the runner on first retreats to the bag after the catch and remains there. Because of the catcher's interference with the swing, however, the umpire calls time; he awards the batter first base, which forces the runner on first to second. By rule, however, because the batter's fly ball was nullified, the runner who scored is returned to third. The manager of the hitting team is then likely to complain, and understandably so, that his team has been unfairly penalized. Why should his team lose a run because the opposing catcher was guilty of interference? At this point, the umpire offers the manager the option of taking the results of the play as it had played out instead of accepting the results of the interference. Essentially the manager can choose: bases loaded, one out, no runs in; or man on first, two out, one run in.

And, of course, even the most familiar rules aren't necessarily held sacred. From John McGraw, whose habit as a third baseman was to hold the belt of a base runner attempting to tag up on a fly ball, to Billy Martin, who once declared that "cheating in baseball is just like hot dogs, french fries, and cold Cokes," to Kenny Rogers, the Tigers' ace whose apparent use of pine tar to help him grip the ball tainted the 2006 World Series, to the spitballers, corked-bat users, and steroid injectors who make perpetual baseball news, it has long been clear that in the major leagues winning trumps fair play as a motivating element. As umpires are wont to remark wryly, "If they played by the honor system, they wouldn't need us."

This shared sense of righteousness, along with the shared sense that they have no other friends, makes for a kind of tribal society. Since 1876, fewer than sixteen hundred men have appeared as umpires on major league diamonds, fewer than five hundred as full-time employees of baseball. The number of big league jobs is minuscule—since the last major league expansion in 1998, there have been sixty-eight—and the men who are in them tend to hold on to them with the tenacity and durability of Supreme Court justices.*

Given the 220 or so minor league jobs, then, there are fewer than three hundred professional umpires at any time—a society, almost exclusively male, of itinerant workers who conduct their business daily in front of thousands if not millions of people, yet as conventional wisdom has it, they've done their job only if you don't notice them. An umpire is only in the spotlight if he has screwed up or someone else has screwed up and blamed it on the umpire. The result is a public argument, usually with a hometown hero who is often childishly demonstrative, that puts the umpire on display as an object of scorn and ridicule.

Indeed, even if umpires were paid well and lived well—the vast majority of them are not and do not—you could still say that their plight genuinely stinks, a symbol of existential unfairness, living proof

---

*Actually, in a peace agreement between the major league owners and the umpires' union, two slots were added for the 2007 season to accommodate Tom Hallion and Ed Hickox, who had lost their jobs in 1999. When Bruce Froemming and Larry Young retired after 2007, no one replaced them, so the roster went back to sixty-eight. Counting Hallion, Hickox, and Bob Davidson, a previously reinstated umpire, the major leagues hired only seven umpires in the first nine years of the twenty-first century.

that no good deed goes unpunished. Umpires exist, after all, only to ensure that the greatest American game is played fairly, and for this selfless endeavor they are universally reviled.

I ended up thinking of them as kind of a cult operating in plain sight, a characterization that umpires themselves have no problem with. In fact, I found it occasionally startling to recognize how fierce and ingrained this attitude is.

"That's pretty close," Doug Harvey told me when I tried out on him my professional-umpires-as-remote-island-inhabitants theory. But it's not exactly true that few outsiders had ever visited the island, he said; *no* outsiders had ever visited. "You can't know what it's like to be a major league umpire unless you were a major league umpire."

I interviewed Harvey at his home in central California; the car in the driveway featured vanity plates saying NL UMP. At seventy-six he still had the full head of white hair that distinguished him on the playing field, where he worked five World Series and six All-Star games, and where his nickname, bestowed by the Chicago sportswriter Jerome Holtzman, was God.

A big man, over six feet tall, Harvey seemed robust, if not the commanding physical specimen he used to be. He'd had throat cancer and looked like a healthy survivor, someone who'd lost weight and put it back on, though maybe not where it had been.

He was known, even among self-admiring umpires, as an egotist, which is perhaps why he said to me more than once that he does not have a big ego, but he shares part of his pride with his colleagues.

"I got cancer in 1997," he said, speaking in a gravelly, authoritative whisper. "And when I went to see the doctor, I asked him, 'What's my chance of survival?' and he said thirty percent. Seven out of ten people die in the first ten months after they discover it. It's called vellecular cancer, cancer of the vellecula, where the tongue attaches to the throat, and it's caused specifically by the chewing of tobacco.

"I said, 'Thirty percent? Fuck that. Don't worry about it, I'll beat it.' Six weeks later, I was sixty pounds lighter. I went from 205 to 148 in six weeks, during radiation. It ulcerated my esophagus, and they had to drill a hole in my stomach below the breastbone.

"When I went back to the doctor, I said to him, 'I told you I'd beat it.' And he said, 'What made you so sure?' And I said, 'Well, because you said the odds were thirty percent, and that didn't sound bad to me.' I said, 'Every day for thirty years I went out on the field with three other gentlemen to umpire a ball game, and there were sixty thousand raving idiots in the stands who all thought they could umpire better than we could, and two ball clubs that didn't care if we lived or died. So I knew I could beat the cancer.'"

As I was leaving, Harvey took out a pad on which he said he was keeping notes for a book, and he read to me a quotation that he had copied from David McCullough's popular Revolutionary War history, *1776*.

"'When asked what he was fighting for, General Washington, in writing to General Thomas, said the object was "neither glory nor extent of territory, but a defense of all that is dear and valuable in life."'"

"He must have been an umpire," Harvey said. "That's what umpiring is about."

This country has maybe one hundred thousand amateur baseball umpires. I've had umpires tell me it's a lot more than that, but a hundred thousand is the estimate of the Amateur Baseball Umpires' Association, a group of (you would think) the most avid of them, which claims between sixteen hundred and nineteen hundred members, depending on the year.

In the phrase "amateur baseball umpires," "amateur" modifies "baseball." Most people who umpire get paid for it, with the fees variable from place to place, league to league, and level to level, regulated by local associations. Some even make a modest living at it, usually young people such as Jim Grillo, a cheerful, round-faced Brooklynite who was a twenty-one-year-old classmate of mine in umpire school, a guy who'd been dreaming of being an umpire at least since he was eleven, when he went trick-or-treating dressed as one for Halloween.

Jim wanted to work in professional baseball but acknowledged that he needed to improve his mobility and to lose about twenty-five pounds. In the meantime, he said, he'd continue doing what he'd done the previous couple of years, working high school and junior college games around the outer boroughs of New York and Nassau County on Long Island, earning maybe $60 or $80 a game, sometimes ten or twelve games a week, from April through October. It was enough to get by on, though of course he was living in his parents' basement.

For the most part, though, these "amateurs" are the mailmen and schoolteachers, the store clerks and factory managers, the midlevel executives and gardeners, the salesmen and lifeguards, ordinary citizens whose recreational life is built around officiating amateur baseball, the men of all adult ages (and women, too, though generally younger women) who call balls and strikes for the local Little League, Pony League, Babe Ruth League, Dizzy Dean League, Stan Musial League, and adult community league; for high school games at the freshman, junior varsity, and varsity level; for independently sponsored travel squads; for junior college and NCAA games; for women's and men's fast-pitch—and even slow-pitch—softball tournaments.

They're a remarkable subculture, people who often spend two or three evenings on the ball field during the workweek, not to mention a tripleheader or two on the weekends. They subscribe to *Referee* magazine, their cars double as parking-lot locker rooms, and they count their number of annual games in the two hundreds or even three hundreds. Just to mention one of them, before the first game I ever umpired myself, in Tallahassee, I met Ken Hayes, a fifty-nine-year-old accountant for the Florida Department of Corrections, who had been umpiring locally for more than thirty years.

"I had a boy on the field the other day, and I realized I'd had his great-grandfather, too," Hayes told me. A couple of years ago, he said, he had a heart attack in the middle of a game. He turned red and overheated, he said, then blanched with exhaustion and went cold.

"I had an angioplasty on a Thursday, and I was back on the field on the following Monday," Hayes said proudly.

I don't have that sort of ardor, but it's arguably a pretty good quality if you want to spend your recreational life as an amateur umpire. Oddly enough, though, the process of becoming a professional umpire is in many ways about stripping that fervor away and looking at the game and your role in it with the opposite emotion, dispassion. The everydayness of professional umpiring, the centrality of a daily ball game in your life, the relentless travel, the persistent haggling on the field with players and managers, the constant harassment of fans, and the harsh and largely unsympathetic scrutiny from the baseball establishment, not to mention the tension attendant to the keen vigilance required for high-stakes pro ball—these are the tribulations that separate the umpire who umpires for the romance and recreation of it and the umpire who umpires for a living.

"People say, 'Gee, you get to travel to all those cities,' or they say, 'Gee, you get to meet all the players,'" Tim Tschida, a major league crew chief, said to me outside a Manhattan hotel before heading to Shea Stadium. We'd been talking about how "glamorous" the job is. He rolled his eyes. "Yeah," he said. "*Get* to."

"People say to me all the time, 'Do you love your job?'" Mike Everitt, a major leaguer since 1999, said to me at the 2007 World Series. "I tell them no. I like it. I don't love it."

John Hirschbeck put it bluntly.

"Umpiring isn't our life," he said. "It's our job."

Imagine the following want ad:

"If you like having every close decision you make criticized, if you like doing your job surrounded by thousands of people ready to blame you for mistakes other people make, every one of them believing they can do your job better than you can, and if you don't mind the only response you get for a job done absolutely perfectly being silence, then maybe you would like being an umpire."

This is the job description written by Ken Kaiser, who worked for more than two decades in the big leagues, in his autobiography, *Planet of the Umps*.

Who would volunteer for this duty? And why?

By now I've asked two dozen umpires this, and there is no consensus. Many umpires use the word "calling" to describe their profession—"It's just like being called to the ministry, as far as I'm concerned," said Jim Evans, though that is perhaps to give the job a gravity that is hard to justify outside the church of baseball.

For most umpires, the answer has something to do with loving the game, though not the way most fans understand that love; the first thing that umpiring does, every umpire says without hesitation, is drum the fan out of you. And it's true, they don't root. (I believe this.) Rather, there's something almost soldierly in the way umpires speak of their task—"centurions of the game" is the phrase Tim Timmons, one major leaguer, used with me—a task they define as the defense of an ideal.

"They don't hire us for our good looks," Jeff Nelson, another big leaguer, said. "It's because we have experience. We know how the game should be played. We know the right way to play the game."

They also spoke of being challenged, having to perform under pressure. A third veteran big leaguer, Fieldin Culbreth, described to me a specific reward, a moment of exhilaration of the sort that anyone would look for in professional life, one in which he stood out, staked a claim against shouting doubters, and was vindicated. His favorite times on the field, Culbreth said, came when he made a close call against the home team and the entire stadium was on his case.

"I've had calls, I knew I was right, but everybody in the park was quite certain I was wrong," Culbreth said. "I'm walking back to my position, thinking to myself, 'All you people just kicked the shit out of that call, and *you're* booing *me*!' How ironic. I'm the one who's right, and nobody's capable of knowing it but me. It's a weird part of me, I know, but I get a kick out of it."

Not until I got on the field myself, however, did I think I got closest to the thing that makes umpires do what they do. When I graduated from umpire school, I asked the instructors, minor league umpires all, what quality of baseball my skills were suited to, and they suggested I begin at the Babe Ruth League level, ages thirteen to fifteen. I did that, and I went on to work—in Tallahassee, Florida, and around New York City—at the Little League, high school, and adult levels as well.

I worked a couple of dozen games altogether, and they were all stressful. I didn't sleep the night before my first time calling balls and strikes—or my second. The games were also physically demanding; anyone who thinks umpiring is not a strenuous enterprise—at least for a man in his fifties with bad knees—is simply wrong. You want to know the truth? I didn't like it. You wouldn't believe the aggravation.

Even so, I worked enough to understand that something connects the lowliest amateur umpire with the big leaguer behind the plate for a playoff game. One play in particular stands out as a revelation about the nature of umpiring, its tightrope walk between the exercise of authority and the exercise of power, and the thing that makes it both alluring and difficult for the people who do it.

I was in Tallahassee, behind the plate in a community-league game for fourteen- and fifteen-year-olds. The game was tight in the middle innings; two were out and two men were on base. The batter hit a hard line drive over the third baseman's head that was clearly curving toward foul territory. I reacted precisely as I had been taught, pulling off my mask as I came out from behind the plate, circling the catcher on the third-base side, and running a few steps up the line. I got as far as I could until I needed to stop so as to be stationary to make the call—like a camera, your eyes get a clearer picture of a play if they're still—and straddled the line.

What happened next I experienced as one of those brief action sequences in life when time seems to slow down and your impressions are so vivid that you can order them. In my mind's eye I can still see the base runner from second heading for third and rounding it; I can still see the third-base coach, an adult, waving his arm in a windmill fashion to tell the runner to keep going; I can still hear the cacophony of the two hundred or so parents and friends in the stands, screaming in excitement.

It's amazing, actually, how much you can take in even as you are focusing on one thing, in this case the flight of the line drive as it settled to the ground, about halfway between third base and the outfield fence. I had a close call to make, but not a difficult one. I saw the landing clearly.

For an instant after the ball hit the ground, it seemed that a silence visited the field, as though everyone had taken a breath at once. And though the base runners and fielders kept moving and the parents in the stands kept exercising their parental interests, there was an interim beat in the action, a hiccup of waiting, as everyone turned instinctively to look at me. The third-base coach was staring into my eyes, I swear.

I extended my arms, threw my hands above my head and slightly in front of me, and bellowed the call: "Foul!" Abruptly, time began again, with half the crowd groaning, the other half sighing in relief. The base runners returned to their bases, the batter to the batter's box. I replaced my mask and resumed my stance behind the catcher, thrilled with my own competence and control, and it was easy, right then, to project myself and that moment into a grander scene—Yankee Stadium, say, during the World Series. It was a feeling of hubris and joy, a moment of great satisfaction for me.

Later, much later, it would dawn on me how dangerous that satisfaction can be, that the feeling is the one that umpires both crave and can't afford.

"This is my game," I was thinking. "*My* game."

CHAPTER ONE

MEN BEHIND A MASK

My favorite umpire is a dead one.
—JOHNNY EVERS

"Strike three!" and I jump.
I'm in a big slump.
I'm down in the dump,
Can't get over this hump.

You cross-eyed old ump,
You're as blind as a stump.
Made me look like a chump,
You horse's rump!
—CHARLES GHIGNA,
AKA FATHER GOOSE

Okay, one more thing about taking off a mask: It's remarkable to realize that you can be a lifelong baseball fan and not know the first thing about umpiring—*literally* the first thing. Baseball, after all, is a sport where everything—everything else, anyway—seems to be under scrutiny all the time, with millions of people gleaning it for new info and insight. Every major league game is televised, as well as many in the minor leagues, and highlights are replayed nationally and nightly. Statistics continue to be invented and historical tidbits unearthed, and both are so voluminous and variously interpretable that a whole academic clan—the Society for American Baseball Research (SABR)—is devoted to them. Reporters, broadcasters, and bloggers exhaust daily stores of news, opinion, analysis, and trivia, and of course literary and faux-literary types have been waxing eloquent, semi-eloquent, and sub-eloquent on the grand subject of baseball for several generations.

All of this has led to a deep pool of common lore and an extraordinary literacy about the game among a wide audience of fans, but for some reason the details of the umpiring craft and the personalities of the men who pursue it remain obscure. Indeed, umpires may conduct their business in public and in plain sight, but most fans can't tell you anything about them except that, to express it benignly, they occasionally err, or that, a little less benignly, they are performing an easy job incompetently. Actually, ask a fan at the ballpark what he knows about umpires—I've done this a lot—and the most frequent response is something like "They fucking suck."

Many of these same people could tell you in an instant what the second baseman is supposed to do, say, with two outs and a man on first when the batter laces one down the line between the third baseman and the third-base bag.

He covers second, of course. In case the left fielder throws there.

But what does the second-base *umpire* do?

The answer is that as soon as the batter touches first—actually, in umpire parlance, he's known as the batter-runner, a designation he takes on as soon as he hits the ball and leaves the batter's box—the second-base umpire positions himself on the infield grass between first and second, where he waits for the play to develop. He is, of course, responsible for a play on the batter-runner at second.

The first-base umpire, meanwhile, has gone to cover home plate for a possible play there, because the home plate umpire has rushed up to cover third for a possible play there, because the third-base umpire has chased after the ball into the left-field corner to make sure no spectator leaning over the rail has interfered with play or the ball hasn't gotten caught under the fence or something else unexpected hasn't happened. So the second-base umpire is also responsible for a play at first, in the event that the batter-runner makes the turn, retreats, and the throw comes across the diamond; he must also be alert for the possibility of a rundown.

Didn't know any of that? That isn't so surprising. Many people who make their living in baseball don't either. On opening day at Shea

Stadium in 2006, for example, on a play identical to the one described above, an umpire's incorrect call helped the Mets beat the Washington Nationals.

With the Mets ahead by a run in the eighth inning, the Nationals' Alfonso Soriano tried to score from first on a double to left and was seemingly tagged out by Paul Lo Duca, the Mets catcher. There was no argument or even a discussion. Lo Duca, however, had dropped the ball, a fact that was confirmed on a videotape replay but had eluded just about everyone in the park, including the umpires.

Umpires make mistakes, of course; that's not the point. (In this case, it was actually understandable. Lo Duca's body had shielded the drop from just about every pair of human eyes in the stadium, and the video replay from only one of four different cameras revealed it.) But when the game was over and members of the press who had seen the decisive replay went to talk to the home plate umpire, Rick Reed, about his mistake, they had to be told that Reed hadn't made the call. The umpires had rotated on the play, properly, and the call at the plate had been made by Tim Tschida, the first-base umpire.

About a month later in Milwaukee I spoke with Robin Yount, the Hall of Fame shortstop and outfielder who was then the bench coach for the Brewers. Yount recalled that in the two seasons he spent as a first-base coach for the Arizona Diamondbacks, he often disagreed with umpires on close plays at first, but on viewing the replay, it almost always turned out he was wrong. It was funny, Yount acknowledged, how your point of view can affect your vision and your decision-making.

"I'd never looked at the game from that angle before," Yount told me, meaning from the vicinity of the first-base bag, and he confessed the perspective threw him off. "I'd see the play differently from the umpire, but then I'd go in the clubhouse and watch the tape and I'd be surprised that almost all the time they were right."

I asked Yount if he'd ever spoken to umpires about why that is, about what they do to see the play properly.

"No," he said. "I never did."

It's often said that the best umpire is the one you never notice, and though that's an arguable point, it is certainly true that umpires are baseball's invisible men. Players are often celebrities, and so are managers, broadcasters, and even some coaches, pointed at on the street, hounded for autographs and pictures. Even lesser lights who play the game can be locally famous in the cities where they play. But umpires are popularly known neither by their names nor their faces, not even by their reputations. I've walked the streets of several American cities with major league umpires, eaten with them in dozens of restaurants, and never once has a stranger recognized any of them. Even at the ballpark, I rarely witnessed anyone ask an umpire to sign a ball or a scorecard, and elsewhere I never saw it happen. Eight umpires have earned places in the Hall of Fame in Cooperstown. But who can name them? Can you name *one*? Not even Bill Klem?

Klem umpired in the National League for thirty-six full seasons, from 1905 to 1941 (a record for longevity that was finally eclipsed in 2007 by Bruce Froemming), and he's generally recognized as the most influential and accomplished umpire of all time, the Babe Ruth of umpiring, if you will.

Klem instituted arm signals for balls and strikes, so spectators in the bleachers, and not just those in the expensive seats near home plate, would know what the calls were. He was the first umpire to disdain the inflated balloonlike chest protector and to wear instead a modified catcher's protector under his shirt. He is credited with several of umpiring's most famous declarations, including "Baseball is more than a game to me, it's a religion" and "It ain't nothing until I call it."

That Klem is a relative unknown is the point. He's alleged to be the first person to aver that a game has been well umpired if you don't know who the umpires were, a sentiment that has become a truism in the game (even if it isn't true). But Klem, who was a substantial egotist even by the standards of an occupation that values egotism, would never have agreed that such anonymity should apply to a career.

Whether umpires should remain anonymous or not, they do. It's weird that they are so little considered in the culture of the game. Nicknames of players, so much a part of baseball's allure—the Sultan of Swat, the Yankee Clipper, Mr. Cub, the Say Hey Kid, the Splendid Splinter, Big Train, the Georgia Peach, Ol' Reliable, the Ol' Perfesser, Peewee, Dizzy, Whitey, Campy, Stan the Man, Yogi, and Yaz, just to name a prominent few—are far more familiar than the real names of Billy Evans, Tom Connolly, Cal Hubbard, Nestor Chylak, Jocko Conlan, Bill McGowan, and Al Barlick, the other seven Hall of Fame umpires.

(Klem, by the way, was called Catfish—for his big lips, the slant of his brow, and his penchant for spitting as he made a point to a player—but only behind his back. He hated the name, thought it demeaning and disdainful, and referring to him that way on the field meant an automatic ejection.)

In dubious circumstances, too, umpires have been relegated to the status of footnotes. Fred Merkle, Ralph Branca, and Bill Buckner are famous as the prominent goats of baseball history. But except perhaps in St. Louis, where anguished fans still blame his erroneous sixth-game, ninth-inning call at first base for robbing the Cardinals of the 1985 World Series title, the name Don Denkinger doesn't raise hackles or even much recognition.

Meanwhile, everyone knows the reputations of Barry Bonds, Roger Clemens, Sammy Sosa, and Rafael Palmeiro are clouded by the suspicion they used steroids, and that Pete Rose and Shoeless Joe Jackson were banned from the game for gambling. But Richard Higham? Who's he?

In 1882, Higham became the only umpire ever accused of dishonesty on the field. He was allegedly in league with gamblers, and on flimsy and dubious evidence (his accuser was a team owner angry about a call) he was thrown out of the sport.

This isn't to say that umpires are morally or ethically pure. Most of them would admit they aren't, and even if they wouldn't, their history is dotted with brutish, scheming, or narrow-minded behavior. George Magerkurth, a habitual barroom brawler who worked in the National League from 1929 to 1947, was suspended for ten days in 1939 when he got in a fistfight during a game at the Polo Grounds in New York with the Giants shortstop Billy Jurges.

Bruce Froemming, who retired after the 2007 season, his thirty-seventh, as the longest-serving umpire in major league history, was suspended for ten days in 2003 when a religious slur directed at an umpiring administrator, Cathy Davis—he referred to her as "a stupid Jew bitch" after an argument over travel arrangements—was caught on her answering machine. And in 2001, Al Clark lost his major league umpiring job after twenty-five years when he was fired for habitually cashing in the first-class airline tickets baseball provides the umpires for coach seats and pocketing the difference. Subsequently, he went to jail for fraud as part of a scheme to profit on phony memorabilia. Clark, who umpired in the 1978 American League playoff game between the Yankees and Red Sox (the game won by Bucky Dent's home run), Nolan Ryan's three hundredth career victory, and Dwight Gooden's no-hitter at Yankee Stadium in 1996, would sign baseballs and authentication documents certifying that the balls were used in those and other games, even though they weren't, then share in the profits of their sales.

Even so, rarely if ever have the acts of major league umpires threatened the honor of the game, though a couple of incidents have come to light showing them tiptoeing up to the line. In 1989, two umpires, Rich Garcia and Frank Pulli, were put on probation after the commissioner, Fay Vincent, learned through baseball's security office that they (along with Don Zimmer, then the manager of the Chicago Cubs) had placed bets with an illegal bookmaker (who was also a drug dealer) on sporting events other than baseball games.

Froemming was among a handful of umpires who were chastised in the 1990s for asking ballplayers to sign baseballs they could then turn around and sell; baseball prohibits this as a conflict of interest, especially since the practice generally includes an implied threat.

"I'm getting ready to pitch—I was about to go out and warm up—and my catcher is trying to prepare for the game," the former knuckleballer Tom Candiotti recalled in 2003 about a game in 1996 when he was with the Dodgers, whose catcher was Mike Piazza. "And Froemming is telling Piazza this story about how one time Johnny Bench wouldn't sign baseballs for him, and Bench went oh for four that day with three called strikeouts, or something like that. So Piazza stopped stretching and signed the baseballs."*

Anyway, the point is not that umpires are well—or badly—behaved. It's that even egregious behavior doesn't do much to raise their profiles. Even sex and death don't seem to put umpires in the public eye. Everyone knows that Joe DiMaggio was married to Marilyn Monroe, and fans of a certain vintage still remember Leo Durocher's wife was

---

*In 2008, I checked with Candiotti, by then a broadcaster for the Arizona Diamondbacks, on this story and he confirmed it, though he said he didn't remember specifically that Bench had struck out three times.

"I also remember feeling good that Piazza signed those balls for Froemming because if he hadn't it might actually have affected the strike zone for me," Candiotti wrote to me in an e-mail.

Froemming, for his part, claimed he wanted the autograph for his dying mother, a Piazza fan.

Laraine Day. Attentive younger fans are aware that, before she got married, Alyssa Milano dated pitchers—she was romantically linked with Brad Penny, Barry Zito, and Carl Pavano—and that Kris Benson, a pitcher for the Pirates, Mets, and Orioles, is married to a woman who has posed for *Playboy* and *Maxim* and made outrageous and attention-getting statements about the sex life she enjoys with her husband. But it's mostly a secret that the onetime National League umpire Dick Stello was married to the 1970s porn star Chesty Morgan, a woman often referred to as having "the world's largest naturally occurring bosom," whose measurements were said to be 73–32–36.

Finally, who is John McSherry? Except among umpires, who revered him, he's forgotten, unless it is as the spur that moved baseball to insist that umpires improve their physical condition. On April 1, 1996, opening day in Cincinnati, McSherry, who weighed well over three hundred pounds, was behind the plate when his heart failed. With the count 1-1 on the third batter of the game, Rondell White, McSherry called time and moved toward the home dugout. He signaled to someone, perhaps the team doctor, then collapsed and died, the only umpire ever to perish on the field.

It was a horrific event, a gruesome tragedy in a public place on an ordinarily celebratory occasion, well within the memory of anyone who can recall the early career of Derek Jeter. Yet far fewer fans remember John McSherry than can tell you about the only player ever killed during a game. That was Ray Chapman, an infielder for the Cleveland Indians who was hit in the head by a pitch from a submarining right-hander, Carl Mays, of the Yankees. The year was 1920.

I find all of this more than a little odd because umpires are anomalous in baseball in so many ways that you'd think this condition alone would draw attention to them. For instance, they're the only ones on the field who don't have any stake in the outcome of the game, but they're also the only ones who are actually on the field for the whole thing. In an environment defined as competitive, they're the only ones who can't win. And there is no glory available to umpires; they're often booed but never cheered, except sardonically, often when one of them is hurt. As Doug Harvey told me, "The player can go from being a bum to a hero. An umpire can't."

Put another way, umpires are the only ones in the park for whom the narrative powers of a ball game are supposed to be irrelevant. For fans, for players, for broadcasters and everyone else, the appeal of a ball game is that it is a story, with characters, a measure of uncertainty and suspense, a beginning, a middle, an end, and in the best of circumstances a climax and a denouement. But for the umpires, the story can be nothing but a distraction. For them the game needs to be a procession of episodes, each only as weighty as the previous one, and it's imperative for them to combat the very human impulse to be drawn into the drama. Complete success in this endeavor is impossible for them, of course. You don't have to be partisan, after all, to feel like a part of things, to be conscious of when the stakes are especially high or the pressure especially intense.

"Sure, you're aware of circumstances," one umpire, Tom Hallion, would tell me. "You know, when the bases are loaded and it's a full count, and you're saying to yourself, 'Holy shit, this is tight!' But you have to push that aside, push it out of your mind and focus on the next pitch. The next pitch. The next pitch. It's always about the next pitch. That's umpiring."

My theory for the general lack of curiosity about umpires is that fans tend to find all the anomalies distancing rather than appealing. They make umpiring too peculiar, too enigmatic, too difficult to analyze. It's not that umpires are hidden exactly, or even inconsequential. Rather, it's as if, both on the field and off, they inhabit a parallel world to that of the rest of baseball. If you watch a game the way you normally do, focusing on the ball and the players who are throwing it, hitting it, or chasing it, the umpires will seem to be absent—it's a little weird, actually; you just don't see them, even though they're often right in the middle of the action. The next time a catcher goes back to the screen for a foul pop, for example, take a moment to look for the plate umpire. You'll find him surprisingly nearby, just a few feet from the catcher, peering intently at the ball as it descends, to make sure it doesn't graze the screen before it hits the catcher's glove.

Conversely, if you look at the photographic negative of your ordinary view of a ball game and focus only on the umpires, you might need an instant replay to figure out what happened on the play. Partly this is because it's often the case that on a given play all the infielders and base runners will be in motion—a sacrifice bunt with men on first and second, for example—but the umpires will stay put.

Just as often, though—if the batter fouls off the bunt attempt, say, and on the next pitch skies one to deep left center—the infielders and the base runners will stick where they are, but the umpires will be flying around. It's as though two different games are going on, or maybe more accurately, as though the umpires are playing a game of their own, within a larger, more familiar game. One story that every umpire tells is about being asked, after a game, whether that catch by the center fielder was the greatest he ever saw.

"I didn't see it," the umpire answers. "I was making sure the batter-runner touched first base."

It doesn't help that umpires are also the only ones on the field for whom fans have none of the tools of comparison and judgment that are customarily used in any serious baseball discussion. I'm speaking of statistics.

Baseball is, of course, a statistics-mad sport, and fans love to pore over and parse the numbers to evaluate players' performances. It's pretty clear that a second baseman who hits .300 is going to contribute to a team more than a second baseman who hits .220.

But there are no equivalent measures to evaluate the quality of an umpire, whose skills are difficult even to define. Yes, there are numbers out there. Las Vegas gambling consultants keep tabs on certain results associated with major league umpires—such as how often the home team has won when a particular guy is behind the plate, or the average total runs scored in games presided over by a particular umpire. But these after-the-fact tendencies don't tell you anything about the accuracy of the umpires' calls. And though it's possible that a sufficient sample of results might be mathematically significant and indicate that the predilection of one umpire, say, is to give the offense more of a chance to score than does another umpire, that isn't a judgment of quality or accuracy, either. (Neither, by the way, does it have anything to do with an umpire's fairness.)

Another array of statistics—similar but more elaborate, available on Internet Web sites such as www.baseballprospectus.com—exists to *describe* an umpire's performance: how many walks or strikeouts per game occur during an umpire's plate game, how many home runs, the total number and percentage of balls and called strikes, etc. The site is a favorite resource for baseball-trivia hunters, obsessive record-ferrets and eccentric theoreticians, as well as more serious researchers (to the degree that baseball research is serious), and the statistics are fodder, just sitting there begging to be interpreted and analyzed freely. But they don't evaluate anything.

Since 2001, Major League Baseball has employed the QuesTec Umpire Information System, an electronic network of video cameras and computers that was installed in a number of ballparks to monitor umpires' calls of balls and strikes. To some degree QuesTec does provide evaluative statistics for umpires. It tracks pitches to see if the ball has passed through the strike zone and, game by game, grades the home plate umpire on the basis of the percentage of pitches he called correctly.

By the time the system was put in place, it had become a common perception that umpires in general were calling a strike zone that was both stretched wider and squashed lower than the rulebook defined it. QuesTec was installed expressly as a corrective measure, to coerce umpires in almost a Pavlovian fashion into returning to the rulebook strike, which is a pitch that passes over home plate essentially between the middle of the batter's torso and the lower border of his knee. (We'll get to the actual definition later on.)

In that regard, QuesTec has been reasonably successful, with most people—players, coaches, baseball administrators, and even umpires themselves—acknowledging that fewer wide strikes and more strikes above the belt are now being called. And Major League Baseball says that the QuesTec scores of every one of its umpires are regularly above 90 percent, the median score above 94 percent.

It is also acknowledged, however, that the QuesTec technology is imperfect and that the system is susceptible to the human error of its operators. And so as not to seem too much like Big Brother looking over the shoulder of its officials, Major League Baseball gives the umpires some leeway. For one thing, when the QuesTec technology locates a pitch within two inches of the strike zone, Major League Baseball says it's close enough to reasonably be called a strike. So QuesTec's usefulness as an evaluative tool is, if not dubious, at least debatable, even in terms of what it purports to measure.

Besides, whether the ability to call a QuesTec strike—or a rulebook strike—is the best measure, or even an appropriate measure, of umpiring skills is another question entirely. Frank Pulli, the baseball official who has most closely been involved with examining QuesTec results, was known, when he was an umpire himself, for calling a strike zone well beyond the rulebook limits.

QuesTec scores are not routinely published; nor are the records that Major League Baseball keeps on each umpire's close calls on the bases. (A summary is made available to journalists each year, but even baseball acknowledges that the results are incomplete. In 2007, for example, baseball estimated that a miscall occurred once every fourteen games, a laughable bit of public relations, when any fan who watches one game a day for a week will count more than that.) So the casual fan has no basis, really, for comparing the accuracy of umpires' calls, which I suppose is the equivalent of a player's batting average or a pitcher's earned run average. Like those measures, though, an umpire's accuracy tells only part of the story.

In the major leagues it is more or less presumed that an umpire is going to get the safes and outs and the fairs and fouls right nearly all the time. Ask major leaguers what they look for in an umpire—I must have asked a few dozen, past and present—and no one ever mentions accuracy. The two words you hear most describe unquantifiable qualities: "consistency" and "control." That is, they want an umpire's boundaries to be clear. What will he tolerate in terms of pugnacious behavior and what won't he? They want the strike zone to be established early and remain unchanged for the duration of the game. And they want to know that the game will be administered with professionalism, briskness, confidence, and authority. Like children with parents, players and managers will try to hoodwink, intimidate, or wheedle the umpires into seeing things their way, but ultimately they know that if an umpire is malleable, he's not operating in their best interest.

When I asked Alex Rodriguez, for instance, why Bruce Froemming kept the players' respect for so long, even though most of them recognized that he couldn't cover the field the way he once had, Rodriguez said, "He's not the most agile guy out there anymore, but when he walks out on the field, you know you're going to have a well-run game. He's like a four-star general out there."

Finally, though, what distinguishes umpires most from the game's other human elements—and what most cultivates the public's indifference, if not disdain, toward them—is that once they come to work, they represent no one but themselves. They follow no one and thus have no following. They support no one and thus have no support. This is no small matter. You can't spend any time around umpires at all without being impressed by their essential isolation from the rest of the game, each crew walking on and off the field together, often to jeers, traveling together, often eating and drinking together in cities far from home. Unlike players, who get to spend half the season in one place, umpires are on the road all season long. It's literally in their job definition that they remain without fans, without people to identify with or root for them.

"I feel bad for them," Jim Leyland, manager of the Detroit Tigers, said to me. "They're the only ones in the park who never play a home game."

The umpire has been around from the birth of baseball. The word comes from the Middle English *umpere,* which was derived from the Old French word *nomper,* meaning one who is not equal, an irony many of today's put-upon umpires would appreciate. The term was applied to the game-by-game overseers of one of baseball's chief progenitors, cricket, which usually employs two of them on the field (and these days, one or more off), whose duties were laid out in the laws of the game established in 1788 at the Marylebone Cricket Club in London. Cricket emigrated from England to the United States in the first part of the nineteenth century, and the idea of an umpire came with it.

As an on-the-field presence in baseball, the umpire was identified in what are generally considered the game's establishing fundamentals, a list of twenty guidelines written by Alexander Cartwright and other members of the Knickerbocker Baseball Club of New York City in 1845. Rule 17: "All disputes and differences relative to the game, to be decided by the Umpire, from which there is no appeal." (An even earlier reference, a similar rule written into the bylaws of the Olympic Ball Club of Philadelphia in 1838, was uncovered by the historian David Block in his 2005 book, *Baseball Before We Knew It.*)

In 1846, a written account of the first game ever played between organized teams, the Knickerbocker and New York clubs, in Hoboken, New Jersey, referred to an umpire fining a New York player named Davis six cents for swearing. (The account didn't specify whether the offending oath was aimed at the umpire.)

As this anecdote suggests, the umpire was initially imagined as a gentlemanly figure—baseball drawings from the first half of the nineteenth century frequently show the umpire in his position off to the side of the batter's box, wearing a top hat and carrying a walking stick—but the job requirements quickly became more rough-and-tumble. The earliest practice was that the home team would choose the umpire—and pay his salary of $5—for which the team, and its fans, generally expected more than a fair shake, which the umpire, for self-preservation if not a simple rooting interest, was often as not inclined to provide.

Major League Baseball gives credit to a Philadelphia man named William McLean as the first big league umpire; he worked the opening game in the nascent National League on April 22, 1876. Three years later, in an effort to combat favoritism, the president of the league, William A. Hulbert, approved the first umpiring staff, twenty men, scattered among the league cities. Only one umpire worked each game back then. Two became the norm during the first decade of the twentieth century (though as many as four were working World Series games by 1909), three by the mid-1930s, and the current practice of four not until 1952. For nearly a century and a half now an umpire has presided over every professional game ever played.

That provenance and ubiquity is another reason that the essential obscurity of umpires is worth remarking upon. It's simply true that when the world looks at umpires, it sees plain-uniformed men who are indistinguishable from one another. They can hide in plain sight; their faces are met with indifference. The home plate umpire's mask *is* seemingly the umpire's face, that is, the representative face of all umpires.

A 1951 cartoon from the *New Yorker* represents this costume-as-character idea perfectly. The captionless image, by Chon Day, shows an umpire in the privacy of the locker room who has either just taken off his mask or is just about to put it on; inside the mask is a whole other face, one fixed in a far sterner expression than the benign-looking one on the man.

Detailed knowledge about umpires may not be prevalent in American society, but an iconography of umpires is. The *New Yorker* alone has published nearly a hundred cartoons about umpires, most using the telltale imagery of mask and chest protector and commenting in some way on the nature of decision-making power, both within the game and beyond it. Moreover, beginning in the nineteenth century, a storehouse of cultural references—in the arts, in advertising, and in public life—makes it clear that umpires may not be well-known figures individually, but they have a collective and useful identity as a representation of faceless authority.

Umpires can be—and are—seen as both icons and iconoclasts; whether they stand for fairness and discipline or hubris and self-importance depends on whom you ask. They've been called tyrants and pawns; a necessary evil and the distinguishing mark of the greatest game there is; kidnappers holding the American pastime hostage and the ballast that keeps the game from sinking under the manipulators and cheaters, the spoiled athletes and craven, greedy owners. Umpires define the level playing field, a huge responsibility, and they do it out in the open, where everyone can see them, yet they nonetheless operate according to the privately held wisdom of the baseball rulebook. They supply the cool voice of reason, yet their most valuable tools are not intellect and erudition but spontaneity and will.

They are the law, but they make mistakes. They've been compared to cops and judges, but their decisions are instantaneous and forever, their mistakes unappealable and irreversible, which makes their law actually sort of lawless. There is something roguish and independent about umpires, so the judicial comparison I prefer is to the itinerant lawmen of the American West, those roving mercenaries who came into a tiny town, cleaned out the cattle rustlers and Liberty Valance–type bullies, and moved on.

Anyway, because they exist only in baseball, the quintessential American game, it's hard not to see them as symbols of something or other. The gorgeous human imperfection of democracy, perhaps? Or the impossibility of true fair play, on the one hand, and the nobility of pursuing it on the other?

Writers, painters, cartoonists, and songwriters, not to mention politicians, clergymen, journalists, and random speechifiers, have found this ambiguous identity helpful over the years in using the umpire to evoke an authority figure that can either be admired or scorned.

On the one hand, umpires have served to represent wisdom, whether in the form of ingenuity, moral gravitas, legal probity, or simple common sense. The convention among genre writers of baseball fiction, the most well-known of which was John R. Tunis, the author of *The Kid from Tompkinsville* and other young-adult novels, is that umpires are authority figures to be saluted, like the flag, and treated with deference, like the school principal. Among the well-regarded baseball stories of Frank O'Rourke—an author of spy novels, children's books, Westerns, and mysteries as well as sports fiction—was "Decision," originally published in 1950, which held up a pair of minor league umpires as skilled men of integrity who refuse to quit in spite of being set upon by an angry mob.

More philosophically, in *A Great and Glorious Game,* his explication of baseball as a blueprint for the idea of America, A. Bartlett Giamatti, the former baseball commissioner and president of Yale University, invoked an image of the umpire as the patriarch of the clan—including pitcher, catcher, batter—that gathered daily at home plate, a ritual recalling the family dinner table.

During his confirmation hearings before the Senate, now chief justice John Roberts compared umpiring to serving on the High Court. Well, actually, it was the other way around; he held up umpiring as a model for the kind of justice he wished to be, reactive rather than proactive, espousing the trademark conservative approach to jurisprudence this way: "I will remember that it's my job to call balls and strikes and not to pitch or bat."

With characteristic American hyperbole, the umpire has also been used to invoke divinity, as Pete Rose did in his recent autobiography, *My Prison Without Bars,* regarding forgiveness for his transgressions. In the book, published in 2004, nearly fifteen years after he was caught betting on baseball games as manager of the Cincinnati Reds, he finally admitted that, yes, he was guilty.

"I've consistently heard the statement 'If Pete Rose came clean, all would be forgiven,'" Rose wrote. "Well, I've done what you've asked. The rest is up to the commissioner and the big umpire in the sky."

Clergymen who are also baseball fans have periodically expanded on this symbolism, often with a seriousness, however tongue-in-cheek, that testifies to how easily baseball has come to serve as a metaphor in American life. In one published sermon from 1973 that can be found in the files of the National Baseball Hall of Fame research library, the Reverend Dr. John C. McCollister, head of the religion department at Olivet College in Michigan, began a call to worship this way:

Almighty God, you who are called the great Umpire, in this game of life we are unsure of what uniform we should wear. While we may be

Angels in spirit, in reality we are Giants in pride, Dodgers of responsibility and Tigers in ambition. When it comes to faith we find ourselves in the minor leagues. When it comes to good works we strike out. When it comes to knowledge of Your word, we are not even aware of the ground rules.

Of course, the contrary image of umpires—as harsh, self-interested, power-mongering, corrupt, and even evil—exists as well.

In fact, the prevailing depiction of umpires in our culture is negative, though usually they aren't portrayed as villainous so much as foolish. In storytelling, especially on-screen, the umpire is usually shown as a marginal figure in a comic setting; generally a bumbler, his ineptitude is his central characteristic. This can be seen in myriad episodes of television series and in cartoons and advertisements that posit umpires as pompously harrumphing authoritarians, fat men who haven't seen their feet lately, hopelessly indecisive milquetoasts or easily distracted incompetents. Probably the best-known example is from the movies, the 1988 cop-story spoof *Naked Gun,* in which the protagonist, a detective played by Leslie Nielsen, at one point in his pursuit of a killer disguises himself as an umpire, sneaks onto a major league field, and inadvertently brings about a brawl.

It may actually be in song that the image of the umpire as a figure of mockery has its most extended history, dating back more than a century. In 1905, a two-act musical called *The Umpire* appeared in Chicago— the review in the *Chicago Tribune* was favorable—telling the story of an umpire who made an unpopular decision in a big game and was forced to leave the country for Morocco, a country, the show's libretto explicitly noted, that had no extradition treaty with the United States. A featured number in the show—music by Joseph E. Howard, words by Will M. Hough and Frank R. Adams—was "The Umpire Is a Most Unhappy Man," which describes the profession most unflatteringly:

An umpire is a cross between a bullfrog and a goat
He has a mouth that's flannel-lined and breast tubes in his throat
He needs a cool and level head that isn't hard to hit
So when the fans beat up his frame they'll have a nice place to sit
How'd you like to be an umpire?

A few years later, in 1909, the celebrated songwriter Jack Norworth checked in with "Let's Get the Umpire's Goat," a jaunty bit of encouragement to fans to make sure the ump knows he is despised. Norworth wouldn't actually attend his first baseball game until more than three decades later, but he'd already proven he had a knack for the lyrics of the game. His previous effort, written a year earlier, was "Take Me Out to the Ball Game."

The popular song wasn't through with umpires in the middle part of the century. Richard Adler and Jerry Ross's lyrics for their 1955 Broadway musical, *Damn Yankees,* included the incantation in the opening number "Yer blind, Ump, yer blind, Ump, you must be out of yer mind, Ump." That was three years after the bandleader Mitch Miller recorded "Take Me Out to the Ball Game" and for the flip side of the 45 composed a novelty number, "The Umpire," which included the voices of actual major leaguers—Tommy Henrich, Ralph Branca, Phil Rizzuto, and Roy Campanella—making disdainful comments about the title character. Among other things, they refer to the umpire as a "horrible monster" and a "nightmarish creature," who is not only blind, but stupid, too. *"The umpire, the umpire, the guy who calls every play,"* goes the refrain. *"We ain't got no use for the umpire unless he calls 'em our way."*

Obscurity, I suppose, has helped keep umpires mired in the role of popular villain. After all, it is easy to disdain a man in a mask, and probably natural to believe that a literally faceless authority is hardly deserving of praise or fealty but rather skepticism, scorn, or worse.

Indeed, the expectation that the umpire is incapable or corrupt is ingrained in American lore. As president, Harry S. Truman recalled that as a boy he'd umpired games in his hometown of Independence, Missouri, a fact generally used to bolster Truman's reputation for honesty and his reverence for fair play, but actually, Truman said, the only reason he was given the job was that his eyesight wasn't good enough for him to actually play the game.

Opposing the umpire is a national custom that is held in some reverence. When General Douglas MacArthur was recalled from Japan in 1951, he made his first public appearance as a civilian at the Polo Grounds in New York for a game between the Giants and the Phillies, where he proclaimed his joy to be home by declaring that he and his wife were "going to settle down now to watch the long hits, mark the errors, and razz the umpire, even if we know he is right."

Antagonism toward the umpire has even been sanctioned by the courts. In 1987, a New York State appeals court resolved a five-year-old lawsuit for defamation brought by American League umpire Dallas Parks against the owner of the Yankees, George Steinbrenner, who had said that Parks was "not a capable umpire" and that "he didn't measure up," criticisms that Parks deemed beyond the pale, worse than the imprecations he was used to hearing at the ballpark.

In a unanimous decision, however, the court ruled against Parks, with an opinion, written by Justice Betty Weinberg Ellerin, that declared accusing the umpire of incompetence to be protected speech, at least in part because of the established tradition of treating the umpire as a public enemy.

"Most fans feel that without one or more rhubarbs they have not received their money's worth," Ellerin wrote.

The language of the general and the judge is, if anything, notably tame. The popular mode for addressing umpires is much more hostile. According to the baseball lexicographers Paul Dickson and Skip McAfee, the earliest citation of fans encouraging bloody murder on the umpire is from 1876, when a writer for the *Cincinnati Star* remarked that the fans who had yelled "Kill him" at the umpire were guilty of bad taste.

The phrase itself, "Kill the umpire," is a uniquely malevolent expression in the American idiom. ("Kill the messenger" is, after all, usually preceded by the suggestion not to.) It dates at least to 1888, with the publication, in the *San Francisco Examiner,* of "Casey at the Bat," Ernest Lawrence Thayer's famously singsong poem about the failure of a local hero to get a timely hit, which, after Casey takes a called strike, proceeds with the following couplets:

From the benches, black with people, there went up a muffled roar,
Like the beating of the storm-waves on a stern and distant shore.
"Kill him! Kill the umpire!" shouted someone on the stand;
And it's likely they'd a-killed him had not Casey raised his hand.

Two years earlier, however, an anonymous poem appeared in the *Chicago Tribune,* invoking if not murder, then certainly mayhem on the person of the umpire:

Mother, may I slug the umpire,
May I slug him right away,
So he cannot be here, Mother,
When the clubs begin to play?
Let me clasp his throat, dear Mother,
In a dear, delightful grip,
With one hand, and with the other
Bat him several in the lip.
Let me climb his frame, dear Mother,
While the happy people shout:
I'll not kill him, dearest Mother,
I will only knock him out.
Let me mop the ground up, Mother
With his person, dearest, do;
If the ground can stand it, Mother
I don't see why you can't, too.

And by 1889, the umpire's place as a cultural pariah deserving of corporal punishment was so firmly entrenched that no less a social observer than Mark Twain could exploit it for satire. In his time-traveling novel, *A Connecticut Yankee in King Arthur's Court,* Twain has his nineteenth-century narrator introducing baseball to the knights of the Round Table.

"At first I appointed men of no rank to act as umpires," Twain writes in the voice of the Yankee, "but I had to discontinue that. These people were no easier to please than other nines. The umpire's first decision was usually his last; they broke him in two with a bat, and his friend toted him home on a shutter. When it was noticed that no umpire ever survived a game, umpiring got to be unpopular. So I was obliged to appoint somebody whose rank and lofty position under the government would protect him."

Like all good satire, the sentiment had its roots in actuality, and the threat to umpires hasn't always been hyperbole. Perhaps the most famous example of violence against an umpire took place in 1907, when Billy Evans, who would go on to have a Hall of Fame career, was struck by a thrown bottle still full of beer, fracturing his skull. But this was hardly an isolated incident. Indeed, it had dozens of antecedents.

Many accounts of the early days of professional baseball have noted that before the turn of the century, umpiring was an especially perilous occupation. In June 1884, for example, two different umpires, one in Baltimore and one in Washington, barely escaped with their lives when mobs unhappy with their decisions stormed the field. Here is the account of one incident, as reported in the *New York Times:*

AN UNPOPULAR UMPIRE ASSAULTED

Baltimore, Md., June 12. There was a very exciting scene today at Oriole Park during the first game of base-ball between the Louisville and Baltimore American Association Base-ball Clubs, and Umpire John Brennan, of Indianapolis, had a very narrow escape from injury. The game was a close one, and at the end of the ninth inning the score was a tie—4 to 4. In the tenth inning Brennan decided Sommers, of the Baltimores, out on third base. The ugly part of the crowd took exception to the decision and about 500 jumped onto the field and made a rush for Brennan. One man drew a pistol and was, with difficulty, prevented from shooting at the umpire. The players of both teams surrounded Brennan and, with bats in their hands, prepared to defend him. Finally the crowd was driven back and the game was resumed. Thirteen innings were played and the score still remained a tie at 4 to 4, darkness preventing further play. As the umpire was leaving the grounds, an unknown man struck him a terrible blow on the cheek. Brennan was carried into the club-house and kept there until the crowd had left the park. He has asked to be released from umpiring any more games in this city. The feeling against him here is very strong on account of a decision he gave against the Baltimore Club in Philadelphia, which gave a game to the Athletics. This is the first disorder that has occurred at Oriole Park this season.

Implicit in the tone and content of this account are a number of prevalent attitudes of the time, with fans viewing umpires as persecutors of their teams and journalists not above justifying or even enjoying this kind of behavior. In his three-volume history, *American Baseball,* David Q. Voigt points out that the men who ran baseball were also not averse to scapegoating the umpires; it was good for business. Albert G. Spalding, the pitcher and sporting-goods magnate who was also president of the Chicago White Stockings, remarked that fans who despise the umpires are merely registering their "democratic right to protest against tyranny." Indeed, in spite of the players in Baltimore rallying to Umpire Brennan's rescue, there were regular incidents of players attacking umpires as well. As Voigt concluded, "By the end of the 1880's, the baseball umpire, that rational symbol of orderly conduct, had become a universal symbol of hate."

The sentiment against umpires, and the kind of general threat to them, persisted well into the twentieth century.

"'Kill the umpire!' is the battle cry of baseball," the great drama critic George Jean Nathan wrote in a 1910 essay in *Harper's* magazine that was largely but not entirely satiric, saying that baiting the umpire (or worse) was the element of baseball that most distinguished it as American and most distinguished it as a game:

> Compared to the umpire, the proverbial fat man is a universally loved individual. If there are twenty thousand men at a ball game, each one of the twenty thousand, as well as all the small boys on the nearby telegraph poles, hate the umpire. They itch to take his life. . . . Other countries have tried baseball, but they have not tried killing-the-umpire. That is probably the reason they have not waxed enthusiastic over baseball. For baseball without umpire-killing is like football without girls in the grandstand.

In 1928, an Italian newspaper, *L'Osservatore Romano,* used the venomous cries of American baseball fans to argue that Christian values in the New World had devolved into paganism, a literal interpretation of "kill the umpire" that might have been laughable if the *New York Times,* in an editorial, hadn't found it necessary to explain the national custom. The tongue-in-cheek tone of the piece is peculiar, to say the least, and does little to make the line between literal and figurative expressions of rage any clearer.

The *Times,* under the headline "We Don't Really Mean It," said:

> It is perfectly true that all over this broad land any Roman editor who might tarry by a village commons or sit in a box at the Yankee Stadium would probably hear from a thousand throats the ejaculation:

"Kill the umpire!" But this does not mean that any of the ejaculators really want the umpire to be assassinated. Some of them would perhaps like to see him slightly injured as reprisal for his manifest injustice against the home team. Others would be willing to have any other spectator launch his fist against the umpire's treacherous eyes. Still others are for various forms of punishment, but not one really desires that the umpire shall pass from the company of mortals.

Today, that line is still a little blurry. "Enemy of the people" is still a label that umpires wear. And as hackneyed as it is, "kill the umpire" is still heard in ballparks from the mouths of adults and children. Fans, of course, never give this a second thought, but the extraordinary hostility of it is not lost on the umpires themselves. In 1998, a time when they were especially embattled, under scrutiny by the media and fending off baseball's mounting efforts to enforce greater discipline on them, *Sports Illustrated* published a cover story excoriating umpires for their ineptitude and arrogance.

The cover line? "Kill the Ump." The photograph on the cover was of Tim Welke, who had been in the big leagues since 1984 and would go on to work the American League Championship Series the year the cover was published.

"Imagine waking up to that," Welke's younger brother Bill, also a major league umpire, said to me. "Imagine having to explain to your five-year-old daughter that no one really wants you killed."

These days umpires say that they rarely worry about their safety on the field, but most major league umpires have stories from their minor league days about having their tires slashed by irate fans or being the targets of other threatening gestures. Jim Evans recalled that once, working a Texas League game in El Paso in the early 1970s, he and his partner had to be escorted from the stadium to safety by the sheriff. When Evans thanked the man, he replied, "Son, if I weren't wearing this uniform, I'd kick your ass myself."

Throughout baseball history there have been a handful of episodes that are reminders of what can happen when hostility is encouraged and misdirected. In 1920, in a famous incident, Ty Cobb challenged umpire Billy Evans to a fight after a game in Washington. The two met under the stands after the game, and Cobb beat him badly.

At Ebbets Field in Brooklyn in 1940, George Magerkurth was

attacked on the field by an ex-convict immediately after a Dodger loss in which Magerkurth had ejected the Dodger manager, Leo Durocher. (It turned out the convict was merely creating a diversion for his partner, a pickpocket who was working the exiting crowd.)

As recently as April 2003, Laz Diaz, working first base at Chicago's U.S. Cellular Field, was attacked by a fan who had leaped out of the stands with an indefinite but malicious intent. When I met Diaz, I asked him about it. The White Sox were playing host to the Kansas City Royals, he recalled, and some drunken nutcase tried to tackle him in the middle of a play.

"I guess the guy was up in the nosebleed section," Diaz told me, "and I found out later that he told his fiancée, 'I'm going to go jump on the field, but before I get knocked down, I'm going to knock down the first person I see.'

"Anyway, it was the bottom of the eighth, two outs, and there was a pop-up to right field. I was at first base, and I turned to go out. And as soon as the ball's hit, everybody's chasing down the line, me and Mike Sweeney, the first baseman for Kansas City, and Sweeney stopped, but I thought he was still behind me, and this guy grabbed me by the waist, and I thought it was Sweeney, and I said, 'Hey, Mike, get out of here.' But then I looked down and I didn't see a uniform."

The man was easily subdued by Diaz with the aid of a couple of players and, eventually, ballpark security.

"It was afterwards that I started to think, 'What if this guy had a knife?'" Diaz said. "I was thinking of Monica Seles, and the guy in Germany who jumped out of the stands and stabbed her, and I just thought, 'Wow, if this guy had had a knife . . .'"

Flesh-and-blood umpires like Diaz are not quite so easy to hate. In the small library of narrative works that treat umpires not as symbols but as actual characters with human characteristics, the depiction is almost always sympathetic. A 1950 slapstick film comedy, *Kill the Umpire,* starred William Bendix (who not only appeared as well in the title role in *The Babe Ruth Story* but played minor league baseball before going to Hollywood) as a virulent fan and rabid umpire hater who, in a cockamamy reversal of fortune, becomes one himself and discovers it is a noble profession after all. Despite a lot of hokeyness, it has some surprises; the story is more thoroughly rounded than you would think.

Written by Hollywood journeyman Frank Tashlin with a reasonably entertaining wryness, it's pretty careful to depict the details of the umpire's job accurately and with respect.

The occasional novelist, too, has found a man behind the umpire's mask. One was John Hough Jr., whose 1986 novel, *The Conduct of the Game,* is an umpire's coming-of-age story, told in the first person, in which the protagonist, Lee Malcolm, works his way up through the minor leagues to the majors, where he discovers that the principles governing an umpire's education on the field aren't necessarily applicable in the world at large. Indeed, one of Hough's unique contributions to umpire lit is not just that Lee emerges as a morally upright fellow, not just that there's more to him than being an umpire, but that other umpires who serve as secondary figures aren't so upright. Solely being an umpire, in other words, is not a definition of character, good or ill.

Another novel that humanizes umpires is *Strike Zone,* published in 1994 and cowritten by Jim Bouton, the former major league pitcher and author of the infamous memoir *Ball Four,* and Eliot Asinof, who wrote the definitive account of the Black Sox scandal of 1919, *Eight Men Out,* as well as the baseball novel *Man on Spikes. Strike Zone* posits an umpire on the fork of a moral dilemma: Should he influence the outcome of a game in order to pay back the man who once saved his life but who has gotten himself in trouble with violent loan sharks?

This plot-heavy book, driven more by suspense than character and utilizing a narrative gimmick of dual narrators—alternating voices between a journeyman pitcher, Sam Ward, and the weary, burdened umpire, Ernie Kolacka—shares with *Conduct of the Game* the idea that baseball is a suitable backdrop against which to sort out nonsporting ambiguities, as well as the idea that the umpire's authority is no inoculation against life's difficult decisions. In both books, the very fallibility of the umpires is their salvation; their crises make them identifiably human, relatives of ours, rather than our natural antagonists.

Two other samples of popular culture are worth citing in this regard. One is from advertising, a television commercial for Budweiser that aired in the late 1980s that skillfully told a thirty-second story about a black umpire who finds his way to the big leagues and earns the respect of a veteran manager by making a tough call and sticking to his guns in the ensuing argument; the umpire's reward comes in the barroom after the game when the manager sends over a congratulatory beer. Not only did the ad humanize the umpire, who had obviously overcome great hardships (racism is merely implicit) to get his chance, but it was a rare acknowledgment in a popular medium that umpiring is a craft that requires training and skill and that umpires advance ostensibly according to a meritocracy.

Finally, perhaps the most enduring image of umpires is the Norman Rockwell painting *Bottom of the Sixth,* which first appeared on the cover of the *Saturday Evening Post* on April 23, 1949. In it three umpires are standing together in Ebbets Field in Brooklyn. The three are modeled on real umpires: Beans Reardon and, slightly behind and flanking him, Larry Goetz and Lou Jorda. (If you've wondered about the fourth member of the crew, recall that major league games did not start employing four umpires until three years later.)

The sky in the painting is cloudy and the first drops of a storm are falling. A scoreboard in the background shows Pittsburgh leading Brooklyn, 1–0, after five and a half innings. Behind the umpires, two men, possibly the managers of the Pirates and the Dodgers, partly obscured and rendered in caricature, seem to be discussing the weather. Reardon, the plate umpire, has his mask in his left hand and his chest protector dangling from the crook of his left elbow. His right palm is out, feeling for rain. The other two have their arms at their sides; all three are looking up, evidently trying to determine if the bad weather will halt the game.

Partly because of their pose, which alludes to supplication, and partly because of their shared facial expressions, somber and uncertain, the umpires seem troubled. The image suggests men of earthly authority seeking the wisdom of a higher one; they're men with a burden of responsibility who are acutely aware of their human limitations. It's touching, really, the seriousness with which the three seem to be taking their predicament, the tenuous weather that has them flummoxed.

Rockwell's images are often criticized as nostalgic or sentimental, and certainly the painting has a surface pathos, but *Bottom of the Sixth* is perceptive about umpires, presenting them as men who are doomed to strive vainly against expectations of their divinity and maybe their own expectations of themselves.

One spring afternoon, I took a major league crew—Tim McClelland, Bill Welke, Fieldin Culbreth, and Marty Foster—out to lunch in Queens, New York, near Shea Stadium, where they were working for the weekend. At the end of a lengthy discussion, I asked them to tell me something they'd been waiting to tell a writer, something that had to be in a book about umpires or the book would be incomplete.

McClelland, the crew chief, who had been in the big leagues since 1983, responded, "Well, it's something I kind of joke about." He paused, as though deciding whether it was smart to actually say what he was thinking of saying. When he continued, he seemed a little embarrassed, but his sincerity was clear, and I was reminded at that moment of *Bottom of the Sixth*.

"It's that umpires are people, too," McClelland said. "We have families, we have emotions. We're not just the ogre that comes out of the ground to make that call. Somebody says, 'Kill the umpire,' and people go, 'Heh, heh, that's funny,' but in order to do that you have to disassociate the umpire from the person. We're human. We're not just robots they send out there."

CHAPTER TWO

"I'M CHASING THE DREAM"

To secure the presence of intelligent, honest, unprejudiced, quick-witted, courageous umpires at all contests in scheduled games has been one of the most vexatious problems confronting those in control of our national sport.

—ALBERT G. SPALDING, 1911

The Osceola County Sports Complex in Kissimmee, Florida, is the spring training camp of the Houston Astros, but every year, before the Astros arrive, it is the home of the Jim Evans Academy of Professional Umpiring as well. It isn't an especially extravagant facility, just a network of ball fields and low-lying administrative and athletic buildings, located across the street from a high school and a small apartment complex, and near enough to Disney World to be within its universe of cheap motels, one of which serves as the academy dormitory.

The surrounding area is oddly spiritless, a kind of limbo on a vast flatland, the outer reaches of the commercial solar system that revolves around Mickey Mouse. The main road through the area, U.S. 192, is a ghastly ribbon of American exterior decor, remarkable for its comprehensive representation of fast-food, lodging, and retail chains. There may not be an uglier or more mercenary stretch of road in the country, and on my arrival I had the thought that baseball, like cockroaches or mold or Wal-Mart, can thrive just about anywhere. Indeed, hundreds of outposts like this make up baseball nation, and as I would eventually learn during my travels, staying in Kissimmee at the Quality Inn was a reasonable facsimile of the lifestyle of minor league umpires, except that

I didn't have to pack up every few days and drive to another mediocre motel a few hundred miles away.

If you're fervid or foolish enough to want to work as an umpire in professional baseball, there's only one way to do it: You have to go to an umpire school, one of the two that have a seal of approval from Major League Baseball. Evans's is one. The other, run by another former major league ump, Harry Wendelstedt, and his son, Hunter, who joined the big league staff in 1999, is only an hour away, in Daytona Beach.

Actually, umpire schools run by major league umpires have been in existence since the early 1930s, and over the years several different ones have been earmarked to feed the professional ranks. Wendelstedt bought his school from another umpire, Al Somers, in 1977. After receiving permission from baseball, Evans started his academy in Arizona in 1990, when two others, Wendelstedt's and that of another umpire, Joe Brinkman, were already operating in Florida. He moved it to Kissimmee in 1993, and in 1998 bought Brinkman's school and folded it into his own.

In 1965, Major League Baseball created the umpire development program (known as UDP or, occasionally, BUD, for baseball umpire development), which for many years consisted of a single supervisor, a man named Barney Deary, who traveled the country observing minor league umpires and gauging their progress. Briefly, starting in 1969, baseball ran its own instruction program—an "umpire specialization course," they called it—for promising young umpires, but in 1974 sold it to an umpire named Bill Kinnamon, who subsequently sold it to Brinkman. The big leagues, through the UDP, did continue to fund minor league umpire supervision until 1997, when the annual investment of $5 million was withdrawn. It wasn't worth the money, Major League Baseball decided, given that, on average, a new umpire was hired only every two years.*

Only since the 1960s have the big leagues prescribed a professional

---

*Jim Evans, whose first big league season was 1972, was the last big league umpire ever hired without having been to umpire school before turning professional. He entered pro ball in 1968 when, while he was working college games in Texas, scouts recommended him to the Florida State League in the low minors, whose president hired him sight unseen over the phone. After his first season, he was a member of the first umpire specialization class.

path for career-oriented umpires. Before that, a guy might get into the minor leagues because some old-time umpire or scout happened to be in the stands at an amateur game and liked what he saw, and a minor leaguer might get a shot at the big leagues because he was recommended through the grapevine to the big league supervisors, who were almost always retired big league umpires themselves. And until 1999, the American and the National leagues recruited and maintained their own staffs.

But these days the first stop for any aspiring umpire is one of the two schools, whose job it is to recommend umpires to the Professional Baseball Umpiring Corporation, aka PBUC (the acronym is pronounced "peabuck"), which administers umpires in the minor leagues.

The Evans and Wendelstedt schools run more or less concurrently, for five weeks in January and early February, and their programs are similar, with morning classroom sessions dealing with rules and umpire responsibilities and afternoon field drills to put the morning lessons into practice. The relationship between the two schools is competitive and testy. Each claims to have the better faculty, the more efficient curriculum, the more successful graduates, and it doesn't take a long conversation with a loyalist from either school to elicit a snide remark about the other. Nothing concrete seems to lie behind the mutual animosity, which exists more among the faculty and major league alumni than anyone else. I chose the Evans school only because the first time I looked into writing about umpires, I e-mailed both schools, and Evans got in touch with me but Wendelstedt didn't.

The differences between the two schools boil down to an essential few. At Evans, more classroom time is spent on learning and discussing the rulebook; Evans is an acknowledged rulebook expert, and his emphasis on the rules is a reflection of his belief that they are an umpire's foundation, that they are what an umpire stands on when he takes the field. Another difference is that at the Wendelstedt school, where the prevailing view is not that the rules are unimportant, but that an umpire's strength is built through game experience, local high school teams are imported to play games so the student umpires deal with genuine competition and, most significantly, work behind the plate with live pitching.

Evans's philosophy is that live games tend to limit the number of circumstances the student umpires will be exposed to; most games, after all, are parades of the run-of-the-mill. So rather than live games, the Evans curriculum concentrates its fieldwork on simulations, the creation of specific game situations, with a combination of students and instructors filling in as fielders and base runners and with a fungo hitter putting the ball in play. This guarantees that student umpires will encounter catcher's interference, obstruction, a balk, or any of the other ball field happenstances they might not see every day, every week, or even every month, but that they have to be prepared to recognize and adjudicate and thus know what they look like and what is required in response to them. One of Evans's favorite tropes is to ask a visitor if he has a driver's license, as he did with me the first time we met. I do, of course, I told him.

"Then you can make ninety-five percent of the calls an umpire has to make," he said. "What we do here is train you for the other five percent."

The evening after my arrival the school's official curriculum got under way at an orientation ceremony in the Astros' low-ceilinged clubhouse. The staff, fifteen or so minor league umpires wearing coats and ties, were milling around, many of them stopping to joke with Dick Nelson, a former minor league umpire and supervisor known to one and all as Sarge. In his seventies, Sarge was Evans's second-in-command and chief field instructor.

There were about 120 of us umpire plebes, sitting restlessly at long tables in long rows—we could have been getting ready to take the SATs—when Evans, with a showman's instinct for making his audience wait just a little, sauntered in. Three decades of standing on ball fields had ground his hip cartilage to dust, and he walked with the rolling and painful gait of a man in need of the surgery he would undergo the following summer. In the school environment, Evans carried the aura of accomplishment and celebrity with him anyway, but his distinctive limp added to it; in the eyes of the students, it made him just a little more intimidating, as though burning oneself out physically were something to be aspired to along with the rest of a big league umpiring career.

Evans was fifty-eight the year I enrolled in his school, seven years past a career on the field that spanned twenty-eight seasons in the American League, nineteen as a crew chief. He had worked in four World Series and three All-Star games, the last one in 1999, only weeks before he lost his job in the union implosion. We'll get to the details later, but of the many umpires who suffered mightily in the aftermath of that season, Evans was among the most severely punished, one of a handful who wanted to resume working in baseball and never got the chance. His annual salary when he left baseball was about $250,000, and he lost valuable years of pension contributions. He had to sell his home and move his family.

None of this was in evidence on the first night of school, however. Evans, who graduated from the University of Texas, where he was once a star debater, was in his element. A smaller man than you might envision—under six feet and compact, though not slight—he had an intelligent face, keen, squinting eyes, and a mustache with a sharp downslope that gave him the aspect of a mischievous badger. A native Texan, he spoke with an amused-sounding drawl, maybe because he was fond of amusing himself when he spoke. When he welcomed us the first night, he set out to test the group wit.

"This is the seventeenth year I've been running my school," he said, sweeping a glance of assessment over the room, "and I can say without a doubt that of all the classes I've had, you are the most recent."

The laughter was sparse. Umpires in general but young ones especially tend to be literal-minded, and though a few students looked at one another as if to check whether Evans was joking, most received the remark as if perhaps they ought to be taking notes. After he finished introducing himself, Evans asked each of us to do the same.

"Tell us why you're here," he said, and the first young man explained his presence and his goal with a simple declaration: "I'm chasing the dream."

This exact locution was a cue picked up on by almost everyone in the room under the age of thirty, which is to say about 80 percent of the class, and was repeated again and again that evening.

"I'm from Des Moines, Iowa," one strapping young man would say. "I've been umpiring for five years, and I'm chasing the dream."

"I'm from Nampa, Idaho," the next would say. "I've been umpiring since I was fifteen, and I'm chasing the dream."

McComb, Mississippi; Rocky Point, New York; Polk, Ohio; Lakewood, Colorado; Bremerton, Washington; Marquette, Michigan; Export, Pennsylvania; Lindsborg, Kansas; Visalia, California; Dallas, Texas; Alcester, South Dakota; Reno, Nevada; Fort Wayne, Indiana;

Omaha, Nebraska; Tomah, Wisconsin; Huntington Beach, California: Coast to coast—plus Hawaii, Puerto Rico, and a handful of foreign lands—the story was the same.

The dream deemed so worthy of the chase is a very specific one, of course—it's about reaching the major leagues—and it is more or less impossible. Most of my young classmates paid lip service to their slim chances—fewer than one in a hundred umpire school students get to the big leagues—but the way the phrase became a casual mantra made it clear they didn't really get (or didn't really give much thought to) what a hundred to one means. Every now and then I wanted to throttle one of them for his optimistic naïveté. During the day you'd pass a guy jogging between the batting cages and the practice fields and one of you would say, "How's it going?" and the other would respond automatically and nonchalantly, "Chasin' the dream."

On the surface, all of this was somehow encouraging and warm-spirited, a kind of testimony to the broadly democratic nature of the professional umpire system. But I don't mean that entirely as a compliment. In 1997, when the owners of major league franchises voted to abandon their role in umpire development, they not only ceded the training of umpires to Evans and Wendelstedt (sanctioning but not supporting them), they also ceded the supervision and administration of minor league umpires to the minor leagues. It was a striking and not-much-remarked-upon act of marginalization. Essentially the owners were saying they didn't care where their umpires came from.

You'd think professional baseball would be on the lookout for talented high school and college umpires, wouldn't you? But the big leagues decided to let the independent schools do their recruiting for them, and with the exception of providing a small number of umpire school scholarships for minorities, that remains the case. But neither Evans nor Wendelstedt has the resources for recruitment, nor can they afford to turn anyone away.

Therefore you don't have to have amateur umpiring experience to enroll in professional umpire school. You don't have to be physically fit, though the schools suggest that if you can't handle moderate exercise, you won't be happy there. You don't even have to have great eyesight; the official requirement for umpiring in professional ball is that your vision must be correctable to twenty–twenty, but they don't do an eye test for umpire school and I know mine, for example, isn't that good.* So if you're eighteen and have the money (tuition and room and board are exceptionally modest, a whole lot less than a midwinter Florida vacation), they're happy to let you in.

You also don't need to be male, though of the 120 students in my class, 119 of them were. The exception was a slightly built Japanese woman who spoke hardly any English, was barely five feet tall, and whose ambition, I learned through a translator, was to become an umpire in international Little League competitions. Everyone called her Bunny, and though she was not without umpiring skills, she was indisputably out of place; the first week in school, she was hit by a golf cart whose driver, an Astros groundskeeper, said he hadn't been able to see her.

Only her gender, not her nationality, made Bunny anomalous, and in most years she wouldn't have been unique for that. According to Evans, between two and six women enroll most years, and Ria Cortesio, the one female umpire then working in professional ball—in Double A—was a regular instructor at the school, though she was recovering from off-season knee surgery the year I was a student.

Bunny was joined in our class by four Australians, four Canadians, and a Swiss. Six other students also came from Japan, which sends a sizable contingent to Kissimmee every year, partly because Evans goes there annually to conduct clinics. Several umpires in the Japanese professional leagues have attended the Evans school as a means of improving their skills or, in the case of Takeshi Hirabayashi and Masaki Nonaka, altogether escaping the profession in Japan, where umpires are treated with considerably harsher disdain than they are here, frequently manhandled physically or spat upon by players, and sometimes forced to apologize publicly for making incorrect calls.

Hirabayashi and Nonaka had both gone through the Evans school as students, and they were now instructors who, like everyone else on

---

*Many professional umpires wear glasses to read and use contact lenses on the field. I wore glasses under my mask, which actually isn't so unusual. In fact, since 1956, when Ed Rommel and Frank Umont became the first flouters of that taboo, a number of big league umpires have been known to do the same. Once, famously, Bruce Froemming was questioned about his eyesight, and he responded thus: "The sun is 93 million miles away, and I can see that."

the academy staff, were working in the minor leagues. I first met them the morning after orientation. They had been assigned to parcel out the equipment allotted to each student, which included a wooden-handled whisk to brush off home plate and a ball-and-strike indicator, the latter of which figured in my very first lesson in how to be a professional umpire, predating even the hat business: Never call it a clicker. (Why? Nobody ever said, but I guess it's like an opera singer's not referring to an aria as a song.)

It's fair to say that both Hirabayashi and Nonaka were better umpires than they were English speakers. Their vocabularies had a heavy emphasis on baseball terms, and their accents had the stereotypical flavor of Charlie Chan. Hirabayashi, a solicitous, sweet-tempered young man whom I came to know as Tak, handed over the indicator and waggled a forefinger at me from behind the counter where he stood:

"No clicka," he said.

Like refrigerator-repair school or stenographer school, umpire school is vocational; the idea is to graduate and to go to work, which is the reason the schools teach the two-umpire system—games in the low minor leagues are officiated by only two umpires, one behind the plate and one on the bases. (Double A and Triple A baseball employ three umpires; only in the major leagues is there an ump for every base.)

But there is a fundamental paradox about umpire school, namely that the vocation it prepares you for is so competitive that it barely exists. The administrative system governing the employment of umpires is truly peculiar and even counterproductive, being essentially a winnowing process that couldn't have more discouragement built in and in which success has as much or more to do with endurance as it does ability.

Here's how it works: The first hurdle for any aspiring umpire is to make it into the top stratum of his class. In early February, at the end of their five-week sessions, the Evans and Wendelstedt schools each select a specified number of their top students, usually around twenty-five, to be evaluated by PBUC, which is responsible for the hiring, supervision, and administration of the umpires who work in the lower minor leagues, from Rookie League to Double A.

In early March, PBUC holds an evaluation camp in Cocoa,

Florida, what amounts to a minor league umpiring tryout. Over ten days, the fifty or so candidates who have been nominated by the two schools are assigned to umpire games played by high school and college teams that have traveled from the North to play ball during spring break. Their performances are scrutinized and judged by the seven PBUC field supervisors (all former minor league umpires), and finally, after each umpire has worked six or eight games, they are numerically ranked from one to fifty. They are hired in order of their ranking, the number who get jobs dependent on the number of jobs that have become available, through promotions and attrition, at the lowest rungs of the minor leagues. That can be as few as a dozen, as many as forty or fifty.

So even if you graduate from umpire school at the top of your class, you're far from certain to land a job. Beyond that, there's a be-careful-what-you-wish-for element to all this, because even if you get a job, you're not likely to make a living. Starting salary for a minor league umpire is $1,900 per month—for five months—and the pay scale doesn't exactly shoot up from there. If you prove to be an exemplary minor league umpire and rise from level to level with regularity, you may reach Triple A in six or eight years, at which time, at maybe thirty, thirty-five, or even forty years old, you'll be making about $20,000 annually. Then, of course, things get especially difficult and frustrating because here, chances are, even for a superior umpire, the road ends. The major leagues just don't have many openings.

It's often said by defenders of this system that umpires are given the same chance as players to rise through the ranks. However, there are eleven times more jobs in the big leagues for players than umpires; the thirty teams have a total of 750 players at a time on their active rosters. In addition, the players' rosters are a lot more fluid, and unlike players, whose talent alone will force their ascension to the big leagues, worthy umpires generally have to wait their turn, sometimes excruciatingly, for forces beyond their control to work in their favor.

For years the umpires have been trying to get baseball to increase their big league numbers, but the owners have resisted, largely because of the expense. In addition to salaries, which are determined by length of service (as of 2008, the majority of major league umpires were earning $200,000 or more), major leaguers get substantial per diem—it was in the neighborhood of $380 in 2008—and unbeknownst to many fans, they are entitled to four weeks of vacation *during* the baseball season.

This creates a rather substantial problem. With two crews per week on vacation, there are just enough umpires on the major league roster to work a full schedule of fifteen games, so if anyone is sick or injured or there's a death in the family, there aren't any readily available substitutes. Baseball's current solution is to designate twenty or so Triple A umpires as major league fill-ins. These guys are the minor league elite, thought of as the pool of next-in-lines for full-time elevation to the big leagues. Of course, whenever they are substituting in big league parks, they fly first-class, stay at ritzy hotels, are treated with a level of deference by stadium personnel they rarely enjoy in the minor leagues, and they receive major league union scale for the big league games they work.

Even so, this status is often a cruel carrot. For one thing, like a sumptuous, requested meal before an execution, it can be a sign that the end is near; every year a handful of these umpires are lopped off the bottom of the fill-in list and usually dismissed altogether as unlikely ever to make a permanent ascent. For a few others it's just an agony of waiting.

Chris Guccione and Rob Drake, for example, two umpires who have been in pro ball for nearly a decade, each worked their one thousandth big league game in 2007, and in 2008 were still minor leaguers, receiving minor league benefits and officially earning minor league salaries. (And remember, these are the best jobs the minor leagues have to offer.) It's no wonder that jobs in the minors turn over at a pretty good rate, sometimes up to 20 percent annually, mostly because people get tired of the crappy life they lead while they wait for a shot at the majors.

Chris Tiller, one of the first umpires I spoke with, put the matter most succinctly. Tiller was then in the Texas League, in Double A—he was later promoted to Triple A—and he was dressing in the tiny umpires' room in Whataburger Field in Corpus Christi. It was midsummer, and at almost 11 p.m. the temperature hadn't receded much from the ninety-five degrees he and his colleagues had just worked a three-hour game in. They were eating the dinner provided by the ball club—a Styrofoam plate full of fried chicken wings, by then cold and doughy. In a few minutes, they'd be climbing into their van for an overnight drive to their next scheduled city.

"Nobody's in this to be a minor league umpire," Tiller said. "Believe me."

* * *

Umpiring isn't something anyone is born wanting to do. Or as Evans put it at orientation, "No father ever lit up a cigar, pointed to his new baby, and said, 'That kid is going to be a major league umpire,'" which isn't quite the same thing, though it implies the same question: How does anybody get turned in this peculiar direction? Usually it has something to do with wanting to be around baseball and not being good enough to play—"I couldn't hit a curve ball, so I decided to call it," Wally Bell, who made the big leagues in 1993, would say to me—and vaguely needing to indulge a craving for competition. But a lot of happenstance is involved, too.

Mike Winters, who joined the National League staff in 1990, said he first thought about umpiring when he was in the sixth grade: "This was the late 1960s and I had a male teacher, which was pretty unusual in elementary school, and he had an indicator, a ball-strike indicator, in his desk drawer. And for whatever reason, this thing fascinated me. And every now and then, I'd sneak over to his desk and play with it and turn the wheels, and finally one day I stole it. I couldn't resist. And after that, every time we played ball in the street, I had the indicator, so I had to be the umpire."

Winters paused, a little embarrassed. "I've still got it," he said.

Ted Barrett, who landed in the majors in 1999, had aspired to be a professional boxer. A heavyweight, he was living in Las Vegas, training and working as a sparring partner for Evander Holyfield, among others, when it finally dawned on him that he didn't have a shot at being the world champion his trainers promised him he could be. His father, who hated that Ted was boxing anyway, staked him to umpire school. Barrett got married to his high school sweetheart in California on New Year's Eve 1988, and the next day he left for the Joe Brinkman Umpire School in Florida.

"Tina was a ticket agent for US Air, so we were able to make a little honeymoon out of it," Barrett said.

The most exotic story, though, belongs to Alfonso Marquez, the youngest umpire in the big leagues—he was thirty-three when I met him in 2006—and the first to have been born in Mexico. His hometown, Encarnación, is a village in the central state of Zacatecas. His father was a tombstone carver until he left the family in 1979, traveling to join his brother in Fullerton, California, where he worked as a gardener to earn the money to bring his family to America to join him.

"We got here in 1980, all of us illegally," Marquez told me during a conversation in Arizona, where he lives. "He paid three or four hundred dollars per person to get us here—my mom, my sister, and myself. I was seven years old."

As a kid in Fullerton, he loved playing ball. One day when he was fourteen and playing Pony League, he hit a ball beyond the outfielders and circled the bases for a home run—but missed second base.

"I knew it, and so did the other team, and they appealed to the umpire, and sure enough he called me out," Marquez said. "And I'm sitting there going, 'There's only two umpires, and one of them is out in the outfield chasing the ball, and the other one is behind the plate. How in hell can they see that?'"

After the game he saw the umpires changing their clothes in the parking lot. "So I went up to them. I said, 'Hey, can I ask you something? How did you see that?' And they started explaining to me what umpires are taught, and I was like, 'Aha!'"

From then on, his romance with umpiring was on-again, off-again. With little instruction, he started umpiring Little League games; it was a chance to earn some money and to bond a little with his father, with whom his relationship otherwise chafed. By the time he was in high school, he was in full rebellion, quitting school, moving out of the house, and quitting umpiring, too.

After a year he began to miss it. He was living with a girlfriend, working a lot of odd jobs in a lot of odd places—a convalescent home, a family restaurant, an auto body shop. During this time he discovered there was such a thing as umpire school, and he wrote to Joe Brinkman, who was running the school that was eventually folded into Jim Evans's. Coincidentally, Brinkman was planning to be in Anaheim shortly; the two men met over breakfast, and Brinkman gave him some advice.

"I told him I'm a legal resident but not yet a citizen, and I said I don't have a high school diploma. He said the resident thing was not a problem, but that it couldn't hurt to get my GED. Right away I went back to school."

In a very real way, Marquez said, "umpiring saved my ass."

The next obstacle was finding the money to pay for umpire school. He got some of it from a fellow amateur umpire, an older man who was umpiring for fun and who donated his own umpiring check to the Marquez school fund.

The rest of the money came even more unexpectedly. At this point he was working in a small factory that made locks and doorknobs, and he had an accident. A glove he was wearing got caught in the spinning cogs of a polishing machine. He nearly lost a finger, but before he went to the hospital, an idea had taken shape: "As soon as it happened, I'm looking at my hand, and I'm thinking—I swear to God I'm thinking this—'If I sue these people, I can pay for umpire school.'"

Happily, it didn't come to that. He found a lawyer who told him the suit wouldn't be worth it, that the company would settle for a small sum, and it did, just enough to send him to Florida. That was 1993.

Six and a half years later, he was in the big leagues.

I heard these stories long after umpire school, of course, and it was interesting to compare them with the stories of my classmates. The formula was the same: a little baseball-philia, a little wishful thinking, a little serendipity.

I was a generation older than just about everyone else in my class, but I wasn't the oldest student. In fact, six of us were over fifty, a dozen or so over forty, a group that Julian Sexton, a fifty-four-year-old Australian, referred to as "the pensioners' club." Sexton, a television cameraman by profession, was a burly man with the musculature of a former athlete, the belly of a hearty eater, and the unlikely physical gusto of someone who dealt with his advancing age by ignoring it. With his smart-ass sense of humor and the thickest of Down Under accents, he was a favorite of both the other students and the instructors, to whom he was wont to snap, "Get back in your kennel," when they argued with him during simulated games.

Sexton was an experienced amateur umpire, though he'd discovered baseball only as an adult. It was actually softball that got him; his children played, and they roped him into umpiring their games. By the time I met him he was working in baseball, the eighteen-and-under division in New South Wales, a high level of competition in a nation with no professional leagues. His wife kept the league scorebooks, and the two of them had become so enamored of baseball that on the second honeymoon they'd taken a couple of years earlier they came to the United States expressly to see the Dodgers play at Dodger Stadium. He

Dodger Stadium. He described a society of Australian umpires that made it sound like a small but avid group of oddball hobbyists who love it that no one understands them. A couple of his umpiring colleagues had been to the Evans school in the past, which is how he ended up there.

"I did quite a lot of boxing when I was young," he said when I asked him what appealed to him about umpiring. "You can't rely on anybody else when you're boxing, and it's that, the aloneness of it, the feeling that you're on your own. That was an exhilarating thing. And umpiring is the same."

Most of the older guys—we had an ex–marine recruiter, a painting contractor, and a cattle rancher who had played college football at Oklahoma, among others—were like Sexton, experienced amateurs looking to improve and maybe move up in their level of competition, from high school to college, where the game is a little faster and more challenging.

"This isn't something you do just for enjoyment," Sexton told me.

The most touching of them was Jim Switalski, a fifty-eight-year-old, chain-smoking Chicagoan with a bad back and gimpy knees, who had begun umpiring Little League games the previous summer after he'd lost his job as a youth employment counselor. He'd wandered over to watch the games at a park near his home one evening in June and was asked to volunteer after the scheduled umpire failed to show up.

"The next thing I knew, I was doing ten games a week," he said. Now he was thinking that while he waited for his pension to kick in, he might be able to scratch out a living doing something with the game he loved. Still, he was having a tough time at umpire school. This was during the second week. His knees were throbbing, his back ached, and he wasn't walking comfortably. He was skipping a lot of the fieldwork.

"It feels a little like boot camp," he told me.

Twenty years earlier, during another period of unemployment, Switalski said he had taken a job as a beer vendor at Wrigley Field, and it transformed a worrisome time into one he recalled as happy. So this year, when he began mulling over going to umpire school to be able to do high school games, he said, his father, a loyal Cubs fan who died just a few weeks later, told him to do it; he deserved to be happy.

"I'm divorced and I've been single for a while," Switalski said.

"Maybe down the line I can move South, and I can do ball games twelve months a year."

He started to cry, suddenly, as if he'd remembered something.

"He asked me to put a Cubs hat in his casket," Switalski said.

Maybe a dozen of my classmates were in their thirties, not too old to be completely without hope of working in professional ball, but with the clock working against them along with everything else. This was the group I identified with the most, I think, foolishly, of course, especially at the beginning, before the novelty of the experience wore off and the grueling reality took root. Like them, it's probably true that I harbored a secret belief that I would prove to have otherworldly, hitherto undiscovered umpiring skills, and also like them (unlike my actual contemporaries), it's also probably true that I relished with childish glee the remote prospect of working on Olympus with the likes of Derek Jeter and Albert Pujols as my colleagues.

They were, of course, savvy enough to recognize the long odds. They knew that, after all, even a terrifically gifted thirty-two-year-old who got all the breaks still couldn't hope to be in the major leagues and making a living wage before he reached forty. But these were the guys who talked about giving themselves a last shot at doing something dream-worthy with their lives before settling down to unthrilling decades in careers they had already begun. One guy was a college financial officer. Another was on leave from the navy. A third was a schoolteacher. We had an insurance agent, a beer distributor, an accountant, a cabinet-maker, a financial planner, a farmer.

"I ended up at the academy because I couldn't take my job," said Joel Cammarata, who'd resigned from a San Francisco architectural firm just a few weeks earlier. He was thirty years old, a balding, slightly built man with at least one dashed dream before he got to Kissimmee: He had yearned to be a painter. He had never umpired a game in his life but was certain he was suited for it.

"You know how you always hear people should do what they love?" he said. "What I love is to paint and watch baseball. And, well, my paintings weren't exactly flying out the door, and the only people I know who get paid to watch baseball are umpires."

This conversation occurred during the first few days of school. In a couple of more weeks, Joel would conclude that he had been crazy to think he could have become a professional umpire, but at this point he was still gung ho. I asked him what had spurred him to come to umpire school in the first place, and he confessed that his ambition was a new one. During the postseason of 2005, he'd watched as several umpires' calls, some of them dubious, affected the outcomes of playoff games. Shortly thereafter, not three months before his arrival in Florida, he came up with his new career plan.

"I used to call a great game from the bleachers of the Oakland Coliseum," he said. "And over a barroom discussion with a friend, I decided to find out where these people come from and what qualifications they have. After a little research I found out all it takes is a high school diploma and attendance at one of two umpire schools and a love for the game."

That was enough for him to make the move he'd been contemplating—throwing in the towel on his first career.

"I tried to not be too specific," he said about how he told his employer. "I said, 'Unfortunately, after the holidays, I'll be out of town, and I won't be returning.' And they said, 'Oh, sorry something's wrong.' And I said, 'Well, nothing's really wrong, I'm going to be going back to school.' And they said, 'Oh, you're going to get your master's in architecture.' And I said, 'No, no, actually I'm going to be attending the Jim Evans Academy of Professional Umpiring.' And you could see all kinds of things going through their heads, but finally it was the same response I got from everybody else: 'They have a school for that?'"

Many in the class were under twenty-one, the majority under twenty-five, and at least three-quarters under twenty-eight, which is the consensus ceiling for a legitimate shot at the big leagues. Some were not even out of their teens and this was their first time away from home. They'd never done their own laundry. They couldn't legally sit at a bar. Some of them were clearly unprepared, either emotionally or physically, and some were shockingly unsophisticated.

"We get guys who show up with their own pillows," Evans said to me once. He didn't really relish functioning in loco parentis, though he acknowledged the responsibility and took it pretty seriously.

The temptation is to say they were a varied group in terms of backgrounds and interests, but that wasn't really the case. A handful were college students, including a couple of guys who were hoping to put off going to grad school—one in economics at UCLA, another in law at Indiana.

But for the most part, my young classmates were solidly blue-collar, decent and competitive young men possessed of the insecurities befitting their age and station, neither scholarly nor clear-minded about the future. When I asked them about the unpromising nature of umpiring as a career, they tended to shrug as though it were of no account. What came across mostly was a fuzzy state of young-adult uncertainty, the hope that something they'd been doing for fun or that simply seemed cool would also turn out to be professionally viable. Asked what it was about umpiring that drew them, almost uniformly they said it just seemed like a great job. "Going to work at the ballpark every day, and just being around baseball," one young man said to me in what could well have been a generic response. "What could be better than that?"

I was disappointed by this. For some reason I thought maybe the nobility of the profession—its law-and-order aspect, the guardianship of the national pastime's integrity—played a role for some of them, but it didn't, not consciously anyway. When I asked if they ever thought about the umpire as a symbol—of justice, fairness, authority, etc.—I got a collective "Naaah, not really."

Still, for many of them, especially the guys I grew to have an interest in, something was going on beneath the surface. Something in the umpire ethos got to them, something about what the umpire stands for that made them want to stand for it, too. They liked the taste of umpire Kool-Aid.

Typical of this attitude were two young guys who couldn't actually have been more different. One was Spencer Flynn, a hulking young man with an outward self-assurance and affability, but who could, in conversation, be cowed pretty easily into confessing his insecurity. He was only nineteen, but well over six feet and two hundred pounds, a self-described redneck who grew up outside San Diego. He'd been a ballplayer in high school—with his massive shoulders and rounded physique he was the prototype of a slugging first baseman, à la Mo Vaughn or David Ortiz—and nothing else gave him the kind of untroubled joy that baseball did. Like just about everyone else at the Evans school, he'd started umpiring locally just to pick up a little extra cash.

Crew-cut and amply tattooed on his upper body with patriotic signs and slogans, Spencer had wanted to follow his grandfather, his cousin, and several of his buddies into the marines. He'd been rejected, he said, because he'd had two steel screws implanted in his knee during surgery to repair a high school football injury. Then he'd spent a semester at a community college but was expelled, he explained, because "I kind of beat the crap out of a kid in my class." His victim had evidently spoken ill of the dead, a friend of Spencer's who'd been killed in Iraq.

This was actually his second time through the Evans school; he'd been there the year before, had been judged irascible and immature, not a suitable candidate for professional ball. That in itself wasn't unusual; a number of hopeful guys without a better idea of what they wanted to do with their lives had returned, having failed to advance to PBUC in their previous visit. This year, however, Spencer was among the top students, and after the instructors selected him to be sent along to PBUC, he told me that umpiring in general, and particularly its tenets as they are espoused by Jim Evans, had steered him away from suicide.

"I was just eighteen when I was here last year, just out of high school," he said. "I wasn't really thinking I'd get a job, and I didn't really think it had much effect on me. But when I got back home, my family had moved to Colorado, and I didn't want to go there. So I was living out of my truck and sleeping on a buddy's couch. I was back working at my old job, at a printing plant, and they were treating me like shit, giving me twelve-hour shifts. And there were problems with a woman, of course. And I debated jumping off the Coronado Bridge. It seriously crossed my mind."

The only thing he had to look forward to, he said, was umpiring.

"One of the guys I was umpiring with had been to Jimmy Evans's school, too, a few years before I went," he said. "And we were talking one day about how life was kicking us both in the ass, and he just said, 'Yeah, well, you know, Jim says, "Control what you can control."' And for some reason I started thinking about that, that I could control where I was working, where I was living, that there was a lot about my life that I could control that I didn't think I had control over."

So he moved out of his buddy's house, dropped the girlfriend who was tormenting him, went to stay with his family in Colorado for a while, and decided to go back to umpire school and to compete seriously for a job.

"I realized there's nothing I love more than being out on this field," he said. "It was just being reminded of Jimmy saying, 'Control what you can control,' that made all the difference for me."

The other young guy was Brian Dubois, a talkative, trim young man from Cranford, New Jersey, who was also back at the Evans school for a second year. He was twenty-four that winter, and he had already been umpiring for literally half his life, beginning as a Little League umpire while he himself was still in Little League.

Around school, Brian seemed especially impressionable; he wasn't quite as self-dramatizing as Spencer, but the eager search for an identity to rely on was equally intense. He took to heart the cautions of Evans regarding the straight-arrow behavior baseball wanted to cultivate in its young umpires, and he paid regular lip service to the seriousness with which an aspiring umpire ought to take the enterprise. He had the quickness and emphatic shiftiness of an athlete when he was on the field, but he always looked sort of grave out there, as if he were performing military maneuvers, and a little bit worried.

"You get to a point in your life where umpiring on your own you can only go so far," he said to me in a characteristically earnest self-analysis. "If you want to take the next step, you have to look into the school. You think you know balls and strikes, outs and safes. But it's a different art form, a different language you have to master in order to advance to the professional level."

Brian was a funny kid, with a personality that wavered wildly between poles of mischief and high-mindedness, swagger and insecurity. He could be self-deprecating one minute, annoyingly smug the next, and he had a surprising and somewhat amusing impulse toward self-flagellation.

I was fond of him. Periodically, after being yelled at by the instructors for an on-field mistake, he'd come to my room at night to moan about how he'd completely screwed up his chance at a future in the game simply because, as the plate umpire with a runner on first, he'd failed to cover third on a single to right.

"I blew it," he said one night, pacing back and forth in my room and nearly whimpering. "It's all over. I blew it."

Along with being a worrywart, Brian also had a remarkable penchant for self-destructive behavior. He'd had the talent the previous year to be at the top of the umpiring class, but by his own admission he'd spent too many evenings at the local bars looking for girls. This was a reprise of some bad habits. He had in the past picked up a couple of DUI arrests, and he'd been thrown out of college, he said with sincere rue, for excessive partying.

When Brian returned to Kissimmee for his second go-round, he arrived with a not-unearned reputation for frivolousness that he was determined to undo. He recognized he had boxed himself into a corner. He was broke, was living in his mother's house, and had had his driver's license revoked indefinitely.

"When I'm not umpiring, I'm actually a stock manager at a woman's clothing store and a waiter," Brian told me, saying he had to walk to both jobs or rely on an infrequently arriving bus. But now he had it figured out. If he earned a job umpiring, he'd be able to get out of New Jersey and start on a career path in baseball. He wouldn't need a car right away because he could be paired with a partner who had one, and he'd finally be able to pay off his fines. It was a perfect solution, he thought, for the mess he'd made of his life, which partly explained why he was so fatalistic about each perceived bad judgment of him on the field. He'd raised the stakes for himself pretty high.

It didn't take me long to recognize that for Spencer and Brian, along with their young colleagues, sharing a nondescript and undistinguished motel room with a stranger in a dull place a long way from home was their idea of an adventure getting under way. From the start they behaved as though they'd been sent to summer camp (albeit one where they could drink beer), whereas for me it felt mildly punitive, like what I imagined reform school to be.

I wasn't entirely wrong. That dozens of newcomers to one another are going to be whipped into a unit of devotees to a cause is a quasi-military idea, after all, and the atmosphere at the school reflected that. The regimentation was pretty fierce. Classes were conducted from 8 a.m. to 6 p.m., six days a week, lectures in the morning, fieldwork after lunch. We were expected to jog from field assignment to field assignment. We finished each afternoon with a "concentration drill," a kind of umpire Simon Says for which we lined up in strict formation and ran short sprints between orders to signal calls.

We had textbooks. We had worksheets. We had exams. We had

homework. We had a school uniform: nondescript gray trousers, a navy T-shirt with the school logo on it, black athletic shoes, and a navy baseball cap with a six-seam brim, which we were forbidden to keep on indoors. If it was chilly in the Florida winter, we were allowed to wear a school-supplied navy windbreaker.

This, in fact, was the weirdest part of things for me, to have to show up every morning dressed not only exactly as you were dressed the day before, but exactly as every other man in the room was dressed. Maybe it's not so weird when you're twenty, but to conform this way for the first time after age fifty makes you feel as if you've become exactly the sort of go-along-to-get-along guy you decided years ago, when such decisions are made, not to be.

This unease was fortified, initially anyway, by the instructors, all of them young men I'd eventually get to know and, for the most part, like. But on the field they were essentially drill sergeants, capable of astonishing vitriol delivered at high volume when we were deemed collectively lazy or distracted, and off the field they held themselves aloof.

It turns out they were ordered by Evans to behave this way, with cool and distant authority, exemplars of the umpire code of professionalism. Most of the time they carried themselves with a vaguely sinister expressionlessness, and they often seemed to be watching over the students like the secret Stasi informers who kept tabs on the citizenry of East Germany. They noticed whose shoes were unshined, who went more than a day or two without shaving, who was habitually, or even occasionally, late for class, who was spending his evenings studying the rulebook and who was fooling around.

The logic to this encouragement of conformity, for good or ill, is that it's the kind of behavior that baseball—both in the minor leagues and the major leagues—expects from its umpires. Baseball frowns on any kind of subversiveness that would draw unwanted attention to the umpires; it wants straight arrows, people who can be pointed to as exemplary, invisible citizens. Evans, for all his cynicism about baseball's administration and its attitude toward umpires, was savvy enough to recognize that he wasn't going to do his students any good by encouraging them to rebel. He said it over and over again: Think of your time at the school as a five-week job interview and conduct yourself accordingly.

Indeed, professional umpires are charged with upholding the public image of the game, which, in the conservative culture of sports, includes emblems of "character" and "values" such as good grooming and "decent" conduct. Once you get to pro ball, you are watched. League administrators and team owners have a pretty good idea where all the bars and strip clubs are in their franchise cities, and in the major leagues the security department actually has a network of local informants. As an umpire, you're judged by the company you keep, and the instructors were, after all, helping select the candidates who might someday be their colleagues or even their partners.

Thus, the instructors were sensitive to renegade behavior, the kind of guy who is likely to bristle at rules, disobey for the hell of it, and cause trouble for everyone. A small example: One afternoon I was chastised for wearing rather tamely striped blue-and-gray socks on the field; they were supposed to be black. My trouser hem rose up during calisthenics, and D. J. Reyburn, a sharp-witted guy with the short haircut and wicked smile of a fraternity president turned drill sergeant, bent down with me as I touched my toes, fingered my socks, and spoke quietly into my ear:

"Umpiring in the circus?" he said.

If I felt somewhat alienated off the field, it was worse on it. Like a lot of ordinary men who once dreamed foolishly of playing big league ball, I still thought of myself as a capable sportsman, with the appropriate instincts, strength, and speed, having missed the point about decades of inaction and how they might have allowed my abilities (such as they were) to go stale. Even though umpires aren't athletes per se, they're out there on the field participating at a professional level in a physically competitive enterprise that requires things that are unrequired of those who earn a living sitting down.

Not that an umpire needs to be fit for a triathlon; umpires are, in fact, famous for being fat or at least out of shape, though by now this image is fast becoming outdated. Judging from what I've seen in locker rooms, it's probably fair to say that squishiness around the middle is an occupational characteristic. But it's also true that professional umpires are generally vigorous, robust men, with especially strong legs.

We didn't do a lot of running, but every day we did a sprint-and-pivot drill around a four-sided course marked by cones (and hence called the cone drill), and every day we spent hours on our feet. I'm not overweight, and I'm reasonably healthy, but by the third day of fieldwork my knees were throbbing so badly that it took two snug neo-prene sleeves on each one to keep me upright for the afternoon.

Still, I expected that. The other kind of discomfort, the mental kind, I had a harder time with. Being a novice at anything at my age was unsettling enough, but as someone who thought he knew baseball, I couldn't believe how at sea I was as a fledgling umpire. The simplest fundamental, signaling a strike, for instance, induced awkwardness. The correct "mechanic," as any signal is known, is to raise your right hand, your arm crooked at a ninety-degree angle, and pretend you're pounding once on a door with your fist, but when I did it, the move-ment felt unnatural and feeble.

The first time I dressed in plate umpire's equipment, I put on my shin guards not only on the wrong legs, but upside down. And in one terri-ble moment that was caught on videotape, the first time I had a close play at first base, instead of signaling safe, I threw my arms excitedly straight over my head—touchdown!

My mistakes, these and others so telling of a tyro, stunned me, and this I attribute not only to self-delusion and hubris, but to being sud-denly introduced to a game that was very different from the one I thought I understood.

After all, from the seat of your pants—in the stands and even more so on the couch in front of the television set—the playing field is a closed box, containable in a sweep of the eyes; you can hold it all at once in your mind. But when you're standing on the field, the reality is that the ninety feet between bases, the sixty feet six inches from the pitching rubber to home plate, the more than three hundred feet to the outfield fence from the batter's box are intimidating dimensions. When you have to cover the ground they describe on foot in order to put your eyes in the best position to see a play clearly, the diamond seems vast, and no matter where you're standing, the terrain seems to run uphill in every direction.

I mentioned my surprise to Jason Klein, an instructor who was the top-rated umpire in Double A ball in 2006.

"The damn field is so big!" I said. "Why didn't I realize that?"

"Yeah, I know," he said. "I call it the scaffolding theory. It's like when they build a building and you're looking up from the ground at the guys on the scaffolding and you say, 'Yeah, that's not so high. I can do that work.' But go on up there, and it's not so easy."

To put it another way, fans take in a ball game in the manner of a museumgoer taking in a painting or a moviegoer at a movie, that is, as a visual whole or a narrative whole or maybe both. The fan's perspective is the long view, the wide embrace. But for an umpire, the game is a series of frames, moments, episodes. Aware as he may be of the grand panorama of the ballpark and the mounting drama inherent in the competition, the umpire must focus on one tiny slice of the game at a time—one pitch, one play, one runner rounding third, one line drive kicking up a tiny white puff on the foul line, one fan interfering with a foul pop, one slide into second interrupted by a sweep tag.

What umpire school does is wean you away from the fan's perspective and toward this different one. The instructors don't put it like this, but for the first three weeks of school, the curriculum is a kind of deconstruction, the morning lectures and matching afternoon drills functioning as a piece-by-piece dismantling of the game so that you're able to see its smallest parts singularly. Then during the final two weeks, when you're prepared to see how the parts potentially fit in the bigger picture, the curriculum shifts to simulated games. In the end it's sort of like teaching auto mechanics to someone whose only previous experience of a car is driving it.

For me, a crystallizing moment came at the end of the first week, late in the afternoon, as a group of us sequestered on a side field were working on the responsibilities for the base umpire with men on base. By this time, we knew the system for afternoon drills: A handful of students had donned fielders' gloves and were playing infield positions. One was stationed on the mound. Six or eight more were lined up near home plate to take turns as base runners. Another half dozen were standing beyond first base, along the foul line, with one at a time venturing onto the infield to be the working umpire. An instructor with a fungo bat stood at home plate, periodically calling out the game circumstances before he put the ball in play.

"None out, man on first," he might say; he'd wait for the base runner to take a lead off first, then lash a line drive to left. Or, "Two out, man on third," he would yell, and then, with the runner in position, smack a two-hopper to short.

When my turn came to work, the situation was men on first and second, nobody out. I took the proper position, to the shortstop side of second base in a small portion of the infield that umpires call the working area. (Not generally known by fans or even players, it's an imaginary—that is, unmarked—rectangular slot between the pitcher's mound and second base that provides umpires in the two-umpire system with positioning guidelines.) John Gelatt, a Single A umpire who was built like Babe Ruth and had the reputation among students of being the most skillful fungo hitter on the planet, slapped the ball on the ground toward the hole between short and third, just to my right.

What I was supposed to do was step forward with my right foot, pivot to face the ball as it was being fielded, then quickly slide toward second base for what was likely to be a force play and potentially the central element of a double play. But I hesitated in reading the ball. For some reason I froze; I was self-conscious about my footwork, then I considered whether the shortstop or the third baseman would field the ball, which might determine where the throw went. This was foolish; with both players going for the ball, no one would be covering third, so the throw would go to second no matter what. The proper read was a certain double-play attempt, the initial throw going to the second baseman who would be hustling over to cover the bag.

As it turned out, the third baseman lunged and snagged the ball, righted himself, and snapped a throw to second. Because of my slow-moving brain, however, when I finally moved toward second, I arrived too late to see the play there, which turned out to be tricky. The second baseman didn't handle the throw cleanly, and not only was there no double play, there was no throw to first. The ball ended up on the ground. But what had happened?

Did the second baseman bobble the throw during the pivot, never gaining control of it, which would mean the runner was safe? Or had he caught the ball and lost the handle attempting to make the throw to first, in which case the runner coming into second would rightfully be out?

I didn't know. Before I'd moved, I'd run through too many scenarios in my head. Who's fielding the ball? If it's the shortstop, will he throw to third? Is it hit hard enough for a double play? Did the runner from first get a good jump? If so, maybe the fielder will simply plant and throw to first. And how many outs are there again?

In other words, I'd acted like a fan, a watcher. I'd considered the situation, parsed the details, and analyzed the possibilities, all before I'd determined where to go. Good umpiring would have been to turn toward the ball and make an instantaneous few slide steps toward second base, to get ahead of the likely play so when the throw went to second, I would be in an advantageous position to make either the routine call or the unpredictable one.

By the time the ball arrived at second, I should have been in or near the cutout—the lopped-off corner of the infield grass around second base—with my head still and the second baseman's open glove in my vision as he made the catch, the pivot, and the throw. But I was still turning toward the base when the fielder dropped the ball; my head was still moving and I couldn't get a clear read on what happened with the ball in the fielder's glove. So I guessed.

Tentatively, I spread my arms, palms flat, and my eyes darted about as though I were a child sneaking cookies from the cookie jar.

"Umm," I said. "Safe?"

Dick Nelson, who was supervising the drill, could've criticized me for just about anything. I'd done about eight things wrong on the play, including not making the call with force and conviction, no matter how uncertain I was. (As umpires will tell you, at worst you've got a 50 percent shot at getting it right, so go for it.) But Nelson got to the heart of the matter, barking at me impatiently from the first-base line like the air force officer he used to be.

"Don't think!" he screamed. "React!"

And that's when I knew why I was having such a difficult time assimilating as an umpire. A fan—the kind of fan I am, anyway—does the exact opposite.

Conditioned by the luxuries of television—the slow-motion replay, the electronically tracked and delineated path of a pitch, the superimposed rectangle that glows like a neon sign directly over the plate—the attentive and experienced fan knows a strike when he sees one. But this is a delusion, and for me it was entirely smashed the first time I put on a mask and chest protector, entered a batting cage, and squatted behind a catcher. This may sound silly, or at least self-evident, but it shocked me nonetheless: The strike zone is invisible, a box of air that you have to locate anew on every pitch.

This is the fundamental challenge for the home plate umpire, but at the Evans school, it isn't even part of the curriculum. Though I had a session behind the plate in the batting cage every day, I went through five weeks of school without calling a single pitch. Evans's theory is that so many variables are involved in pitch-calling, so many nuances that can only be assimilated through long repetition and experience, it makes more sense to spend the limited time at school impressing on students the proper technique. It's the umpire school version of the theory that if you give a man a fish, he'll eat today, but if you teach him to fish, he'll eat forever. Learning to call pitches is thus not about making tricky, instantaneous judgments in widely varying and often unpredictable circumstances; rather it's about various body parts and what to do with them.

To begin with, some background. The best way to position yourself to call balls and strikes is a matter of some debate in umpire-dom, and if you watch major league games, you'll see some variety, though generally the stances are variants of two fundamental styles. One is known as the scissors, in which one foot is placed well in front of the torso, the other behind; the position is often referred to as vertical, meaning your legs are in line with the path from the pitcher's mound to the plate.

The front knee is bent and the umpire leans forward, his weight on the front foot and supported by the front-leg quadriceps. For many years, this was an approved position throughout baseball, especially advocated by Ed Vargo, who, after a long career in the big leagues, was the sole supervisor of National League umpires between 1984 and 1997. When I met him, not long before he died in 2008, he explained to me that the scissors indisputably gives an umpire the best look at a pitch, and that "anybody who tells you different is fuckin' horseshit."

Vargo's inflexible view notwithstanding, lately the scissors has generally gone out of favor as ergonomically deficient, as it puts unnecessary strain on the neck, the lower back, and the knee, and leaves the umpire more vulnerable to being struck under the chin by a foul ball. It also provides a less-than-natural foundation; when I tried it, I simply couldn't keep my balance without concentrating. So these days the schools teach only a more squared-off position to the pitcher, a stance sometimes called the box, which is becoming more and more the prevailing style throughout the game.

At school your plate stance is a matter of great precision and intense scrutiny, from your location, aligned in the "slot" between the plate and the batter and close enough to the catcher to touch his back; to the position of your feet, which need to be broadly based, i.e., wider than your shoulders, for balance, and nearly but not quite parallel, with the toes of one foot—the one farther from the batter—aligned with the heel of the other; to the height of your head, which as the pitch is released, should bring your chin precisely to the level of the top of the catcher's head; to the placement of your hands, with one resting just above or just behind the rear-foot knee, and the other in a soft fist with the forearm curled just below the chest protector, protecting the stomach.

Mastering the stance means being able to fall into it naturally, pitch after pitch—without checking your feet, your distance behind the catcher, your relationship to the plate and the batter. It means trusting the catcher to catch the ball, not flinching when a pitch comes in high and seemingly right at your nose. It means keeping your head completely still and "tracking," that is, following the ball with only your eyes until it disappears in the catcher's glove.

It means staying in your crouch to call a ball, vocalizing the call just enough so that the catcher hears it; to call a strike, it means rising up with authority to make your pound-the-door mechanic as well as projecting your voice forcefully as if declaiming your decision to the whole ballpark. The coordination of all this is on the order of patting your head with one hand and rubbing your stomach with the other, then switching; it requires a specialized effort every time, an engagement of the mind, and dozens of repetitions, to establish the muscle memory.

So each afternoon, in teams of four, we traipsed into the batting cages for stance instruction. The ritual quickly became entrenched: One of us loaded the pitching machine; one crouched behind the plate as a catcher; one stood in the batter's box with a bat on his shoulder, and the fourth was the umpire. No matter where the pitches were, the umpire called four balls, then three strikes. Then the batter switched sides of the plate and the umpire called four more balls and three more strikes. It was all about repetition. Then we rotated positions.

All of this was observed by two instructors. One sat in a chair, alongside a videotape machine, about fifteen feet in front of the plate and just off to the side, to watch the eyes of the umpires and make sure we were tracking properly and that our timing was right. (In umpiring the use of the eyes is rather confusingly known as timing, because when you use your eyes properly and follow the ball all the way into the glove, it keeps you from making a call prematurely.) The other instructor hovered around the umpire, using a straight ruler to measure his head height and check the alignment of his feet. We had the chance, in the evenings, to watch the videos of ourselves, and I found it painful to see how I looked behind the plate. I regularly winced at my hesitations, my awkwardnesses, the thinness of my voice.

Still, as I watched myself on videotape nightly, I could see the improvements. My balance was better, my strike mechanic more straightforward and insistent, my body language more cogent. Two weeks into school, I began to grow impatient to put my new skills to practical use, and just about then Evans himself came to watch me in the cage for the first time. When I finished, I asked him when we were going to begin calling actual balls and strikes, and instead of answering, he told me to keep my mask on. I was flinching on pitches, he said, and he hauled me off to the side for a drill that he promised would cure me of the habit.

"You've got to trust your equipment," he said, taking a baseball in one hand and rapping it hard against the front of my mask. Then he grabbed a bucket of balls and backed up a few feet, but only a few.

"Get in your stance," he said, and I did, and he began hurling baseballs at me, hard, from barely an arm's length distance. One after the other, they glanced off my mask, and after a dozen or so I found I could stare the ball into the mask and absorb the blow without even blinking.

"Not bad," Evans said.

If Jim Evans's fall from big league grace was remarkable, his ascension to it was equally so. When he was elevated to the American League in 1972 (at a salary of $10,000), he had spent only four seasons in the minors, and at just twenty-three he was one of the youngest men ever to reach the pinnacle of the profession. (The youngest was Billy Evans, no relation, who was hired at twenty-two—in 1906.)

The way the system for hiring umpires has evolved, the days of the twenty-three-year-old big league umpire are long over.* This fact of Evans's biography has stuck in my mind because I remember what I was like at twenty-three—what most of us are like, I would submit—namely, how I still had the instinct to defer to my elders and how I walked around in the world with minuscule achievements, small confidence, and no authority whatsoever.

How was it possible that he was able, at such a young age, to stare down a hundred-mile-per-hour Nolan Ryan fastball and call the likes of scowling future Hall of Famers such as Carl Yastrzemski and Frank Robinson out on strikes? When I asked him about this, he just shrugged and said umpiring was umpiring, and it had never occurred to him to be intimidated by the identities of the guys on the pitcher's mound or in the batter's box, which is why, I suppose, he was able to do what he did at twenty-three and why I couldn't no matter how old I got to be. Did it ever occur to him that he had students, at the age he entered the big leagues, showing up at umpire school with their own pillows? He laughed. It didn't, he said.

More pertinently, Evans's tenure in the game made him a bridge between umpiring generations. The old-school umpires, characterized by the likes of Doug Harvey and the Hall of Famers Al Barlick and Nestor Chylak, the latter of whom was Evans's first crew chief, were a blue-collar bunch who exercised tyrannical power on the field but were helpless in their dealings with the management of baseball and who never had to cope with the daily scrutiny of television cameras and instant replay. The younger generation, many of whom Evans not only worked with but taught at his school, are generally better-educated men for whom technology, and the substantial benefits accrued by years of union negotiations, are accepted as part and parcel of their professional lives.

Evans's own background is a hybrid, half-redneck, half-sophisticate. He grew up in rural Texas, the son of a carpenter, and he's fond of describing a rugged, dust-bowl upbringing. But his father had eight sib-

---

*Alfonso Marquez and Mark Wegner were both twenty-seven when they reached the big leagues in 1999, but these days it's much more likely an umpire will have reached at least thirty before he arrives at the top. Of recent hires, Lance Barksdale was thirty-nine when he was hired in 2006; Dan Iassogna was thirty-four in 2004, as was Jim Wolf.

lings, seven of whom were teachers, and one of them, Luther Evans, was appointed Librarian of Congress by President Harry S. Truman and later became director general of UNESCO. And though he's an umpire through and through, with all the hawk-and-spit earthiness of an uncomplicated tough guy, in addition to his umpiring pedigree, he was considering going to law school to become a trial lawyer when he decided to give umpiring a shot first.

Evans's degree was in education, and he often spoke to me of umpiring and teaching as twin passions. He told me that he would never forget when Bill White, then the president of the National League, told him his application to run an umpire school was going to be approved. It happened in the umpires' locker room at Anaheim Stadium, just moments before Evans went out to work behind the plate for the 1989 All-Star game.

"I walked out on the field a very happy camper," Evans said, "and not because I was working the plate in an All-Star game, which I was honored to do, but because I was going to see a dream come true."

All of this is to say that Evans was an accomplished teacher, a natural pedagogue, though his talent has been heavily flavored by his experiences in baseball. It would be hard to imagine him in any academic setting with, say, a mixed-gender atmosphere or a lot of scholarly decorum.

I've seen Evans be surprisingly courtly around women—he met his wife (his second) when he took a class in ballroom dancing and she was his instructor—but he's clearly most at home in the company of men. His jokes are often blue, his language salty, and his humor, though genial, is indisputably sexist. Part of this is a function of being in baseball, whose idiom is thoroughly and cheerfully profane, thoroughly and cheerfully heterosexual and earthy. But Evans always seemed a little self-conscious using dirty words in a school setting, as though he were a cowboy suddenly invited to a ladies' tea party, aware of an impropriety but uncertain of the preferred decorum.

"Now, you're gonna hear 'cocksucker' on the baseball field," Evans said to the class once. "And you'll hear 'motherfucker.' When a manager comes out to argue with you, the first thing he says, ninety percent of the time, is 'What the fuck is going on?' That's just the way it is. But here at the academy, we don't like to use those words."

Mainly, he explained, this was so visitors to the academy, usually several every day, parents and tourists and such, wouldn't be offended.

Instead of curse words, he said, they would use names of fruits, and you would know what you were being called by the number of syllables. Thus did angry shouts of "Raspberry!" and "Huckleberry!" occasionally ring out over the practice diamonds of Kissimmee, though instructors were more likely to forget themselves and tell you that you looked like a monkey fucking a football out there.

Like a lot of umpires, Evans liked to take a drink, and when he did, he became especially expansive and comradely. He poked you when he talked, laughed aggressively, and liked being the center of attention. The swagger to his personality that served him well as an umpire swelled up a bit, as it did in the classroom, which made me think that teaching, like drinking, made him feel good. Evans's old-fashioned maleness certainly played well with an almost entirely male audience, young guys who aspired to his career and were eager to benefit from his experience and influence.

Of course, Evans's tales of life in the big leagues, some serious, some not (and probably some apocryphal), were offered as frequent carrots, highly entertaining and nearly always thrilling reminders of the mythology the students ached to participate in. He was behind the plate for Nolan Ryan's first no-hitter and Don Sutton's three hundredth victory; he was at first base in Fenway Park when Bucky Dent hit his famous home run for the Yankees in the 1978 playoff game against the Red Sox; and he was at second when the ball went through Bill Buckner's legs in the sixth game of the 1986 World Series, opening the way for the Mets to win the championship.

Most of his tenure in the game came during an era when baseball's prime cheaters weren't injecting illegal substances into their bodies, but applying them to the baseball. For pitchers and umpires, this created a kind of cat-and-mouse chicanery, a game of catch-me-if-you-can within the game. Once, Evans recalled, he was working behind the plate for a game pitched by Sutton, who, during his Hall of Fame career, was often suspected of doctoring the baseball with a substance that he hid somewhere on his body or else with a nail file he kept in his uniform.

"So I went out to search him this one time, and I said, 'Let me see what you got in your pocket,'" Evans said, "and he pulls out a card and gives it to me, and it says, 'You're getting warm.'"

Of course, Evans was also a veteran of psychological combat with baseball's most legendary umpire baiters. Billy Martin, he said, once sent him a Christmas card saying, on the outside, "I hope you and your family have a wonderful holiday season," and continuing on the inside, "because you sure had a horseshit summer."

In the middle of a typical screaming rant by Earl Weaver, he recalled, he once pulled out the stopwatch he used to time the between-inning breaks and showed it to Weaver to indicate he was timing his tantrum. Weaver snatched the stopwatch from his hand and flung it into the dugout, where it lodged under the bench. Evans had to retrieve it from beneath Frank Robinson, who was pretending to keep a straight face.

Before one game, when Ralph Houk was getting close to the end of his tenure with the Detroit Tigers, Houk came to a home plate conference with the lineup card and his zipper undone. "And I said to him, 'Hey, Ralph, your flag is at half-mast,'" Evans said. "And I thought he'd thank me, you know. But he looked up at me and he said, 'Only a cocksucker would notice something like that.'"

Most of his stories were like that, with him getting the worst of it. But occasionally he let one slip where the umpires got their revenge. One involved Harvey Kuenn, who hit over .300 during a fifteen-year major league career and won an American League batting title in 1959. Kuenn was a successful manager and coach as well, but he had some medical bad luck and had to have his leg amputated after a blood clot in 1980. Six months later he returned to coaching, and in 1982, as manager of the Milwaukee Brewers, led them to the pennant. He occasionally irked the umpires, though.

"If he wanted to argue, we'd walk away from him," Evans told us one day. "We'd make him walk all the way out to second base on his artificial leg."

In addition to his practiced storytelling, Evans was a clever teacher who brought to class a whole portfolio of tricks and tropes. Long mornings in a lecture hall were punctuated by competitive quiz games; film clips of major league umpires' mistakes; and the use of silly props, such as the windup teddy bears singing "La Vida Loca" he let loose one morning as we took a written test, one of the many gambits he employed to challenge our powers of concentration.

His pedagogical style had the kind of earnest, exhortatory simplicity that inspirational speakers have turned into an industry. Like evangelists of every stripe, he counted on sentiment. Patriotism, big among all umpires, is a pillar of Evans's character; one morning he delivered a somber lesson in how to stand for the national anthem. Later, when I asked him if he had an overall philosophy of umpire training, his response was military: "The more you sweat in training, the less you bleed in war."

I told him I thought maybe this metaphor was a little over-the-top, and he laughed agreeably.

"What I mean is you've got to stay in the moment or something bad's going to happen to you," he said. "There are all these distractions that occur during a game, and one of the things you've got to learn is to control that. For example, the first inning. If you're still thinking about something that happened at the hotel when you checked out that morning and had an argument over your bill, or if you're still ticked off that the cabdriver got stuck in traffic going over the bridge to Yankee Stadium and you were late getting to the locker room, you're going to miss something. It's like a pitcher; I remember something Tony LaRussa"—the longtime big league manager—"once said, that the toughest thing for a pitcher is coming into the game in the first inning, because he's been warming up on a different mound and he's not into the game yet. And certain pitchers do have the reputation of struggling in the first inning and hitting their stride for the next eight. Well, umpires can be the same way. So when you walk on the field, you've got to be able to turn that switch on and turn all the other ones off. That's why I teach the national anthem is important, by the way. It's not just paying homage to our countrymen, but it's a time when you really turn the switch on and tell yourself, 'Okay, this game has *started*.'"

In class, Evans offered a number of practical rules on how to think on the field. "Anticipate all of a play's possibilities but not its outcome," he would say. Or, "The call is a mental process and the signal a physical one; separate the two." Beyond that, there were homely tenets, the kind that an umpire's wife might embroider on her husband's chest protector. "The umpire's greatest enemy is surprise" was a favorite.

He was fond of the fable as a teaching tool. One of his most elaborate illustrative metaphors was what he called the mousetrap theory, which began with a tale from his childhood, when his grandmother sought to rid the kitchen of an unwanted rodent, baiting a mousetrap and putting it behind the refrigerator. The first couple of days, the mouse nibbled at the cheese without getting caught, but the third day, when little Jimmy Evans checked the trap, there was the mouse, who had tempted fate once too often. For this reason, Evans preached to his class of aspiring umpires, you shouldn't take shortcuts in your umpiring:

"You can be out of position and most of the time get the call right. You can be lazy and get away with it most of the time. You'll get away with it for a month. You might even get away with it for a whole season." But eventually, he said, emphatically if unnecessarily, your carelessness, your lack of vigilance, your lack of hustle, will cost you and maybe even cost you big.

"Believe me," he said, "you don't want to end up like that mouse."

The entertainment value of all this was considerable, and probably necessary, because the morning classes could otherwise be soporific, early wake-ups followed by four hours of being yakked at, a lot of the material necessitating the kind of rote memory work you associate with learning the state capitals or the elements of the periodic table. Some part of every morning was devoted to umpiring responsibilities: man on first, one out. The hitter singles to right. What do the base and home plate umpires do? (Among other things you need to know is that if the throw goes to third, the plate umpire is supposed to be there to make the call.) These lessons, usually from 8 a.m. until about 9:30, were led by the instructors. Then, after a short break, Evans would come wandering in like a celebrity guest lecturer, rulebook in hand, and the more serious business of the morning would begin.

I called Evans the Rebbe (a term I had to explain to him) because he is baseball's equivalent of a Talmudic scholar. Known around the game as a rules expert, he's actually written an annotated version of the rulebook that runs to 750 pages and identifies some 250 errors and omissions. The idea that the rulebook, which is only about 125 pages long, would be so demonstrably imprecise is amazing, but try reading it.

Baseball's rulebook is a highly unruly document that is written in faux legalese, that hasn't been wholly revised since 1949, and whose original awkwardness has since been layered with dozens, maybe hundreds, of piecemeal modifications. Every year there are rule changes. First a proposed change is implemented on the field as a yearlong experiment; after a year, if it is approved by baseball's rules committee and by the Major League Baseball Players Association, it goes into the next rulebook revision. In 2008, for example, the requirement that first- and third-base coaches wear batting helmets was implemented, a result of a minor league coach, Mike Coolbaugh, having been killed in 2007 by a line drive.

Some of the errors noted by Evans are marvelously arcane and inconsequential. For example, the rulebook defines the infield as a ninety-foot square, but it isn't quite. Second base is centered on the intersection of the extended lines defined by the outer edges of first and third, which means three-quarters of second base, part of the infield, is not within the square, whose other two sides are the first- and third-base lines.

Some errors are inconsistencies or out-and-out contradictions, as in the conflict between Rule 3.02, which says a pitcher who delivers a discolored or damaged ball is to be ejected from the game and automatically suspended for ten days, and Rule 8.02, which says that, for the same offense, "the umpire shall call the pitch a ball, warn the pitcher and have announced on the public address system the reason for the action."*

Some errors are simply careless. The first clause of the rulebook's first sentence, Evans pointed out, has been obsolete since 1973.

"Rule 1.01," he said. "'Baseball is a game between two teams of nine players each.' Well, what about the designated hitter?"

Yes, he was a little obsessive, the way experts in arcana tend to be, but the rules, he said, are not only the backbone of the game but the backbone, too, of the umpire's craft. His obsession, I realized, was a sign of his reverence for the umpiring enterprise. For two hours each morning, sometimes more, Evans would read the rulebook aloud and lecture on its wording, its practical meaning, its alternating clarity and cloudiness. We were tested on these lectures—and graded on the tests—a couple of times a week. (A sampling of test questions appears at the end of this chapter.)

During the five weeks of school, Evans covered the rulebook's every clause, interspersing his speechifying with Socratic-method quizzing:

---

*In 2007, this disparity was corrected, and the rules now call uniformly for the ejection of a pitcher who taints the ball.

"The batter swings and ticks the catcher's glove, but hits the ball into right field for a single and the runner on first goes to third. Brian Dubois, place the runners." (If Brian was paying attention, he'd respond that the runners stay put on first and third. The ticking of the glove constitutes catcher's interference, which gives the batter first base and pushes ahead every runner who would be subject to a force, *unless* the batter reaches first of his own account and every runner advances a base. Then the interference is negated.)

If it sounds grueling and a little mind-numbing, well, sometimes it was, but it was also a terrific demonstration of what a complicated game baseball is and what a poor grasp most people have on its complexities. The fan's rulebook, I came to understand, is a vastly pared-down version of the real thing.

One reason that many of the regulations remain obscure is that they are so rarely applicable in actual play, even though they describe situations that might determine the outcomes of games. Did you know, for instance, that with less than two out, if a player makes a catch and falls into the stands, every runner is awarded a base? This means that with one out and a man on third in the bottom of the ninth inning of a tie game, if the catcher makes a sensational play on a foul pop and flips over the railing the run scores and the game is over. The catcher's reward for his great play is he costs his team the game.

Many rules are so intricately stratified that no one would bother to keep the possibilities straight if he didn't have to. For instance, when a ball thrown by a fielder sails into the dugout or the stands, no single dictum applies for placing the base runners. Where the runners end up is determined either by where they were when the ball was pitched or when the ball was thrown by the fielder, depending on the nature of the play.

Some rules—such as those for placing the runners after one of them has missed a base and been declared out on appeal; or for figuring out what happens after batters have batted out of order—are simply befuddling in the way abstract mathematics is. To wit, Rule 6.07 (d) (2): "When an improper batter becomes a proper batter because no appeal is made before the next pitch, the next batter shall be the batter whose name follows that of such legalized improper batter. The instant an improper batter's actions are legalized, the batting order picks up with the name following that of the legalized improper batter."

Beyond all that, the rulebook is full of minutiae that no fan bothers to keep in mind or even cares about while watching a game. Who, in the stands or on the living room sofa, is aware of the particulars of uniform and equipment requirements? (You can't use a bat longer than forty-two inches, for example. Nor can the visible sleeves of a pitcher's undershirt be different lengths.) Who knows what constitutes a legal substitution? Or is aware of the difference between interference (which can be committed by a batter, a runner, a catcher, an umpire, or a spectator) and obstruction (which only a fielder can commit), not to mention the difference between the two kinds of obstruction? (One occurs when a play is being made on the runner being obstructed, the other when not.)

The prescribed dimensions of the field are laid out in the rulebook with the detail of an architectural blueprint. Home plate—or "home base," as one of the rulebook's many archaic locutions would have it— is described, for example, as "a five-sided slab of whitened rubber," in the shape of "a 17-inch square with two of the corners removed so that one edge is 17 inches long, two adjacent sides are 8½ inches and the remaining two sides are 12 inches and set at an angle to make a point." Why this might be of concern to an umpire is that it means that the black rubber border of home plate is not included in the seventeen-inch diameter and thus not officially considered part of the plate or part of the strike zone. Most fans will tell you that when a pitch is "on the black," it is thought to be a strike, and though most umpires will consider it a strike, at least according to the literal rule it is not. (In the early days of baseball, home plate, like the other bases, was a square, and it was oriented so one point faced the pitcher, one faced the catcher, and the two others defined the horizontal limits of the strike zone. What has survived from this configuration is a bit of jargon that today is literally nonsense: that the plate has an inside and an outside corner.)

In the confines of the classroom, the rules often seemed so picayune, esoteric, and beside the point that you wondered if the lessons were practical, worth the time we were spending on them. You'd hear guys grumbling occasionally, the way high school students do about algebra, that what they were studying wasn't going to be of any use, and each week I noticed a few more guys cutting morning classes.

I understood their impatience to be done with their pencils and their notebooks and out on the field, but I was weirdly fascinated by the rules, even in the abstract, though I learned, as all umpires do, that the abstract has a way of becoming discomfortingly concrete. In one of my first games as an umpire, I was behind the plate for a high school game on Long Island when the batter hit a line drive past the pitcher that hit my partner in the shoulder before he could duck.

The ball ricocheted off him, bouncing right to the shortstop, who threw to second for a force play that ended the inning. That's what we allowed to happen, anyway. The proper call, according to Rule 5.09 (f) is that the ball is dead, and the batter is awarded first base, which in this case would have pushed the base runner to second. Studious as I had been at the academy, I simply forgot the rule. (I don't think my partner ever knew it, and evidently the teams' managers didn't either.) My uncertainty gnawed at me, though, and I looked up the rule when I got home. It was especially unsettling to learn of my mistake because the team that I cost a chance to score lost the game by a single run.

Lapses like that are amateurish, but they aren't entirely the province of amateurs. In early May 2007, the Baltimore Orioles were playing in Cleveland when the umpiring crew, led by one of baseball's most senior umpires, Ed Montague, realized in the sixth inning they had erred about an hour earlier and awarded the Orioles belated credit for a run they should have had in the third. The run went up on the scoreboard in the bottom of the sixth, leading one local newspaper to report, "Only in Cleveland could the Indians go from a tie game to being a run behind—while they were batting."

The Orioles ended up winning the game handily, but the umpires were not only embarrassed, their reversal led to a protest of the game by the Indians, and it was all set in motion when they collectively forgot a rule. With one out in the top of the third and Orioles on first and third, the batter hit a fly ball to the outfield, and the runner on third tagged up but the runner on first did not and was doubled off, called out by first-base umpire Marvin Hudson. The umpires acknowledged that the runner from third crossed the plate before the runner from first was out, but they disallowed the run, saying the out at first was a force play.

"Gross umpire error," said Bill Miller, who was on the crew that day, when I reached him by telephone. "That's about all I can say about it."

That they corrected themselves—during the game, publicly, in spite of the embarrassment—was to their credit; it was Montague's doing, Miller told me. What they forgot was the section of Rule 2.00 that defines a force play and deals with this precise situation—known, in umpire parlance, as a time play because whether the run counts depends on when the out is made—describing it and declaring in no uncertain terms, "Not a force play. . . . If, in the umpire's judgment, the runner from third touched home before the ball was held at first base, the run counts."

When I heard about this, I called Evans at his home in Colorado, wanting to cluck a little bit, I suppose, because it wasn't my mistake.

"If you make that error the last week of umpire school, you don't get sent to PBUC," he said. "I'm telling you, you gotta keep brushing up on the rulebook."

THINK YOU KNOW THE RULES?
TEST QUESTIONS FROM THE JIM EVANS ACADEMY
OF PROFESSIONAL UMPIRING

TRUE OR FALSE?

1. Runner on second, two out. The batter hits a home run, scoring R2 (the runner on second), but the B-R (batter-runner) is declared out for missing first base. Only one run counts.
2. An outfielder may wear a first baseman's mitt in the outfield.
3. A B-R can never be declared out when he is hit by a thrown ball as he is running in foul territory.
4. There is no penalty for throwing a glove at a fair ball.
5. The ball always becomes dead immediately when a balk is called.

CATCH OR NO CATCH?

6. A fielder secures possession of a batted ball in flight, then falls into the stands but comes up immediately displaying the ball in his glove.
7. The center fielder appears to have made a great catch running to his right. Before he can gear down, he collides with the left fielder and the ball pops out of his glove and hits the ground.

FAIR OR FOUL?

8. A line drive hits the pitcher's rubber and deflects into foul territory near the first-base on-deck circle.
9. A batted ball strikes third base and ricochets back into foul territory near the third-base on-deck circle.

10. One out, runner on first. The batter hits a sharp one-hopper to the first baseman. The first baseman tags R1, who is standing on first base, then tags the base before the B-R arrives.

    (a) Double play.

    (b) The B-R is out when first base is tagged. The runner is safe since the force was removed.

    (c) The B-R is out on the force. To complete the double play, R1 must be retired at second base.

    (d) The B-R is declared out. R1 is safe since he is not forced until the B-R touches first base.

11. With a runner on first and one out, the batter hits a pop-up to the second baseman. He gets under the ball, then backs up and lets it fall untouched in front of him. He turns an easy double play.

    (a) The umpire should invoke the infield fly rule.

    (b) The double play stands.

    (c) The ball is ruled dead.

    (d) The batter is declared out on the intentional drop and the runner may advance at his own peril.

12. No outs, runner on first. A hot grounder is smashed up the middle. The shortstop fields the ball but throws it wildly trying to retire R1 approaching second, and the ball rolls into the first-base dugout just after R1 has rounded second and the B-R has touched first. Place the runners.

    (a) Both runners score.

    (b) R1 scores; B-R is awarded third.

    (c) R1 scores; B-R is awarded second.

    (d) R1 is awarded third; B-R is awarded second.

13. Rain causes a suspension of play in the bottom of the seventh with the home team leading 4–3. During the suspension of play, the lights fail. After the lights are fixed, the field is found to be unplayable because of the rain. The game is . . .

    (a) a suspended game to be resumed at a later date.

    (b) called because of rain with the home team declared to have won, 4–3.

    (c) declared no game and to be replayed in its entirety.

    (d) a suspended game to be replayed in its entirety.

14. The batter swings and misses for strike three. The pitch touches him as he swings and the ball drops to the ground. What is the ruling?

    (a) The batter is out. The ball remains alive and in play.

    (b) The batter can run and possibly reach first base safely.

    (c) The ball is dead and the batter is out.

    (d) The ball is dead and the batter is awarded first base.

15. Runner on third and no outs with a 1-2 count on the batter. The runner attempts to steal home, and as he is sliding across the plate, he is hit by the pitch within the batter's strike zone.

    (a) The ball is alive and in play. All play stands.

    (b) The ball is dead and the batter called out on strikes. The run scores.

    (c) The ball is dead and the batter called out on strikes. The runner returns to third.

    (d) The ball is dead. This is a double play. The batter is out on strikes and the runner is out for interference.

Answers

1—F. The out at first base is considered a force play, so no run counts.

2—F. The allowable dimensions of a first baseman's mitt exceed those of the gloves of other fielders.

3—F. If the batter running to first base in foul territory outside the runner's lane is hit by a true throw to first, the batter may be declared out. (This might occur, for example, if a batted ball has been deflected by the pitcher into foul territory and has been picked up by the catcher. Or it could occur on a dropped third strike when the catcher is throwing from foul territory.)

4—T. A penalty of three bases for each base runner applies only if the thrown glove touches the ball.

5—F. If the balk is committed when a pitch is imminent or a pickoff is being attempted, the ball remains in play until all play ceases. Only then is time called and the balk rule applied. The ball is not automatically dead at the time of the balk.

6—Catch. The out stands but all runners are awarded one base when the fielder leaves the playing field.

7—No catch. A fielder must have complete control of his body and firm and secure possession of the ball for it to be considered legally caught.

8—Foul. A batted ball that enters foul territory and has not reached a base must be touched by a fielder or settle in fair territory to be considered fair.

9—Fair.

10—A. Once a fair ground ball is hit, R1 is forced to vacate the base; he is no longer the legal occupant of first base, no longer entitled to be protected by standing on it, so he's out when tagged. The B-R is out because the base was tagged before he got there.

11—B. The infield fly rule applies only with men on first and second or the bases loaded, and the intentionally-dropped-ball rule applies only if the fielder touches and drops the ball. The play stands.

12—D. When the first play by an infielder on a batted ball is a throw that goes out of play, the batter and all runners are awarded two bases from their position at the time the pitcher pitched the ball—not at the time the fielder threw it.

13—B. If the game were unable to be completed simply because the lights had failed, it would be declared suspended and completed at a later date. However, weather conditions take precedence over mechanical problems. A game is considered complete if, after four and a half innings, it is called because of rain with the home team ahead. Therefore the game is over and the home team has won.

14—C.

15—B. This occurrence is specifically discussed in Rule 6.05 (n). If two are out, the third strike ends the inning and the run does not score.

CHAPTER THREE

"Fix It!"

Don't let anybody call you horseshit.
—Dick Nelson

Jim Evans is fond of saying that umpiring is half-art and half-science, which may be elevating the craft a bit, but it's not hard to see what he means. The science is a kind of spatial engineering: Your job is to divide up the field into manageable slices so as to commandeer it effectively.

This was illustrated for us daily, beginning with our first day on the field, when the lesson focused on the most rudimentary of plays, conventional batted balls with no one on base. On contact, both umpires must take a moment to assess the play, then leap to action. You don't move instantaneously, but you don't dawdle. You act with alacrity, but with clear purpose. The progression is drummed into you: Pause, read, react. For the novice umpire it becomes a mantra. Pause, read, react.

With no one on base, the starting position for the base umpire is along the right-field line, just beyond the first baseman. From there, you can race into the outfield on a batted ball that is potentially troublesome for the fielders—for instance, if it appears it will fall between them and roll to the fence, or require a shoestring catch, or create any other circumstance where an umpire might want a close look. You pause; you read. If your judgment is that the ball is a "trouble ball," you turn and race toward it. If you judge it will be an easy catch or an obvious base hit, something clear enough for your partner behind the plate to see, you react by racing into the infield to monitor the batter-runner, to make sure he touches first base as he rounds it and to be in position to call a tag play at first or second in case an outfielder gathers up the ball and makes a quick throw.

On the other hand, if the ball is hit on the ground to an infielder, your responsibility is to position yourself for a call at first, a spot dependent on where the ball is hit—or more specifically, from where it will be thrown. You want to locate yourself fifteen to eighteen feet from the bag, with your line of vision at a ninety-degree angle to the path of the infielder's throw.

For a first-timer, even if you've played a lot of baseball, the experience of reading and reacting to a batted ball as an umpire is disorienting. Not only does the perspective give you a literally different view of the game than you've ever had, but you have to make a play on every ball, even though it never comes to you.

This is especially perplexing on infield grounders. It takes practice to get a quick and accurate read on the angles and arcs of batted balls that are almost always headed away from you; and judging the path of a thrown ball that isn't thrown to you is a wholly unfamiliar skill. As the first-base umpire, you have to be able to decide, while the ball is in the air, whether the throw from the shortstop to the first baseman is true—and to react accordingly.

For the plate umpire, the task is seemingly simpler. Essentially, he's the troubleshooter. He circles the catcher and follows the runner up the first-base line, stopping in time to be still when the throw arrives. The idea is to be in position to discern whether the runner commits interference; or, in the event of a wide throw resulting in a catch and swipe-tag attempt by the first baseman that is out of the view of the base umpire, whether the tag was made in time; or, in the event the throw gets by the first baseman, whether and when the ball goes out of bounds—that is, into a dugout or otherwise beyond the field of play. The difficulty is that the plate umpire is looking for the unexpected and unpredictable, for what *might* occur, a kind of anticipatory thinking that fans never bother with and that players often eschew. They can usually afford to—how often do the outfielders back up infielder's throws?—but umpires never can.

Virtually every situation has its equivalent two-man prescription, which means that for umpires, every play involves coordination and teamwork, its own explicit choreography. Our drills concentrated on one situation at a time: an extra-base hit with the bases empty; a force play at second; a single to the outfield with a man on first; a steal of second, etc. By the end of the first week or so I was holding six or eight different plays in my mind and felt I knew how to umpire each of them from either behind the plate or on the bases. I was beginning to get comfortable with the idea of the two-man system, appreciating that every play takes place within the context of the whole field, and that my partner and I were sharing responsibility for anything that might occur on it.

It was a good feeling, but it didn't last because for the next couple of weeks complications were added daily—multiple base runners, rundowns, balks, catcher's interference, time plays, appeal plays, intentionally dropped balls, the infield fly rule. I can't pinpoint the exact moment I got overwhelmed, but I equated the experience with my long-ago college days, when I briefly thought I was going to be a mathematician. I made the leap from trigonometry to calculus well enough, but when the degree of difficulty ratcheted up again, and calculus morphed into abstract algebra, I was left behind by those who simply got it.

Similarly, there are those with a natural predilection for seeing the game as an umpire must, and by week three you could begin to tell who they were, the guys who were good, the guys who adapted quickly and seemed to own the baseball knowledge immediately on its being passed along to them. You could see it in their body language, the confidence and stature that emanates from the demonstration of skill. Brian Dubois was one of them. So was his roommate, A. J. Johnson, a former college pitcher from Mississippi, with a thick Southern accent and a garish wardrobe; I remember in particular an orange shirt with a flared collar. So was Kelvin Bultron, a burly Puerto Rican who enjoyed singing between innings on the field and liked to pass the time talking about women; he had once been an infielder in the Mets' and Astros' organizations but failed as a player, he said, because he'd had a terrible attitude and was always getting into fights. And so was Adam Hamari, a string bean of a guy from the Upper Peninsula of Michigan whose preternatural ease on the field and graceful, authoritative signaling were the envy of his classmates. Two years later, A.J., Kelvin, and Adam were still in the game and advancing nicely up the umpire ladder.

It interested me that my most gifted young classmates seemed so

much older on the field than they did anywhere else, and that I felt precisely the opposite. I was always nervous. As I awaited my turn on the
field, I paced up and down along the right-field line, my thoughts racing through the possible plays I might have to handle and the responsibilities I'd thus have. It was a schoolboy's panic at the test, the speaker's
fear of the microphone, the actor's unwillingness for the curtain to
rise—a palpable sense of being neither gifted nor prepared.

When it was my turn to work, I would trot out to my position with
my stomach churning, like the last kid chosen in a pickup game who
ends up in right field praying the ball won't be hit to him but is certain
that the moment of his undoing is merely a matter of time. Eventually
I knew I was going to run to the wrong spot, forget about a runner,
misapply a rule, miscall a balk, lose track of the number of outs, or fail
to help out on a rundown. When I finally took my position, trying to
see everything, I had a lot of blind spots.

Instructors were noticeably shrewd about recognizing our weaknesses, and they'd often give you the same play late in the afternoon
that you'd screwed up just after lunch or the previous day. It was the
umpire version of déjà vu. One afternoon I was at home plate with a
man on second and the batter singled through the left side of the
infield. The runner was off at the crack of the bat, and I came up from
my crouch, whipped off my mask, made sure the runner from second
touched third as he rounded the base, and positioned myself along the
extension of the first-base line for a possible play at the plate. Everything done exactly as it should be, except that I didn't notice that the
third baseman, entirely in my line of vision, had wandered into the
base path and forced the base runner to alter his stride and go around
him, causing a glancing collision that threw the runner off-balance.

This is textbook obstruction, which requires the umpire, when the
play is over, to place the runner in such a way as to nullify the infrac-
tion; that is, to figure out how far the runner might have advanced had
the fielder not got in his way.

This precise situation was presented to me again that afternoon and
I reacted the same way: I saw the collision but didn't acknowledge it as
something of consequence. I suppose I was too busy focusing on something else—the whereabouts of the ball, perhaps. Or maybe I was anticipating what would happen next. In any case, the two plays ended

differently. Once the runner was thrown out at the plate, and once he didn't even attempt to score because he'd lost his balance in the collision. I didn't call time-out either time, as I should have; nor did I score the run either time, as I should have. I simply let the play stand.

Had this happened in an actual game, I'd have been faced with an apoplectic manager; obstruction is one of the leading causes of the kind of volcanic brouhaha that umpires call a shithouse. But I was confronted only by an instructor, Darren Hyman, who was then working in Triple A, in the Pacific Coast League.

Darren is a small man—his height, five feet six inches, worked against his promotion to the big leagues, which never happened (he became a cop in Scottsdale, Arizona)—but he carried himself with charismatic aplomb. A former marine with *GQ* looks and penetrating blue eyes who had worked as a model and a movie extra—he appeared as a Harvard student in the Reese Witherspoon vehicle *Legally Blonde*—he was the staff prom king, the guy you wanted to like you, who could make your day with a sparkling smile or ruin it with a dismissive spit.

After my first screwup, he simply walked out to talk to me and pointed out the mistake. The second time I could see the anger in his gait as he left the dugout and approached me. I immediately began constructing an alibi.

"Didn't you see that obstruction?" he began, pointing at the spot where it happened as if the act were frozen there. "It happened right in front of you. That's twice."

"I saw it," I said.

"Then what the fuck? Why didn't you call it?"

"It didn't have a bearing on the play. The runner would have stopped at third, anyway."

Darren shook his head in mock disgust and turned and walked away from me, and I figured I'd survived. But then he stopped and turned back, with less disdain and more disappointment, which was maybe worse.

He put his hands on his hips and cocked his head to the side. "Is that what you really think? That he wouldn't have scored?"

"No," I said.

"Didn't think so," Darren said.

* * *

Fans tend to think that an argument is something an umpire brings on himself, the consequence of a bad call, but umpires know that disputes are inescapable, that you can't get every call right, and that even if you could, you'd still be an object of scorn.

"It's a lot easier to argue if you were right," Evans said in class one day. "But you could be Jesus Christ himself, and when you shave and put on a blue shirt and gray pants, they're still going to give you hell."

It's hard to overstate, I think, the distinction, and the psychological burden, this confers on umpiring as a profession. Is there another line of work—prison guard, maybe?—where the workplace is so steeped in hostility? Or where being right is no defense against attack? For most of us, an argument is something out of the ordinary and something that we try to win, but umpires go to work expecting to be derided and disdained.

In the professional lexicon, the euphemism for arguments and/or the circumstances that might result in them is "situations," as if to underscore that they aren't things to be won or lost but handled. This means spotting trouble on the horizon so as to sidestep it whenever you can, and when it descends on you anyway, not making it worse.

From the outside, it seems plain screwy that though the rules of baseball give umpires decision-making authority, the game's practices and traditions do everything they can to undermine it. It is the only sport in which nonplayers are even allowed on the field to dispute with the officials. In any other context, sporting or otherwise, one grown man raging at another in apoplectic frustration, kicking dirt on his shoes, throwing his hat on the ground and stomping on it, would be considered either ridiculous or childish, not to mention grounds for being punched in the nose. Baseball managers, though, do these things routinely, and most of the time they're cheered for it.

Television analysts are fond of saying that when managers such as Bobby Cox or Lou Piniella lose their temper in an especially extravagant manner, they do it as a ploy, to rouse their team, stir the players' competitive juices, which might momentarily be running a little sluggish. Perhaps that's true, though Jim Leyland of the Detroit Tigers scowled when I asked him if he argued to motivate his players, saying he didn't play those games and that any player who needed firing up that way didn't belong in the big leagues.

More to the point was Leyland's implication that for a professional, baseball is an enterprise to be taken with utter seriousness and pursued with relentless competitive drive. Though that concept meets with knee-jerk acknowledgment among fans, I think it's actually not so easy to absorb. For someone who has a job that is just a job, it's likely to seem that baseball is just a game, but in the big leagues especially, the game matters to the people who play it by at least an order of magnitude greater than it does to anyone else; for professional teams, prevailing on the playing field is not simply a reward to be pursued but a defining way of life.

Once you understand that, it shouldn't be surprising that it's not just the opposing team that players and managers want to defeat; they want to get the better of anyone in their way, the umpire included. This essential aggression is built into the game, and it's something an umpire has to recognize and accept before he can handle himself effectively on the field.

"Nobody has more respect for umpires than I do," Evans said often, "but if I were a manager, I'd get thrown out of a game three or four times a year just doing my job."

An umpire has thirteen automatic grounds for ejecting someone in professional baseball: If a player or coach makes physical contact with you; kicks or throws dirt at you; spits at you; flagrantly throws equipment in obvious protest at a call; questions the honesty or integrity of you or your partner; draws a line in the dirt—usually with a bat to indicate the path of a pitch—in an obvious attempt to show you up; throws objects from the dugout onto the field; leaves a field position to argue balls and strikes; doctors the baseball; uses a doctored bat; intentionally throws at a hitter; charges the mound and gets as far as the dirt circle; and perhaps the most frequently invoked, uses profane language directed at you or your partner.

"People always want to know whether there's a magic word," the umpire Gary Cederstrom would tell me later. "Is it 'cocksucker'? Is it 'asshole'? No. The magic word is 'you.'"

The list seems to cover a lot of territory, suggesting that all you have to do is familiarize yourself with it and you'll have a pretty good grasp on how to control a game. Of course that isn't so. Every baseball fan has seen all of these circumstances arise over the years, but in the grand scheme of things, they are rare.

Far more numerous are the occasions when a manager or a player tiptoes up to the line of automatic ejection and stops just short of it, or even winks and backs away. Players and coaches grouse at you from the dugout with regularity, but how much do you put up with? You have to allow managers to come out and complain, but when do you engage and when do you walk away? And what's okay to say to them? When do you owe them an explanation and when a rebuke? When is a rejoinder cleverly squelching and when does it further inflame?

Most of what an umpire does to enforce his authority on the field has to do less with power than with a kind of diplomacy. Above all, an umpire does not wish to do anything to unduly influence the outcome of the game. What he wishes for at the beginning of the game is not to be blamed for anything at the end of it.

"There's a monkey running around out on the field, and it's going home on somebody's back," Evans yelled to us more than once. "Don't let it be yours!"

Indeed, if the difference between an amateur and a professional umpire is that the latter can make all the calls when the game is played at the professional level, then the difference between a minor league umpire and a major league umpire is that the latter has the experience to handle situations with skill and judgment. Beginning with the third week of school, a good part of every afternoon was taken up by instructors pretending to be managers or coaches and reacting to umpires' decisions, generally assuming one or more of a variety of angry behavioral modes: manipulative, illogical, furious, threatening, profane, tricky, belittling, abusive, or misleading, to name a few. Students had to react to the instructor's display of temper, resolve the situation, and put the game back on track.

We were given a few practical hints: Don't bait anyone. Avoid the impulse to get in the last word. Don't call the manager "sir"; it puts you in the position of supplicant. Don't call him "Coach" either; he'll take it as an insult. Call him "Skipper," if you have to call him anything, or better, call him by his name. Conversely, don't let anyone call you "Blue"; that's for amateurs.

If a guy starts kicking dirt, don't just stand there; walk onto the grass where there's no dirt to kick. Don't get too close to anyone chewing tobacco unless you want to get sprayed, but if a guy does go nose to nose with you, make sure the bill of your cap is under the bill of his, so he can't rap you in the forehead with it, an act known as beaking.

But beyond these suggestions, the situation exercises left us on our own, relying on our wits, our common sense, our ability to listen and react and behave like responsible human beings. If I had to summarize the proper attitude as a tenet, it would be this: Be gallant and forceful simultaneously, which is as close to a contradiction as it is to good advice. Don't be a "red-ass," that is, too imperious, too inclined to throw people out of the game. But don't be a target, either.

"You can't stand there like a mummy," Sarge said, "but the more you say, the more you give them ammunition to use against you."

The instructors generally delighted in this role-playing, bringing to it a verve and imagination that were otherwise scantly in evidence in their behavior on the field. So antic dramas, featuring circular arguments, dirt-kicking, hat-throwing, obscenity-laced tirades, warnings that we'd never reach the big leagues—"You'll die here!" is a favorite taunt of minor league managers—and even occasional chest-bumping, were enacted again and again.

For most of the students, the threat of being challenged added a huge element of uncertainty to the umpiring enterprise, and the similarity to an improvisatory acting workshop was not subtle. Placed in an artificial circumstance, you were asked to react in character to the unexpected actions and remarks of someone else. The instructors had the advantage of holding the script—"I don't think I've said anything on the field here that hasn't been said to me by a manager somewhere," Darren Hyman said to me—and they were looking for us to show, with quick thinking, a cool demeanor, and an expedient segue to the resumption of play, that we didn't need one.

These were exercises aimed at bringing the psychological elements of the job into sharp relief, and the results were sometimes painful. A guy would make a mistake, an instructor would come storming out of the dugout and ask—at top volume—for an explanation, and the demeanor of the young umpire, fumbling for a reason where none existed, would simply crumble. The exercise would come to a halt, demonstrating to the humiliated young man and to dozens of us standing on the sideline what can happen when an umpire fails in his authority and unduly influences the game.

The instructor would let the moment sink in, then scream, "Fix it!"—a signal for the two umpires on the field to huddle, decide what went wrong, and make the appropriate correction. As a phrase, "Fix it!" became something of grim joke. A guy would drop a beer glass at a bar at night or show up somewhere with a shoe untied: "Fix it!" someone would yell.

I had much more natural ability at the arguing part of umpiring than the call-making part. As inept as I often was on the field, standing up for my decisions—whether or not they had been proper—put me suddenly at ease. Maybe I shouldn't have been surprised. As a writer and a reporter I'd practiced verbal fencing daily for decades, so understandably I felt more comfortable repelling complaints and taunts than I did making the judgments that brought them on. The skepticism that is part of a journalist's natural perspective also let me look upon the raging instructor/manager as just a little ridiculous, taking the events of a ball game so seriously as to carry on as though they were matters of life and death. More than once I wanted to throw up my hands and say simply, "Are you kidding me?" or "What are you doing out here?" or even "What the hell's wrong with you, a grown man behaving like this?" Usually the angrier they got, the easier it was for me to remain calm because the dynamic felt to me as it would to a parent about to enforce a time-out on a hysterical child. During one argument with me around first base, Brent Persinger, a fire-hydrant-shaped Triple A umpire, bent over to pull the bag out of the ground and couldn't do it; it stuck, and he ended up sitting on the dirt with the base fixed between his outstretched legs like a dinner plate at a picnic. It was a rare moment of triumph for me.

"Had enough?" I said, bending over to speak in his ear. "Good. You're out of the game."

Of course, I was older than just about everybody I had to argue with, except Evans and Sarge, and the idea that, say, a twenty-eight-year-old was trying to intimidate me in a debate seemed illogical. And, of course, I wasn't competing for a job. All of this contributed to making my arguments last a while; I talked too much, didn't pay enough attention to warnings against baiting and getting in the last word, and I'd perpetuate discussions until an ejection became inevitable.

Actually, I thought ejections were great fun, and they quickly became their own temptation. Ridding yourself of a yammering pest is incredibly satisfying, especially when you think of it as a sudden expression of joyous power, usually after a period of increasingly difficult restraint. To call it orgasmic is only to make an unseemly metaphor, not to be misleadingly descriptive.

Of course, the ejectees don't always accommodate you and go when you tell them to. Once they're out of the game, they have little else to lose, and they figure they might as well air their grievances fully. To illustrate this, Evans showed a video of one of the more famous arguments in umpire lore. In Baltimore in 1980, in the first inning of a game between the Detroit Tigers and the Orioles, the first-base umpire, Bill Haller, called a balk on the Oriole pitcher. That brought the Oriole manager, Earl Weaver, out of the dugout. When he reached first base, he said that Haller's reasoning for the call was "bullshit," and then he got personal.

"You're here, and this crew is here, just to fuck us," Weaver told Haller, and Haller emphatically thumbed him from the game, pointing to the dugout and exclaiming, "Boom!"

But that's when Weaver got going. His memorable tirade went on for a full seven minutes, as he repeatedly headed for the dugout, then thought better of it. Haller did what we were taught to do in such a situation, turn and walk away—don't keep relighting the fuse—but it didn't work, and Weaver trailed Haller back and forth across the infield like an annoying puppy, grousing and cursing, grousing and cursing. The dialogue, much of which was about who had poked whom, was pricelessly idiotic:

Weaver: Well, that's good, that's great.
Haller: Ah, you shit.
W: You couldn't wait to throw me out.
H: You run yourself, Earl. You run yourself.
W: Get your finger off me.
H: You hit me?
W: Yeah, 'cause you put your finger on me.
H: Good, I'm glad you did.
W: You're here for one goddamn specific reason.
H: What's that, Earl?
W: To fuck us.
H: Ah, you're full of shit. Fuck you.
W: And don't you ever put your finger on me again.
H: You hit me, Earl.

W: You put your finger on me.

H: That's okay.

W: You're goddamn right. If you touch me, I'm going to—

H: You ain't gonna knock nobody on their ass.

W: You do it again and I'll knock you right in your nose.

H: I didn't touch you.

W: You pushed your finger—

H: I did not. Now you're lying. You're lying.

W: No, you are.

H: You are lying.

W: You're a big liar.

H: You're a liar, Earl, a liar.

W: You are. I'll tell you something, you're here for one reason, to fuck us good.

H: Wrong.

W: That's the only reason you're here.

H: You are wrong, Earl.

W: And you'll have your chance tomorrow.

H: Oh, what is wrong with you?

W: You ain't no good.

H: Nah, you aren't either.

W: You ain't no good.

H: You're no fucking good either.

W: You stink.

Sophisticated stuff.

We did have a lesson in properly signaling an ejection. You use your right hand and make a pointing and tossing gesture, usually with an accompanying shout: "You're out of here!" or "You're gone!" or, most idiomatically eloquent, "You're done!"

I never got it exactly right, though I had a fair amount of practice. One other student umpire, but only one—a guy who threw out an entire lineup's worth of instructor/players at one time for collectively arguing balls and strikes from the dugout—had more total ejections than I did. One day I threw out opposing managers on the same play.

Still, I'm left-handed, and as the moment for an ejection approached, my excitement generally got the better of me and I could never remember to use my right hand. And because I was gesturing from a mirror opposite of the expected direction, two or three times I surprised the instructor I was tossing and cuffed him under the chin, leaving me in an umpire-uncomfortable position of having to apologize for nearly knocking him out as well as throwing him out.

During the last two weeks of school, the fieldwork every afternoon was devoted to what Evans called camp games. These were nine-inning-game simulations, each half-inning consisting of a dozen or so serial plays set in motion by a fungo-hitting instructor and presided over by a different pair of student umpires. Other instructors were serving as base runners, fielders, and pitchers (with students filling in the empty slots) as well as managers and coaches, and they were all equipped with microphones and earpieces, a network of communications.

You would see them speaking into their shirt collars, coordinating their plans. For each umpiring crew they contrived a mishmash of plays—some conventional, some unusual, some outright outlandish. (One brisk and windy afternoon, for example, one of the instructors, as the pitcher, pretended to be blown off the mound by a stiff breeze during his delivery.) Each crew would be attempting to handle the routine plays and unpredictable situations with confidence, even temperament, smooth authority, and wrinkle-free teamwork, thus to emerge from the inning having prevailed over the exigencies of the game.

When your number was called, you and your partner worked two half-innings, one each as a plate umpire and a base umpire. Every day each of us worked with a different partner. Though on one of our final mornings we also had a two-hour written test, the camp games felt like the real final exam, a long and ongoing one whose results, everyone knew, would largely be responsible for the list of "honor students" to be recommended to PBUC.

The pressure on my young classmates became palpable. You could see it all over the place. A lot more of them were smoking. They were getting snippy with one another, sulking after every criticism on the field, and worrying their camp-game performances to death. The instructors made things tougher. They were meeting in the early evenings to discuss the individual students' progress and rate them as candidates; meanwhile, on the field, their attitudes grew more militantly aggressive.

"Doesn't *anybody* here want a fucking job today?" Darren Hyman screamed one afternoon after a string of students made careless mistakes. The instructors told me later this was by design, the purpose being to simulate the hostile atmosphere a professional umpire often has to endure.

As the judgments on their umpiring futures grew imminent, a few obviously competent and confident young umpires seemed to know they were going to make the cut. The older guys like me were basically trying to perform well for the hell of it, because we'd put in the time and wanted to show ourselves what we could do. A few guys were content to fail and, reverting happily to their natural slackerdom, skipped class occasionally, stayed out late at night, and weathered the barbs of the instructors with sheepishness and a shrug. And then there were the maladroit and initially misguided guys, on whom self-knowledge was dawning; you could see the hope draining out of their faces as they realized they'd been fooling themselves all along.

But that left maybe seventy or eighty young men who weren't sure where they stood, for whom the last two weeks were a progressively ratcheting-up drama. One of these was a twenty-eight-year-old Ohioan named Greg Brown, who cut a strapping athletic figure on the field but whose inexperience was showing. Greg had floated around between school and odd jobs—he'd been a short-order cook most recently—and umpiring, which he'd done to pick up extra cash for several years, had suddenly and fiercely grabbed hold of him as a career idea like nothing else ever had. His first camp game was solid, but his second was less so, and he had assessed his situation, accurately, as being on the bubble. That is, he wasn't a sure thing either way, but he might earn his way into the group going to PBUC by climbing the learning curve and showing improvement in his remaining camp games.

With a little more than a week left, however, he pulled a thigh muscle when he slipped on a wet infield, and he had to sit out a few days, which drove him bananas. You could see the tension in his gait, limp and all, as he paced the sidelines, half watching to see how his classmates/competitors were making out, half-afraid of what he would see, because he knew he was supposed to be a good sport and root for them, but he couldn't help hoping just a few more guys would screw up. The second day I asked him how he was doing.

"I can't stand just standing around," he said, dragging desperately on a cigarette. "I want this job so bad. I should do like the pros do, get a shot of drugs and just go out and do the job. This is my one chance."

Poignantly, Greg and Brian Dubois had become friends; they spent their Sundays together at the home of Greg's parents, who had moved to Lakeland, about an hour away, where Greg's mom did their laundry. They talked about what they would do when they were both in pro ball, maybe, if they were lucky, even as partners.

They were unlikely bedfellows, very different guys. Greg was blond and wide-shouldered and well over six feet tall, Brian, brooding and slight, four years younger and about six inches shorter.

Brian was more verbally deft and clever, but his harsh self-critical gene made him prone to moody drama in the way of someone who expects things to go badly. During camp games, he told me he was quitting because he'd messed up an appeal play, something he thought the instructors would feel he should be able to handle in his sleep. His need to be so fiercely accountable for his mistakes was touching, sort of, though it would have been more so if it were a little more measured and a little less loopy.

But he was sunny about his friend's chances, admiring the formidable posture and raw athleticism Greg brought with him onto the diamond.

Greg did, in fact, carry himself with the ease of a man used to being the biggest, best-looking guy in the room, which made it especially striking to see him so agitated, though unlike Brian, he never seemed discouraged or fatalistic. He figured Brian's experience—it was Brian's second year at the school, and he was helping Greg daily with the nuances of the rulebook—would make a difference. Brian, Greg thought, was a shoo-in.

The drama of these two young men seemed especially intense, and I watched with interest as they approached a moment together that each felt had the power to change his life. After a few days of rest and heat treatments, Greg returned to the camp games, but the layoff had undermined him. His timing was off, his concentration seemed to vanish, and faced with situations, he looked baffled. Even his fellow students saw that he wasn't saving his candidacy. When he didn't make the cut, he left school bitterly.

Brian, meanwhile, was selected to attend the PBUC camp, and he did so in March, traveling to Cocoa, Florida, with forty-nine other aspiring umpires. His attitude remained the same, simultaneously hopeful and pessimistic, and when I went to PBUC myself to look around, from what I could tell, his work on the field was competent. Still, when his tryout was over, his evaluation turned out to be only fair to middling, which broke the barrier of his self-control. That night he got drunk and argued with some of his classmates, a disagreement that ended with someone urinating on someone else's bed. The next day Brian was upbraided for his actions by the director of the Cocoa Expo Sports Center, PBUC's landlord, and he argued back. Word of all this filtered back to the PBUC executive director, Mike Fitzpatrick, and Brian was more or less blackballed.

Agonizingly for Brian, he had picked exactly the wrong time to behave so badly, and what eventually happened to him was a bit like a bad movie in which a sympathetic character suffers irrevocably from a moment of weakness, an oops that he can't undo and that turns into a personal calamity. A month later, at the beginning of the 2006 season, minor league umpires went on strike for better pay, which caused dozens of veteran umpires simply to leave the game in disgust. An inordinate number of umpiring jobs were thus open when the strike ended in June.

Too late, Brian wrote an abjectly apologetic letter to Fitzpatrick, acknowledging his bad judgment and pleading to be forgiven for his lapse, but he received no response. I called Fitzpatrick myself, intending to speak on Brian's behalf, but when I mentioned his name, Fitzpatrick simply said, "No, no, no, no, no," and refused to say anything more. But Brian understood that his immaturity had cost him what he most wanted. Every single umpire who attended the PBUC camp that year was offered a job in professional baseball, except Brian Dubois.

For months afterward, Brian was despondent. He moved back to New Jersey and lived with his mother for a while, having to take the bus to look for work because he was still forbidden to drive. Once we went together to a minor league ball game in Coney Island, where Brian spent much of the game obsessively checking the messages on his cell phone in the forlorn hope that Fitzpatrick might finally have responded to him. Afterward, we went to visit the umpires in the dressing room, which struck me as emotional scab-scratching, a lot like going to visit your ex-girlfriend and the guy she had just moved in with. He was heartbroken and I was heartbroken for him.

I lost touch with Brian for a while after that, but about a year later

I heard from him. He'd gotten his driver's license back and had been working as an associate in a mortgage business, which sounded hopeful, but he still ached to be an umpire and he was full of self-recrimination. "I did this to myself," he said sadly.

Meanwhile, after Brian's terrible faux pas, Greg Brown got a call at home from PBUC. More umpires than predicted had resigned in the aftermath of the strike, and positions in the lowest minor league were open. Was he interested?

So it was Greg who would end up as the working umpire, while Brian spent the season at home, their friendship unsoldered as quickly as it had been forged.*

My own camp-game experience wasn't so bad, or at least it could have been worse. I'd learned a few things, and many of an umpire's fundamental responsibilities had made their way into my muscle memory. At long last, it had become second nature for me, as the plate umpire with a man on first, to cover third on a base hit to the outfield. As the base umpire, I'd gotten better, if not yet good, at finding the precise angle and distance for a throw to first base, and I'd disciplined myself to keep my chest facing the ball, even on a drive to the outfield with runners careening around the bases and every instinct I had misinforming me to follow them.

In my second camp game, I correctly invoked the intentionally-dropped-ball rule. (An infielder is allowed let a fly ball drop in front him on purpose, but he's not allowed to glove it and drop it; if he does, the ball is declared dead, the batter out, and the runners are returned to their original bases.) In my third camp game, I recognized a tricky time play. With runners on first and third with one out, the batter grounded to the first baseman, who stepped on the bag, recording the second out and removing the force play at second. So when the throw was made to

---

*Brian Dubois's story had a happy ending. After another close call behind the wheel, he wised up and entered rehab. Some time later, in November 2007, I went to see him in York, Pennsylvania, where he was then living, and took him to lunch. He seemed bored but chastened. We talked about his going back to umpire school, for a third time, and perhaps earning forgiveness from PBUC, and in January, several months sober, that's what he did. In Kissimmee, he stuck to the task at hand, and Evans and his staff sent him to Cocoa, where he performed well. To its credit, PBUC determined that Brian deserved a second chance, and for the 2008 season he went to work in the Gulf Coast League. His name has been changed—Brian Dubois is the only pseudonym in this book—to guard his identity on the field.

second, the runner reversed his field and headed back to first, where the tag was made to complete a double play. It was also the third out of the inning. Before the tag, however, the runner from third had crossed the plate. Properly, I counted the run.

My satisfaction at these small triumphs was, of course, mitigated by calamities. Once, with the bases empty, lined up behind first, I was too slow to decide whether to follow a line drive into the outfield or to come into the infield, and I ended up colliding with the batter-runner as he rounded first and tried to stretch his hit into a double. In the same half-inning, I called consecutive balks on a pitcher for not coming to a full stop in the stretch position before propelling himself toward the plate, but I hadn't been paying attention—he'd been using the same motion for a half dozen pitches before I made the call—and anyway, his motion, with an infinitesimal stop, was probably legal. My partner thought so, anyway—as he told me after I had to fend off an instructor who came out to argue. Then, probably gun-shy, I compounded the error by *not* calling an egregious balk on a pickoff throw to first.

Anyway, it went like that. Sometimes I felt in control of the game, sometimes not, which means, of course, that I never was. In the camp games I got a glimpse of the umpire's job from the inside and, from that perspective, recognized for the first time what a mass of contradictory qualities it required. Suddenly I understood how crucial it was to be both relaxed and vigilant; to be both rigid enough not to shirk any responsibilities and flexible enough to adjust when a play took an unexpected turn; to know the rules backward and forward so as to be prepared for anything they cover and yet be ready to extemporize when the rulebook falls prescriptively short; to actually see and register what's in front of you and simultaneously anticipate the immediate future; to be confident enough to hold the balance of the game in your hand and humble enough to avoid deciding it; to hold firm opinions and to keep your mouth shut; to remember baseball is just a game and to take it very seriously.

I understood, too, that as the umpire you are neither inside the game, as the players are, nor outside it among the fans, but that the game passes through you, like rainwater through a filter, and that your job is to influence it for the better, to strain out the impurities, to make it cleaner, fairer, and more transparent without impeding it, corrupting it, changing its course, or making it taste funny.

*   *   *

On the last day of school I had my last camp game, and Sarge took me aside before my stint as a base umpire and told me he was going to go overboard, that he was going to bump me during an argument. Why he felt it necessary to warn me I'm not sure, probably because he didn't take me all that seriously and maybe was afraid I'd take offense at such overt aggression or that I'd think he was trying to embarrass me in front of everybody. This would have been consistent with Sarge's personality—he couldn't have been more sweet-tempered off the field or more military on it. "I love you, you know that," he'd say, but then if you lined up in the wrong position or turned your back carelessly on the ball, he could get ridiculously angry, as though you'd wandered too close to a land mine and endangered the lives of your platoon.

Whatever the reason, when the moment happened, it was so weirdly, confusingly real that I had the experience that I've heard actors talk about, when they're onstage and the script suddenly dissolves and they're up there having an actual conversation and not acting at all.

The catalyst was a double-play ball grounded to the shortstop, who threw to the second baseman, who bobbled the throw and dropped it during the pivot—the same kind of play I'd screwed up on in front of Sarge a few weeks earlier. This time I did everything I was supposed to do and was in position to see the second baseman receive the ball. I watched it settle in his glove, and I watched him juggle and lose it, but only after he pulled the ball out with his throwing hand. I made the proper signal, a demonstrative and exaggerated mimicking of a fielder yanking a ball out of his glove, repeated it twice, and shouted, "He's out, he's out, he's pulling it out!" Then I banged on the imaginary door with my right fist—a perfect umpire-school out mechanic.

That was when Sarge came tearing out of the dugout, howling, "What the fuck is going on out here?"

The dialogue went something like this:

"He was pulling it out of his glove, Skip," I said. "You saw it as well as I did."

"Bullshit!" he screamed. "You didn't see it. You weren't even in position."

"I was right where I had to be, Skip. Don't tell me I'm not doing my job."

That ratcheted up his temper.

"Don't tell me what to tell you!" he yelled, and with his hands on his hips and his chin tilted up at me and his face contorted in rage, he charged me and our chests bumped hard.

"That's a bump, Sarge." I stepped back and threw my right hand and arm over my head and toward the dugout. "You're out of here."

Instead of leaving, he stepped in closer to me, until we were just about nose to nose and I could smell his breath.

"I'm out of here?" he said. "I'm out of here? We're busting our asses trying to win a pennant, and you're screwing it up for us, and all you can do is throw me out? That's horseshit."

"All right, all right, that's enough. You've had your say. Now go sit down."

"I'll tell you when it's enough."

And so on and so on.

I may be recounting this from memory, but someone snapped a photo of the scene and sent it to me, and I have it here in front of me as I'm writing. It's amazing. I rarely get so demonstrative or loud in anger—I'm too self-conscious, generally, to release the governor on that kind of emotion—but Sarge and I are really going at it, and the fury in the moment is unmistakable. It's a close-up shot, cutting us off at the shoulders, taken from the side and just a little bit in front of me. Sarge is a few inches shorter than I am, so his head is tilted slightly upward and mine is tilted down, but I've got the bill of my cap under the bill of his. Our noses are maybe two inches apart, and both our mouths are going, pursed in the exchange of bile. His chin is jutting aggressively. One of the cords in my neck is bulging, and the one nostril of mine you can see is flared.

The photo makes it perfectly clear that either our acting is extraordinary or our emotion is real; either way, in that moment we were hopping mad at each other, and finally, when Sarge stormed off the field, he kept looking over his shoulder and yelling. I do recall exactly what he said to me then.

"That's all you can do, throw people out," he said. "You make a bad call and I get thrown out?"

I stood there with my hands on my hips and watched him go, trying to keep a placid expression on my face.

"You'll never be a major leaguer," he said. "Put *that* in your fucking book!"

CHAPTER FOUR

WELCOME TO
PROFESSIONAL BASEBALL

One of the best days an umpire can have is if nobody knows he's there.
—BUD SELIG, commissioner,
Major League Baseball

An umpire leads a lonely life. He has few human contacts save with his partner. He is as isolated as a monk in a monastery.
—HARRY "STEAMBOAT" JOHNSON,
minor league umpire, 1910–46

When umpire school ended, I spent some time visiting umpires in spring training in both the Grapefruit League (Florida) and the Cactus League (Arizona). In March I went to the PBUC evaluation camp to see how my classmates would fare in their competition with the umpire candidates from the Wendelstedt school and to see if anyone I knew would get an actual job. And I worked some games myself.

It's fair to say my umpiring beginnings were modest. My first game was a Little League contest; I was on the bases. And my first call of any consequence I got wrong on purpose. The team at bat had scored a dozen or so runs in the third inning, largely because the first baseman had dropped three perfectly good throws, and with the score something like 20–1, the poor kid finally held on to one. The runner, however, had beaten the throw by a stride and a half. I did my job.

"He's out!" I bellowed.

The reactions were interesting. The center fielder, sprinting by on his way to the dugout, said, "Thank you, thank you, thank you, Mr. Umpire," with the plaintive gratitude of a squirming boy who'd been excused early from an overlong church sermon. One of the parents on the sideline growled at me, "You're kidding, right, Blue?"

"I'd had enough, hadn't you?" I said.

"That's bullshit."

My partner, one of the league's regular umpires, stared daggers of disgust in my direction and didn't talk to me for the rest of the game, which thankfully ended, owing to a local slaughter rule, after the fourth inning.

Afterward, the coach of the winning team came over and shook my hand and winked at me. "Nice job on that call," he said.

I didn't think a lot about it at the time; it became just a small, funny story I enjoyed telling. But in retrospect it was a good introductory lesson in the distinctions among an umpire's authority, his power, and his job. Is an umpire only supposed to get it right, with nothing to come between him and the pure call? Or does he more appropriately consider context? Things such as sportsmanship, the personality of the players, just deserts, the way the game "ought" to be played? And if it is okay to consider context, is it always okay? And if it's not always okay, when isn't it? What sorts of calls should or shouldn't be affected?

Anyway, I thought I did the right thing: I still think so, though obviously not everyone agreed. The point is that ambiguity, ethical ambiguity, is much more a part of umpiring than anyone ever acknowledges, except, of course, when the umpires themselves, experienced ones, look in the mirror. Longtime baseball watchers will be aware, for example, of "the neighborhood play," something that has always catalyzed a certain amount of outrage on the part of fans but that has mostly, though not entirely, disappeared from the big leagues because of slow-motion instant replay on television.

The neighborhood play occurs on an attempted double play, when the pivotman takes the throw as he gets to second base and throws to first, but in so doing does not actually touch the bag with his foot, or he touches it but not at the same time he has the ball in his possession. He just gets close, either physically or temporally; i.e., he's in the neighborhood. For most of baseball history, umpires tended not to be sticklers about this call, allowing the fielders some leeway, on the logic that the pivotman is at some risk of being hurt because a base runner is often bearing down on him, and while he is catching and throwing, he is unable to get out of the way or protect himself against being upended.

"If you want to break down what you mean by 'neighborhood,' yes, there's a neighborhood play," Tom Hallion would explain to me later that year. "If the throw, the fielder, and everything stays in an ordinary progression of what's supposed to happen, what should happen, what normally happens, I'd say, yeah, you would give him the call even if he's not right on the bag. Let's say the fielder drags his foot and misses the bag, but the throw is there, the fielder doesn't have to reach or make an extraordinary fielding motion, everything is normal. Then it's an out. Because if I call the guy safe, here's what they say: 'Do you want this guy fucking killed?'

"But nowadays you can't give them as much, you can't give them a foot off the bag. Your life's on the line to get it right because they have sixteen freakin' cameras on you. I had a play in Minnesota the other day, guy on first base gets picked off, he goes down to second, slides in, and the second baseman just takes the glove and does a lazy, lazy tag on him, goes down, tags him up here, on the shoulder, like it's just a formality."

Ordinarily, an umpire would give the defense the benefit of the doubt, Hallion said, a reward for the pitcher who had skillfully separated the runner from first base with a crafty pickoff throw and didn't deserve to have his good move erased by a teammate's lack of effort. Nonetheless, Hallion called the runner safe.

"Well, the guy should have been out, he got picked off," Hallion said. "But I said to the second baseman, 'You're killing me with that tag. You gotta give me something better than that. I can't give you that.'

"This is the kind of call you make from experience," Hallion concluded.

My own experience turned out to be minimal that spring because after just a handful of games I sprained my ankle rather badly—not umpiring, alas, just falling off a curb as I was crossing the street. I had stepped up a bit in level of competition, doing not only some Babe Ruth League games, but two high school games and a few adult-league contests on Long Island, where the players, mostly former college athletes now in their thirties and forties, could still catch and throw the ball pretty well—the pitchers were throwing about 80 mph—and hit with power. They couldn't run the way they used to, though, which made things a little easier for a fledgling umpire. But I'd just embarked on my life on the field when it was curtailed for several months. I'd pick it up again in September.

In the meantime, I began my minor league travels with a limp.

On an early summer Thursday, the Boise Hawks lost to the Tri-City Dust Devils, 1–0, at the Devils' home stadium in Pasco, Washington. The crucial moment of the game came in the top of the eighth, when a Hawks outfielder, Alfred Joseph, laced a ball down the third-base line with a man on first and two out. The home plate umpire, Ben Robinson, called the ball foul, incurring the considerable irritation of the Hawks in general and their manager, Steve McFarland, in particular, who was still miffed about it when I met him the following Tuesday.

"Ben didn't react quickly enough," McFarland said to me. "The ball was hit too hard down the line for him."

"I told him, 'I'm standing right on the line, where I should be,'" Ben said in his defense. "'You think you've got a better view from the dugout?'"

After the argument, Joseph was then retired. In the Hawks' judgment, Robinson's call had cost them a run and very possibly the game, and a tone was set for the week to come. Even though the Hawks won the next two games, tension was evident between the umpires and the Boise club. After Saturday night's contest the Hawks took the team bus home, where they were to begin a series the next day against the Yakima Bears, and under most circumstances they wouldn't see Robinson and his partner, Phil Henry, again for maybe a couple of weeks. But as a quirk of the schedule would have it, Robinson and Henry, newly minted rookie umpires, were headed to Boise, too.

The low minor leagues confront umpires with an endurance test of almost comic dimensions, and for Phil and Ben, the next few days would provide an apt welcome to the life they'd chosen. It's not quite three hundred miles to Boise from Pasco, which is in the south-central part of Washington (the other two of the tri-cities are Kennewick and Richland, if that helps you locate it), about a five-hour drive.

That's not so bad, really, in the minor league universe, where, for example, the fourteen-hour drive between Corpus Christi, Texas, and Springfield, Missouri, is a Texas League staple, and most of the time, has to be done between games on consecutive nights. The umpires gave the Hawks a head start, waiting until the next morning to make the trip, but about two-thirds of the way along, somewhere in the hills of eastern Oregon, Phil's road-weary Pontiac began to rattle under the hood, and soon the steering wheel was shaking so violently that the car became undrivable.

In Double A ball, the leagues provide vans for their three-man umpiring crews, and in Triple A the umpires frequently travel by plane, with cars or vans available to them once they arrive. But this was the Northwest League, a level of baseball known as short season A, one step from the bottom rung, Rookie League. Here, where the two-man crews are yoked together like oxen for the season, no transportation is provided.

Instead, the leagues offer a mileage allowance—forty-four cents per mile in 2006—and make an effort to pair up an umpire who owns a car with an umpire who doesn't. Other things being equal, in some leagues where the distances between cities are substantial, owning a reliable automobile is an excellent credential for an umpire's résumé. This is among the many reasons that umpires say the higher you climb up the baseball ladder, the more dignified and the less stressful—the easier!—the job gets.

Phil and Ben now had a serious problem. At midday, the temperature in the nineties, they were about a hundred miles from Boise, where game time was 6:15. But well schooled in and slightly intimidated by all the league rules and regulations that governed them—"Every umpire I've ever known has wanted to please the boss," the big league umpire Bill Miller told me once—they did what they were supposed to do. Happily, by walking to the top of a rise, they were able to get a cell phone signal.

First they called a tow truck. Then they called the general manager of the Boise Hawks to let him know what was going on so he could line up a couple of local amateur umpires in case they couldn't make it to the park on time. Then they called the league president, a Boise lawyer named Bob Richmond.

This was a dicey matter because their relationship with Richmond hadn't really been established yet—they'd met him once, at an orientation meeting—and league presidents, who oversee umpires, have extraordinary power over them. They have different reputations, some as umpire friendly, like George Spelius of the Midwest League in Single A ball, whose daughter married one of his umpires (Marty Foster, who is now in the big leagues), some as umpire hostile, like Randy Mobley of the Triple A International League, who was an active adversary of the umpires' union during contract negotiations when the minor league umpires went on strike in 2006. Richmond's rep was somewhere in between, that of an okay guy who recognized that umpires were people but who generally condescended to them and wouldn't take their side when any of the ball clubs complained about them.

Richmond, who had been the Northwest League president since 1991, told me that the operating budgets for the league's eight teams ranged between $1.5 million and $2.5 million. Of that, $12,000— between .5 percent and .8 percent—fed the league's fund to support its eight umpires, the minimum number needed to officiate four games in four different cities on the same night.

When I suggested to Richmond that not providing cars for the umpires seemed chintzy and that it might save a lot of headaches in a league where the distances between ballparks are often measured in the several hundreds of miles, he shrugged and said he didn't really think so.

"For us to lease cars, it doesn't work out," he said. "Believe me, we've looked into it." Anyway, he said, car troubles like Phil and Ben had were rare, which struck me as either incredible good fortune or a rosy spin on things. It's not as if these guys were driving new BMWs; when Phil's 1994 Firebird broke down, it had 183,000 miles on it.

Anyway, umpires didn't have to use their own cars, Richmond said; they had the option of renting. He didn't say that the rental fee—for a midsize, say—for the eleven-week season would be about $2,000, not including gas, and that first-year umpires earn less than $6,000, so no one rents.

"I have a soft spot for these kids, I really do," Richmond said. "We tell them this is a great way to start your life out, no matter what career you end up in."

Stranded on the side of the road, Phil and Ben hadn't had much interaction with Richmond yet, so all they had was the common presumption that league presidents want nothing from their umpires so much as freedom from administrative irritations, like having to find replacements. The general belief among umpires is that if you don't show up for a game, or if you merely cause the first inning to be delayed, even with a good excuse like car trouble, your job becomes instantly in jeopardy.

The tow truck, a well-weathered pickup with a winch affixed to the back, eventually arrived, driven by a fat man whose wife, also fat, was keeping him company. The cab had no backseat, so for the two-and-a-half-hour ride to Boise, Ben and Phil were jammed in the front seat with them. It was uncomfortable and expensive, but at least it got them to the game in time. With about forty-five minutes to spare, they hopped out of the truck in front of Boise's Memorial Stadium.

No garages were open; it was the July Fourth weekend. So Phil didn't have any choice but to trust the tow-truck operator to drop his car in the parking lot of a repair shop and to bring his keys back to the ballpark. (He did.) With no time to check into their hotel, Phil and Ben stored their belongings in the umpires' dressing room, a closet-size space under the third-base grandstand with no windows and no air-conditioning that had clearly been intended for use as a one-stall restroom.

They didn't have a chance to eat, and no pregame meal would have been provided, anyway. Afterward, three hours later, a teenaged clubhouse boy would bring them a couple of cold hot dogs wrapped in tinfoil. On the field they were met by a full house, about thirty-five hundred people, a local crowd known for being knowledgeable and highly partisan. As in a lot of small ballparks, there wasn't much room behind the plate or in foul territory, so the spectators in the good seats were close enough to the field that they didn't have to raise their voices much to make objections.

"This is probably the worst place to umpire in the Northwest League," McFarland, the Hawks manager, would tell me later. "I've seen a lot of crews who were glad to be out of here."

Sitting in the front row, just on the first-base side of home plate, was a large, bearded man wearing a Hawks cap. He was the kind of fan who is a fixture at almost every minor league park, a guy who calls attention to himself in appearance and manner, who presumes a casual familiarity with the home-team players and calls them by their nicknames, who considers himself a strategy expert and acts as the self-appointed spokesman for the home fans. In the first inning, Phil, who was taking his turn behind the plate, called a close pitch against a Boise hitter, and the man delivered a stentorian warning.

"Blue, you don't get on the ball and this could be a long week, son," he boomed out. "I'm here every night!"

Ben Robinson and Phil Henry had been professional umpires for exactly thirteen days.

For fans, especially those who come from big cities, the romance of minor league baseball is irresistible and real and specifically American, and you can't travel around in its infectious ambience for long without being infused with a kind of patriotism. The team nicknames alone describe a singsong American poetry that is worthy of recitation: the Lansing Lugnuts and the Clinton LumberKings, the Kannapolis Intimidators and the Winston-Salem Warthogs, the Albuquerque Isotopes and the Altoona Curve, the Arkansas Travelers and the Asheville Tourists, the Modesto Nuts and the Montgomery Biscuits, the Scottsdale Scorpions and the Greensboro Grasshoppers, the Burlington Bees, the Buffalo Bisons, the Birmingham Barons, and the Bakersfield Blaze.

Sprinkled about the continental landscape, you'll find Rock Cats, River Cats, Hillcats, Mudcats, Snowcats, Fisher Cats, and Valley Cats, not to mention Rock Hounds, River Dogs, Muckdogs, Sea Dogs, and Desert Dogs. You've got Shorebirds, IronBirds, Pelicans, Owlz, Loons, and Osprey; Snappers, Catfish, Hammerheads, and Manatees; Sidewinders and Timber Rattlers; Knights and Wizards; Dragons and Lake Monsters; Zephyrs, Cyclones, Thunder, and Storm; AquaSox, Baysox, Sky Sox, and Solar Sox.

Boise Hawks doesn't add much in the way of invention to this music—not like Lancaster JetHawks, Oklahoma Red Hawks, or South Bend Silver Hawks—though its three-syllable straightforwardness is pleasingly punchy. And like the name in the minor league lexicon, the place itself sits with comfortable anonymity in the minor league atlas, which describes a nation of small cities and big towns, places where local pride tends to be palpable, the ballpark is often a community gathering place, and the players are celebrities in the local pizzerias and bars—that is, if they're old enough to drink.

Teenagers come to a minor league ballpark to hold hands and eat junk food (though I suppose that describes anyplace teenagers go), and parents bring their young children to enjoy an outing together as a family and to relax in a place where they know the proprietor is going to work hard to entertain the kids. Every minor league franchise courts families with mid-inning activities for children, like quiz competitions, sing-alongs, giveaways of T-shirts or food (generally involving ice cream or maybe bratwurst, though I witnessed a butter-eating contest in Fresno), races around the bases, and games in which contestants have to toss, say, plastic lobsters into a lobster trap, or roll a tire-size foam-rubber hamburger around an obstacle course.

Mascots are big. Every team has a purple burro or a lime-green coyote or some such creature stalking the roofs of the dugouts and collecting high fives from eight-year-olds. Then there's the patriarch of mascots, the Chicken, aka Ted Giannoulis (whom I encountered in Des Moines), who has made a substantial living dressing up in a bright yellow chicken suit to taunt umpires and perform other antics at dozens of ballparks a year. (Umpires always speak well of the Chicken, who rewards them for their cooperation with gift certificates from department stores.) It tells you a lot about why people come to minor league ballparks that as of the 2006 season, Giannoulis was commanding $7,000 a game, a lot of tickets at maybe eight bucks apiece; this was according to a league president, though he looked a little nervous as soon as he said it.

"Please don't print that; the Chicken'll kill me," the man said. (It was the same guy who explained to me that the most important thing about running a minor league team is to keep the concession stands and the restrooms clean. "If Mama sees they're not spick-'n'-span, she won't bring the kiddies back," he said.)

The point is there's something about a minor league ballpark, with its manageable size and ticket prices, the mingling smells of mown grass, grilled franks, and spilled beer, that gives off the sense that it is the great American carnival, with a ball game coincidentally being played in the vicinity. This is precisely what it was like for me in Boise.

Memorial Stadium wasn't much, an undistinguished structure made up of three concrete grandstands laid out in a wide U and set down on the outskirts of Boise's commercial sprawl. A trailer park was nestled in the trees beyond the right-center-field fence. But it was, in many ways, typical, with the familiar and comforting quality of a postcard. Its prime virtue was that it faced northwest, so patrons got a fine view of the foothills of the Sawtooth Range beyond the outfield, though when the summer sun was low, if you were sitting on the first-base side, the glare was brutal.

The day I arrived was the day following Phil and Ben's tow-truck adventure—they recounted it for me in all its awful detail—and that evening at the ballpark it was Happy Birthday Idaho Night, featuring postgame fireworks (a minor league staple that most club owners will use any excuse for). Before the first pitch, the fans were asked to sing along to the hymnlike state song, "Here We Have Idaho." And between innings, an announcer with a microphone roamed the stands and quizzed patrons for prizes: What was the state's first capital? (Lewiston.) What is the state bird? (The mountain bluebird.)

It was a gorgeous night, hot but clear. I drank a beer, stood for the national anthem, and was feeling very much at home, an honorary Idahoan, when I heard the first insults leveled at the umpires. "Hey, Blue, poke a hole in the mask!" someone yelled at Ben, who was behind the plate and hadn't even called a pitch yet, and suddenly the hostility that umpires live with seemed newly clear to me because it fit in so seamlessly with the ballpark atmosphere, as part and parcel of the evening's entertainment. Indeed, in every league, there's at least one ballpark—it didn't happen in Boise—where the clever organist plays "Three Blind Mice" when the umps take the field, and everywhere fans find the same catcalls (some of them quite vulgar) endlessly amusing. It occurred to me in Boise, when someone screamed, "Bend over and use your good eye, Blue!" that, however publicly accepted, this is generically hateful behavior, the equivalent of ethnic slurs against people defined by their color. I'd had the name leveled at me by teenagers and adult amateur ballplayers, and it hadn't occurred to me to be irritated, but it was then I understood why professional umpires bristle at being called Blue.

For umpires, working in the minor leagues has always meant living a beleaguered life, its relentless unpleasantries constituting a tradition, of sorts. Ask any umpire, working or retired, about his minor league career, and the tales of indignities endured come out, usually told, though not always, with the comic tinge that distance allows. The stories are a fraternal glue.

Some of them are about the enmity hurled at them on the field and the consequences of making close calls against the home team. It's true that the bad old days when their physical safety might be in question are over. You can read about them in the first umpiring memoir, *Standing the Gaff,* written in 1935 by a lifelong minor leaguer, Harry "Steamboat" Johnson (the nickname was a reference to his foghorn voice) and from which it is evident that fistfights and pop-bottle bombardments were routine enough to be considered working conditions.

These hardscrabble days are not so long gone that I didn't hear more than one current major leaguer remember his tires being slashed or an ominous note being left on his windshield: "We know where you sleep!" But now most umpires complain far more about the abuse they have to take from the game's participants than from the spectators, especially in the low minors, where many of the players haven't yet reached adult maturity and even the managers and the coaches throw regular tantrums. Andy Russell, who was one of my instructors at umpire school, quit umpiring suddenly in the middle of the 2007 season, his third in pro ball, the day after a player threatened to kill him.

The previous year, Andy and his partner had been the object of a tirade by the manager of the Asheville Tourists, Joe Mikulik, that was so demonstrative it made local newscasts across the country—as well as the *Tonight* show. After Andy called an opposing base runner safe on a steal of second—it happened to be Koby Clemens, Roger's son— Mikulik argued vociferously enough to get himself ejected, then stalked about the field, pulling second base out of the ground and hurling it into the outfield, throwing bats from the dugout into foul territory, and piling dirt and pouring water on home plate and slapping the water bottle down on top of the mess he'd made.

After the game, Mikulik said that mannequins from Sears could umpire better than Andy and his partner, Stephen Barga. But what Mikulik said to Andy on the field—"You are fucking horseshit!" and "You have no fucking balls!" among other things, according to the ejection report Andy was required to file with the league—wasn't made public, nor was that when Mikulik left the field, he barricaded the umpires' dressing-room door with clubhouse detritus—folding chairs, a watercooler, a pitching screen, and a large metal dustpan.

A mild-mannered guy and a promising umpire—he was ranked sixth among all A-ball umpires when he quit—Andy told me the Mikulik incident didn't figure in his decision to walk away, though frankly I think he was kidding himself. We talked a couple of weeks after his abrupt retirement, and he said he'd been considering it for a while, that for months he hadn't been enjoying going to the ballpark because he put himself under so much pressure to get everything right.

"Every single pitch," he said. "And I would judge every game by how it went, you know, how much they were screaming at me, and I just got to a point where I couldn't deal with it anymore. I'd be on the field and I'd look at the scoreboard and go, 'Jeez, we're only in the sixth inning?' If I get a few gripes here and there, I can deal with it, but it was about how I was handling it on the inside. I can appear as though nothing is bothering me, I'm real good at that, but my mind is going like crazy. I don't have a lot of self-confidence, I guess. It was affecting my well-being."

In mid-July 2007, during a Carolina League game between the Myrtle Beach Pelicans and the Winston-Salem Warthogs, he reached the end of his tolerance. In the bottom of the eighth with two out, a Myrtle Beach runner stole second. Andy called the runner safe on a close play, and the next batter hit a home run.

"That's when the catcher came sprinting out and went off on me," Andy said. "He said, 'That's on you.' And he said, 'You don't even know, I'm going to effing kill you.' If there were any more signs that I needed, that was it. I'd had enough."

Mostly, though, the minor league stories you hear from umpires have to do with life away from the park, the low-rent living that the chosen profession foists on them. Part of it has to do with boredom and isolation, which was also foreshadowed by *Standing the Gaff*. Indeed, for all of the bump-and-bruise episodes recounted by Steamboat Johnson, his most affecting passage was in a chapter titled "The Umpire—A Lonely Chap," in which he summarized the umpire's day after the game is over, a simply declared account that rings pretty close to the life that minor league umpires feel themselves consigned to today:

> We undress and take a shower, then dress and go at once to our hotel. There we fill out a report card for that game. The card has blanks for the date, home team, visiting team, weather conditions, ground conditions, time game started, time it finished, and remarks on the conduct of the players, fines imposed, players sent out of the game and anything else of an unusual nature. . . .

After making our report we have dinner, our second and last meal of the day. We usually dine in a quiet restaurant and try to dine alone. Occasionally friends invite us out to their homes for dinner and that is a real treat. After dinner we usually go back to our hotel. Attending the movies sometimes hurts our eyes because squinting into the glare of the sun all day often makes our eyes very tired. When our assignment ends in that town, we go on to the next and repeat the process from April until October.

Even today, what most umpires convey when they talk about the minor leagues is precisely this sense of unprivileged monotony. The paperwork, especially after a game in which there is an ejection, is especially tedious. (Even so, ejection reports, which are supposed to be detailed and dispassionate, can make amusing reading. Here's an excerpt from Andy Russell's ejection report of Mikulik: "Joe then walked over to me and yelled at me: 'You need to call some fucking strikes.' He then kicked dirt three times on me as he passed me, walked over on top of the plate and covered it with dirt. Joe then walked to his dugout and threw four bats out on the playing field. After this Joe walked back out on the field and poured water on the dirt-covered plate and wiped it off while looking at me yelling, 'Can you see the fucking plate now?'")

What seems most to stick in the minds of umpires, however, even long after their minor league days are over, are the petty humiliations of making do on unconscionably low wages, meager benefits, and bare-bones amenities.

Barry Larsen, for example, a Double A umpire in the Texas League, told me about his regular routine in Springfield, Missouri, where the roadside motel the league put the crew in didn't have a complimentary breakfast, so every morning he crossed a divided highway to eat surreptitiously at a different hotel that did have one. He spoke of this as if it was both amusing and pathetic, and indeed it was. Larsen, who had recently been married, was twenty-eight years old at the time and was earning $2,500 a month.

This small story is of a piece with the uncomfortable memories that all big league umpires seem to have of their minor league years. Rick Reed, a major league crew chief, remembered that during his first year in baseball in 1973, in Bluefield, West Virginia, in the Appalachian League, the umpires dressed in the equipment shed for the grounds crew.

"They would keep opening the door as we were getting dressed, saying they had to get the lime to lime the field," Reed said. "'We need to do the batter's boxes. Everybody decent?'"

In Medford, Oregon, in 1989, Ted Barrett and his partner had to dress for a game in the general manager's office because "the regular dressing room went fishing," Barrett said. Ordinarily the umpires changed clothes in a double-wide trailer parked behind the ballpark, but one day the guy who owned the trailer and who was evidently just lending it to the ball club took his family on a vacation.

"That was my first year in baseball; my second year was when they started paying for our rooms," Barrett went on. He was still working in Single A ball, in the California League, and the leagues had just determined that they could save money if, instead of including lodging costs in their umpire per diem, they chose the hotels and arranged payment themselves, often bartering with advertising space on outfield fences and in programs.

"So we no longer got to choose where we stayed," Barrett said. "And some of the places they put us in were absolute dumps. I'm not a picky guy. If I've got a bed and a TV, I'm good to go, but some of these places just flat weren't safe. That first year in the Cal League, the hotel they had us staying in Bakersfield, the crew went in there and we were sharing the place with drug dealers and prostitutes. We called the league office, and a guy from the league came to check it out, and he was driving a Cadillac. Well, the cops pulled him over. And he explained to them who he was, but they said to him, 'If you're down here, you're here to pick up a hooker or buy drugs, so get out of here.' They switched hotels on us the next day."

It's likely that umpires wouldn't find baseball's cheapness in their care and feeding so irksome—"It's a business, I understand that" is a sentiment I heard often to mitigate their complaints—if the message that such treatment represents a more general disrespect didn't also come through with a disheartening regularity. Virtually every minor league umpire who has been in the game for a few years has a story of being rushed back to work after an injury or an illness by an impatient league president who was tired of the inconvenience and expense of finding local replacements. One umpire worked in 2007 with a squint after returning too soon from a bad case of shingles. Another retired because after his girlfriend miscarried their baby, his request for a leave of absence to be with her for more than a few days was refused by the league and PBUC. The brief communication he had from PBUC concluded with a brusqueness and chilliness that seemed to me all too characteristic of the way these young umpires are treated as a matter of policy.

"Please let the Eastern League and I know as soon as possible," the executive director wrote, "if you desire to accept the offer of a few days off, if you wish to follow your umpire schedule as assigned or if you wish to resign from your position as an umpire. Thank you."

The most notorious story of all was that of Bill Miller, a friendly, beefy Californian with red hair and, unlike many of his colleagues, a college degree, a BA in history from UCLA. Miller reached the big leagues for good in 1999 after being a vacation replacement for a couple of years, but in 1995 he was a rookie in Triple A, having been elevated to the International League that season, his sixth in the game. He had made steady but unspectacular progress, was twenty-eight and married with a child on the way.

Now, umpires do tend to carry around a martyr complex. There's a lot of woe-is-me in umpire culture. But for Miller, his grim tale told over a pregame meal in Philadelphia, in detail and with visible emotion, was still vivid more than a decade after the actual events.

On this particular night, he and his crew were in Norfolk, Virginia. They had arranged, after the game, to meet and go out for a drink, and Miller was getting ready in his room at the Days Inn—it opened onto the street—when there was a knock on the door, and thinking it was his fellow umpires, he answered it. Three men broke in, put a gun to his head, and robbed him of all his belongings.

"They tied me up and threatened to kill me," Miller said.

We were in a garrulous sports bar, a burger-and-wings kind of place, and we'd been having a lively conversation about umpiring before this memory became his subject. His voice went suddenly dull, his face ashen.

"I can still feel the barrel on the back of my head," he said. "It was a bad, bad ordeal."

Afterward, Miller said, the league president, Randy Mobley, was largely unsympathetic.

"The way I was treated was reprehensible," Miller said. "I'd had a major trauma, and I was a wreck. I might as well have gone to the loony farm—uncontrollable sobbing, the whole thing. I was away from home and my wife was two weeks away from giving birth to our first child. We ended up moving hotels, there was no way I was going to stay there, and we went and got a hotel where the ball club was staying. They were staying at the Omni down on the waterfront, but the umpires were at the Days Inn, because the league traded advertising for the hotel room. It wasn't safe. And then the league president chewed my partner's ass for moving hotels."

Miller was left without clothes or money, but the league made no offer to help him out.

"I didn't work the next night," Miller went on, "and he understood why. I told him I was feeling a little bit better, but then I regressed. I *wasn't* doing better, and the next night he called and said, 'You told me you were doing better. How come you're not working?' I was in the hotel room, underneath the covers, just going, 'I'm not doing too good, I don't know if I'm going to be able to make it.' He was so mad, so mad.

"We went from Norfolk to Richmond, but I was done, I was a wreck, there was no way I could work."

He borrowed $500 from the general manager of the Richmond Braves for a plane ticket home.

"So then, I'm at the airport, and I get paged: 'William Miller, pick up the white courtesy phone,' and Randy Mobley is screaming at me. 'Who gave you the right to go home? You have no right to do this!' I mean, he was *screaming* at me. It was unbelievable."

Later, I spoke to Mobley about the incident. He remembered the robbery but not the airport page.

"I know he did have feelings that we weren't compassionate enough," Mobley said about Miller. "But I think the story as it's been reported to you is a bit exaggerated."

At one point in my minor league travels, I asked Frank Burke, the owner since 1994 of the Double A Chattanooga Lookouts, about Fay Vincent's idea that the major league owners felt umpires were like bases, a necessary expense, something you couldn't do without but didn't care to pay much attention to. Was it applicable to the attitude of Burke's colleagues in the minor leagues as well?

"That's a pretty fair characterization," Burke said.

The answer didn't surprise me. In encounter after encounter with minor league officials, I had found them largely indifferent—or worse—to the working environment of their umpires. Burke, actually, seemed more umpire-friendly than most. After umpires objected to conditions at the downtown motel the Lookouts had put them in, Burke upgraded their accommodations for the 2007 season, even though it meant kicking in a few thousand dollars on top of the usual advertising considerations. But when I asked him, "Shouldn't they be paid more?" he grimaced.

"If I went on the record saying umpires should be paid more, there are eight or nine guys who would kill me," he said. "But the amount they are paid is awfully tough to live on."

Given the long history of their frustration, it's a little surprising that minor league umpires didn't get around to organizing until 1999. (And it's ironic, of course, that this was the same year that the Major League Umpires Association imploded and dissolved.) But they have always been hampered by a revolving membership.

The union they finally formed, the Association of Minor League Umpires (AMLU), struggled. Its main problem was that the majority of the members were the younger umpires in the low minors, who were naive, excited to be working in pro ball, and hadn't been in the workforce long enough for their enthusiasm to be mitigated by the earned dignity of workingmen. Though they were generally respectful of the union concept, the union hadn't found a core issue or core strategy that would prove to them its usefulness. So there remained two disparate factions—the younger guys who didn't care all that much yet about making a good living, and the older ones who did.

I didn't realize it at the time, but when I enrolled in umpire school, the collective bargaining agreement between the minor leagues and the AMLU had recently expired and the union was threatening to strike. The main issue was compensation.

Amazingly, minor league umpire salaries had not been increased in a decade. Introductory pay for umpires was $1,800 per month for the season, and the top pay in the minor leagues was $3,400 per month. That's an annual range of about $5,000 in the rookie leagues and short season A ball, where the season is not quite three months, to about $17,000 for the five-month Triple A season. Per diem was offered as well, with the youngest umpires given $19 a day for food, and the most experienced umpires $27.

While I was in Kissimmee, I heard my instructors talking about the labor issues, and in February, not long after I graduated, I went to see Pat O'Conner at his office in St. Petersburg, Florida. After the 2007 season, O'Conner would become president of Minor League Baseball, the head honcho, but at this point he was the chief operating officer, in charge of negotiating with the umpires.

Since 1997, the minor leagues have borne the cost of umpire development, O'Conner said, and they've done it without gleaning any benefits. After six or eight years in the minor league system, after all, an umpire either becomes a legitimate candidate for a major league job or he's dismissed or he retires. In any case, he doesn't stick around in the minor leagues long enough to give the organization that trained him the benefit of his experience. So while the umpires have no incentive to stick around in the minor leagues, from O'Conner's perspective the minor leagues have no incentive to make the job of minor league umpires worth holding on to.

"They are the first line of defense for the integrity of the game," O'Conner said to me. "I respect the hell out of these guys. They're doing something I couldn't do."

In that case, I said, why are they paid so poorly?

They aren't, O'Conner said; there is simply a difference of opinion about their stature as employees. That is, the umpires think of themselves as being on a professional career path, and the minor leagues consider them to be neither full-fledged professionals nor full-time employees. Rather, their time in the minor leagues, he said, is an apprenticeship; their contracts are for seasonal work.

"Our program is not designed for them to be able to live on their salaries for twelve months a year," O'Conner said. "To want to change that is to change the financial underpinnings of the entire minor league system. That being said, not many employers pay seasonal workers what we pay them."

O'Conner was refreshingly straightforward. He was aware of the fury that the two words—"apprenticeship" and "seasonal"—incited in umpires, but he was neither defensive nor apologetic.

"I'm the devil incarnate to these guys, I understand that," he said, adding that he didn't know the umpires personally, didn't care to know them. But that's an improvement, he said. Since taking it over from the major leagues in 1997, O'Conner said, PBUC had made minor league umpiring a meritocracy, dismantling the old-boy network in which promotion from league to league and ascension to the majors was largely a function of social contacts and personal influence.

"You don't wish bad on anybody, and you want to see guys do good," O'Conner said. "But I don't know any of these guys. From the standpoint of the rank and file, that may sound cold. But it's in their best interest."

O'Conner seemed indifferent to the imminent strike. The games would go on as scheduled, he said, with local amateur umpires replacing the union guys, the quality of the competition on the field wouldn't suffer much if at all, and in the end, all it would prove was that the "apprentice" umpires are less essential to the game than they think they are.

"I want to work with the AMLU umps," he said. "We've invested in them. They're a quality product. But I don't *need* them."

The Professional Baseball Umpire Corporation, a wholly owned affiliate of the National Association of Professional Baseball Leagues, aka minor league baseball, oversees the umpires in sixteen domestic minor leagues, encompassing 186 teams at six levels of professional baseball.

Well, really there are three levels—A, AA, and AAA—with several fractional gradations at the bottom. The lowest rung of the ladder, restricted to players in their first or second professional years, is known as rookie ball, and it's played in four leagues spread around the country: the Gulf Coast and Appalachian (sometimes called the Appy) in the East, the Arizona and Pioneer in the West.

The rookie league season is abbreviated, seventy-six games running from mid-June through the first week of September, essentially to accommodate players who are still in school, and the same is true of the next level up, known as short season A, which is also made up of very young players, though a handful of them have had a couple of years of professional experience. The two short season A leagues are the Northwest, where Ben Robinson and Phil Henry were working, and the NY-Penn in the Northeast.

Starting with plain old A ball, with two leagues (the Midwest and South Atlantic, also known as the Sally League), the seasons are not quite twice as long, 140 games, beginning in April. The next step up,

Advanced A, is an unofficial distinction, but within baseball everyone recognizes that the players in its three leagues—California, Carolina, and Florida State—are slightly better, slightly more promising.

At the top are three Double A leagues (Southern, Eastern, and Texas) and two Triple A leagues (International and Pacific Coast).

The network is pretty complicated, with eighty-five or ninety games going on every night, spread out in every corner of the nation and all of them needing umpires, who often have a long way to travel to get to the ballpark.

PBUC's specific functions include the selection of umpires for these jobs, a process begun every March at the evaluation camp in Cocoa, Florida. PBUC also assigns umpires to particular leagues and is responsible for the observation, evaluation, and ranking of their performances, and decisions on promotions and releases, dismissals and leaves of absences. (When an umpire reaches Triple A, though he still reports to PBUC regarding his scheduling, his evaluations are made by the major league umpire office.)

This translates to a huge amount of power over the lives of minor league umpires, which is wielded by what many working umpires think is a petty, small-minded, and vindictive bureaucracy. PBUC has a staff of nine, seven of whom are former minor league umpires themselves, and the general belief among working umpires, both in the major and the minor leagues, is that they enjoy their control far too much. The bitterness of umpires toward PBUC is both widespread and deeply felt, though no one will express these feelings without assurances of anonymity for fear of retribution.

"What you always have to remember is that all of these guys were rejected by the system they now have a hand in," one major league umpire told me.

"The worst part is, they don't even care about you, not as an umpire, not as a person," one minor leaguer said.

I had a difficult time figuring out PBUC; it's not an organization that welcomes scrutiny, and its employees, some of whom are cordial, nonetheless make it pretty clear that reporters aren't their favorite people. They'll talk readily enough about umpiring technique, but ask about how decisions are made to promote umpires or rank them or release them, or why they seem to treat umpires with such condescension, and they shut down.

The executive director, Mike Fitzpatrick, for example, had spent twelve years on the field in the minor leagues, finishing his career in Triple A in the late seventies before becoming a field supervisor in Major League Baseball's now defunct umpire development program. An outwardly affable man in his sixties, he invited me to the 2006 evaluation camp and spoke genially in the Florida sunshine about the observation of the candidate umpires. But afterward, when I called him to ask about what had happened to Brian Dubois, he became considerably less affable and, from that time on, never returned another phone call.*

I recognized he was following his own advice. During the introductory meeting for the umpire candidates at Cocoa, Fitzpatrick gave the welcome and then the last word. After the advice offered by the staff on such things as physical conditioning ("Shin splints, gentlemen, come from not stretching"), conduct on the road ("It's not a safe world out there anymore, gentlemen, so you've got to watch out for your partners"), equipment, especially the bucket mask, a plastic helmet resembling what a hockey goalie might wear ("If you start to take a lot of shots to the head, if you're feeling dizzy or nauseous, think about changing to the bucket"), and general maturity ("If you think your time here means drinking, picking up girls, and pulling high school pranks, we're here to tell you you're wrong"), Fitzpatrick offered this tidbit about speaking to the press: "Here's a helpful slogan. Silence cannot be quoted."

The Cocoa Expo Sports Center, where the PBUC evaluation camp is held, is a sprawl of ball fields, one of which is a legitimate, if somewhat dilapidated, stadium that has been used by major and minor league teams from time to time. Located on the unglamorous touristy fringe, a half hour from the Atlantic and within driving range of Cape Canaveral, it's a year-round facility, sponsoring tournaments and clinics and other baseball-related events (soccer, too), but in March it is a kind of spring-break mecca for high school and college teams from the Northern states that need a warm-weather place to prepare for the season. These are the games the PBUC umpires work.

---

*Fitzpatrick stepped down before the 2008 season and was replaced by one of his staff supervisors, Justin Klemm, who was no more forthcoming with me, though he did make the umpires themselves more comfortable.

During the ten-day camp, the aspiring umpires from the Evans school and the Wendelstedt school get to meet one another, compare notes about their educations, and check one another out. One thing everyone notices right away is that the Wendelstedt umpires tend to conform to more of a physical type, strapping and athletic, young men whose physiques are natural aids in the struggle for authority.

This has long defined a philosophical division among umpires, some of whom think a hulking, intimidating guy has an advantage on the field. Such was the working theory of Cal Hubbard, a Hall of Fame umpire who first had a career as a tackle in the National Football League—where he also earned a place in the Hall of Fame, making him the only guy enshrined in both—and who spent much of the 1950s and 1960s as the chief administrator of American League umpires, building a staff of large men like Hank Soar and Frank Umont, both of whom also played pro football.

Harry Wendelstedt arrived in the majors in 1966, with Hubbard in the final years of his stewardship, and though Wendelstedt worked in the National League, he was a chip off the Hubbard block, tall and burly. Jim Evans, on the other hand, might never have been hired by the American League in 1971 if Hubbard hadn't retired two years earlier. Evans once told me that, yes, umpiring is probably not a profession for an undersize man, but his own example led him to recognize that you didn't need to be a giant to be an umpire; relative to the Wendelstedt students, his graduates were of more assorted shapes and sizes.

The two groups, while maintaining a healthy loyalty to their schools and chief instructors, melded rather easily. When Pat Barbour, a Wendelstedt grad, had his right elbow broken by a foul ball as he worked his first game behind the plate and finished the game anyway, making his calls with his left hand, the admiration came from all sides. Overall, they were more like one another than not, more birds of a feather than rivals, and before long they began to unite against a common enemy—PBUC—which would give them their first inkling that baseball doesn't love umpires.

The PBUC camp had a basic-training feel to it, with the supervisors pushing the idea that umpiring, like, say, being a marine, is a profession with stringent standards that can be met by only a few good men. The level of attention to umpiring detail was high, and the details were frequently compelling—real inside baseball, so to speak.

PBUC publishes a couple of umpiring manuals, one with remarkably precise instructions for most plays an umpire might encounter—a whole section, for example, titled "Swipe Tags at First Base with No Runners On"—and the other with commentary and situational procedure: "After a home run is hit out of the playing field, the umpire shall not deliver a new ball to the pitcher or the catcher until the batter hitting the home run has crossed the plate."

You couldn't help being impressed by the arcaneness of it all, how expert it was possible to be on the subject of umpiring. In the mornings, the supervisors often held demonstrations, classes that were essentially refinements on the lessons that were taught at umpire school. For instance, instead of taking plays at the plate on the third-base side of home, from a few feet in foul territory and along an imagined extension of the first-base line, the PBUC umpires were taught, as a play developed, to move to an interim spot directly behind the point of home plate and to read the throw home. Then they could shift position according to the throw—a few steps toward first base if the throw required the catcher to make a sweep tag from fair territory, or toward third if the throw left the catcher in a position to make the tag straight on.

I was especially curious about what the supervisors looked for when they watched the umpires work. Some of it was seemingly mundane, or at least what you would expect, though it often turned out to be more complicated than it appeared. Though they lectured on the requirement of calling a rulebook strike zone and showed a video made by the major leagues in 2001 when the commissioner's office was making a concerted effort to enforce greater uniformity in calling balls and strikes, on the field they didn't exactly watch to see if an umpire's strike zone was accurate or consistent. That would require a supervisor to focus only on that and essentially to call the game himself from behind the batting cage.

Instead, as Jim Evans had, they were looking to see if a home plate umpire kept his feet in proper position, his shoulders square to the plate as the pitch came in, his head still and held consistently at the right level. This is what gives the umpire the best opportunity to call an accurate, consistent strike zone.

One morning, standing behind the home plate cage with one of the veteran supervisors, Larry Reveal, I watched a batter hit a foul pop-up along the third-base line and out of play, nothing much to take note of, except that I saw Reveal make a note. So I asked him what he had just seen.

The umpire wasn't following the pitched ball all the way into the catcher's glove, Reveal said.

How do you know that? I asked.

"When you see the ball hit," Reveal said, "you want to see the umpire's head move right away—Boom!—in the direction of the ball. If it doesn't, if he's looking for the ball when it goes up, you know he wasn't following it all the way in, or he was flinching."

With the same batter in the box, Reveal pointed to his stance—and the umpire's. The batter was holding his hands well out from his body, creating a wide alley between himself and the plate, and the umpire, reading that and assuming he could take advantage of it, had taken a position of his own halfway between the batter's body and his hands. This lane of vision, known as the slot, is generally the clearest path for watching a pitch. But Reveal said the umpire was too far off the inside corner and therefore had a poor angle on an outside pitch; he had to move his head slightly to get a good look at the corner. When the hitter swung at the ball, the umpire's head was moving, Reveal said, and when it was fouled off, he had to search for it.

"Too far in the slot," Reveal said. "That's what I'll tell him."

Tidbits like this aside, I became suspicious of the way Fitzpatrick and his supervisors wielded their authority, with more than a dollop of haughtiness and disdain. The level of scrutiny brought to bear on the young umpires seemed not just intense, but burdensome. An implied threat was always hovering: Do things our way or perish!

And I noticed that the supervisors did seem to relish ratcheting up the pressure.

"We take this very seriously and you have to, too," one supervisor, Jorge Bauza, said one morning as he paced up and down in front of the umpires gathered along the first-base line of a practice field. "You don't know how to communicate? You're not responsive? We don't want you here. You're gone."

Tension followed the young umpires everywhere, on and off the field. Many of them were clearly unnerved by running into a supervisor around the motel or at a local restaurant. One supervisor, Denny Cregg, chuckled as he remarked at a local restaurant, "They could sell a lot of Preparation H these ten days, these kids are so tight."

*   *   *

Jobs in professional umpiring come available for two reasons. Every year poorly performing umpires are dismissed as unlikely to climb to the next level. And every year a handful decide to hang it up on their own, looking in the mirror and recognizing that they'll never reach the big leagues. This is what happened to Chris Hubler, the senior instructor at the Evans school, who, after nine years in baseball, knew that 2006 would be his last. At the school graduation dinner, Hubler stood at the lectern and delivered a speech that left him in tears and served as a warning for my young classmates, for whom Hubler had been a role model the previous five weeks.

"Barring a major miracle, I'll never work a major league game," Hubler said. "I guess I wasn't meant to."

Every year the umpires who are still around fill the slots from the top level down, so that generally the handful of available jobs—maybe two dozen in an ordinary year—are in the four rookie leagues, which, all told, employ forty umpires.

The morning of the final day of the PBUC camp, the fifty aspiring umpires gathered, as usual, in an administrative building at the edge of the Cocoa complex. They knew this was the day their fates would be revealed to them, but they didn't know how. The supervisors were sitting at a long table in the front of the room, and Fitzpatrick announced they would confront the umpires one at a time to deliver their evaluations.

In the meantime, everyone had to leave the room by a back door that opened onto an enclosed meadow. One by one, the umpires were called in to sit in a chair in front of the long table of supervisors to listen to the verdicts on their performance and learn whether they'd be given a chance to join the umpiring profession.

I hadn't been privy to the deliberations of the supervisors, and they didn't let me in the room, so I stood outside in the meadow with the guys who were waiting, some for almost three hours, to hear what the supervisors had to say. There was no place to sit, so the guys just stood around on the dewy grass, as if in a holding pen, pacing, some of them smoking, not talking too much.

The umpires had no choice but to remain there, docile and uncomplaining as sheep, knowing that they were either about to embark on a career in baseball or about to have to think of something else to do.

Max Guyll, a burly, amusingly blunt guy I had met at the Evans school, was thinking about his girlfriend back in Indiana, a young woman his umpiring friends all made fun of because he was always on the phone at night palliating her. Max had been admitted to Indiana University law school, and his girlfriend wanted to marry someone with a solid future who could be counted on to come home at night, like a lawyer, not a peripatetic baseball man who would be counting on her to support him, at least for the first ten years, while he pursued the unlikely possibility that he'd actually make it to the big leagues. Every time you mentioned law school to Max, he rolled his eyes back in his head and looked panicky. That's how he looked that morning.

"How you doing, Max?" I asked him.

"At least I'll get my girlfriend off my back," he said.

You couldn't have created a more discomforting situation for these young men if you'd tried, and I realized that the passive-aggressive power of PBUC was perfectly displayed here.

Every few minutes, a guy who had gone in through the back door would exit through the front and walk off, heading away from us. You could try to guess by his posture and his gait whether he was buoyed or disappointed, but none of the umpires who'd received the news circled back to share it with the guys who were still waiting, so I didn't hear the results until later.

Ironically, after all that, there were none.

The candidates had been aware, of course, that a strike of minor league umpires was likely, and they had been worried that any job offer from PBUC would come with the caveat that they serve as replacements: Congratulations, you have a job in Minor League Baseball as long as you spurn the union and go to work.

Happily, PBUC wasn't so manipulative as that; for one thing they didn't want to foist on the higher minor leagues a load of young and largely inexperienced umpires. But because of the impending strike, PBUC decided to wait before offering anyone a job and chose not to reveal the candidates' rankings. They gave each umpire only a vague idea of where he stood in relation to his classmates—near the top, somewhere in the middle, not in the top third, somewhere below the midpoint.

So the fifty aspiring umpires left Cocoa in March not knowing much more about their futures than they knew when they'd arrived.

No one was allowed to feel assured of employment. No one knew how many jobs would be available when the strike was over. No one was told in what order the jobs would be doled out.

In April, the strike came to pass. As the season began, the 220 or so AMLU members decided not to go to work, and they forced the minor leagues to use replacement amateur umpires for the first two months of the season. Predictably, minor league officials claimed that the games went on without interruption, and without any effect on the quality of play, but the anecdotal evidence indicated this wasn't so. Newspaper accounts of games from around the country were full of askance references to the officiating, and a handful of events drew wide public attention to players running amok in the absence of effective on-field authority.

On April 26, Delmon Young, an outfielder for the Triple A Durham Bulls, was tossed from a game in Pawtucket, Rhode Island, for arguing a called third strike, and on his way back to the dugout, he flung his bat at the home plate umpire, Richard Cacciatore, whose experience was largely in small-college baseball, striking him across the chest. (Young was suspended for fifty games, but the incident didn't do much to derail his career. He was promoted to the big leagues later in the season.)

Then on May 7, Chris Cron, the manager of the Birmingham Barons of the Double A Southern League, pulled his team off the field in the seventh inning of a game against the Jacksonville Suns—even though his team was behind and he was essentially forfeiting the game—after a series of beanballs resulted in three bench-clearing brawls.

"I've been in the game a long time, and I've never seen anything like this," Cron told the *Birmingham News*. "It was out of hand. Nobody was in control. So I took my guys off the field."

During the strike, I went to several minor league games in different parts of the country. For one thing I wanted to see if I could tell the difference between the amateurs and the pros, though an obvious distinction was that most minor league umpires are young and in pretty good shape and a lot of amateur umpires are not. Once in New Britain I sat in the stands with some picketing umpires who kept up a running commentary in my ear about what the replacements were doing wrong in front of my eyes, but frankly it was pretty small stuff, like not getting close enough to the bag when they were making a call on a tag play, or not straddling the line when making a fair-foul call, or not making demonstrative enough signals.

But aside from the occasional "Stee-ball"—a signature amateur moment that results when a home plate umpire doesn't wait long enough on a pitch, starts calling it a strike ("Stee—") and changes his mind—I couldn't tell from the stands whether the replacements were adequate. So I started asking around among the players. A few were glad to have the replacements, who they said had none of the arrogance that many in baseball see as an occupational characteristic of umpires.

"Yeah, they miss some, but so did the other guys," Phil Seibel a left-handed pitcher for the Portland Sea Dogs, a Double A affiliate of the Red Sox, told me. "And these guys, the replacements, are easier to talk to. They're more approachable. The other guys, so many of them were arrogant. They think they have something to prove. The players, we're arrogant, too, I'll be the first to admit that, but these guys act like they're the game, that the fans came to see them."

Still, by the end of May, most of the players and coaches I spoke with were pretty fed up. They particularly focused on the strike zone—this was especially true of the pitchers—and how the replacements didn't have the same firm grip on it as the pros.

"They're consistently inconsistent," Randy Beam, a pitcher for Portland, told me. "They're just not good enough for this level of ball."

Matt Anderson, a right-hander for the Triple A Fresno Grizzlies, said: "The inconsistency is a problem. When you throw a close pitch, you never know whether you'll get the call. You might get a few more pitches off the plate, and that's nice, I guess, but I don't know if it helps you in the long run."

Kasey Olenberger, a right-hander for the Salt Lake Bees, also in Triple A, told me: "At this level the game is too fast for them. You throw a sharp slider and the catcher catches it like this"—he made a motion with his glove, as though sweeping a pitch off the corner—"and he calls it a ball, but it got a lot of the plate."

And Jeff Heaverlo, another right-hander for the Bees (once known as the Buzz, and then the Stingers), added: "As a pitcher, you're trying to throw from here to here, the top of the kneecap to the bottom of the kneecap, and when you execute that and they don't call it, it's like, 'Now what do I do?'" He drew two lines in the air with a hand, one at the thigh, one at the waist. "I can't throw up here. Guys at this level, they hit that pitch, even if you're throwing ninety-seven or ninety-eight."

Partly to protect the replacement umpires, who were crossing picket lines to work, and partly to keep the public relations war from tipping too terribly against them, the minor leagues did not release the names of the replacements and forbade them to talk to the press. As the strike went on, they also tried to gag the managers.

In late May, when I approached Todd Claus, the Portland manager, and asked about the umpires, he looked terrifically uncomfortable, hemming and hawing as though tamping down an urge to spill the beans before he finally settled on a kind of code. "I have a career in the game," he said, "so when we've been told not to comment on the umpiring situation or the umpires, I won't. I can't." I asked him whether, if he had his druthers, he'd like to see the professionals back, and he said: "Druthers? You always want the best possible conditions, the highest level of professionalism available. These guys don't have anywhere near the professional experience that the regular guys had. Does that answer your question?"

But with other reporters, other managers were less able to keep their lips buttoned. Dave Trembley, manager of the Ottawa Lynx of the Triple A International League (he became manager of the Baltimore Orioles in mid-2007), said to the *Ottawa Sun* that the umpiring was "the worst officiating I've seen in twenty years of professional baseball," calling it "an embarrassment to the International League and an embarrassment to me as the manager here."

And Bill Massey, the manager of the Double A Trenton Thunder, said to the local paper, the *Trentonian,* "The umpiring is an absolute joke. That's the bottom line. It is absolutely not professional baseball that we're playing out there. This game can get turned around on one pitch. I'm not saying professional umpires don't miss pitches—obviously, they do. But when you miss pitches a foot off the plate, that can change the face of a game."

Massey wasn't through: "Major League Baseball should be absolutely ashamed of themselves for letting this happen over freakin' nickels. Pennies and nickels. You know who I would call to arms? The owners of the teams. These are guys spending millions of dollars on kids that they signed, and they're not playing with the same strike zone that you play with in the major leagues. It hurts pitchers, it hurts players. What happens if some kid gets called up from Double A? He's got no idea where the strike zone is. Everybody knows it stinks."

In sum, the umpires proved their point, namely that the game is better with them than without them, and that their training in professional ball distinguishes them from their amateur counterparts. But it didn't matter. The minor leagues, seemingly indifferent to the on-field complaints, held fast to the piddling concessions they had offered before the strike got under way, and the union finally buckled. The least experienced among the umpires were eager to get to work and prove themselves, even at less-than-subsistence wages. Swaying the vote, they overwhelmed the resistance of their elder brethren. In early June, 62 percent of the membership voted to accept the leagues' offer—a $100 a month raise across the board, plus an average $3 boost in per diem, though with a corresponding increase in their insurance deductible.

The settlement didn't satisfy anyone, really. Many experienced umpires simply decided that given such a slap in the face by their employers and the shortsightedness of their younger colleagues, pursuing the long-shot wager that they might eventually reach the big leagues was no longer worth it. Dozens resigned. In all, the minor leagues hired upward of fifty new umpires in 2006, more than twice the usual number. Even the veteran umpires who remained did so with a lot of bitterness.

"In the umpires versus baseball, baseball won, that's for sure," said Jason Klein, a union member then in Double A who voted against the settlement. "And everybody's justifying every clause in the settlement so it seems like we gained something. But I'll tell you, I'm not buying dinners or drinks for younger umpires anymore. If they're happy, if they think they're making enough money, so be it."

CHAPTER FIVE

PHIL, BEN, AND RIA

I guess they're okay as people, but they got to make better calls.
—ALFRED JOSEPH, outfielder,
Boise Hawks, July 2006

I feel like I just got out of a bad marriage.
—RIA CORTESIO, October 2007,
just after her release from baseball

Phil Henry and Ben Robinson had been classmates of mine at the Evans school, though before I got to Boise, I hadn't known either of them very well. Each was tall and lanky with a short haircut, each had a respectful manner, and neither was easy to get a rise out of. They presented themselves as calm, respectful, and serious; their humor was dry. If you didn't know they were umpires, you wouldn't be surprised to learn they were soldiers. But they weren't really alike, and they hadn't been much more than acquaintances before they became partners.

This, of course, is another hazard for umpires in the low minors, the enforced brotherhood between two young men who don't know each other and not only have to work together nightly in an environment where it is the two of them against the world, but also live together— in A ball, umpiring crews share a hotel room—and travel together around a circuit of cities where chances are they're far from home and don't know anyone but each other.

"Have you been to Eugene?" Phil asked me, as if he'd just returned from the moon. "They don't wear shoes. It's a lot of hippies driving VW buses." He gave me a deadpan look. "We had to carry tambourines for protection, so they didn't think we were too conservative."

Then, too, it's never too far from their minds that they're rivals as well as allies, competing for advancement; at the end of the season, all the umpires at each level are ranked, with the rankings used to determine promotions and dismissals. Phil and Ben would eventually begin to grate on each other—at one point, they didn't speak to each other for two or three days until they presided over a brawl on the field and had to discuss which players to eject—and it didn't surprise me when, a few weeks after I left them, I called Ben and asked how the two of them were getting along. "The season will be over soon," he said.

But that was later. In Boise, a city neither had been to before, they were still getting acquainted, not only with each other but with the rhythms of their new life and the demands of their new job.

Ben, twenty-six, was the older of the two. He'd been to umpire school previously, a couple of years earlier, and had been disappointed not to have been recommended to PBUC, but he was a quietly single-minded guy and being an umpire was the idea he had when it came to a career. Between his two stints at the Evans school, he worked high school and junior college games in the Denver area, where he lived, and for a while he moved to Lincoln, Nebraska, where a job as a store manager for OfficeMax had opened up and where he lived for several months in monklike deprivation specifically to save money to take one more shot at umpire school and professional umpiring.

In Kissimmee and again at Cocoa, he'd struck his classmates as aloof, maybe a little bit haughty. He himself used the word "businesslike," and I came to recognize the severe face he presented to the world as a bit of a shield. He was actually pretty sensitive, and the combination of an opaque mien and tender feelings would draw trouble to him on the field. He would have twenty-six ejections over the course of the season, more than any other umpire in all of the minor leagues.

Ben told me he knew he wasn't well liked; he said that his aim all along had been to get a job, not make friends. I thought he was a little too quick to express disdain to be as self-confident as he wished to appear, but the standards he applied to other people he readily applied to himself as well.

"What amazed me was the breaking pitches," he said when I asked him about his first professional game behind the plate. "I was tracking pretty good, but I was surprised that the pitches moved so much. And there could have been a bonfire going on in the bullpen and I wouldn't have noticed, I was so focused on calling pitches. At one point it started getting dark, and I forgot to tell them to turn the lights on. They did it on their own, but that was kind of embarrassing. I guess I thought I was horseshit, but nobody seemed to notice."

After a pause, he went on, "As unhappy as I've been with my umpiring so far, I feel like I belong here."

Phil was from a small town in Missouri, not too far from St. Louis, where his father was on the grounds crew at the airport. He was twenty-four, and he'd been working for Federal Express, handling hazardous materials, but he was a college graduate, from the University of North Texas in Denton, where he still lived; he'd studied music, of all things, jazz trumpet. His demeanor was self-deprecating and he had a bashful kind of charm.

I found I could make him blush by teasing him about his narrow shoulders or his new hairdo. He'd gotten a buzz cut just before he left home, and his scalp had fried almost immediately. Naturally pale anyway, he was peeling furiously by the time I met him in Boise, leaving him itchy and constantly running a palm over his skull. I said to him at one point that umpiring was a strange vocation for someone who had been a trumpet player, and he ducked his head as though I'd wildly overcomplimented him.

"Trumpet owner is more like it," he said.

Still, umpiring obviously suited him. I'd noticed this at school, that he didn't seem to have any swagger about him at all, except on the field. Taking his position, he'd pull his mask down over his face with an emphatic snap, his posture would suddenly improve, and in an instant he'd be carrying himself with seemingly newfound surety. But Phil was also capable of going along to get along. He was one of the few young umpires I met who spoke of PBUC without resentment, and who seemed to buy into the umpire ethos with a kind of gratitude, as though in discovering umpiring he'd found a behavioral model he could live in comfortably. He took on the us-them view of the world of umpiring as if it were natural.

"We hate it when they call us Blue," he said. "I tell them, 'My name's Phil.' They'll learn."

When I asked him, in Boise, about his first impressions of professional umpiring and how it was different from the high school games he was used to, he was shrewd and specific: "It's little things, mostly. Like with a guy on second and he's going to steal third. I'm used to high school kids—clomp, clomp, clomp—they're so clumsy you can hear them. But these guys are *quiet.*"

He was speaking to me as a former classmate, knowing I'd know that as the base umpire, with a man on second he'd be lined up behind the pitcher to the shortstop side of second, with his back to the runner.

"The first time it happened, it caught me sleeping, and it caught the fielders sleeping," he said. "Usually, the guy runs and the fielders are going, 'Runner! Runner!' and that's a clue, too, you know? But this guy took off, and I didn't hear him, and nobody said anything, and when I finally saw him out of the corner of my eye, I was only able to get a step or two towards third. I was lucky. The ball was hit into left field, so I didn't have to make a call, but I would have had a horseshit look. That was a pretty good lesson."

Phil said the months following the PBUC camp had been agonizing for him. He'd returned to Denton and gone back to Federal Express, thinking he'd done well. At his evaluation, he said, even though no one was being offered jobs, "They said, 'We look forward to having you in the system.'"

For the next several weeks, he said, he just waited, checking Internet sites like umpnews.com for strike information. He knew he'd be in a short season league, which didn't begin until June, but as time went by, he was worried.

"I was thinking I'd have to work at FedEx all summer, that it was all a waste, all this time, all this work, all this money," he said. "I was thinking, 'What if it doesn't get settled this year? Would I have to go back to umpire school and start all over again, and would I do it if I had to?'"

It didn't come to that, of course. Phil and Ben got their calls from PBUC in early June, soon after the strike was settled. Phil was told he'd be going to the Gulf Coast League, Ben to the Arizona League. But over the next few days, the poststrike exit parade of older umpires began, so Phil and Ben were promoted—from rookie ball to short season A—before they'd ever worked a game. With just a weekend before they were to leave home, both of them were redirected to the Northwest League, which is how they ended up together on the road to Boise, sharing the front seat of a tow truck with a fat man and his wife.

Professional baseball in the low minors, entry-level ball, is fun to watch but often excruciating to umpire. You'll find players with major league gifts for throwing, running, and hitting, but the gifts are immature, so the quality of play is wildly inconsistent.

At this stage, players make a lot of mistakes, which often gets umpires in trouble because a player's ill judgment or bobble makes the umpires' anticipating a proper play, which they are taught to do, into a liability. An infield capable of turning acrobatic double plays might also commit half a dozen errors in a game, and a slugger who belts a 450-foot home run on a fastball in his first at bat won't come within a foot of the ball when the pitchers feed him a diet of curves. Games tend to be rhythmless—which makes it difficult for umpires to do their job as the metronomes of baseball, enforcing a pace on the proceedings—and they tend to be long, which umpires abhor.

Especially pertinent for umpires is the lack of refinement in pitchers and catchers. A pitcher with genuine major league prospects might well strike out the side in the first inning, then walk five in a row in the second. Young pitchers, even those with the most powerful arms—maybe especially those—have to learn to harness their power, no mean feat at the level of professional ball where every strike is not necessarily a good pitch and every good pitch is not necessarily a strike.

By a pitcher's standards a good pitch is one that puts the hitter at a disadvantage. Generally that means it is placed in some remote county of the strike zone, or just out of the zone but tempting enough to get the hitter to chase it. "Locating," as the baseball idiom has it, therefore means not only getting the ball over the plate consistently, but also sharpening one's control within and around the strike zone, being able to put the ball precisely where you want to.

Rare in the low minors, a pitcher who can locate is a gift to umpires because the ball will be around the plate and therefore they know where to look for it. It keeps them focused on a manageable area rather than having to employ the sweeping vision of a sailor in a crow's nest. It allows them to follow pitches without their heads moving or their eyes darting, and it makes them more attentive to the nuances of the strike zone. Umpires also feel safer when the pitcher can locate, less likely to be ducking out of the way of a head-high fastball bound for the backstop or skipping to avoid the skitters of a breaking ball bounced in front of the plate and past the catcher, who may not be all that proficient himself.

But perhaps the most trying condition in A ball, and it's easy to overlook, is that because the players are young, because they are competing for the first time for career advancement as well as for victory, and because they are without the calming experience of professional everydayness and have yet to learn professional decorum, the atmosphere on the field is electric with testosterone.

If you're watching closely, and listening, you can sense the palpable tension on just about every call: the pitcher's glare when he doesn't get the call on a close breaking pitch, a hitter's taut grimace as he reacts to a called strike and resists turning his head around to object, or the catcher's tautened forearm as he "sticks" a pitch on the outside corner, holding it there for an extra beat to let the ump know he missed it. The chatter from the dugout is persistent and hostile:

"I had that down, Ben, bring it up!"

"Where was that pitch, for crissakes?"

As much as anything, the constant provocation contributes to the trial-by-fire experience of fledgling umpires because it makes establishing a level of tolerance an immediate, crucial issue. Reputations spread quickly from team to team: If you hear and react to everything, you'll be known for "rabbit ears," an especially malign term of disrespect. Yet if you ignore the complaints and name-calling, it will only get worse. The umpires, inexperienced, too, are still learning how thick their skin is, how sensitive their antennae to challenge and insult, how much steel is in their spines. Among themselves, they disdainfully refer to the players as rats. (In the same lexicon of disparagement, players' girlfriends are known as rat cheese.)

The managers and the coaches are generally experienced at higher levels of baseball, where the umpiring is more polished, so they are prone to frustration with the untested umpires they're saddled with in A ball. In addition, they're obliged to protect their players, so their fuses are ready to be lit. All this results in a pepper of arguments, many of them seemingly gratuitous, all of them threatening to blow up into a shithouse.

To wit, at my first game in Boise, with Ben behind the plate, it took only a couple of innings for an argument to erupt over something triv-ial—a call of time. The Yakima hitter asked Ben for time before the first pitch, and it was granted, but then, after Ben put the ball in play, the hit-ter still wasn't settled in the batter's box and asked for time again. This time it wasn't forthcoming, however; the pitcher threw, and as the bat-ter stood and watched, off-balance, Ben called the pitch a strike. A small jawing match ensued.

"He said, 'I had fuckin' time,'" Ben recalled for me later. "And I said, 'That's funny. I didn't.'"

But the more consequential spat came after the hitter swung and missed the next pitch for strike three and threw a few sneering words over his shoulder as he walked to the dugout.

Ben took off his mask and took a step or two toward the retreating hitter—not a good move, he would later admit—and sensing trouble, the Yakima manager, Jay Gainer, who was coaching third, hustled in and intercepted him. They were soon nose to nose, though the exchange was brief.

"I don't know why I got so aggressive with them," Ben said. "But I guess if I don't throw them out, I can at least try and shut them up."

Gainer, a former minor league outfielder who spent a brief time—"a cup of coffee," in baseball parlance—with the Colorado Rockies, was in his second year as a minor league manager, and he sounded exasper-ated when I spoke to him the next day.

"It wasn't the enforcement of the rule, it was the way he enforced it," Gainer said. "What are the umpires so uptight about? I guess they're new, so they want to send a message, but you can't even talk to them before they want to scold you or worse. It's like that's what they're taught. I just went over to Ben and asked him what was up, and he got all over me."

Later in the game, after a batter fouled a ball into the dirt around home plate, the Boise first-base coach, Kevin Green, asked Ben to check the baseball, wanting to make sure it wasn't so scuffed up that his hitter would have a hard time seeing it. Once again, Ben reacted testily. This time the argument escalated, and Green got testy himself.

"When the ball came off the bat, I said, 'Excuse me, could you check the ball?'" Green recalled for me. "I didn't swear at him. Yet. He said to me, 'I don't need your help. Get back in your damned box.' He says that to me, and I go, 'Well, fuck you, do your job!'"

Ben threw him out of the game.

The next afternoon, as his team practiced on the field, I spoke with Steve McFarland in the home-team dugout. Even though the Hawks had won, their fourth victory in a row, the manager was steamed about the ejection of Green, blaming Ben for needlessly escalating the mood to one of high dudgeon, which made McFarland think about the call along the third-base line in Pasco five days earlier.

"In the last three days, I've had to back off," McFarland said. "I was on Ben so hard the first night that I had to hold a team meeting and tell them not to get on the umpires. One of my jobs is to teach these guys how to deal with the umpires, but it's frustrating when the level of umpiring doesn't match the level of play."

McFarland said umpiring was less than stellar throughout the minor leagues, but especially so in A ball, where the umpires were just out of umpire school, and especially this year, when guys like Phil and Ben, who would ordinarily have been assigned to rookie ball, had been elevated ahead of their capability.

"Consistency is the biggest thing," McFarland said. "They don't have it. The biggest discrepancy is in the pitch that's down; from one pitcher to the next the zone seems to change. Maybe it's that the release point changes, maybe it's the arm angle, but do they pick up each pitch the same? Probably not. Do they have the feel to be consistent? No, they don't."

McFarland also said the game was too fast for Phil and Ben. "I'm trying to get these two guys to loosen up a little bit. But I can tell when they walk to home plate, they're afraid of screwing up."

I asked McFarland if he'd been thrown out yet.

He said he hadn't. "I got close last night. We'll see what happens tonight."

What happened was this: With one out in the ninth inning, a Boise hitter grounded to the shortstop, who bobbled the ball momentarily before throwing to first, just long enough to turn the play into an impossibly close one, a "banger" or a "whacker," as umpires call it. McFarland, most likely frustrated by his team's play—they were behind, 7–5, largely the result of having committed seven errors—couldn't resist. He sped across the diamond from his place in the third-base coach's box and launched a plaintive argument in Ben's face, subsequently removing his hat and waving it about and pointing demonstratively at the first-base bag.

The gist, Ben told me later, was that McFarland was insisting that a tie goes to the runner.

"They got there at the same time, Ben," McFarland said. "Same means safe."

"So I said to him, 'What is this? Little League?'" Ben said. "I'm surprised he didn't go nuts when I said that, that was pretty disrespectful, but I just explained there was no such thing as same time, the ball either beat the runner or the runner beat the ball, and I had it that the ball beat the runner. He just kept saying, 'Here's what you gotta remember: Same time means safe.' Then he said, 'You're fucking crazy.' That's what I ran him for."

Ben was right, at least about Rule 7.01. It declares: "A runner acquires the right to an unoccupied base when he touches it before he is out." In other words, the runner has to beat the ball to the base to be declared safe, which implies one of two things: Either there isn't any such thing as a tie, or, contrary to popular belief, a tie goes to the defense.

Professional baseball isn't exactly color-blind when it comes to umpires; only six African-Americans have been on the major league umpire roster in the history of the big leagues, the first not until 1966, nineteen years after Jackie Robinson was a rookie with the Brooklyn Dodgers.

So it was noticeable to me that Ben never mentioned being black during our time together in Boise; at one point I asked him if he thought it affected the way people saw him on the field and he shrugged. Nah, he said. A few months later, after his first season, I asked him again, and he told me that he didn't feel being black had had any bearing on his umpire experience at all, that the only racial comment he'd heard on the field came from a black coach, who during an argument had called him "bro." That bothered him, he said, the presumption that they had a bond.

My impression is that Ben isn't unique in that way. I'll have more to say about the dearth of black umpires in baseball a bit later on, but the black umpires I met in both the major and the minor leagues were uniformly unwilling to accuse the game of institutional racism. Sure, there are racist fans, they said. A couple of umpires working in Southern leagues said they occasionally heard racist remarks from the stands—"Go back to picking cotton!" was a favorite, they said—but within the confines of the game they were just umpires, and umpiring is tough on everybody: white, black, green, yellow, polka-dot. On the field they were all blue.

Well, maybe not all. Baseball does have a problem with female umpires, and Ria Cortesio is a case in point.

At the midpoint of the 2006 season, Ria was one of the four umpires chosen by PBUC to work the Futures Game, an annual showcase of promising minor league players that is part of the big leagues' three-day celebration of the All-Star game. For minor league umpires, the selection is considered a gold star, a signal that your work is being approved, that, like the players, you've got promise.

It's also a taste of the big time, with all its perks. You stay in a luxury hotel, you're given a brand-new set of equipment, from mask to plate shoes, you're a fêted guest at all the festivities. You get to work in a big league stadium (in 2006, it was PNC Park, the comely home of the Pirates in downtown Pittsburgh), dress in a big league locker room, eat a big league postgame meal. These are no small things for minor league umpires accustomed to dinner at Denny's and a double bed in the Days Inn. The previous year, when Chris Tiller returned to his Texas League crew in Wichita, Kansas, from working the Futures Game in Detroit, I was there when he walked into the locker room. One of his crewmates asked him how it went.

"You wouldn't believe it," Tiller said. "They fed us lamb chops."

For Ria, the only female umpire then in professional baseball, however, an appearance at the Futures Game was far more complicated than being simply an encouraging professional reward and a few good meals. It was a reminder of baseball's two-facedness toward her, its public pride in her stick-to-itiveness and its own ostensibly meritocratic system on the one hand and its private impatience with her on the other, its wish that she would just go away. The honor of her Futures Game selection came with a concomitant under-the-table slap; though she was the senior umpire on the crew of four, which would ordinarily mean she'd be given the responsibility of working home plate, instead she was assigned third base, the least prestigious spot.

Ria pointed out the slight to me herself. Umpires are fervent readers of tea leaves—they're always trying to figure out what the supervisors are thinking, which umpires are rising or falling in the rankings—and they're often paranoid, too. So it's possible she was being oversensitive. More likely, having grown accustomed to being patronized, she simply assumed a snub was coming, even on the heels of a compliment. By that time she was twenty-nine, in her eighth season in pro ball, her fourth in the Double A Southern League, which was a longer tenure at that level than that of any other umpire, so she knew she was being treated differently from everybody else.

For the next year of her life, the pattern would continue. At the end of the 2006 season, she was ranked fifth among the forty or so umpires in Double A, which meant she stood a good chance of being promoted to Triple A, where umpires finally escape the purview of PBUC and come under the supervision of the major league umpire office.

During the winter, four Triple A umpires either retired or were released so the top four Double A umpires were promoted, which meant that as the 2007 season began, Ria was next in line. One more retirement, one more injury, and she'd be a Triple A umpire. In March, she was invited to major league spring training. No woman has ever worked a regular-season major league game as an umpire, but on March 27, 2007, in Tucson, Arizona, Ria worked on the bases for a spring training game between the Chicago Cubs and the Arizona Diamondbacks, only the second woman ever to appear on a big league diamond and the first since 1989.

Her predecessor was Pam Postema, the only woman who ever made it as far as Triple A, and who was kept from the big leagues, it is generally believed, only by tragic ill fortune. Had A. Bartlett Giamatti, then the commissioner of baseball and a supporter of umpires in general and Postema in particular, not died unexpectedly on September 1, 1989, the theory goes, he would forcefully have urged one of the league presidents to name Postema to the next major league opening. The new commissioner, Fay Vincent, did not have Giamatti's muscle with the leagues, and instead of being promoted, she was released. All told, Postema spent thirteen years in professional baseball.

The news coverage of Ria's spring training appearance was substantial. Most accounts on television and in print spoke optimistically about her potential for breaking the glass ceiling and featured the encouraging comments of the Cubs' manager, Lou Piniella: "I think there is a place for women in the umpiring ranks. They're certainly as qualified as anybody else"; and the comments of the Cubs' star first baseman, Derrek Lee: "I think it's about time. Female eyes are as good as male eyes."

When Ria entered pro ball in 1999, straight out of the Jim Evans Academy, she was the fifth woman ever to work as an umpire in the minor leagues, and she eventually became the longest-serving female umpire after Postema. With the exception of 2003, when Shanna Kook worked a season in the Pioneer League as the sixth member of this tiny sorority, Ria spent her entire career as, "yeah, the only chick."

Those were her words, characteristically flip, but they hardly convey what I came to understand as her deep isolation. Umpires are used to living in a kind of quarantine, separated from the world by a curtain of scorn, but Ria's situation was unique, a quarantine within a quarantine.

"It is a horrendous work environment if you're a woman," Ria told me after her Futures Game appearance. "Not so much on the field. On the field is a safe haven. But baseball as a whole, minor league baseball, the supervisors, PBUC, there's a systematic targeting of women."

I was a little surprised by the matter-of-factness of her anger. But as I traveled around the umpire world over the next year, crossing paths with Ria on a handful of other occasions, I came to see she might not be wrong. "Systematic targeting" was a stretch, perhaps, but Ria was alone among umpires in that she didn't even have the support of her colleagues. At umpire school I had gotten the first real inkling of what her life must be like when I went out one night with the instructors and we all got drunk, and I asked them what they thought of her. Their response was to fine me $1, the penalty for anyone who ever mentioned her name.

I would later discover that umpires assigned to work on a crew with her considered it a hardship and that berating her, especially after she became crew chief, was umpire sport. During one game, in early 2007, her two partners, both younger than she, turned their back on protocol and refused to stand with her at home plate during the national anthem, saluting the flag together from the outfield instead. This gesture of disrespect was not only noticed by the teams on the field but was passed around among all umpires and considered an example of a weakness. If she'd been authoritative enough with her crew, been able to command their respect, the argument went, it would never have happened.

None of this was lost on Ria. Indeed the slights had built up over a long time, and when she expressed her resentment to me, it was in the language of pure disgust: "I'll tell you, I've been in the game nine years, but it was evident after two that my biggest disappointment in the game was going to be the quality of the people in it. And just within the umpire community, well, some treat you more horribly than others, but there's not one umpire who would stand up for me. Not one, in all of professional baseball, who would defend me or stand up for me. You know that umpires call players rats, right? Well, hands down the biggest rats I've ever encountered in my life are professional umpires."

Generally, the criticism I heard of Ria was based on her work, or at least it was couched in those terms. She wasn't authoritative enough, I heard. She wasn't a good partner; she didn't support her partners in arguments. She made mistakes, then left her partners to deal with the fallout. The comments were consistent, and I have no reason to distrust the sincerity of the speakers, many of whom were men I liked and respected.

Still, the case against her seemed flimsy to me. I watched Ria umpire in eight games—a five-game series in Huntsville, Alabama, in 2006 and a three-game series in Chattanooga, Tennessee, in 2007. She was working with two different crews, and both times she was the crew chief. Not once on the field did I see even a hint of conflict or confusion among the umpires, nor did the umpires lose control of any game. In fact, there was hardly a ripple in any of them. It was disappointing, to tell you the truth, not very dramatic to write about, but as umpires will tell you, that's what happens when they do the job right.

Granted, that's probably not enough time to get a full appreciation of an umpire's ability, but eight games is about the same number that PBUC supervisors spend observing individual umpires over two seasons. And one veteran manager who had seen her much more often than that, Jayhawk Owens of the Chattanooga Lookouts, spoke to me at some length about her and confirmed my feelings.

"I've had Ria three years in this league," Owens said to me after I'd watched her work the bases and the plate on consecutive nights. "The first time I saw her, it was 'Wow, a female ump.' But she's paying her dues and she's definitely getting better. She's better at slowing the game down, and that's when umpires take a step forward."

Perhaps because he played in the major leagues as a catcher, Owens was most observant regarding her plate work.

"She does a really good job on the bases, but the toughest part of umpiring is balls and strikes. I'll say this: Basically she's consistent, and she's got an average strike zone. Umpires usually have a strike zone you could call tight or big, but an average major league strike zone is what she's got. That's good."

We were sitting in the first-base dugout of AT&T Field in downtown Chattanooga. Owens raised his hand and sliced it across the letters of his uniform.

"She probably needs to bring it up a little bit. Up here. As far as getting to Triple A," he said.

He meant that the higher you climb on the minor league ladder, the closer you must hew to the major league strike zone. For the previous few seasons in the majors, umpires had been encouraged to call higher strikes, to bring the actual strike zone, the one that's called in games, closer to the boundaries that are defined in the rulebook.

"But I have confidence in her ability," Owens said. "Could she cut it at Triple A? Absolutely."

I asked about Ria's spine, her conduct in an argument.

"People get in her face, sure, and she handles herself pretty well," Owens said. "I remember one call she missed. It was a home run call in Carolina. I knew it was a home run; it was plain as day. But she said no, and I really lit her up, got up in her grill pretty good. And she let me say my piece, and she said her piece. My players were freaking out, and it was my job to get thrown out if I had to so they didn't get thrown out. She knew what I was doing there. And that was that. I'll tell you something else. I've never seen her hold a grudge."

In the end, I couldn't help thinking that all of the qualities that other umpires seemed to feel lacking in Ria were of the kind that are especially relished by bands of brothers—foxhole buddies or astronauts, say—describing a distinctly male value system that specifically excludes women. In the locker room, even if she was comfortable changing clothes in the same cramped space as her male colleagues—usually behind a jerry-rigged curtain—they sometimes weren't. And it was especially telling that guys who had never worked with her were willing to offer an opinion about her, either that she was a lousy umpire or that she slept around, with umpires and with players.

There was a lot of "I hear" in the talk about Ria, and finally I'd heard it enough that at one point I held my nose and asked her directly: Had she ever slept with a player? She seemed to be expecting the question. She hadn't, she said. She acknowledged a profligate youth, but said she had renounced premarital sex before she got into baseball.

"It's funny," she said. "When I got into the game, I thought everybody would think I was gay. Instead they all think I'm a slut."

After being released from baseball, Pam Postema wrote a memoir, *You've Got to Have Balls to Make It in This League.* It was a bilious and vindictive book that made her sound a little like the shrew that baseball cast her as. But it also showed that simply by being female and exemplifying the indispensable umpiring trait of being difficult to discourage, she disrupted the easy order of things in the baseball universe and made the men around her behave in preposterous ways. In one episode, she described what began as a perfectly routine conference at home plate before a 1987 game in Buffalo, with the managers of the hometown Bisons, Steve Swisher, and the visiting Nashville Sounds, Jack Lind.

"Lind usually was a quiet and subdued guy," Postema wrote. "He rarely argued and when he did it was always without much fanfare. I thought he was harmless. . . . Swisher and Lind handed me the lineup cards. I looked them over and handed them back. Suddenly Lind snatched my mask, gave it to Swisher, and in one hurried, shocking motion, grabbed my waist, bent me over backward and proceeded to give me a five-second kiss in front of a stunned stadium. Worse yet, Lind was trying to slip his tongue into my mouth."

Ria didn't claim anything quite so openly demeaning. But her presence did make things more complicated and confusing for the men who inhabit the minor league baseball world, at least in their view. At the home plate conference, whenever a player ferries the lineup card to home plate instead of the manager, he is charged by tradition with telling the umpires a dirty joke, but many wouldn't do it in front of Ria. On the field, both young players and set-in-their-ways managers and coaches had to get used to taking orders from—gasp!—a woman.

Early on, she was called a bitch, of course. (The fans were often more inventively cruel. "'Pull out the bloody rag,' I heard that the other day," she said to me once. "That was a new one.")

In the offices of the various minor leagues and the administrative offices of PBUC, where the uniqueness of her situation was perceived as nettlesome rather than opportune, Ria's existence was resented and her presence unwelcome.

"Thank God she's not my problem," Tom Kayser, the president of the Texas League, said to me when I asked what he knew about her.

For baseball officials it was a rare moment of candor. (Kayser recognized this, too; he immediately requested that I keep his knee-jerk remark between us, though I didn't see any reason that I should.) Otherwise, when I asked about Ria in the offices of minor league baseball, the responses were virtually always preceded by a tentative pause and, when finally uttered, were entirely benign to the point of meaninglessness. Usually some generic praise, often delivered with a whiff of condescension, was followed by some vaguely belittling caveat that made it clear the speaker wasn't entirely supporting her.

Perhaps the speaker would denigrate her character; one Southern League team owner told me outright that Ria had had a sexual affair with his catcher. Perhaps someone would say she didn't have the toughness for the job, but it wasn't her fault; no woman did. More often, I'd be offered the stereotypical criticism of female umpires that they "chase the ball," a code phrase meant to suggest that women don't have keen enough baseball instincts to be umpires.

The reasoning goes this way: Women didn't grow up playing ball, so while male umpires are honing the baseball knowledge they first gleaned as children, women are still learning fundamentals. They're always behind, the way an adult who learns a second language is always behind someone who learned it in childhood. You need to have absorbed the game before you can learn to umpire because, after all, positioning for an umpire is often counterintuitive; you see the ball go somewhere, and while the player instinctively moves toward the ball, often the proper umpiring response is to go somewhere else. But women always lag behind men in this learned skill; they chase the ball.

Such is a blueprint of thought that has been applied not just to Ria, but to all of the women umpires who have made it to the minor leagues. From Bernice Gera, the woman who broke the gender barrier in 1972—she sued to be able to work as an umpire in pro ball, won the suit, worked the first game of a doubleheader in A ball in Geneva, New York, then quit before the second game—to Postema, the judgment has been the same: Women can get to be pretty good at calling balls and strikes, but they're weak on the bases.

Ria was nearly six feet tall and a little bit gangly, with the lithe but densely packed figure and the sinewy arms of a tennis player. Her hair was dark blond, and she kept it short, not quite to her shoulders. Early in her career, she had cut off the ponytail that drew irrelevant and distracting attention to her behind the plate.

At the ballpark she went out of her way to cloak her femininity—behind the plate it isn't all that hard, I suppose—but away from it she didn't, and she could be a striking young woman. She had an intelligent face, with a broad nose and eyes that occasionally reflected defiance, occasionally amusement. You wouldn't call her gorgeous, but—and here let me be briefly chauvinistic to satisfy the chauvinist in all of us—she looked good. She liked strappy sandals and heels, favored snug jeans and tops with spangles, and often wore a stud in her tongue and several in her right ear.

Seeing Ria in street clothes, you wouldn't be surprised to learn she was an athlete. But in uniform (without the plate umpire's armor, that is), in the unisex blue shirt and cap and those awful trousers, she appeared slight compared with her crewmates. This was the first thing I noticed when I saw her on the field in Huntsville, where I went after the Futures Game for a series between the hometown Stars and the visiting Mississippi Braves. Granted, her partners, Tom Clarke and Brett Cavins, were big guys, but even so, standing behind the first baseman as the first game of the series began, Ria seemed, well, physically out of her league. I didn't want to think this, but it was unavoidable, and I wasn't the only one. I was seated between home plate and first base, and from early in the game, a man and woman in their twenties seated in front of me seemed to be making a study of her. They sensed something unusual, but they didn't know what it was.

"He's so skinny," the young woman of the couple said of Ria. "And he has long hair. He looks like a girl."

That's when I leaned forward and said, "She *is* a girl. The only one in professional baseball."

"Really?" the young couple said in unison. "Cool."

Ria was born in Davenport, Iowa, and she grew up mostly across the Mississippi River in Rock Island, Illinois, where she still lived when we met. Her family was a talkative, contentious one, half-Greek, half-Italian—her full name is Maria Cortesio Papageorgiou—and it included nearby cousins who were in and out of the house. She was a tomboy, a good athlete—she rowed on a high school crew and played basketball—and a baseball fan. It was in 1993, a summer of floods in the Midwest, that umpiring first occurred to her. The field at the local minor league stadium, in Davenport, was underwater, so games were being played at a nearby high school, and she and her cousins would go to the games. There, one day, Ria came across the umpires, changing their clothes in the parking lot. She was sixteen.

"The key was that everybody was accessible at that little high school field," she said, "and we were there every day, so everyone knew us, the team, the front office, everyone. And the bullpen guys all knew us—because that's where we'd sit and spread out our blanket. There were no locker rooms or anything, and one day between games of a double-header, we see the umpires. And it hit me, like, 'Gee, they're not old and fat and grouchy looking, they're just normal-looking, midtwenties guys, just normal.' And it challenged my stereotype. And from then on, being the kids that we were, we went up and said hi to every crew that came through, and we'd talk to them a little, and I came to think, 'You know, this is something I've never thought about before, and it's interesting.' And the more I learned, the more interested I became. And near the end of the season, one of the umpires who was an instructor at umpire school sat me down and explained everything to me about going to school and how you get in the game. And it felt very possible to me, and that's when I got the idea that I was going to do it."

She went to Rice University in Houston—her plan was to study civil engineering and design highways, she said—and after her sophomore year, when she was nineteen, she took a semester off and went to Jim Evans's school. She returned to Houston afterward and finished at Rice, also umpiring local amateur games and intrasquad games for the college team. Then in 1998, she enrolled in the Evans school a second time, graduated, and was sent to PBUC. Her memories of PBUC are bitter—"my first experience with true, honest-to-God discrimination," she said—and she was placed on the waiting list for a job.

Halfway through the season, suspecting she was being purposely passed over, she placed querying phone calls to a handful of lawyers, including the prominent women's rights lawyer Gloria Allred.

"I never paid any of them a cent," she said. "And I wasn't going around telling everybody about this, but I must have told a couple of people because suddenly everybody knew, and what do you know? Suddenly there was a job open for me in the Pioneer League."

Ria's rise up the minor league ladder was slow. Before her unusually lengthy sojourn in the Southern League, she spent two years in the Pioneer League at the rookie league level and had also worked in the Midwest League and the Florida State League, in advanced A. During our talks, she aired a litany of complaints, tales of ugliness aimed at her, enough so that I began to detect a confirmed mind-set; I realized I was getting a jaded perspective. But that's not to say I didn't believe her. That she had been brought back to the Southern League for a fourth year, neither promoted nor released, was a clear sign that PBUC didn't know what to do about her.

"She's a good umpire, she really is," Don Mincher, the president of the Southern League, told me in 2006. "And she's gotten better every year she's been here. But it's up or out. She may not be returned to the field next year, and I'll be ashamed if she's not returned, but PBUC does things its own way."

Of course, PBUC did bring her back in 2007 for a fifth year in Mincher's league—despite the collective-bargaining agreement's stipulation that after four years it is "up or out"—using as a reason that she had missed the final month of the 2006 season, having suffered a serious concussion after getting hit with a foul ball. As the season began, she was number one on the list for promotion.

Funny thing happened, though. No openings occurred in Triple A through April, May, and June, just long enough for the midseason evaluations to come out, in which Ria had slid from number one to number seventeen.

"Significant improvement must be made for the remainder of the season for consideration for advancement to Triple A," the evaluation read, in part.

In October, her year-end evaluation came with her dismissal. It cited insufficient improvement and, in language that was clearly meant to be dismissive and insulting—"You still display attributes of a lesser experienced umpire"—presented a litany of skills she had failed to master and standards she had failed to meet.

"Finally," the evaluation read, "your interaction with your fellow crew members and with the league office too often lacked the professionalism needed to be a successful umpire and to have a cohesive umpire crew over the course of a long season."

In other words, baseball was saying what she already knew: We just don't like you.

The day after Ben Robinson finally tossed Steve McFarland from a game, as though he and Phil needed a little more scrutiny, Mike Felt, a PBUC supervisor, arrived in Boise for the first of two evaluations the young crew would receive during the season. Felt, who was in his forties, was a compact man with silver-gray hair and a facial resemblance to Art Carney back when he was doing *The Honeymooners,* and a more earnest true believer in the craft of umpiring you will never meet. He spoke of umpiring technique with patience and exhortatory passion in the manner of the best junior high school algebra teachers and was wont to punctuate most, if not all, of his lessons with a query—"Does that make sense?"

"Muscle memory means what?" he said to Ben and Phil the morning after he arrived. He'd gotten the two umpires up early for a lesson in a local park on covering tag plays at home plate. "Lack of thinking. Anytime you think in the game, you're going to find yourself in trouble. Does that make sense?"

I spent two nights watching ball games with Felt—the first with Ben behind the plate, the second with Phil—and we walked all over the park, spying on the action from different angles. Felt made voluminous notes and answered most of my questions, though he had the signature PBUC reluctance around someone with a notebook, and he never seemed certain whether he was supposed to be talking to me. He told me both Phil and Ben were doing pretty well in calling balls and strikes, but they had a ways to go with their technique on the bases and their teamwork on balls hit to the outfield.

Felt had arrived from Spokane, where he'd been evaluating another crew. His plan had been to wait for Phil and Ben, who were scheduled to travel there after the Boise-Yakima series, but because of Phil's car trouble, Bob Richmond had told them to stay put through the week, so Felt rerouted himself to Boise as well, arriving in time for Wednesday night's game, the first of three between the Hawks and Tri-City. It was a relatively quiet affair, for the umpires, at least.

The next night, however, was another matter. Early in the game, a Boise batter lined a ball to center field, and Ben, at first base, misread it as a sure base hit. Instead of racing to the outfield to rule on whether the ball was fairly caught, he came into the infield to monitor the batter-runner. But the ball hung up in the air long enough for the center fielder to make a play on it, diving for the ball and snatching it up on a short hop. Because Ben wasn't out there and was focused on the batter-runner instead, Phil had to make the call from just in front of home plate, and he mistakenly called the batter out. The fielder caught the ball on the fly, he said.

An argument naturally ensued. McFarland asked Ben to overrule the call because he was standing closer to the ball than Phil, but Ben had to tell him it wasn't his call to make, essentially a lie. Then McFarland got into it with Phil.

No one was thrown out, but the argument was embarrassing to the umpires because they had clearly been out of position.

Interestingly, Felt wasn't angry at the missed call or even at Ben's misread: "Reading line drives to the outfield is the toughest thing a young umpire has to learn," he said.

Rather, what Felt was concerned about was the damage to the umpires' authority that the incident caused. You never want to be in the position of defending your competence and training, Felt said; it's much easier to defend your judgment.

"You can never win an argument if you're arguing over where you were standing," he said. "If Ben had gone out and made the call, the argument would never have been 'How can you call it from there?' It would have been 'He didn't catch the ball.' Does that make sense?"

It did make sense, though Felt couldn't actually hear what was said on the field, and his presumptions turned out to be wrong. Later, after Felt made the point to the umpires, Phil told me that McFarland had actually argued that the fielder didn't catch the ball and never said a word about Phil's—or Ben's—position.

"He kept saying, 'How did he catch the ball, Phil? How did he catch the ball?'" Phil said. "And I said to him, 'What do you mean how did he catch it? He caught it with his glove.' But he kept going, and I finally said, 'Enough, Steve. I ruled it a catch.' "

That McFarland had another blow-up that night shouldn't be surprising. It happened, once again, in the ninth inning, on a play at first. A Boise hitter slashed a ball down the first-base line, where the first baseman, playing deep, dove toward the line and snared it. He got to his knees and flipped to the pitcher, whose foot couldn't find the bag. However, the pitcher wisely swept his glove around, attempting a tag on the batter-runner who, in desperation, dove headlong toward the bag. It was a very tight play. Ben, who had been in position behind the first baseman down the line, had called the ball fair, then hustled onto the infield dirt. He did well to get as close as he did, the dust from the play enveloping him as well as the two players.

Still, as the pitcher caught the throw, he seemed to get his body in the line between Ben and the bag, so Ben couldn't tell exactly when the batter's hand reached it. He called the batter out, and the ballpark went nuts.

Recognizing an imminent dispute, Ben appropriately turned on his heel and walked away from the play, toward the middle of the field and away from the enraged base runner, but he was intercepted by McFarland, who rushed to meet him from his spot in the third-base coach's box. A furious discussion followed in the base path between third and short, fully five minutes long, in the early stages of which McFarland was ejected once again.

"You are just a joke!" McFarland yelled. "You don't belong here, Ben! If you are going to be this fucking bad, it's going to be a long, long summer."

The game ended a few minutes later. Felt had a plane reservation early the next morning, so he met with the umpires immediately afterward to give them his impressions, a verbal evaluation that would eventually be reflected in the written one they would receive at the end of the season. The idea, he told them, was to take his suggestions and make changes in their technique, so when another evaluator came to see them in a few weeks, they wouldn't be making the same mistakes.

"One guy listens and makes the adjustment, another guy doesn't," Felt said. "That's the difference between being promoted and not."

When the meeting was over, it was about midnight, and I took Phil and Ben out for a late drink to hear about it. Not a whole lot is going on in Boise at midnight on a summer Thursday, and we walked the quiet streets of downtown until we found an open restaurant. We ordered pizza and beer.

They were glum and exhausted, irritated at some of Felt's picayune criticisms, defensive about their performances.

"I'm horseshit," Phil said. "He said my plate stance is inverted. My out mechanic is all fucked up."

"He told me I have to slow down when I'm on the bases and read the play a little longer," Ben said. "Why couldn't Felt have shown up three days earlier? I'm usually fine, and tonight I was horseshit."

Phil laughed at their similar self-assessments.

"Everybody agrees," he said. "I was walking off the field and going past some of the players and one of them said, 'You're horseshit, Blue. Don't quit your day job.'"

The tow into town had cost $600, and the repairs on the car another $300, adding up to about a week's pay for each of them, which the league did not reimburse. They had one more game in Boise the next night, after which they'd be driving all night to Vancouver, a six-hundred-mile trip in Phil's fresh-from-the-repair-shop jalopy. They'd sleep all day, then work another game that night.

They hadn't been to Vancouver yet, though Phil said they had collected some information from the other umpiring crews who had already worked there—what the hotel was like and where to eat and drink after the game, the stuff that is the meat of a minor league umpire's life.

Phil asked me if I knew the city; I didn't. He smiled hopefully.

"I hear they have good strip clubs there," he said.

CHAPTER SIX

BALLISH STRIKES
AND STRIKELIKE BALLS

I would say umpires are capable of calling a ball within an inch of where it is. As a hitter, I felt I could tell within a half-inch.
—TED WILLIAMS, HITTER

If the Constitution is what the Supreme Court says it is, then the strike zone is what the umpires say it is.
—GEORGE WILL, WRITER

The damn pitch is coming at you one hundred miles an hour, and you don't know what's coming, where it's moving. I'm not trying to be smart; it ain't that easy to see.
—MARTY SPRINGSTEAD, UMPIRE

I can't really describe what a strike is, but I know it when I see it.
—RON DARLING, PITCHER

Calling balls and strikes makes umpires unique in officialdom. There really isn't anything else like it in sports. For one thing it distinguishes one official on a crew and makes him unequivocally more important than the others. More significant, it's the only task in sports that asks an on-the-field official to demarcate the field of play itself. The strike zone is defined in the rulebook, sure, but on the field the architect of its precise dimensions is the umpire.

Doug Harvey, who was a professional basketball referee before he made it to the major leagues as an umpire—he worked in the original American Basketball Association—thundered at me when I asked him to compare the two.

"I've done forty-seven years of baseball, twenty-seven years of basketball, including four professional, and twenty-two years of football, in high school and college, and if you think football and basketball are tougher than baseball, you're full of crap," he said. "I mean, the first thing they hand you is the strike zone. Now, you tell me where the hell the strike zone is, when you got Frank Howard, who was six foot seven, and then the little guy who was with Pittsburgh, Fred Patek, who was five foot four?"

I'm not sure Harvey was saying that being an umpire is harder than being, say, a basketball referee or a line judge in football. Many of the calls those officials have to make—hockey refs, too—verge on the impossible, after all. You could, it seems, call a foul just about every time a guard drives to the hoop or a forward crashes the boards. The difference between a holding call on an offensive guard on first and ten and the lack of one on second and twenty is just as likely to be that the line judge is watching the tackle this time as it is that the guard isn't doing the same thing all over again.

But unlike in those sports, in which the officials are on hand largely to point out infractions, in baseball the umpire is a critical element of every play. Moreover, it is a far more linear game than those are, with more or less one thing happening at a time: a pitch, a swing, a hit, a catch, a throw, a tag. Along with the absence of a clock, these things are what most distinguish baseball from other games and make officiating it so idiosyncratic. With the exception of a few situations—a play at a base, for instance—the umpire is generally dealing with only one thing in motion: the ball. Is it fair or foul? Is it over the fence or in play? Was it caught or did it hit the ground? And, of course, the most common question of all: Was it over the plate?

Thus we come to the strike zone, a unique and notorious entity, a three-dimensional container of empty space located somewhere in midair a foot or so off the ground, between five and six cubic feet in size (depending on the height of the batter) and in the shape of a large vertical shoebox—say thirty-two inches high, seventeen inches deep, and though officially seventeen inches wide, probably closer to twenty.

For more than one hundred years, the strike zone has been accepted as the central battleground of the game, the turf, so to speak, for which the pitcher competes with the hitter, as pivotal in any at bat as the Normandy beaches during World War II. It's the focal point of baseball. And irony of ironies, everybody is staring at it all game long even though it quite literally can't be seen.

I've mentioned that this queer quality of the strike zone, its invisibleness, was a revelation to me the moment I crouched behind the plate for the first time. It's the same for anyone, I think, when he begins to umpire. Now, whenever I go to the ballpark just to watch a game and the maniac next to me in the upper deck is screaming bloody murder at the home plate ump, I think: This is someone who has never umpired; this is someone who has never come upon the sudden understanding that the strike zone is malleable by the mind, that every pitch is a puzzle, that just about every ball has strikelike qualities and almost every strike is ballish.

Anyone who thinks a strike is a strike is a strike ought to recall that the strike zone is like the fulcrum of a seesaw. It sits at the swivel point of baseball, between pitching and hitting, between offense and defense, and if it isn't precisely situated, the game is thrown out of balance and one side is left up in the air.

It's worth remembering, too, that even though the strike zone has become a familiar and crucial element of baseball, the game wasn't born with it. After the first game between organized teams, twelve years passed before there was even such a thing as a called strike, a concept introduced in 1858. Before that, a pitch over the plate that wasn't swung at was just a do-over.

According to baseball's rules, circa 1876, the year the National League came into being, pitchers pitched underhand from a distance of forty-five feet, and a batter informed the umpire, who in turn informed the pitcher, his preference for a high or low pitch: The batter specified he wanted the ball over the plate (which was then only a foot wide) and between his shoulders and waist, or over the plate and between his waist and an imaginary line a foot from the ground. (A hitter who had no preference for either a "high ball" or "low ball" could request a "fair ball," which meant either would do.)

If the pitch was in the specified area and the batter didn't swing, the umpire called a strike unless there were already two strikes, in which case the batter was warned that he better swing at the next one or he'd be called out. Only every third pitch delivered not in the specified area was called a ball, with three balls allowing the batter to reach first, meaning that it took effectively nine balls for a walk.*

In 1887, in recognition that the pitchers were at a disadvantage, the hitters' requests were dispensed with. That same year came the legislation that made a called strike resemble, for the first time, what we have today. Rule 23 of the National Playing Rules of Professional Baseball Clubs declared: "A Fair Ball is a ball delivered by the Pitcher while standing wholly within the lines of his position and facing the batsman, the ball, so delivered to pass over the home base, not lower than the batsman's knee, nor higher than his shoulder."

The official definition of the strike zone remained the same for more than sixty years. But then in 1949, the rulebook was codified and rewritten, and starting in 1950, what had long been called a strike was different, with the strike zone defined anew as "that space over home plate that is between the batter's armpits and the top of his knees when he assumes his natural stance."

This was a huge alteration. For one thing, in stripping a couple of inches from the strike zone at the top and bottom, it gave a monumental gift to hitters. (Major league run production jumped 5 percent in 1950.) But perhaps more crucial from an umpiring standpoint was the final qualifying clause: "when he assumes his natural stance." It was added to legislate against the potential unfairness of a hitter's affecting an exaggerated crouch. But its more far-reaching effect was that by introducing a temporal element to the definition—*when* the hitter takes his stance—the strike zone was acknowledged, for the first time, to exist in time as well as space. In other words, from then on the rulebook would imply that not only is the strike zone invisible, it's also evanescent.

Since then baseball's fickle rule writers have been unable to stop adjusting and readjusting the strike zone's upper and lower limits. After shrinking it in 1950, they enlarged it slightly in 1963. In 1969, still dissatisfied, they returned it to its 1950 dimensions. Then, almost

---

*Three strikes and four balls did not become the norm until 1889, five years after pitchers were allowed to throw the ball with any motion they pleased. The plate took on its current size and shape in 1900.

two decades later, they made it smaller than ever, at the same time seeming to acknowledge that any real precision is impossible.

The "upper limit" of the zone, the rulebook declared, beginning in 1988, is halfway between the top of the hitter's shoulders and the top of his pants, which not only requires a certain amount of visual triangulation but seems to give altogether too much influence to a batter's tailor, not to mention how snug he likes his trousers in the crotch. That language remains in the rulebook today (that is, as of 2008), and in 1996, the definition of the lower limit of the zone was changed as well, evidently so it would be equivalently fuzzy.

"The strike zone is that area over home plate," Rule 2.00 of the current rulebook says as of this writing, "the upper limit of which is a horizontal line at the midpoint between the top of the shoulders and the top of the uniform pants, and the lower level is a line at the hollow beneath the kneecap."

What?

So it was more than a joke—though it was a good joke—that umpire Durwood Merrill, who retired from the American League in 1999 after more than two decades (he died in 2003), wore kneepads one postseason with a mischievous diagram sketched on them. Two lines were drawn across them, one just above the knee, one just below. Above the top line was written "Strike." Below the bottom line was written "Ball."

"I'm the one who gave Merrill those kneepads," John Hirschbeck told me. "I was on his crew and he was working the playoffs that year, and I went and got him the nice kneepads, and we wrote the lines in with a Sharpie. And in between, this area right here"—Hirschbeck indicated a two-inch slice on the lower half of the knee—"it said, 'Not sure.'"

The rulebook makes another distinction, a refinement of the temporal aspect of the definition: "The Strike Zone is determined from the batter's stance as the batter is prepared to swing at a pitched ball." Though this is not terribly precise—"as the batter is prepared"?—it has an accepted interpretation: as the hitter strides to swing.

This clause and its enforcement are among the many reasons that the strike zone is so widely misunderstood. When a hitter steps toward the ball, after all, his body height contracts and his strike zone consequently lowers by a significant amount and may even shrink up to a few inches, depending on how erect the batter stands in the batter's box and how long his stride. Over the past twenty-five years, as television has become the way most ball games are presented to most fans, and the view from the center-field camera has become the familiar way of seeing the pitcher facing down the hitter, the strike zone has seemed to be palpable, a rectangle superimposed on the screen. But the rectangle, fixed in place, is never adjusted to a hitter's stride. That, as much as anything, has led fans to underestimate the dicey and complicated enterprise of calling balls and strikes.

The point of all this is that the strike zone isn't, nor has it ever been, set in stone, or even sand. It's set in air, a concept, not a thing. It can't be transported from one ballpark to another, but like the memory of a secret code it has to be formulated by each umpire each time he squats behind the catcher, every game, every pitch. The umpire's job is not so much to enforce the rulebook as to represent it, to set the fulcrum of the seesaw—to *be* the fulcrum of the seesaw—and make sure the duel between the pitcher and the hitter is properly balanced. Though fans and broadcasters may treat the plate umpire as if he were a mere ballot counter, punching the ticket of each pitch as it crosses the plate and acknowledging its ostensibly obvious credentials, in truth he's much more of an arbitrator, keeping the most contested area on the ball field from being taken over by one side or the other. More than one major league umpire spoke to me of calling balls and strikes as a kind of political enterprise, an activity requiring will and conscience and a point of view.

"It's like the Constitution," Gary Cederstrom said to me. "The strike zone is a living, breathing document."

When I asked Tim Tschida why balls and strikes provoked so many arguments and so much enmity, he responded by comparing the rulebook strike zone to one of the most controversial Supreme Court decisions of the twentieth century.

"Have you ever read *Roe v. Wade*?" Tschida said. "It's very clear. What it says is *very* clear. And we've still been fighting for twenty-five or thirty years over what it means."

Everyone likes strikes.

It's a baseball bias, a secret that is essentially shouted during every game: Strikes are better than balls. They're cooler. They're more desirable. They're sexier.

Strikes are the engine of a ball game. They propel it forward. Without strikes, outs are rare. Without them, a game has no conflict, no drama, no story. Indeed, the game cannot proceed—or end—without strikes.

Pitchers, of course, love them. So do their catchers. Pitching coaches *really* love them.

Managers love strikes, especially when their team isn't at bat, though they're not opposed at all to an opposing pitcher throwing strikes, which lets the hitters dig in with confidence and forces them to be aggressive. Even hitters themselves like to see strikes; they are, after all, at the plate to hit, and a strike is, by definition, more hittable than a ball.

Fans prefer strikes, too. They're more dramatic than balls, which can occur, after all, only if specific things *don't* happen: if the pitch doesn't pass over the plate, if the hitter doesn't swing, if the umpire doesn't raise his right hand. Strikes, on the other hand, promise action. Whether it's the first pitch of an inning or the count is full and the bases are loaded, a ball is simply less exciting than a strike. Should the 3-2 pitch be called ball four, the runner ambles home from third, and even if the home team is scoring, the reaction from the crowd is closer to relief than ecstasy. But on strike three—called or swung at and missed, it doesn't matter—the place goes ballistic.

Strikes, in sum, are the pretty girls of baseball; they get a lot of attention and a lot of favor. And maybe no one likes strikes more than umpires do. Pitchers having control problems elicit universal umpire scorn. Even the lexicon of umpires reflects their collective yearning for a well-paced game in which pitchers are always around the plate and hitters are swinging the bat and not waiting out every count. Home plate umpires speak about finding strikes, looking for strikes, hunting for strikes. "I could have grabbed a few more," an umpire might say, discussing his work after a game. More than one umpire talked to me about a game they play with themselves, keeping umpire score, as it were.*

"It's impossible to call a rulebook strike zone; it is," said Chris

---

*In 2001, concerned that some umpires were calling too small a strike zone and that as a result games were going on too long, Sandy Alderson, then baseball's executive in charge of umpires, sent an e-mail to at least one umpire urging him to "hunt for strikes." It set off a small furor, the umpires disingenuously claiming this was an outrageous attempt to get them to go against their judgment to speed up games.

Guccione. "It's a game within a game. That's the whole thing. You're playing the scoreboard. You're the strikes and the visitors are the balls. You don't want to go crazy obviously, but you want to make it to where you get the strikes ahead, just to make the game move along. There's a pace you have to keep, you've got to get a flow for the game, keep it moving. You can't be so fine that you're always calling balls."

I thought Guccione—everybody called him Gooch—might have been reckless in our interview; we were talking during spring training in Arizona. Frequently in discussions with me, especially with a tape recorder going, an umpire would say (usually with some sanctimony) something like "A strike is a pitch that passes over the plate between here and here." And when I'd hear things from umpires that echoed what Gooch was saying, they'd usually ask that I keep their names out of this discussion because they were uneasy about what the commissioner's office would say.

But Marty Springstead was even less circumspect than Gooch was. Springstead was a venerable figure in umpire-dom, having worked twenty years on the field, later becoming the executive director of umpires for the American League. He was still on the supervisory staff when I met him. He was a famous baseball character, a voluble guy with an excitable manner and a lisp—think of the vocal style of Sylvester the Cat ("Thufferin' thuccotash!"). He also had a reputation for being savvy, for being a sharp teacher of young umpires, and, in general, for being a no-bullshit guy. He told me that calling a third strike on a big league hitter was the hardest thing for a young umpire to learn. That takes big league confidence, he said, and a lot of guys in Triple A don't have it.

The strike zone is there to make sure the pitcher doesn't have an advantage over the hitter, and the hitter doesn't have an advantage over the pitcher, Springstead told me. It's your job to enforce that, but that's not your only job; at the same time you can't let the game grind to a halt.

"You want to keep the game going," Springstead said. "Why do they tell you 'hunt for strikes'? Because if you're squeezing the plate, they'll never swing. The Yankees are famous for it now, they take every sonovabitching thing. Take, take, take. But you want them to swing the bat, that's how you keep your games going. You can't sit up there and just call fucking balls all day."

Our conversation took place over breakfast at a Bob Evans restaurant just off a Florida interstate, as though we had chosen the proverbial nondescript location to hide in plain sight as we discussed state secrets. But Springstead attracted attention from neighboring tables, chewing his eggs noisily and waving his arms to indicate when he was discussing pitches that came in nose high or a foot outside.

"Now, you can't help a guy"—a pitcher, he meant—"who's up here and out here, but you can help a guy who's around there someplace." Springstead held his hand a couple of inches off the edge of our table. "Let's put it this way. The plate's seventeen inches, right? Well, the hitter's got his arm, which is three feet, and you got another thirty-two to thirty-six inches with the bat. Now, if you can't hit a pitch that's nineteen inches away, you got serious problems, big boy."

Not only hitters come in different shapes and sizes; umpires do, too. Often, a guy like Tim McClelland, who is six feet six, is going to get a different perspective on a pitch from, say, Ed Montague, who is maybe five feet ten. Their height affects their stances, for one thing. To get down to the optimal height for viewing a pitch—with your chin at the level of the top of the catcher's head, as they teach you in umpire school, or with your eyes at the precise level of the upper limit of the strike zone, as I've heard some umpires say—McClelland needs a deeper crouch. However, he has the advantage of being able to stand back farther from the catcher and raise up higher without losing a full view of the plate. Many umpires will do this anyway, from time to time, as a kind of last-moment improvisation when the catcher rises up or shifts from side to side and blocks their view of the plate.

Then there are the variations in stances. Wally Bell, among the few who still use the scissors, is distinct in that he gets down on one knee to call a pitch. Most umpires are square to the plate, but if you watch closely, you see wide differences in depth of crouch, height of head, and angle to the plate. Some umpires habitually set up directly behind the catcher, looking at the plate over the catcher's head, the theory being that you get the best view of the plate straight on; the downside of this is that you have to set up a little higher and get a less advantageous view of the low pitch. Other umpires prefer the slot; your view from there is unimpeded, but you're looking at the pitch from a slightly off-center perspective, which skews, minutely but perceptibly, your view of the outside corner.

The difference between peering over the catcher's head and peering from the slot may result in, say, a centimeter or two shift in the strike zone, but on a pitch at the knees or off the black outside, a centimeter or two could easily make the difference between a strike and a ball, no? Bruce Froemming put it this way: "You and I don't see the same. When you're behind the plate, what might be a strike to you is a ball to me."

That's the same argument umpires make to explain their dislike of the center-field camera that television uses to illustrate balls and strikes on the air, essentially that the camera is in a skewed stance. It's usually situated well above the height of the strike zone, and it's never directly behind the pitcher because if it were, the pitcher would be in the way. The view from the camera, umpires say, is close to accurate, but only close.

Further, the zone as it is represented on the television screen has a number of obvious shortcomings. One is that it isn't adjusted for the stride of the hitter. Second, the television strike zone is two-dimensional but the strike zone is three. Usually, the represented zone is set on a plane at the front edge of the plate, which means that any pitch that doesn't pass over the plate's front lip won't show up on the screen as a strike; in the big leagues especially, pitches break so sharply that they frequently go around the front of the plate but enter the strike zone from the side.

"You know, the strike zone is a funny thing," Mike Winters said, "because it looks real easy when they put that box up on TV. It's like, 'How could anybody *miss* that?' Well, that box isn't there, you know, the strike zone's invisible, and you've got a ball being thrown x miles an hour and it's moving vertically and laterally. There's a lot of room for disagreement. When you put that little box up there, it looks like an absolute piece of cake, but trust me, it's not."

The television zone merely reinforces the notion among fans that the umpires aren't the best judges of what's going on. It's never been easy to convince the yahoo in the upper deck (or the managers in the opposing dugouts, for that matter) that the umpires actually have the best possible view of a pitch, and the center-field camera only confirms their doubts. (The umpires are correct on this issue: The television strike zone "is for entertainment purposes only," said Justin Shaffer, baseball senior vice president for new media.)

"It gives the fan a general idea, but I don't think it's accurate," said Randy Marsh, a big league crew chief. "I don't think it's far off, but if according to their machine it missed the line, and I'm saying it hit the corner, then the broadcasters get going. Some of them are fair, but some are butchers up there on us, and they go, 'Oh, that pitch was inside.' Give me a break."

In calling balls and strikes, particularly at the big league level where pitchers are able to throw the ball regularly in the very near vicinity of where they want it to go, the umpire's job is to find the most precise view of the strike zone they can get. In many ways, the task is akin to a hitter's; both have to be able to cover the zone, and like a hitter, whose weaknesses are often spoken of as holes in his swing, an umpire can have blind spots.

"I think when I came up to the big leagues, I hadn't really gotten to know the inside corner that well," Alfonso Marquez told me. "It gets crowded in there. The catcher's set up inside and the batter's up on the plate. You're taught to set up in the slot and follow the ball all the way into the glove, but when the catcher crowds you—when he moves into your slot—you lose the plate, and if the batter is crowding the plate, too, you lose the pitcher's release point. So if you stay where you are, you're only going to see the ball"—Marquez snapped his fingers—"for that long. In the minor leagues, I was kind of guessing."

I asked him how he solved the problem, and he said just about every umpire made the same discovery—I confirmed this with others—that you have to shift your position counterintuitively, not getting down lower or squeezing your head in a narrower crevice of space closer to the plate, but by easing off just a bit, creating a different angle from which to look at the pitch. It requires practice; you need to train your eyes to appreciate a different perspective on the plate, but at least you get a longer look—you see the ball from the time it leaves the pitcher's hand to the time it hits the catcher's glove.

"What I do now when they crowd me is back up and rise up," Marquez said. "I set up higher so I can look over the catcher's head. That way, if he does shift and block me, I've already made sure my nose is right on the inside part of the plate right on the corner."

He made his hand into a divider and placed it lengthwise along his nose. "If the ball comes in here"—that is, anywhere to the right of his nose—"it's a strike."

The lesson came in handy in one of Marquez's most prominent plate assignments—game three of the 2003 American League Championship Series, Boston versus New York at Yankee Stadium.

Not only was it a highly anticipated game, pitting two ace pitchers, Pedro Martinez and Roger Clemens, against each other, but it turned out to be a famous game as well, in which the long-standing rivalry between the Yankees and the Red Sox flamed into a brawl. After Martinez hit a Yankee batter, Karim Garcia, with a pitch, Garcia was forced at second and, as a measure of revenge, slid hard into the Boston second baseman, Todd Walker. The next inning, Clemens, notoriously unafraid to throw at batters, pitched high and inside to the Red Sox slugger Manny Ramirez. The pitch wasn't really that close, but Ramirez either believed he was being thrown at in retaliation, or else he was so primed for such an occurrence that anything close would have set him off. He dropped his bat and headed for the mound.

Both benches cleared, as did the bull pens, and in the ensuing melee with dozens of players pretending to fight and several actually doing so, the Yankees' seventy-two-year-old bench coach, Don Zimmer, charged at Martinez like an insane, bald Santa Claus, and Martinez, essentially defending himself, seemed to grab Zimmer by the head and throw him to the ground. Neither "bizarre" nor "surreal" is too strong a descriptive word for the scene, but amazingly—and impressively, for the umpires—no one was ejected, partly because the umpires didn't want to decide the game and the series by tossing out any of the stars, and also because it became impossible to assign real blame.

"After Pedro hit Garcia, Clemens came out and he told me, 'I'm going to hit somebody,'" Marquez recalled for me. "He said, 'Fonz, I gotta protect my guys.' I told him, 'Okay, Roger, I'm just telling you, the benches have been warned. You've been warned. You do what you've got to do, but I'm going to do what I got to do.'"

Marquez was telling Clemens he understood the players' code, but he was also saying that if Clemens hit a batter—or even threw at anyone—he'd be ejected. In retrospect, the warning kept Clemens, and probably several other players, in the game. Clemens's pitch to Ramirez was, in fact, likely a message—that is, it was close enough to let Ramirez know Clemens was capable of vengeance—but it wasn't a knockdown pitch. Marquez was quick to make that fine distinction—and to recognize that no action was necessary. He'd married his knowledge of how to see the inside pitch clearly to his knowledge of handling players. Savvy umpiring.

"Roger ended up not hitting anybody," Marquez said. "He didn't have to. They were scared shitless of him up there."

Among players, suspicions about what goes into the calling of balls and strikes are many, from a rooting interest to vendettas to a simple desire to get the game over with.

"You play a day game in Chicago on getaway day, and these guys have to leave same as we do," said Jeff Blauser, who played shortstop for Atlanta in the eighties and nineties, and who was managing the Braves' Double A farm team when I met him in Huntsville, Alabama. "It all plays into it. Wrigley to O'Hare isn't the easiest trip in the world at five p.m. on a Wednesday."

Ozzie Guillen, the volatile manager of the White Sox who played infield for them from 1985 to 1987, had a lot to say on the subject of umpire bias, essentially that star players get star treatment. He was standing around the batting cage during spring training in 2006, holding court for a bevy of reporters.

"Everybody has their own strike zone," Guillen said. "This year they come to us and say, 'We're gonna call the strike zone from here to here'"—he sliced the air at the knees and the letters—"but they have to say something every year to make us think they're working. But if Roger Clemens or Pedro Martinez or Greg Maddux, Tom Glavine, is pitching, it's a strike. Jose Cruz pitching? It's a ball. Same way for hitting. You're fucking Wade Boggs? That's a ball. You're Frank Thomas? That's a ball. Ozzie Guillen hitting? Strike, get the fuck out."

Current umpires, of course, say this is ridiculous, though some old-timers will tell stories with a wink. Marty Springstead, for instance.

I had wanted to ask Springstead about how the strike zone has changed over the years, and especially about QuesTec, the system of cameras and computers that baseball has employed since 2001 to measure and evaluate umpires' plate performances. He told me a story from thirty-five years earlier, about umpiring behind the plate for a game between the Tigers and the Twins.

"This was back in the seventies," he said. "The Tigers had Denny McClain, Mickey Lolich, and they had another pitcher, a converted out-fielder named Earl Wilson, and they sent up Wilson to pinch-hit in the ninth inning. It's a 5–0 game, and Dean Chance is pitching for Minnesota, and I'm saying to myself, 'Even if he hits this son of a bitch to downtown Minneapolis, twenty miles away, it's only going to be 5–1,' so I wasn't going to waste a whole lot of time with Earl Wilson. He's a pitcher, anyway, he doesn't care about his batting average. He gets into the batter's box, and the first pitch from Chance comes in and it's a fastball, cock high, but it may have been a little outside"—Springstead put his hand eight inches off the table edge—"maybe it's this far outside.

"I said, 'Strike one.' And Earl Wilson looked down at home plate and shook his head. He knows what's going on, and he said, 'Man, I sure wish I was pitching this game.'"

Springstead laughed. The story was his way of telling me how umpiring—and baseball—had changed. As television brought fans closer and closer to more and more games, the power of umpires to use the strike zone to keep control over a game, both for good and frivolous purposes, was diminished. They still do it, to the much smaller degree that it's possible, though they're less likely to admit it these days. Even some of the old-time umpires I spoke with cling to the public position that all strikes are created equal, but enough of the others enjoyed telling such tales as Springstead's that the truth was pretty clear.

The best anecdote actually came from a former player, Bob Uecker, who is much better known as an actor and a broadcaster, the longtime voice of the Milwaukee Brewers. Uecker was a noted baseball humorist, if that isn't too much of an oxymoron, and maybe he embellished this tale, which he told me in the Brewers' home dugout before a game against the Mets, but it sounded genuine to me. He wasn't checking to see if I thought it was funny.

During his rookie year, 1962, Uecker said, he was pinch-hitting for the old Milwaukee Braves against the Dodgers. The home plate umpire was Jocko Conlan, and though Uecker wouldn't swear to it, he thought he remembered that Don Drysdale was pitching. Conlan, who would make it to the Hall of Fame, was a crusty bantamweight, notorious for an Irish temper—once, when Leo Durocher kicked dirt on him, he famously kicked back, catching Durocher in the shin, maybe accidentally, maybe not—and for brooking absolutely no disputatiousness over balls and strikes, especially from rookies.

"So the first pitch comes in and it's in the other batter's box, and Conlan says, 'Strike one!'" Uecker recalled. "And I'm going, 'Jeez, how am

I gonna hit that?' So I stepped out and I looked back and I said, 'That wasn't a strike.' And Conlan doesn't even look at me. He just says, 'So's the next one.'"*

A brief side trip on a related subject: For an umpire, the skill that most resembles calling balls and strikes involves judging when to suspend play because of rain, and subsequently when to call off the game. There are guidelines for this but no rules and tons of unforeseen variables that end up affecting the decision. It takes experience; it takes a sense of being able to draw an imaginary line, in this case between tolerable and intolerable playing conditions. And it involves balancing the concerns of different constituencies. You don't really learn how to do it until you've done it a number of times. Anyone who saw the 2008 World Series and watched baseball's administrators, umpires included, become flummoxed by the weather—rain caused game three to be delayed by more than two hours and game five to be suspended and resumed two days later—will understand that.

The rulebook leaves the authority to delay a game before it begins in the hands of the manager of the home team (though in reality it's more often the general manager's call, especially in the minors). Once the game gets under way, however, it's the crew chief's call, and his concern is generally focused on whether the conditions are hazardous for the players. Is the field too slippery? Is the ball too slick? Are there puddles in the outfield or on the infield? Is the field draining properly? Is it raining so hard that the players' vision is impaired? Is someone likely to get hurt? And these are largely the governing issues in amateur baseball.

In professional baseball, however, economic concerns often complicate the decision. When a game is delayed and then postponed before it is an official game, the customers are entitled to refunds, the teams may have to revise travel plans, the television schedules need to be rejiggered. These things drive cost-conscious team owners and general managers crazy, so from the early days in the minor leagues, the umpires are instructed to push to get the games in, not to be aggressive

---

*Uecker's memory might be a little faulty. On April 13, 1962, he did, in fact, make his big league debut for the Milwaukee Braves, pinch-hitting against Don Drysdale of the Dodgers in the ninth inning and grounding out. Jocko Conlan, however, was not behind the plate. He was at first base. I think it's a good story anyway.

in clearing the field, to let the players play through squalls, to wait through long delays. Meanwhile if the game is official—once the trailing team has had five complete at bats—the team that's ahead will be howling that a shower is a monsoon and the team that's behind will be shrugging and suggesting a cloudburst is a mere sprinkle.

"Am I out here to get the game in? Yes," Adam Hamari, a classmate of mine at umpire school who'd made it to Double A by the end of 2008, told me. "But it gets to the point where it's not fair to the pitcher or the hitter. It's not easy."

Indeed, the umpires often feel as though their authority is at its most fragile when it's raining because while the teams are often lobbying them toward different ends, the umpires are often laboring under instructions that undermine their own instincts. The little voice in an umpire's head that is telling him, "This is insane, it's pouring out here," is directly contradicted by the league president's warning that team budgets are strained and they've got to get the games in, or the knowledge that the general manager of the home team has the league president's ear when it comes to umpire evaluation.

Jason Klein recalled that once, in Double A, he consulted with such a general manager during a rainstorm, and the man said to him: "You gotta do your job, Jason. I hate you right now, but you gotta do your job."

How an umpire learns what to do in a rain delay is illustrated by a story Hamari told me. Toward the end of his first season in Single A, as the pennant race heated up, he recalled, the league president was so unwilling to leave the decision to call off a game in the hands of his rookie umpires that he instructed them never to do so on their own. First, they were required to get the permission of the home team general manager and the field managers of both teams, a set of circumstances pretty close to impossible.

That dictum led to an occasion on Staten Island in New York City, in which the home team, the Staten Island Yankees, was leading the Batavia Muckdogs by a run in the late innings, and a storm caused Hamari and his partner to clear the field. After a delay, Hamari determined the game should be called; he got clearance from the Yankees, but the manager of the Muckdogs refused to agree. It didn't have anything to do with the game really, Hamari said.

"He just hated the Yankees manager and wanted to stick it to him," Hamari said.

So, as instructed, Hamari called the league president in St. Petersburg, Florida, to adjudicate. The president checked the weather radar on his computer and informed Hamari, who was soaked, that it wasn't raining on Staten Island. It took Hamari awhile to finally persuade him that it was, in fact, pretty wet where he was standing and the president finally told him, Okay, wait another half hour and if it hasn't cleared, call the game. The visiting manger was fine with the decision. The Yankees manager went nuts.

"You're going to let that SOB in Florida tell you what to do?" he screamed at Hamari. "That's horseshit!"

"I had to tell the guy, 'Well, yeah, he signs my paycheck.'"

They waited half an hour, and the rain was still falling. Hamari informed the home team manager he was calling the game, then went to tell the visitors.

But he couldn't find them. They'd already packed up and left.

Talk to umpires about what does go into calling balls and strikes and contradictions abound. Umpires will argue that pitches are like snowflakes, that you can't compare one to another because they're all different. Yet they'll talk about categories, too, as if pitches come in bulk. "Maddux always wants that pitch," they'll say about Greg Maddux, the great control pitcher who is known for being able to place the ball just off the outside corner, where he expects the umpire to reward him by stretching the plate.

They'll say calling strikes is paramount, but they'll withhold a strike call from time to time—if the pitcher badly misses the catcher's target, for example, even if the ball might still graze the zone. If the catcher sets up outside and the pitch is up and in, the umpire ethos says the pitcher doesn't deserve a close call for doing a poor job. Besides that, he's made the catcher lunge; his glove probably moved out of the strike zone, which means it'll *look* like a ball from the dugout, which means the umpire will be getting an earful if he calls a strike.

Or they'll say, "You can't call that pitch," meaning that if a ball breaks downward as it crosses the plate so the catcher has to turn the pocket of his glove upward to catch it, it's not a strike, even if it clipped the front of the plate at the knees.

Why? Once again, from the dugout, such a pitch will appear to be low, and the players will complain loudly. It's always the same stuff, too, from the low minors to the majors: a sardonic exhortation like "Concentrate, now!" A declarative correction: "He's bowling out there!" An exasperated, plaintive question: "Where do you have that, Gary?"

Not quite arguing. No ad hominem abuse. Yapping, umpires call it, and it comes across as a sandstorm of criticism, flecks of vitriol flying out of the dugout as if in a hot wind.

As an umpire you can't let them continue. Squawking about balls and strikes is forbidden, an ejectable offense, not to mention that it's just plain irksome. But unless you want a reputation for being easily rattled, you can't make a habit of walking over to the dugout to figure out who said what and making a big show of your authority.

So you find a way to make it stop, and though it will no doubt irk some fans to learn this, yielding to popular opinion on a few ball and strike calls is preferable to an umpire's risking his control over the game. When I asked Gary Cederstrom how he learned the strike zone as he was coming up through the minor leagues, he said: "I called everything a strike until they started yelling."

"When you start out working in rookie ball or A ball, it's trial and error," Cederstrom said. "From umpire school you know where the zone *supposedly* is, but the first time you call a pitch up, in the zone but up, they burn down the damn house. So you go, 'Well, okay, maybe that might not be a strike.'"

I got similar responses from many umpires, the implication being that umpires are not exactly the manipulators of the strike zone and the abusers of authority they are often thought to be. Rather, they're reactive, at least in part at the mercy of the teams on the field.

This helps explain how the strike zone became so warped during the 1990s. Everyone recognized it; umpires weren't calling strikes on any pitch above the belt, and to compensate, they were giving back some airspace off the outside corner. The result was a strike zone that, in practice, tipped the rulebook zone on its side; it became wider than it was high.

The change is usually blamed on the umpires, but umpires say, rather sensibly, I think, that it was a collaborative effort, that they would have no motive for changing the strike zone on their own; they add that they were simply reacting to what the players and the leagues demanded.

That the warp of the strike zone evolved over time and wasn't declared by some umpire conspiracy is hard to refute. It certainly didn't change overnight. As film from the 1960s and the 1970s attests, the zone was called much more tightly on the corners than it was in the 1980s, and with strikes as high as the letters. By the mid-nineties it had evolved so the high strike had more or less vanished and the outside edge of the plate was being extended as far as four or even six inches.

The umpires' explanation for the shape-shifting of the strike zone was unexpected—and also counterintuitive. That is, it may seem obvious that an umpire who won't call a high strike is a boon to hitters, but it's the pitchers and the pitching coaches, several umpires told me, who forced the strike zone down.

The high strike is the easiest pitch, after all, to hit for power. It encourages hitters to swing for the fences and yields a lot of home runs. For most pitchers, it's also the most difficult pitch to throw for a *swinging* strike. Unless you have an exceptional fastball, say, 95 mph or above, you're rarely going to throw a high strike past a major league hitter. Through the 1980s and 1990s, home run production was steadily increasing, and it behooved pitchers and pitching coaches to ban the high strike from their repertoires and to put across the idea that throwing above the waist in the strike zone is a mistake. They didn't want the umpires to call the high strike.

"If the umpires don't call it, the hitters are going to stop swinging at it," said Jim Evans. "The batter is going to take that pitch and work the count instead. A pitcher can be hurt a lot less by a walk than by a home run."

The pitch that pitchers do want, of course, is the low strike—the lower, the better—but certainly the one that just shaves the southern border of the knee. Sometimes they get it, but the low strike is especially affected by the stance and position of the umpire. Generally speaking, the lower a guy gets in his crouch, the easier it is to gauge—and call with confidence—pitches at or near the Antarctic extremity of the zone.

As the top of the strike zone was being tamped down like tobacco in a pipe, it was also growing wider. Part of this, no doubt, was the umpires' willingness to compensate for the lost area of the zone above the belt, an adjustment in the fulcrum of the seesaw. Though the plate has two sides, of course, umpires are loath to extend the zone inside because a pitch that is off the plate inside is unhittable. Even if the hitter gets the bat head around quickly enough to connect solidly, he's almost certainly going to pull the ball foul. More likely, he'll hit the ball off the handle. The odds are so stacked against the hitter, in other words, that the delicate balance of pitcher and hitter is spoiled.

As Marty Springstead suggested, however, a pitch two or even four inches or more off the plate outside is still easily reachable by a hitter with the barrel of the bat. So, in this region, umpires felt comfortable employing their, um, individual interpretations of the strike zone.

For most of baseball history, nobody minded this. Pitchers expected an umpire to have a point of view. Hitters were fine with it, too, as long as they knew what the umpire's strike zone was and he called a consistent game for nine innings.

"When I was pitching, a crew would come into town and we'd run out to the dugout to see who was at first base," said Jim Kaat, who pitched in the major leagues from 1959 to 1983. "If it was Ed Runge, we knew we had a good pitcher's umpire the next day. Ed would say, 'Boys, I didn't come here to see you walk. Let's swing the bat.' Anything close they knew they had to swing. Eddie Hurley, though, we knew we might as well throw it down the middle."

The problems arose when it became evident the umpires were taking too much license, especially with the outside of the zone. When the vertical shoebox of the strike zone seemingly became horizontal, the media took notice, accusing umpires of usurping the authority of the rulebook, and baseball became determined to rein the umpires in. The tipping point came when a 1997 playoff game between the Florida Marlins and the Atlanta Braves was umpired by Eric Gregg with such a wide strike zone that it indisputably altered the quality of the game, which ended with twenty-five total strikeouts. Baseball seemed to take Gregg's performance as a challenge to do something about umpires who were, collectively it seemed, officiating a game of their own design.

Umpires can't claim to be innocent of overextending their authority, but some of them do. The evidence on videotape notwithstanding, some of the older umpires would disagree that the strike zone ever changed.

"When you tell me, or whoever tells me, that the strike zone has evolved, I say, 'That's your perception, not mine,'" Jerry Crawford, a thirty-year veteran, told me.

When I asked Randy Marsh how the strike zone shifted so drastically, he said, "A lot of people blame the Maddux and Glavine era, when they were with the Braves."

I heard that frequently about Tom Glavine and Greg Maddux, two likely Hall of Fame pitchers, how they made a living by stretching the zone outside. Neither could throw terrifically hard, but with deceptive breaking pitches and exquisite control, each would go on to win more than three hundred games. Each was capable of putting the ball exactly where he wanted, and each could turn a game into a psychological battle with the umpire.

In any game, actually, the opening innings involve the pitcher and the catcher negotiating the parameters of the strike zone with the umpire, with the hitters going back to the dugout and delivering information, warning teammates to swing at the ball off the outside corner, for instance, because the ump is calling it a strike.

But Maddux was especially good at this; he'd throw a pitch just off the plate and see if it was called a strike; if it was, he'd throw the next one just a little farther out. If that was called a strike, he'd go farther out still. When he finally got a ball, he'd bring it back in. He also had his manager, Bobby Cox, a notorious yapper, providing dugout support.

"Maddux would tell Javy Lopez," Marsh said, naming the Braves' regular catcher of the nineties, "'I want your cock right on the outside corner of the plate, and just catch it here.'" Marsh moved his hand three or four inches to illustrate a point off the plate. "So Maddux just kept throwing outside there and kept hitting the glove, and when he didn't get a call, Cox would be screaming from the dugout."

"Maddux, Glavine, if I have those guys, I just go, 'Oh, I'm gonna have a headache after this game,'" said Chris Guccione. "They work your ass off on the outside corner, creeping, creeping, creeping. And the Braves always had great catchers, they just sit on the corner and they're so soft-handed."

Guccione mimicked a catcher catching three pitches in succession. "Puck, puck, puck," he said. "And then he'll just kind of scoot over a little, and puck, puck, puck—and the next thing you know, it's like six inches outside and the batter's going, 'Whoa!' And you're like, 'Yeah, that might have been a little too wide.' So you ball the next one and here they come, right back in. And it's like this all game, outside corner, outside corner. Oh, my God, it drives you nuts. You just sit there and go, 'I cannot wait till they pull them out of the game.'"

Grant Secrist may not be the only person in the world who ever considered the potential effect of the end of the Warsaw Pact on baseball, but he was the first I ever heard of. An aerospace and military consultant in Cedar City, Utah, he lobbied the major leagues for more than a decade to improve its methods of training and evaluating umpires, largely to no avail. The end of the Cold War, he told me, was the impetus for his campaign.

A genial, talkative academic, Secrist was in his late sixties when we met in Cedar City, a remote and lovely college town, a two-and-a-half-hour drive from the nearest air hub in Las Vegas, almost all of it gradually uphill into the high desert of southwestern Utah. Zion National Park and Bryce Canyon are nearby. The school is Southern Utah University, where Secrist helped create something called the Human Performance Technology Center.

Secrist had a couple of advanced degrees in gibberish-sounding subjects—human factors engineering and industrial/organizational psychology—but he was basically a kind of efficiency expert, focusing on professions that require high-speed, high-volume information processing. A bit of a pedant, he was used to feeling that his knowledge is arcane and so was always on guard against being misunderstood. You could see why baseball officials might find him annoying, as some did.

Nonetheless, his résumé was impressive. Secrist spent twenty-two years in the air force, including some time in the 1960s as a launch officer for ICBMs in the Strategic Air Command. Then, after he resigned his commission, he spent most of the 1980s working with air force funding as a research scientist, studying the perceptual and cognitive abilities of fighter pilots and developing technology and training methods to enhance their awareness and decision-making time in combat situations.

"But with the dissolution of the Soviet Union in the late eighties and early nineties, the funding for research and development in the military changed quite significantly," Secrist said to me. "And there was a big move to transfer technology that wasn't extrasensitive to commercial applications."

One of those applications was baseball. Secrist's specialty was high-demand performance, which is the study of why some people respond to avalanches of stimuli better than others, especially in high-stakes or high-stress situations. Obviously fighter pilots fall into this category, as do other military occupations, air traffic controllers, and to some extent commercial pilots and police officers. But athletes do as well. Of course, the stakes aren't life-and-death, but for quarterbacks reading defenses in the face of a rush; point guards racing up the court and deciding whether to pass or drive to the hoop; hockey goalies staring down a power play; and hitters wondering what's coming next from the likes of a Josh Beckett or a Johan Santana—a 97 mph fastball, a 92 mph slider, or a 78 mph changeup?—the required skills are parallel. And the research questions are essentially the same. What kind of person can move most quickly from perception to cognition to action? And what can be done to train already skilled people to do it better?

Secrist had a lifelong interest in sports and liked the idea of studying athletic performance. But he also knew that the testing and training of athletes was already an international industry. Secrist's partner, an air force scientist named Bryce Hartman, suggested that the sports official might benefit from their expertise as well.

"Dr. Hartman said to me, 'You know the athletes get everything, but the people who officiate the games essentially get nothing,'" Secrist recalled. "'Why don't we see if anybody's interested in moving what we do to that side of sport?'"

So in June 1992, the pair sent queries to the NFL, the NBA, and Major League Baseball, explaining who they were and how they might improve the performance of league officials. The first two were lukewarm in their responses; if baseball went ahead, they'd monitor the results. But baseball's interest was legitimately piqued. The commissioner, Fay Vincent, wrote a letter to Hartman and Secrist saying he was impressed with the design of their program and the plans described in their proposal, the sexiest element of which involved an electronic flight simulator that was already being used to train fighter pilots. Essentially a highly sophisticated video game that tested and measured pilots' reactions in simulated battle situations, the machine that Secrist and Hartman had developed could be adapted, they were certain, to allow umpires to practice calling big league pitches in a virtual environment. A 98 mph fastball is, after all, the umpire's equivalent of an incoming missile.

Vincent was their natural ally. Like his two predecessors, Peter Ueberroth and especially A. Bartlett Giamatti, he was an admirer of umpires. His father had been one—an amateur, that is—and had fixed in him the idea that umpires were proud, working-class men who genuinely felt the importance of making sure a game was played by the rules and who ought to be treated as pillars of the sport.

"My father would make twenty-five bucks on a Saturday doing a high school game," Vincent recalled for me. "During the week he'd go out after a day's work to umpire a softball game, for which they paid him five dollars. He smoked cigars, and he explained to me, 'If I do a few softball games during the week, I can buy my cigars.' I used to go with him sometimes, and I learned how serious they were about what they did, and how upset when something went wrong. Whenever somebody yelled out, 'Kill the umpire,' I felt bad. It was my father."

What appealed to Vincent most about the Secrist/Hartman proposal was that it treated umpiring seriously, as a legitimate profession, with respect for its complexities and nuances. The first element of the proposal was for a detailed study, based on extensive interviews with umpires, of the work that they do, in order to break down the profession to its parts, its individual tasks and individual required skills, in much the same way that a kinetics- and physiology-minded batting coach would break down the mechanics of hitting.

"The key to developing any effective training is understanding the performance requirements, and that takes a lot of front-end analysis," Secrist explained to me. "A lot of research. A lot of spending time with people who are very effective at these positions to begin with. And that's seldom done except when the stakes are great, like in the military. I don't believe anyone had ever brought that kind of thinking to officiating before."

As the commissioner, Vincent had been astonished by the disdainful attitude that the men who hired him, the major league club owners, expressed toward the umpires. He thought it was inexplicable and mean-spirited, not to mention wrongheaded, bad business. It's not that the owners were against umpires, exactly, Vincent said; they just saw them as low-level employees, no more necessary or significant than groundskeepers, janitors, or popcorn vendors—human expenses.

"When I came in, the attitude of the owners was really bad, and it's only gotten worse," he said, when I met him in 2006. In fact, he was still railing about their dismissiveness and condescension toward the men who were literally their representatives on the field.

"No other sport organizes its officials this way," he said. "No other sport depends on individuals paying their own way into schools you have to go to. But the bigger theme is umpiring is one of the last vestiges of nineteenth-century structure in baseball."

Unfortunately for Secrist, that September, just weeks after expressing interest in his proposal, Vincent resigned as commissioner following a vote of no confidence by the club owners. Bud Selig, then the owner of the Milwaukee Brewers, replaced him, and his view of protecting "the best interests of baseball," as the commissioner's role is defined, set the stage for the confrontation between umpires and baseball in 1999.

But that's getting ahead. Even after Selig took over, Secrist had reason to think baseball would remain interested in his umpiring plan. In November 1992, he submitted an update of its technical aspects, specifically a detailed description of the adapted simulator, to Bill Murray, then baseball's executive director of operations. Murray was intrigued enough that a series of meetings ensued over the next eighteen months between various baseball officials and various faculty from Southern Utah University. The meetings took place all over the country, in New York and Denver and most crucially, in August 1993, at Brooks Air Force Base in San Antonio, where Marty Springstead, then the American League executive director of umpiring, his associate Phil Janssen, a former minor league umpire, and Ed Lawrence, the head of baseball's now defunct umpire development program, witnessed a demonstration of the specialized flight simulator for fighter pilots— known as the Situation Awareness Training System (SATS)—that Secrist and Hartman had designed. Springstead actually got in the simulator, and more than a decade later he recalled how realistic and furiously paced the experience was.

"I had to shoot tanks and planes—this was around the time of Desert Storm, remember," he told me. "Believe me, I didn't even have a chance to pull the trigger, those things were moving so fast past me."

The excitement from that meeting, according to Janssen and Springstead, was palpable. They heard Secrist explain (as he would to me) that the key to succeeding in a high-performance task is experience; for example, the more missions a fighter pilot flies, the greater his chance of survival. The idea is to build the kind of familiarity with what needs to be done so that you do it with seeming mindlessness. It's not mindless, of course, Secrist told them; you just get so accustomed to looking for certain mental cues that you're able to pick them up and process them with increasing alacrity. That's what the simulator is for, to give pilots a sense of having been in a dogfight before they get in one for real, and between battles to keep their human instruments tuned.

"Repetition is critical and there's a good analogy," Secrist said. "In weight training, the same way physical reps build muscle, mental reps build cognitive processing power."

This is equally true for umpires. But unlike a hitter, a pitcher, or a fielder, an umpire can't practice, at least not on his own. He needs a game. A major league umpire who works thirty-five plate games in a season, a reasonable number, will call roughly fifty-six hundred pitches.* Theoretically, Secrist said, with simulators available in every umpire locker room, umpires could see the equivalent of that many pitches every week. But Secrist emphasized that the simulations needed to achieve verisimilitude.

"You're teaching people to respond to very subtle cues that are present for very, very brief periods of time," Secrist said. "What you train them on has to look exactly like it does in the task environment. For a fighter pilot in penetration mode, flying six hundred miles per hour fifty feet off the ground, your training method has to look just like it looks out the windshield. So if you're going to develop an umpire training system, that ball coming over the plate has to look just like it does from behind the plate."

The effectiveness of the simulator, therefore, would depend on detailed information provided by umpires in research interviews. And the simulator was only a piece of what Secrist saw as a thorough revamping of baseball's system of training and evaluating umpires.

The machine would have graduated levels of difficulty, and one could, theoretically, program specialized situations. If an umpire was having trouble, say, fixing the upper limit of the zone, he could watch five hundred pitches in a row just above or below the letters. If he was struggling with hard breaking balls from a left-hander, he could dial up a diet of Randy Johnson sliders. If he was going to face a knuckleballer the next day, he could insert the knuckleball CD-ROM and watch knuckleballs until he went cross-eyed. If he had a bad game against, oh, Roger Clemens, the next time his crew went to Boston—this was 1993, remember, Clemens was still with the Red Sox—he could prepare by watching Clemens's last three games beforehand.

---

*In 2007, major league games averaged 287 pitches, but on average only 159.4 were called balls or strikes. The rest were swung at.

"We left there, and the idea was we were going to build these simulators and put them in the locker rooms," Springstead said of the meeting in San Antonio.

Ed Vargo, Springstead's counterpart in the National League, didn't share in the enthusiasm. He was an old-school umpire with Luddite tendencies for whom the ways of umpires would never change. And he was perfectly representative of his staff, which was older than the American League's, tied to the leadership of the union, and deeply suspicious of anything that would alter long-established tradition.

Vargo, who died in 2008, was known for his stubbornness and his foul mouth, but when I met him at his home in Butler, Pennsylvania, he couldn't have been more charming. He told me a story about Fred Hutchinson, the old-time manager of the Cincinnati Reds who died of cancer in 1964 and stayed in the dugout nearly to the end of his life. Hutchinson was renowned as a tough, tough guy, especially brutal on umpires, who hated him and respected him equally. During one game in the months before he died, Vargo threw him out of a game. "I hope you get what I got," Hutchinson screamed back at him in anger.

"But when the game was over, we left the field and there was a knock on the door, and it was Fred Hutchinson," Vargo said. "He was crying. He said, 'I'm sorry I said that to you, kid. You don't deserve it.'"

Vargo passed his antipathy for the simulator along to most of the umpires in the National League, as well as to Len Coleman, the league president. It was one of many issues that divided the two umpiring staffs, which, like Democrats and Republicans in the Senate, served together but sat on opposite sides of the aisle. The opposition to the simulator was partly pride—why do we need a machine to help us do what we do better than anyone else in the world already?—and partly a fear that baseball's administration would use it not to help umpires but rate them.

"The umpires were divided," Bill Murray said. "Those that didn't like it would say, 'How do you know how it's gonna be used?' or 'The hell with it, I don't need it.' And there were others who were afraid of it, afraid they'd be graded."

Even so, by mid-1994, Secrist was certain that baseball was on the verge of funding an umpire training program based on his proposals. Murray was a supporter, especially regarding the simulator, though he predicted that amassing the software—the individual games and pitches to be simulated—would be time-consuming and labor-intensive.

"I liked it," he said. "I had wanted to build a virtual room, where you could call balls and strikes off a screen that gave you depth perception. But I liked the way [the simulator] was designed. The technology was there. It was a question of getting the library material together. And I always felt the money was not that great, not in comparison to what you'd get, an improvement in a guy behind the plate, an improvement in the quality of the game."

But later that summer, on August 12, with the collective bargaining agreement between players and owners having expired, major league players went out on strike to protest the owners' demand that they accept a team salary cap in the next agreement. The walkout lasted until the following spring and forced the cancellation of nearly a thousand games, including the whole 1994 postseason. It was the first time in ninety years baseball hadn't had a World Series, and the financial hit absorbed by the owners caused them to call in all their risky chips. Forward-looking projects, such as a new training system for umpires, were nixed.

"We had a full-blown technical proposal to build an umpire training simulator; we called it UTS," Secrist said. "In August, it was ready to be approved. Bill had asked for résumés on the R-and-D team. Then the strike happened and everything changed. Everybody wanted to know about money then."

Phil Janssen was a tightly wound former college ballplayer and minor league umpire who had long been convinced that professional baseball's development of umpires was inadequate. By the time I met him, in 2006, he had become the administrator of the World Umpires Association, the major league union, but in 1993, he was working for the major leagues' umpire development program, a precursor to PBUC.

Janssen first encountered Grant Secrist at the simulator demonstration in San Antonio, and impressed by Secrist's scientific approach to the umpire training, he became something of a protégé. The two men began to work closely in developing a comprehensive program for umpire evaluation, which ultimately became the basis for Janssen's dissertation for a doctorate in education that he submitted in December 1996.

Written in the jargon of academe and replete with data analyses and field survey reports, Janssen's dissertation is not exactly a readable document, but it does provide, in highly specific detail, a set of standards for umpire performance and a method for observing and measuring individual umpire skills, something baseball had never had. Even so, when Secrist presented the program to baseball, it was received with indifference.

By then, Janssen had gone to work for Marty Springstead as coordinator for umpire operations in the American League, and he and Secrist—especially Secrist—embarked on a sincere effort to badger baseball into accepting their plan. For the next four years, Secrist sent letter after letter and proposal after proposal, first to Bill Murray, then to Murray's successor, Sandy Alderson, to try to convince them it was in baseball's best interest to invest in a scientifically based program of umpire development. According to the detailed notes he kept on the process, he made little progress.

"The NL and AL presidents have shown little interest in the field test findings and new umpire performance rating forms," he wrote in August 1996. "MLB continues to use haphazardly developed umpire performance evaluation tools."

In April 1997, Secrist and his colleagues at Southern Utah submitted an offer package to Major League Baseball that included a description of the simulator, a phased schedule for its development, and a budget. Baseball demurred; instead of investing in umpire development, the owners voted to withdraw its funding for umpire development altogether, relegating training and supervision entirely to the minor leagues.

Secrist and Janssen were profoundly dismayed that baseball didn't respect the science of their program, which they viewed as proof that they could improve umpire training with the multipart program they had devised. They also felt they had been misled by baseball's administration about its interest in their work, which ended up costing them a lot of time and money. Finally, in February 1999, baseball requested that Secrist and his corporate partner, Sygenex/SCS Technologies (which would build the machines from Secrist's design), deliver a formal proposal for the financing and construction of the simulator (UTS)—and an additional system for measuring the strike zone and assessing umpires' ball/strike decisions, which Secrist would call SilverStrike. (In essence, it was a version of QuesTec.)

For the next two months, according to a summary of events written by Secrist in 2008,

> intense scientific-engineering effort and substantial financial resources were invested to design a UTS simulator that . . . could deliver many thousands of repetitions of realistic game situations and related field awareness, situation assessment, and real-time decision demands. The UTS simulator was designed to present authentic game situations from multiple visual perspectives, field positions, viewing angles, and distances. The UTS design also included provisions for realistic environmental conditions including: (a) day or night games; (b) daylight conditions ranging from bright sunlight to total overcast; (c) unique night lighting associated with actual stadiums; (d) glare resulting from low sun angle, haze, and stadium lighting; (e) and weather such as mist and rain. A formal technical and cost proposal that included the foregoing design features was submitted to MLB on 27 April 1999.

While development work continued on both SilverStrike and UTS, Sygenex and baseball negotiated over the purchase and appropriate deployment of the technology. But an agreement was never reached, and in early 2000, the negotiations were abandoned. The 1999 union implosion had resulted in a new hierarchy administering the umpires (see Chapter 7), and according to Phil Janssen, baseball wanted the simulator and was prepared to pay $2 million for it. It was not, however, prepared to assure Secrist that it would be used as part of the entire program they had designed, and he turned the offer down.

For one thing, Secrist didn't simply want to sell the simulator; he had expected to be involved in setting up baseball's new model for umpire development. But second, as a scientist, Secrist thought it was anathema for baseball to pick and choose the elements it wanted from a system that had painstakingly been developed as a whole. Without proper training for the umpires in the simulator, without the prescribed training for umpire evaluators, and without the application of performance standards developed by Janssen, he thought the simulator would end up being not much more useful than video games.

He also saw the possibility that, as some umpires had feared, baseball would use it to evaluate umpires rather than train them, which is exactly what happened with QuesTec, the pitch-calling technology that baseball did finally invest in.

"Our goal was to provide umpires with the advanced training technology to reach full performance potential," Secrist wrote.

> In the process, the means of achieving this goal would be placed in the hands of individual umpires. Our leadership approach emphasized scientific principles and ethics, open and honest communication, objectivity and transparency, and meaningful umpire involvement. Our goals and means were in *complete opposition* to the new umpire administration's insistence on total control, autocratic management, and arbitrary decisions. Under such conditions, there was a real danger that our . . . technology would be used to consolidate power, exploit individual umpires, and promote cronyism—clear violations of scientific ethics.

Instead of making a deal with Secrist and Sygenex, baseball made a deal in 2001 with QuesTec Inc., a digital technology company based on Long Island that had financial problems—it was undercapitalized—and whose founder and major stockholder, Edward J. Plumacher, had a history of unpaid debts and dubious stock deals for which he'd been investigated by the Securities and Exchange Commission and barred by the American Stock Exchange from working for any member of the exchange. His company had been fined twice by the New York State attorney general. The baseball deal, which was reportedly worth $520,000 for five years (and was reportedly signed without alternative bids), was an agreement to develop "a state-of-the-art pitch measurement and reporting system," as the company refers to it, and it gave the company, which was founded in 1987, its first profitable quarter.

The QuesTec Umpire Information System is a network of cameras set up in the stands along the first- and third-base lines whose photographs are analyzed by computer to track the path of a pitch and determine where it passed by the batter, in or out of the strike zone. The system operator records the umpire's calls, and the calls are matched against the system's results, which the company says are accurate to within one-half inch.

The day after an umpire works behind the plate in a ballpark where the QuesTec system is installed, he is provided with a CD-ROM on which all of his called pitches have been recorded, their paths charted and diagrammed. The umpire is graded on his accuracy.

The system was implemented for the first time, ostensibly on a trial basis, in Fenway Park in Boston in 2001, and in eight stadiums in 2002—through 2008 it had never been in more than thirteen of the thirty ballparks—and it caused immediate mayhem. The umpires were confused and nervous about being watched and graded. They said the system was inaccurate and that it was unfair to have non-umpires operating it. One thing the operators had to do was set the upper and lower boundaries of the strike zone for each hitter, and they were inconsistent in their settings, the umpires said, and often just plain wrong. A series of lawsuits and filings for arbitration ensued.

The players weren't happy either; they were frustrated by what they perceived as different strike zones being called in QuesTec parks and non-QuesTec parks, and they complained that umpires were apologizing to them for calling the strikes well above the belt the electronic system insisted they call, and for not calling the ones just off the plate that the players were used to. The pitcher Curt Schilling, then with the Arizona Diamondbacks, became so irritated that in May 2003 he destroyed a QuesTec camera with a bat.

Eventually players either adjusted or didn't. For some pitchers, older ones whose fastballs had tapered off and who needed the outside strike as a weapon—the left-hander Al Leiter is an example—QuesTec and the new strike zone hastened the end of their careers. Tom Glavine, who moved from the Braves to the Mets in 2003, had the two worst seasons of his career in the first two years of QuesTec, but by 2006 he was back at the All-Star game, where I met him. It took him more than two years, he said, to change his pitching patterns and become effective again.

"I had to learn to stretch the zone north and south instead of east and west," he said.

For umpires, much of the adjustment was colored by resentment; the union fought legal battles over QuesTec for three seasons, and in the end baseball was forced to concede that at least some of the umpire complaints were legitimate. In the compromise that was eventually reached, baseball allowed umpires a two-inch buffer around the edges of the strike zone, meaning they could call strikes two inches off the plate and still be graded acceptable by QuesTec.

The first several years, Frank Pulli, a former umpire, examined the

QuesTec tapes and counseled umpires afterward, urging them to be more careful, say, on pitches outside and low. When Pulli, in poor health, retired in 2007, the job was taken over by a non-umpire in baseball's New York office, Fred Seymour. The contract with QuesTec had meanwhile expired, but it was being extended year by year while baseball was developing its own system.

I went to see Seymour in the spring of 2008, and he demonstrated his job for me, explaining how he adjusted the scores by examining the film of each pitch that the system had determined was incorrectly called by the umpire.

A diligent young man, Seymour told me: "I want to get every pitch right, just like the umpires do. Conceptually, there are a few ways to adjust a pitch. You look at one low in the strike zone, but it's caught so low that public perception would say it was too low to be called a strike, even though it passed through the QuesTec strike zone. In an instance like that, both are correct, the machine and the umpire. So it wouldn't count as an incorrect call."

He went on: "Then there's something called catcher influence, when the catcher makes an extreme reach, where he has to reach across his body, and the umpire is influenced by that in calling the pitch a ball."

That, too, Seymour said, rates an adjustment.

In other words, umpires still weren't being required to call a rule-book strike zone. The outside strike was reined in a bit; the high strike was called more often. But beyond that, umpires were allowed to do pretty much what they were doing before QuesTec came along. By 2006, baseball was routinely bragging that all its umpires had QuesTec scores well above 90 percent, but with all the adjusting, that doesn't mean much, does it? It's not as if arguments over balls and strikes have receded from the game.

In the end, QuesTec changed the shape of the strike zone modestly, encouraged more uniformity; it marginally improved the public perception of umpires, perhaps, but it was never supposed to help the umpires themselves or to improve umpiring, and it didn't.

Secrist didn't have any quarrel with QuesTec; in fact, his own system, SilverStrike, was based on similar technology, and he was willing to give it to baseball free as part of the implementation of his training and evaluation program. What Secrist abhorred, of course, was how

QuesTec was developed—without umpire participation—and deployed.

He wrote a critique of the system, one of a myriad of papers and analyses he produced between 2000 and 2008, most of them vehemently critical of baseball's administration.

In July 2002, for instance, he sent one such analysis, entitled "Mismanagement of Professional Umpires," to Larry Gibson, then the lawyer for the World Umpires Association, which had taken over as the umpires' union after 1999. By December, he was writing to Gibson again, but this time to criticize the union for its complicity in baseball's sins against umpires. "There is a perplexing disconnect between the severity of MLB's mismanagement and the timidity of the WUA response," he wrote.

By July 2003, when he sent off the QuesTec critique—to the union, its lawyers, and to Sandy Alderson—his effort had begun to seem quixotic.

"MLB erroneously believes the strike zone can be changed by edict," he wrote. "Well-defined strike-zone decision standards, an appropriate training paradigm, deliberate practice, and intense repetition are required to change an umpire's mental model of the strike zone and re-establish high-level performance. This is an arduous and intensive process."

In 2006, when I met Secrist, he was still at it; he'd just finished a critique of baseball's newest effort to recruit more blacks into umpiring, a youth academy in Compton, California. I asked him why he persisted after baseball officials had made it clear they weren't interested in what he was trying to sell.

"One thing is a real interest in the science of a high-demand profession," he said. "But second, I've always been fascinated by the guy in the arena, the guy that actually has to perform under great stress. The guys carrying the freight always interest me, and I have very little patience for people who were charged with leadership for those individuals and didn't do it well."

Phil Janssen had another explanation: "When Secrist made his presentation to umpires back in the nineties, he made a commitment. He said, 'I'm a scientist and won't do anything to hurt the profession. I'm going to develop something to train you, make you better, put your destiny in your own hands.' And he stuck with that. Stuck with it so much that there is no simulator right now."

CHAPTER SEVEN

THE 22

We've always had turmoil. We've always had fans against us. We've always had baseball management against us.
—JERRY CRAWFORD, September 2006

You can't replace Ken Griffey Jr. You can't replace Alex Rodriguez. You can't replace Willie Mays. But the umpires?
—REGGIE JACKSON, July 25, 1999

After a decade of one embarrassing defeat after another, Major League Baseball finally found the union it could kick around. . . . So now here are Bud Selig and Sandy Alderson pounding their sunken chests over the firing of 22 men who lost their jobs for no other reason than baseball really needed to beat up on somebody.
—WALLACE MATTHEWS, *New York Post*, September 3, 1999

Okay, 1999.
     For major league umpires it was the Flood, Armageddon, the Civil War—a dividing line in history. Even a brief synopsis of the events of that season gets confusing. But its chief consequences were the consolidation of the umpire staffs of the two leagues, which had been separate entities for a century, and the assumption of authority over the umpires by the commissioner's office.

This was an idea that had been around since at least 1992 as a solution to what baseball administrators thought was a renegade umpire culture, one that fostered too much independence among individual umpires and allowed them too much discretion in reigning over the games on the field. Baseball officials believed that the umpires were generally but not universally skilled and professional, that standards of accountability were not high enough, and that the public perception of the umpires, fed by a disdainful press corps, was that they were arrogant, overweight, lazy, and incompetent.

The solution to all of this, baseball believed, was to enforce greater uniformity on the umpires—in the way they called the strike zone, in their attitudes toward players and managers, in their on-field responsibilities, and in the way they took care of themselves and otherwise conducted themselves off the field. To do that baseball had to eliminate the two-staff structure. And to do *that* baseball had to confront the umpires' union, which is what finally happened.

But like any pivotal event, the umpire cataclysm of 1999 can be properly understood—or at least better understood—only in a historical context. The entire decade of the 1990s was contentious between the umpires and baseball. And the relevant history goes back a lot further than that, to the evolution of the American and National leagues, their separate umpire cultures, and the crosshatch of loyalties and enmities that arose as a result.

The rivalry dates to the first third of the twentieth century and the two leading umpires of the day, Bill Klem of the National League and Thomas Connolly of the American, both Hall of Famers. Men who saw themselves as lordly giants, they might well be credited with establishing the unassailable demeanor that umpires still, to some degree, believe is required to take the field. But each conceived of his profession in very particular and peremptory terms. Klem, for example, instructed his staff to call balls and strikes from the viewpoint of the slot, whereas Connolly insisted that his staff set up directly behind the catcher.

Klem made sure all National League umpires wore chest protectors inside their jackets, while Connolly favored the outside, balloon protector. Not until the 1970s did the American League begin insisting that all newly hired umpires go to the inside protector.* The reputation of the American League umpires for calling higher strikes than their brethren in the National League—the result, it was always said, of their

---

*The last umpire to use the balloon, Jerry Neudecker, retired after the 1985 season.

restricted ability to crouch with the balloon protector—persisted well into the 1990s.

For decades, the leagues left the hiring, firing, and scheduling of an entire staff to one supervisor apiece, men who vied to hire the best umpires in the minor leagues, a competition that had all the civility of pissing dogs marking their terrain. It was understood that if the American League supervisor took notice of a particular umpire in the minor leagues, that umpire was off-limits to his counterpart in the National League and vice versa. The practice preserved the independence of the two leagues but often worked against young umpires, delaying the opportunities for many to advance to the major leagues.

The differing cultures were cemented in 1963, when the first umpires' union was formed by National League umpires, and the American Leaguers remained unorganized. Five seasons later, in 1968, two American League umpires, Bill Valentine and Al Salerno, were summarily fired by league president Joe Cronin, ostensibly for incompetence, but more obviously because they'd made it clear they intended to join the union and persuade their fellow American Leaguers to follow suit. Afterward, the American League staff was absorbed into the National League union and the Major League Umpires Association was formed.

By tradition, the National Leaguers held themselves superior, partly because they were the first to unionize, partly because the American League—long known as the "junior circuit" because it was founded in 1900, twenty-four years after the National League—was seen as an upstart, even most of a century later. Especially between 1965 and 1985, a period when the Yankees, significantly, were mostly in decline, the National League was widely viewed as superior, with more quality teams and better players overall—during that stretch, the National League won nineteen of twenty-one All-Star games—and better umpires, too.

"Even the work ethic was different in the National League," said Mark Letendre, who was a trainer in both leagues—first for the Yankees and then the San Francisco Giants—before joining the major league umpiring staff as a medical supervisor. "I can't explain why; it just was. And my challenge now, with the American League guy of old, is to try to get him to work, and with the National League guy is to try and get him off the field. So when a guy becomes injured today, if he's an old American League–thinking guy, I've got to push him a little bit. And on the other side, I got to yank the National League guy off the field."

Indeed, by the 1990s, it was widely assumed—and even asserted by general managers and club owners—that the National League umpires were simply more skilled and more authoritative.

"With a few exceptions, all the good umpires were in the National League," Fay Vincent told me.

Whether true or not, many umpires acknowledge this perception had an unhealthy effect on the fraternity as a whole. And it was not entirely a surprise that when the union fragmented in 1999, it was mostly umpires from the American League who led the revolt, and a powerful faction of National Leaguers who were most resentful.

This was only part of the collective umpire psyche, however. In interviews with me, more than one umpire used the term "dysfunctional family" to describe the relations among the former staffs of the two leagues, and one point of the comparison was that just as in a squabbling family, when a threat emerged from the outside, unity tended to prevail.

"The umpires' ability to be symbiotic with baseball just never existed," Mark Letendre said with a shrug.

Indeed, umpires as a whole had long felt that baseball was the enemy, that the game's administrators treated them generally with disdain, rarely supporting them and their actions on the field. For their part, many baseball officials, especially the club owners and general managers, had long been resentful of the umpires, whom they viewed as a separatist cult.

"You never had a good working relationship, in my view, between management and umpire," one umpire with more than a dozen years in the big leagues told me. "They are always looking down at umpires, putting you down, and umpires are always fighting for respect."

The conflict is in some ways endemic to the relationship; the umpires are literally the representatives of baseball's administration on the field, and they believe they should be treated with the collegiality and respect that implies. The club executives nonetheless tend to see umpires as a secondary, diminutive line of authority, sort of the way the police view neighborhood crossing guards. This is especially true of the owners, who, with the imperial instincts of chief executives, are not authority sharers by nature, especially with people at the lower echelons of their payrolls.

By 1999, these innate hostilities had been mounting steadily for two decades, ever since a strike in 1979 had won the umpires the first of several advances in compensation and benefits. Their union leader, Richie Phillips, who was hired as executive director in 1978, had already presided over two other work stoppages, in 1984 and 1995, and established himself as a relentless irritation to baseball's club owners and front-office personnel. Between 1984 and 1992, he was in many ways aided by three commissioners—Peter Ueberroth, A. Bartlett Giamatti, and Fay Vincent—who were hired by the owners from outside baseball and were relatively sympathetic to the umpire cause.

According to Ralph Nelson, an assistant general manager for the San Francisco Giants who would eventually become baseball's vice president in charge of umpiring, the problem of reining in the arrogant and independent umpires was on the agenda at the annual general managers' meeting every year during the 1980s. The concern wasn't about their field work, Nelson told me. Complaints from club management, he said, were only minimally about the umpires' calls or their ability to make them; rather they were about "image, work ethic, hustle, and, most frequently, attitude."

In a 1995 letter to National League president Leonard Coleman, Nelson wrote of "the umpires' lack of trust and respect for leadership" and of an existing public perception "that the industry lacks control over it's [sic] own umpires." In particular, he wrote, "The 'confrontational' demeanor of particular umpires is constantly discussed at the club level."

The letter was accompanied by a proposal Nelson had submitted once before, a detailed plan for revamping the administration of umpires throughout organized baseball. Nelson had first circulated the proposal in the late fall of 1992, when he'd sent it to, among others, Bud Selig, the newly installed commissioner of baseball.

In September of that year, after Fay Vincent had been forced to resign as commissioner, the owners had replaced him with Selig, who, as then owner of the Milwaukee Brewers, was one of their own.*

---

*It was initially an interim appointment, but Selig hung around and hung around in it, and he was officially given the job in July 1998, at which point he transferred ownership of the Brewers to his daughter; the team was later sold. As of 2008, no end to his commissionership was in sight, and he has frequently been referred to, either with disdain or admiration, as commissioner-for-life.

Then, six weeks or so after Vincent stepped down, instant replays showed umpires clearly missing two calls during the World Series (one negated a triple play), and a debate arose in the press about how umpires were chosen for the postseason, with players and writers objecting to the rotation system then in place, which meant the best umpires were often sitting at home during baseball's ultimate games.

Shortly thereafter, Nelson wrote to Selig with an elaborate thirteen-point agenda to reorganize the administration of umpires. Nelson may have been the first to recommend the consolidation of the staffs of the two leagues, and his plan was commended by Selig and several general managers, including Frank Cashen and Joe McIlvaine of the Padres. Fittingly, though everyone seemed to agree the umpires were a problem, they were thought to be a back-burner problem. Other concerns—namely the threat of a players' strike, which eventually occurred in 1994—kept baseball from actively addressing it, at least for another few years. In the meantime, the cold war between the umpires and their employers remained at full chill.

What was probably the pivotal umpire event of the decade occurred during the final week of the 1996 regular season. During a game in Toronto on September 27, home plate umpire John Hirschbeck called Baltimore second baseman Roberto Alomar out on strikes on a pitch Alomar felt was outside, and the two men got into a heated argument, during which Alomar spit in Hirschbeck's face.*

Alomar was suspended for five games, which umpires felt was far too lenient a penalty, and they were especially incensed that he would not serve the suspension until the beginning of the next season so as to be allowed to play in the Orioles' postseason games that were to begin a few days later. In protest, the umpires threatened a walkout, but they were ordered to work by a judge who ruled they'd otherwise be in violation of the collective bargaining agreement. Instead, they settled on a more modest demonstration of their indignation: The umpires working the first two American League playoff series delayed the starts of the games. One crew held up the Baltimore-Cleveland game by seventeen minutes, the other the New York–Texas contest by ten minutes.

---

*Whether Hirschbeck precipitated the act by calling Alomar a name—"faggot," as some lip-readers suggested at the time, or "fucking spic," as one umpire and a former baseball official told me—has never been established.

At the end of 1997, tensions between baseball and the umpires flared publicly again. On October 12, during game five of the National League Championship Series, Atlanta Braves pitchers Greg Maddux and Mike Cather struck out ten hitters, and their counterpart for the Florida Marlins, Livan Hernandez, set a playoff record by striking out fifteen, including Braves slugger Fred McGriff, looking, to end the game, on a pitch that seemed to be at least a foot outside. As was evident on television, the strike zone of home plate umpire Eric Gregg had been so wide all game long that it seemed to warp the very nature of the competition. The Braves were especially flummoxed, managing only three hits and often waving feebly at pitches that were far off the plate but that they were afraid would be called strikes.

"It wasn't like any other game I ever played in," Jeff Blauser, who played shortstop for the Braves and struck out twice that day, told me. "We got out of our game and had to become umps ourselves."

"Eric Gregg caused more trouble at that one game!" Fay Vincent said. "What he did was unspeakable, and baseball has never recovered from it. The umpires never have. The older guys will tell you, it was an unbelievably bad episode. I don't think Eric had a clue."

Gregg, who died in 2006 before I could interview him, was known as a voluble guy, and he compounded the outrage when he boasted after the game: "If you know me, you know my strike zone."

Of course, everyone in baseball knew that umpires saw the strike zone in different ways, at least minutely, but Gregg's statement explicitly violated a taboo. He seemed to be claiming the authority to usurp the rulebook and determine the strike zone on his own.

"That was a big-time blunder," Randy Marsh recalled. "He couldn't wait to get in the interview room and be on national TV."

Even among umpires like Marsh who knew and liked Gregg, his performance that day was viewed as preposterous—and as a catalyst for much that was to follow.

"God bless Eric Gregg," Bill Miller said. "But that was the death knell. That's where all the trouble started."

The 1998 season was a resounding success for Major League Baseball; The Yankees won 125 games and the world championship, one of the great team performances in history. Mark McGwire and Sammy Sosa spent all season in a frantic home run parade, chasing after Roger

Maris's season record and surpassing it. We found out later, of course, that their power was more than likely fueled by illegal steroids, but at the time it was thrilling: "Chicks dig the long ball!" was the pop phrase of the year. Finally banished was the resentment over the players' strike of 1994. Fans came out in droves, beginning the surge in attendance and profits that persisted for the next decade.

It was, however, a dreadful year for umpires, at least in the public eye.

"Kill the Ump" was *Sports Illustrated*'s cover line on October 19. Its story began: "The 1998 baseball season might be the best ever, but the millions of fans tuning in the World Series should be warned that the same cannot be said of the umpiring." Calling for greater uniformity in the strike zone, citing a litany of missed calls, quoting baseball officials who wished to find a way to fire some umpires for incompetence and lamenting the rotation system for postseason assignments, the story was a willfully provocative rant, specifically accusing American League umpire Ted Hendry, "generally considered to be a below-average and over-the-hill ump," of incompetence (without actually making the case) and leaving no doubt that baseball fans should be outraged that the officials of their game were undermining its integrity.

Correct or not, the story certainly caught the extant spirit in the clubhouses and front offices of baseball. When the World Series was over, the players' union indicated to baseball's administration that it was tired of waiting for baseball to improve umpiring and that it intended to publish the results of a players' survey in which umpires were rated.

But the union was dissuaded by Selig—the survey would not appear in print until the following year—who told the union that baseball intended to take steps on its own to rein the umpires in. Selig then named Sandy Alderson, the former general manager and president of the Oakland A's, who had just been hired as Major League Baseball's executive vice president for baseball operations, to take on the oversight of umpires as part of his portfolio.

For the umpires, this was especially ominous. The collective bargaining agreement between the union and Major League Baseball was due to expire at the end of 1999, and with hostilities at a simmer, both sides knew that negotiations were going to be acrimonious. Now the umpires had to deal with Alderson, a former marine with a no-nonsense bearing who had long been known as an umpire critic. He was certain umpires played favorites. He abhorred both the warped strike zone that had evolved in the 1990s and the lack of uniformity with which even that was called. He had blamed the failure of a highly touted pitching prospect in Oakland in the early 1990s, Todd Van Poppel, on the umpires' reluctance to call his best pitch, a curve ball that caught the front lip of the plate before diving toward the ground, a strike.

"There's no question that during my tenure at Oakland there were pitchers who were favored with the strike zone and pitchers who were not," Alderson told me in 2006 in San Diego, where he had taken over as chief executive of the Padres. "Van Poppel had this pitch, a sort of twelve-to-six breaking ball, which was so big that it was impossible to get it called a strike. And that had to do with where the ball was caught, rather than where it passed through the strike zone."

In January 1999, Alderson met with union leaders to discuss the future of baseball's relations with the umpires, and he left a clear impression that baseball wanted to assert more control over them, confirming what had widely been suspected: The commissioner intended to dissolve the league offices and to consolidate the two leagues' umpires under one administration out of the commissioner's office.

The umpires were determined to resist this. They liked their relations with the leagues and the league presidents. The two staffs liked being independent of each other. Most important, perhaps, the veterans of each league liked their routines. They were comfortable in the separate and relatively small circuits of cities they traveled around during the season, and they felt that if they had to double the number of ballparks they needed to be familiar with, and especially the players and managers they would need to know, it would not only be inconvenient for them, it would make their jobs tougher than they already were, probably resulting in lower-quality performance.

In the January meeting, Alderson told Richie Phillips, along with the long-time National League umpire Jerry Crawford, who was then the union president, that he was aware that no official changes could be made in 1999, because to reconfigure the administration of umpires would contravene the existing basic agreement. Nonetheless, he said, they should prepare for a day when umpires would be rated on and held accountable for their performances. In an analogy that would become notorious among umpires, Alderson compared them to Boy Scouts.

Much of what occurred during the next nine months would be

detailed during a subsequent series of arbitration hearings. In one of them, Crawford testified that Alderson had said, "If you have twenty Boy Scouts in a room, out of those twenty you're going to get five Eagle Scouts, you're going to have probably ten who are going to remain Boy Scouts, and you're going to have probably five juvenile delinquents, and what you do is get rid of the juvenile delinquents."

In his own testimony, Alderson took issue not with Crawford's recollection of what he'd said, but with the interpretation of it. He denied the intention was to fire umpires; an evaluation system, he said, would be used "to identify weaknesses" and to give people an opportunity to correct them.

"Yes, at some point there may have to be termination," he said, "but the whole effort is to make sure that that doesn't happen or it happens as infrequently as possible."

Alderson disagreed with Phillips's contention that umpires who reached the major leagues should be anointed forever as the best in the profession. It's human nature, Alderson said, "that people progress or regress on an individual basis," and management's responsibility was to make sure that people kept their performance level high.

"I didn't believe in the notion that once selected as the best, someone remained the best for the next thirty-five years," Alderson said.

The January meeting turned out to be only an opening salvo by baseball management. In February, Alderson sent a memo to umpires and insisted that they begin calling higher strikes, up to the level of two baseballs above the belt, a dictum perceived by the umpires as a redefinition of the strike zone, essentially a rewriting of the rulebook, an act not within the jurisdiction of the commissioner's office.

At the same time, Major League Baseball was arranging a series of exhibition games between the Baltimore Orioles and the Cuban national team, a dicey enough enterprise, umpires aside, that required negotiations with the Players Association, the State Department, the Department of Naturalization and Immigration, and Fidel Castro. But the umpires were never consulted, no financial incentive was agreed upon, and they were unilaterally assigned to the games.

The umpires balked at treatment they considered dismissive and refused to work the games, which were held in Havana in March and Baltimore in May; Cuban umpires and American amateur umpires were used instead. Meanwhile baseball presented the umpires' refusal as a bald and greedy play for money.

In March, another memo from Alderson, this time to the general managers of all major league clubs, ordered each to assign a representative to chart the pitches at every home game "in order to monitor compliance with the strike zone directive of February 19." This memo incensed umpires because teams would be assigning people with no umpiring experience to what amounted to a supervisory role. Later that spring, the commissioner's office stung the umpires again by hiring two amateurs—men who had worked as replacements in the big leagues during union work stoppages—as evaluators for minor league prospects.

These were all thumbs in the eye, wedged between the bars of the collective umpire mask. Finally the umpires were ready to take a stand, and on June 30, the union's board of directors authorized a strike vote.

Then on July 2, Tom Hallion, a fourteen-year veteran, was suspended for three games by National League president Len Coleman for having allegedly bumped a catcher and a coach of the Colorado Rockies during an argument.

Umpires felt that the suspension was a retaliatory gesture, meant to caution the umpires against moving to strike; the game in which the Hallion incident had taken place occurred before the strike vote authorization, but the suspension ruling came afterward. It was almost certainly meant as a warning that stricter accountability and tighter discipline were on the way; no umpire had ever before been suspended for actions during an argument. In fact, in 1990, Fay Vincent intervened to *prevent* the suspension of Joe West by the National League president at the time, Bill White, after West had had an altercation with a Phillies pitcher, Dennis Cook, and Cook ended up on the ground.

Besides, there was some question whether Hallion actually did what he was supposed to have done; his crew chief, Terry Tata, claimed there had been no contact at all.

"If any discipline was warranted," Richie Phillips told the *New York Times*, "it should have been levied against the pitcher, catcher, and manager who incited the situation, physically and verbally threatened the umpire, and flaunted"—he meant flouted, of course—"the umpire's authority."

In sum the episode was an almost perfect representation of the blustery standoff between baseball and the umpires, with each side flexing its muscles and asserting a kind of sovereignty, both recognizing that a climax was imminent.

On July 5, a letter was sent out over the signatures of Phillips and Crawford to all members of the union, declaring that "the relationship between the Major League umpires and Major League Baseball has degenerated to an all-time low." It listed the offenses of the previous months, derogated the league presidents—Coleman and, in the American League, Gene Budig—for not standing up for umpires, and summoned all members to a meeting to be held during the All-Star break.

"It is painfully obvious," they wrote, "that Baseball evidences little or no respect for its umpires and their enormous contribution to the game. It is equally obvious that Baseball is engaging in deliberate acts of provocation in order to pander to misguided media pundits and the Players' Association."

The meeting took place in Philadelphia on July 14, and it changed major league umpiring forever. Though an informal poll of union members indicated that they felt baseball had transgressed the basic agreement and that therefore a strike was called for, Phillips thought a work stoppage, which was expressly prohibited by the agreement, might well be forbidden by the courts, as had happened following the Hirschbeck-Alomar incident. He was fearful that public opinion would tilt away from the umpires even further and be seized upon by baseball as an opportunity to dismantle the union.

So he proposed an alternate strategy, namely that the umpires resign their jobs en masse, as of a specified date in the future, September 2, with each of them laying claim to a severance payment that the basic agreement mandated for voluntary termination.

The logic was that the owners would thus be motivated to open contract talks before the resignation deadline—the termination pay for all the umpires would amount to $15.5 million—and the union could begin to address the issues that worried them. Phillips also proposed that the umpires form their own company, Professional Umpire Services Incorporated, and give baseball the option of relinquishing the administration of the umpires altogether and simply outsourcing the job to the umpires themselves. Union members voted to accept the strategy.

In twenty-two years of representing the umpires, Phillips had won mammoth gains for them in compensation and benefits—umpire salaries had increased by nearly 500 percent—and earned the admiration and loyalty of many union members. But not all. His closest associates among the umpires, Bruce Froemming and Jerry Crawford, were National Leaguers, and he had a friendship with Len Coleman, the National League president.

But a handful of umpires, largely in the American League, were critical of Phillips's autocratic control of union matters, his belligerent personal style, and the exorbitant administrative fees and commissions he was taking for his services. Over the winter, a small faction, led by John Hirschbeck and Joe Brinkman, had already begun lobbying other union members to support them in a bid to unseat Phillips.

Those who remained loyal to Phillips believed Brinkman and Hirschbeck were motivated by petty selfishness. Phillips had stood in the way of an appearance by Hirschbeck and other umpires on the game show *Family Feud*, and Brinkman was irked that Phillips hadn't lobbied harder to protect his status as crew chief. Whatever the case, in the end, the lack of unity behind Phillips became his undoing.

"There had gotten to be such animosity between Richie and the league office that a lot of guys thought that limited his effectiveness," Randy Marsh told me. "He got real vehement at times; there's a story about him throwing a chair against a wall. It's more businesslike than that now, no more of the ranting and raving."

Accounts of the July 14 meeting vary. Phillips, whose lawsuit against Major League Baseball was still being litigated when I tried to reach him, has rarely spoken to reporters since 1999, and he was seriously ill. His law partner, Patrick Campbell, didn't respond to my interview requests. I did speak to Jerry Crawford.

"We discussed strategy for four or five hours with the membership," he told me. "We had a good frank discussion, and when we came out of there, we were unanimous, with the exception of the guys who didn't show up. It ended up being a failed strategy because we didn't stick together, and that's really the end of the story. It happened under my watch, and it's something I'll regret till the day I die."

But Jeff Nelson, who had just joined the umpiring staff of the National League that spring, recalled feeling bullied.

"It was my first union meeting," Nelson said. "It was the first time I met Richie Phillips. There had been kind of a growing drumbeat through the rumor mill that a crisis was coming up, that baseball wasn't going to negotiate with us. But I've since realized that there are certain people who create panic so they can come in on the white horse and save the day. Am I talking about Richie Phillips? Yes."

The strategy to resign, Nelson said, was a surprise to everyone in the rank and file, and in retrospect he felt manipulated.

"Create a panic situation, offer a drastic, rushed solution, and get people to quickly sign on the dotted line before they have a chance to sort it all out," Nelson said about Phillips's strategy that day. "I regret my decision to resign. It was a mistake on my part, but I trusted the attorneys to have researched and thought this out. I assumed they were competent and that they had a strategy that was well planned and that they thought of contingencies. I was very nervous about it. I'd worked ten years to get my job and three months later, I was resigning it, walking the plank. I assume responsibility for what I did, but I also think it was a huge mistake, and I have serious issues with the way the meeting was conducted and the way things were run."

At the end of the meeting, fifty-four umpires—thirty-four National League umpires, twenty American League umpires—signed resignation letters, which were forwarded to the league offices on July 15.

Sandy Alderson's immediate reaction was widely quoted: "This is either a threat to be ignored or an offer to be accepted."

Over the next week, as the reality of what they had done began to sink in, the resolve of the umpires began to come apart. Wives, appalled that their husbands had resigned their jobs without consulting them, put pressure on them to reconsider; checking with their personal lawyers, many umpires learned that Phillips's strategy was a probable loser, that they were in danger of having committed career suicide. The press was astonished at and disdainful of the hubris.

In only a day or two, rumors began flying about which umpires had rescinded their resignations and who was being contacted by the league supervisors. Most accounts indicate that Marty Springstead, the American League supervisor, was counseling umpires to rescind, and Paul Runge, the National League supervisor, was counseling umpires not to. Wherever the impetus was coming from, by the end of July 22, a little more than a week after the meeting, thirteen umpires had rescinded their resignations, eleven of them from the American League.

The anger that had always simmered in the divisions between the American and National leagues, between the old-guard umpires and the younger generation, between the Phillips supporters and the Phillips detractors, boiled over quickly and furiously, and by the end of July it was out in the open. In the most egregious example of publicly expressed fury, Marcia Montague, the wife of senior National League umpire Ed Montague, wrote a letter to Denise Hirschbeck, wife of John Hirschbeck. In it she referred to John, an American Leaguer who had not attended the meeting and had not resigned, as "a Judas in our midst, who sold us out for twenty pieces of gold" and "an embarrassment to all real umpires."

"You must be very proud of your husband for undermining twenty years of work from an association that has reaped him so many benefits," Ms. Montague wrote.

Meanwhile on July 22, Bud Selig presided over a meeting in Milwaukee that included Alderson, league presidents Coleman and Budig, other baseball officials, and a passel of lawyers. According to testimony at the arbitration hearings, the group was divided. One faction, including Coleman and Budig, advocated a patient and peacefully negotiated resolution to the crisis. There was, after all, no rush, they said; the resignation date was still six weeks away. But the other faction, including Alderson and Selig, were determined to use the occasion to break the union, or at least to assert their control over the umpires. Selig ordered Coleman and Budig to begin hiring replacements immediately. That day. One of the first National League hires was Brian Runge, the son of Paul Runge, the National League umpire supervisor.

Budig allegedly called the order "the vilest thing" he'd ever had to take part in. Nonetheless, he did it, and four days later, the American League staff was once again full. Letters to nine veteran umpires—Greg Kosc, Richie Garcia, Jim Evans, Ed Hickox, Mark Johnson, Dale Ford, Ken Kaiser, Larry McCoy, and Drew Coble—went out over Budig's signature. Their resignations were accepted. As of September 2, they were done.

"Thank you for your service to the American League and I personally wish you the best in your future endeavors," the letter concluded.

The next day, July 27, the union, conceding its actions to have been hasty and ill-advised, withdrew all the resignations, too late to help any of the above nine, but throwing the situation in the National League, which up to that time had received two rescissions and had hired thirteen new umpires, into complete chaos. It had nineteen remaining vacancies and thirty-two veteran umpires wishing to fill them.

Richie Phillips argued that the only appropriate way to fill the slots was by seniority, but Coleman rejected that idea and said he would decide on the basis of "merit and skill." The thirteen umpires who didn't make the cut were Gary Darling, Bob Davidson, Bruce Dreckman, Eric Gregg, Tom Hallion, Bill Hohn, Sam Holbrook, Paul Nauert, Larry Poncino, Frank Pulli, Terry Tata, Larry Vanover, and Joe West.

But that was far from the end of it. The union took legal action, among other things suing in federal court and filing an unfair-labor-practice complaint with the National Labor Relations Board to halt the terminations of the twenty-two contracts, neither of which was successful. Finally, at the end of August, the union filed a demand for arbitration with the American Arbitration Association, and Alan Symonette, a Philadelphia lawyer and experienced arbitrator, was agreed upon by baseball and the union to hear the case. The hearings began that November and, in seventeen separate sessions, many of them contentious, continued through August 28, 2000.

Much of the testimony in the hearings involved Coleman's application of the "merit and skill" standard in determining which umpires would be allowed to rescind their resignations and which would not. Coleman himself would resign in early 2000 because of the reduced responsibilities of the league presidents and because he and Alderson, to whom he was to report, held a mutual disregard for each other. It emerged in the testimony that Coleman was not happy about having to do the firing and hiring. It also became clear that the job was impossible to do satisfactorily.

Coleman rejected several suggestions made by Alderson—including that senior umpires Bruce Froemming, Jerry Layne, and Dana DeMuth be let go, and that Tom Hallion, Frank Pulli, and Paul Nauert be kept—and came up with his own list based on a kind of free-floating set of priorities, including keeping a balance of experienced and young umpires and maintaining an ethnically diverse staff. But there were other, seemingly more whimsical criteria. Hallion was let go, for example, because he had had temperament issues, Coleman said.

Symonette's ruling, issued in May 2001, satisfied neither side. He said that in some cases Coleman "abused his discretion" and ordered baseball to restore the employment of nine umpires.*

In the middle of all this, further complicating the matter of "the 22," as the dismissed umpires came to be called, were the dissolution of the Richie Phillips–led union, the Major League Umpires Association (MLUA)—it was decertified in a vote by union members in November 1999—and the formation of a new union, the World Umpires Association (WUA), in February 2000. Not only did several Phillips loyalists refuse to join the new union, which was led by John Hirschbeck, but the two bodies continued to clash, a dispute that cost several umpires, including Jim Evans, their best chance to return to work. In the summer of 2000, as part of a new collective bargaining agreement, Hirschbeck negotiated a deal with baseball in which ten of the twenty-two would be rehired, six would receive buyouts, and six would retire.†

Under federal law, however, it was the MLUA that remained the authority in the grievances of the twenty-two, and Phillips rejected the deal, saying he wouldn't accept a compromise that sold out some of the union members for the sake of some others. Instead, they'd wait for Symonette's ruling. In that case, Hirschbeck responded, the WUA would go ahead and negotiate a new contract without making a solution to the issue of the twenty-two a priority.

"I, frankly, am not surprised that John Hirschbeck stands ready to cut the twenty-two loose," Pat Campbell, the lawyer for the MLUA, was widely quoted as saying. "I never thought he cared about the twenty-two, anyway. The MLUA never trusted John and was always suspicious of his professed concern for the twenty-two."

At about the same time, however, Richie Phillips gave a speech that seemed designed to undermine any hope that the remaining members of the twenty-two would get the satisfaction they sought. The *Milwaukee Journal Sentinel* reported that Phillips, speaking in mid-August in front of the Fraternal Order of Eagles in Ontario, California, called Bud Selig "the most vile and mean-spirited individual" of his acquain-

---

*The nine who were offered their jobs back were Coble, Darling, Hohn, Kosc, Poncino, Pulli, Tata, Vanover, and West. Coble, Kosc, Pulli, and Tata opted to retire.

†Under Hirschbeck's proposal, the ten who would have returned to work were Coble, Darling, Davidson, Dreckman, Evans, Garcia, Hallion, Hohn, Poncino, and Vanover.

tance, who may have made a fortune in the used-car business but who "gives used-car salesmen a bad name." Phillips said the dismissal of the veteran umpires and the hiring of replacements was "a nefarious, insidious plot hatched one black day in Milwaukee, Wisconsin."

Selig was said to be infuriated. And from that point on the twenty-two were essentially dissolved as a unit for anyone to care about or negotiate for. Between 2002 and 2007, additional legal actions and negotiations resulted in the piecemeal reinstatement of six more umpires.* But Jim Evans, Dale Ford, Eric Gregg, Mark Johnson, Ken Kaiser, and Larry McCoy, men with 142 years of major league experience among them, not only never got their jobs back, but had their severance pay delayed, lost valuable years of vesting in their pensions, and missed out on a significantly better pension plan that was negotiated in the next bargaining agreement.

This was the lingering mess that I walked rather innocently into in 2006. Most of the legal wrangling had been resolved, but the same couldn't be said of the hurt feelings or the personal animosities. Beyond that, the umpires were still accommodating themselves to the new regimen that the commissioner's office implemented for them in 2000 and began, under the supervision of Sandy Alderson and Ralph Nelson, to enforce.

An umpiring handbook, covering all aspects of an umpire's duties, including his attitude and demeanor, was compiled by Nelson and a committee of supervisors and umpires and published in 2002. Its very first page—indeed, its first paragraph—addressed the problem of the perception of umpires by the public and the press:

"Major League Baseball expects energetic and earnest work from each umpire on the staff. MLB Umpires should be focused on every pitch of the game without regard to factors such as the score, inning, weather or standing of the teams involved. MLB Umpires should display hustle, concentration, and an alert, confident demeanor in order to project a professional appearance on the field."

Umpires would be expected to call a uniform strike zone and be held accountable if they did not. Games were taking too long, in the commis-

---

*Dreckman, Holbrook, and Nauert returned for the 2003 season; Davidson, Hallion, and Hickox were reinstated in 2007.

sioner's view, and umpires would be expected to quicken the pace of things; the time between pitches in their plate games would be monitored, averaged out, and used as part of their evaluations. They'd be expected to hustle more, do more running, especially into the outfield on balls near the fence and between fielders; baseball wanted to combat the popular notion that umpires were fat and lazy. There would be no more special treatment, no more coddling of senior umpires.

These dicta, decided on and enforced by Alderson and Nelson, were not unreasonable, really, but they were received by umpires as condescension and chastisement. By the time I met the two men, both had moved on to other jobs, but it's fair to say the umpires still weren't crazy about them.

I spoke to Alderson in his office in PETCO Park in San Diego, where he had become CEO of the Padres. In a wide-ranging conversation, he said that by the time he was called in by Selig to address umpires, their "situation" had gotten out of hand, the result of baseball's long-term negligence of umpire management and Richie Phillips's potent manipulations.

"Historically I don't think the umpires reacted well to friendship," Alderson said. During the 1980s and the early 1990s, under the commissionerships of Ueberroth, Giamatti, and Vincent, "those commissioners who reached out to them," he said, "I think basically the umpires took advantage of these men and their inexperience. Certainly I think Richie Phillips took advantage of that, and I think baseball relied too much on this personal outreach and didn't devote enough time, attention, and resources to the umpires. So what happened was more of an indictment of Major League Baseball than it was of the umpires. If people aren't managed, they'll figure out a way to manage themselves. Someone will fill in the void. Richie Phillips filled in the void. And at some point, I guess like a lot of things in life, the pendulum swings too far in one direction and it has to come back in the other direction."

I said to Alderson that I thought something had been taken away from the game with the various assaults on the umpires' independence, and he nodded. I mentioned a conversation I'd had with the former Mets pitcher Ron Darling, who'd said that during his career, which spanned the years 1983 to 1995 and included time in both leagues, he wanted to know two things when he got to the ballpark: Which way was the wind blowing and who was behind the plate? The variation in the umpiring, he'd told me, was part of what made the game fun.

"You knew Frank Pulli was very aggressive with the first pitch, so if you were anywhere near the plate, you'd get a strike," Darling said. "You knew if Lee Weyer was back there, you'd have a nice big zone. I used to love Dutch Rennert and his histrionics behind the plate. You could hear him in center field. It was a beautiful time for players and umps. Did you get in fights? Yes. Get thrown out? Yes. But let's say you had a tough inning. You thought he'd missed a couple. In those days you could say, 'Hey, Frank, those pitches were outside?' He'd say, 'Ronnie, I had them just off the corner.' He was telling me, 'Move it over a little.'"

Alderson nodded again, but he said baseball had changed. With thirty teams now and the leagues no longer having separate umpiring staffs, not only were there more umpires, but they visited each ballpark fewer times.

"So Ron Darling might come to the ballpark now and say, 'Who's working the plate?' And somebody will say, 'Guccione,' and Darling'll go, 'Who?'" Alderson said. "The point is that predictability is even further reduced nowadays, and the only way you have any ability to enforce the rules is to have everybody get as close as they can to the rule. There's no question you're going to have human variability. But to me, players and fans have a right to some level of accuracy and consistency. And that goes to credibility. The fact is that umpiring today is not what it was back in 1945. Or even 1965. Why is that? Because every game is televised. Because there is instant replay. Because there is something called a K zone." He was referring to a television graphic feature that charts pitches.

"And I used to tell the umpires, 'What I want to happen here, when any new technology is adopted by ESPN or Fox or whomever, is that it'll be used in a telecast to demonstrate just how good you are as opposed to how lousy you are.' That was the goal. Everything else we did was a function of that. Now you have maybe 280 pitches in a game, and 150 or so are called ball or strike. And you can't have respect and credibility if an event that occurs 150 times in a game is totally unpredictable. Umpires have to be credible. And credibility is often a matter of perception."

Whereas Alderson was the chief executive of the umpire operation, the policy maker and theoretician, Nelson was the implementer. He kept track of daily problems, kept tabs on who was having a good year and who was struggling. He gave out the playoff and All-Star assignments, oversaw the knitting together of crews and the construction of the travel-schedule jigsaw puzzle.

"Right after I got the job, there was an article about me in *Referee* magazine," Nelson said to me over dinner near his home in Scottsdale, Arizona. "And they pulled out a big quote: 'My entire goal is to remove politics from umpiring. I want it to be based on merit.' And that was my thing."

But to Nelson, who was by then working for a private company that trains and advises officials for many different amateur sports, that turned out to be a winless proposition. He told me the following story, and though self-serving, it had the ring of veracity:

"This is my favorite story ever, about umpires. I was meeting with the Joint Committee on Training"—the group that wrote the handbook—"which at that time was Tim McClelland, Randy Marsh, and Mark Hirschbeck on the umpire side. And I was the chairman. And these guys come up to New York, and the meeting starts with McClelland pulling out a piece of paper and reading to me thirteen reasons why the morale on the umpire staff is low. I don't remember the last twelve. But number one was that I give Bruce Froemming special treatment, kiss his ass: 'Bruce gets away with things more than the rest of us can get away with, and if you want this staff to be good, you gotta treat him like everybody else.' Well, later on that year, which I think would have been 2000, maybe it was 2001, but later on that year, we had instituted something that had never been done in baseball, and that was we brought the seventeen crew chiefs to the winter meetings. We'd have the thirty managers from all the teams in a meeting, close the door for three hours, Sandy and myself sitting at the front of the table, and the thirty managers, from, you know, Joe Torre on down, on one side of the table, and the seventeen crew chiefs on the other. We'd talk about the strike zone, and then we'd just open it up for communication. It was great! So this one year was in Boston, and now the meeting is over, and Sandy and I want to thank the crew chiefs for flying in during the winter to do this, so we have a luncheon. And so we're sitting around the room, and I'm sitting somewhere having lunch with whoever, and I get a tap on the shoulder and it's Bruce. And he says, 'Can we go talk in private?' So we go into this little ante-room, and it's just he and I sitting at a little conference table, and he says, 'I've gotta talk to you,' and I say, 'Okay, talk to me.' I'd assigned him the first round of the playoffs that year"—not the league championships or the World Series, in other words—"and he looked me right in the eye and he said, 'I was going straight to the Hall of Fame until you got this fuck-ing job.' And I said, 'Excuse me?' And he said, 'You and I've been friends for twenty years, and now that you're my boss, all you do is fuck me. You get every opportunity to fuck me, you screw me, you don't give me the right assignment. I was gonna be a Hall of Famer, then you got this job, and I'm nothing but a first-round umpire.'"

Nelson laughed. "That's Bruce. I said, 'Bruce, let me tell you something. A month ago, the Joint Committee came in and told me their number one complaint was that I was giving you special treatment. And now you're sitting here telling me all I ever do is fuck you. That indicates to me that I must be right down the middle, which is exactly where I belong.'"

That's Ralph.

For his part, Froemming said a conversation took place, but vehe-mently denied ever mentioning the Hall of Fame.

Not surprisingly, it was the older umpires who felt most acutely oppressed by the new rules and regulations.

"It's not as much fun as it used to be," Ed Montague told me at the 2007 World Series, when you'd think he'd be having a great deal of fun. "It's all just a business now."

"I think it was the press," Jerry Crawford said. "The press wanted some kind of accountability. And perception, that was another big word in baseball in '99. Reality didn't matter. I don't believe we were out of control. I do believe we were the only guys out there having fun in the game. Everybody else was turning baseball into a business. So they won. Now we're all doing it as a business, too."

Crawford was probably the staunchest of the old-order guys. As of 2008, he was the only umpire who hadn't joined the new union, the World Umpires Association, whose president, John Hirschbeck, he didn't respect. Nor did he like the path the union had taken, which he saw as appeasement. He believed baseball sought to take the authority of running a game out of the hands of the umpires, and the new union was letting it happen.*

"It's not my idea of a union; it's a company union," Crawford said. "There are more controls on us today than there were back when I ran it, I can tell you that. We have a book today that tells us where we should stand. I understand having a system, but now baseball dictates what side of the base we move to? Come on.

"And baseball gets around it by saying we participated in making the book. But they set down the ground rules. They wanted specific things in the book and they got them. It makes you a robot. And that's really what baseball wants—robots, not umpires."

Of all the umpires affected by the events of 1999, Tom Hallion was probably the guy whose career rode the wildest roller coaster. Hallion was one of three umpires—Ed Hickox and Bob Davidson were the others—who lost their jobs and, to reclaim them, had to return to the minor leagues and retrace the slog up the ladder to the majors.

But Hallion's was a singular case. It was two weeks before the mass resignation, remember, that Hallion got into an on-field argument with a handful of Colorado Rockies during a game in San Diego, during which it was alleged he bumped into a catcher, Jeff Reed. It was, according to Hallion and the other umpires who were present, a fierce but not extraordinary set-to, business as usual on a major league ball field. Nonetheless, it became something of a cause célèbre.

"Mike DeJean was pitching for the Rockies, and there was a check swing," Hallion recalled for me. "And I went to the third-base ump, who was Terry Tata, and he said no swing. And then the guy got a base hit."

Jim Leyland, then the Rockies' manager, came out of the dugout to take DeJean out of the game, Hallion said, and as Tata started down the left-field line toward the bull pen to signal the relief pitcher, DeJean was coming off the mound and yelling at him.

*To lead its bargaining team with baseball, the union had hired a Baltimore lawyer and player agent named Ron Shapiro, who was largely known for a best-selling business book on the art of negotiating called *The Power of Nice*. The Richie Phillips era was over indeed.

"So I go over to DeJean and I said, 'Hey, let's go,' and he went off at me. And I said, 'Get the fuck out of here.' So we went nose to nose, face-to-face. Jeff Reed was catching, and he got between DeJean and me, and he was leaning into me. They said I pushed him."

For initiating physical contact, Hallion was suspended for three games; in 2006, when I spoke to him, he was still angry about it.

"The thing is, there was a lot of shit going on then. Baseball was trying to control the umps, and the American League and National League presidents, baseball was trying to get rid of them," Hallion said. "So Leonard Coleman and Paul Runge viewed this as a way to show Major League Baseball that they had control of umpires. If you look back into that '98–99 time frame, the code word was 'accountability'; 'There's no accountability in umpiring' is what we heard all the time. So what they said was 'We're going to suspend you, to show the commissioner we have accountability.' Should I have been suspended? No. But this was Coleman's and Runge's way of trying to save *their* jobs."

Later that summer, of course, it was Coleman and Runge who determined which National League umpires who had resigned and rescinded would be kept on.

"Not only did they not do what was fair and what was right, they did what was in their best interest," Hallion said.

Hallion worked until September 2, and then flew home to Louisville, Kentucky. "I had my wife and two of my closest friends with me, and we took the red-eye home. And I remember thinking, 'We'll get through this. I won't work the rest of this year, and next year I'll be back at spring training.' But it never happened."

Hallion's case was considered in the Symonette hearings, but though Symonette restored some jobs, Hallion's was not among them. According to his ruling, baseball had been within its rights to consider Hallion a disruptive influence.

"In the end there were three of us," Hallion said. "Me and Hickox and Davidson. We were the only three that wanted to come back, that had a chance of coming back, that physically could come back. But we didn't get our jobs back. We didn't get anything. We were shit out of luck."

By the time 2002 came around, Hallion was working in Louisville as a stockbroker when a possible reprieve emerged. He was told that, along with Hickox and Davidson, he might be considered for readmission to the big league roster if he returned to the minor leagues and proved his mettle all over again.

"I was looking for some way to get back in the race," Hallion said. "I mean, if I'm not in the race, I can't get to the finish line. So one day Jerry Crawford called me and he says, 'We're trying to get you and Bob back.' He told me what would be involved, that I'd have to go back to umpire school. And I said, 'No way.' This was in the fall of 2002. But as we progressed into January and February of 2003, I became more receptive."

At some point that winter, Hallion called Ralph Nelson. "I said to Nelson, 'This is what I'm thinking. Is it a good idea?' He said it would be. But he said there were no guarantees."

Hallion escaped the humiliation of returning to umpire school, but he did have to swallow a large amount of pride. In June 2003, he was hired as an umpire in the New York–Penn League, in short season A ball, near the bottom of the baseball ladder, where he worked the games of the Staten Island Yankees, the Brooklyn Cyclones, the Williamsport Crosscutters, and the Batavia Muckdogs.

"You talk about demoralizing, humbling, embarrassing," Hallion said. "I was back to the two-umpire system. My first partner was an older guy—he was thirty-four—and I worked a month and a half with him, and then the last half of the season, they put me with another guy, a younger guy. They were using me to help him out. I remember there was a Sunday-afternoon game in Oneonta, and afterwards I said, 'Let's go out for a beer,' and he said, 'I can't, I'm only nineteen years old.' I was forty-six, and I was sharing a room with a nineteen-year-old."

In 2004, Hallion took one step up, to the South Atlantic League—still A ball, still the two-umpire system, but a full-season schedule. And that winter, John Hirschbeck, the new union president, called him and said the union had negotiated a deal to bring him back to the big leagues, but it was dependent on some other umpires retiring.

However, not all of them did, so the deal fell through. Instead, Hallion became a substitute, still officially a minor leaguer, but guaranteed a hundred major league games as a fill-in. When I met him in September 2006 in Chicago, during an important series between the White Sox and the Tigers, he was nearly two seasons into this arrangement. He was fifty years old and it had been seven years since he'd lost his secure position in baseball. A compact, dark-haired man with a blunt jaw and a blunt manner, he described himself as a "typical jock" who was "all about being challenged."

His aggressive openness with me was striking. He was personable in that he knew he had a good story that he could tell confidently, and he felt righteous about telling it. He'd been screwed and he wasn't about to take that from anybody, the same way he wouldn't take a lot of guff from players on the field.

"Do I have animosity towards Richie? Absolutely, but not like I have for Runge," Hallion said. "I never got along with Paul. He always had that California ego and awe about him, and he thought he was better than you. I never kowtowed to him, though, and that winds up being another reason that I'm here."

He also had little good to say about John Hirschbeck, a disapproval that was especially grating—for others as well as Hallion—because of Hirschbeck's high profile within baseball. As if the Alomar spitting incident weren't enough, the following season Hirschbeck was the subject of a Pulitzer Prize–winning story by a *Baltimore Sun* reporter, Lisa Pollak, which really was a profile of a grievous and heartbreaking family situation. John and Denise Hirschbeck's two young sons, John Drew and Michael, both suffered from adrenoleukodystrophy, a rare, inherited nervous system disorder that leads to progressive brain damage; it had killed the elder boy, John Drew, in 1993 before his tenth birthday, and Michael's life was in peril. (Happily, when I met him in 2006, he was relatively healthy.) Hirschbeck, nonetheless, squandered a great deal of the sympathy many of his colleagues had for him when he led the opposition to Richie Phillips in 1999.

"When did Hirschbeck get spit on, 1996?" Hallion said. "I'm assigned to work the division series the week after that, but we decide we're not going to work, because we're going to show support for Hirschbeck. Baseball gets a court order, which said we had to go back, but we were all willing to strike, give up working, possibly get arrested. Yet where is John in 1999? You say, well, okay, that's the kind of person he is."

Hallion said we'd have to talk further. He had documents, he said, from the period after the July 14 meeting and a transcript of the Symonette hearings that he'd be glad to share with me. This story needed to be told thoroughly and honestly, he said. He gave me three different phone numbers where I could reach him during the off-season, and through the fall we talked several times, if briefly, trying to arrange for a transfer of documents, and he apologized several times for not having gone up to his attic to find and organize them. I offered to go to Louisville and pick them up myself, even look at them there without taking them.

Shortly after the new year, I called and he didn't respond. Then I called again and the same thing happened. I probably called a dozen more times over the next month, but the calls were ignored. I would learn later that he'd gotten his job restored. Evidently he was nervous about incurring baseball's disapproval for sounding off. The last time I spoke with Hallion, he was in his office, where his secretary usually answered. She must have been at lunch, though, because he picked up his own phone.

"Tom?" I said.

He told me to hold on, waited a few moments, then came back on the line and said he wasn't there.

As of 2008, in the entire history of the major leagues—that is, since 1876—pitchers had pitched only seventeen perfect games: twenty-seven batters up, twenty-seven batters down, no runs, no hits, no walks, no errors, no base runners. The sixteenth of them was pitched by the Yankees' David Cone in an interleague game against the Montreal Expos on July 18, 1999, four days after the Philadelphia meeting in which the umpires had decided to resign.

The home plate umpire that day was Ted Barrett, an American League prospect, a fill-in who had been going up and down from Triple A for several seasons. He hadn't been to the July 14 meeting; he wasn't a union member. But he knew he'd be hired as a replacement if replacements were, in fact, hired.

In 1998, Barrett had been in line to get one of the four jobs that came into baseball with its expansion to franchises in Tampa and Phoenix, but had lost out when the owners voted to realign the leagues a bit, shifting the Milwaukee Brewers—and the new umpires—to the National League. At the end of that season, Don Denkinger retired, but Ed Hickox was named to take his place. Still, three more umpires—

Larry Barnett, Ted Hendry, and Durwood Merrill—were scheduled to retire at the end of 1999, and Barrett was expecting to fill one of those vacancies.

But after July 14, Barrett was faced with the prospect of possibly replacing an umpire who didn't want to be replaced, a potentially serious dilemma. Should he take the job that he would have gotten three months later anyway but help screw the umpires who'd be losing theirs? Or should he turn it down and effectively lose any chance of ever again having the opportunity he'd been working ten years for?

"The games became secondary," Barrett said. "And it wasn't just me, believe me. Guys weren't concentrating. Umpiring was probably at its all-time worst, but we didn't care."

On July 22, when Gene Budig, the American League president, called and offered Barrett the job, he first said no.

"He says, 'Congratulations, we're going to hire you for the major league staff,' as if it had nothing to do with anything," Barrett said.

It took the logic of several veterans—Tim McClelland, Mike Winters, and Jim Evans—to turn him around. The guys knew him, they said, knew he deserved his shot. He wouldn't be considered a scab, they said.

But none of that had been settled on July 18, and it was definitely on his mind when he took his place that afternoon behind the plate.

"It was already a weird day," Barrett said. "I was working with Evans, Meriwether, and McCoy, and it was a getaway day, but we had a strange schedule. We had Atlanta in New York on Thursday, Friday, and Saturday, and then Montreal was coming in on Sunday, Monday, and Tuesday. We were going to do the first game of the Montreal series and then leave. So we were leaving the hotel that [Sunday] morning and we couldn't find the car. Somebody had taken it the night before—it wasn't me—and put it back in the wrong parking place and it had been towed.

"So it just happened that Larry McCoy had his future son-in-law with him, and we piled into his rental car, an SUV-type thing, and because I'm the low man, I'm sitting all the way in the back, crunched in there like the family dog, and I remember pulling into the stadium, peering out the back window like a little kid, my chin on my knees just about, and I'm thinking, 'Hi! I'm the home plate umpire!'"

Occasion and coincidence haloed the game. For one thing, it was the only perfect game in history interrupted by a rain delay. For another, it was the birthday of Joe Torre, the Yankee manager, and Joe Girardi, who would succeed Torre in 2008, was the Yankee starting catcher. For a third, it was Yogi Berra Day at Yankee Stadium, a celebration of the Hall of Fame catcher who was returning to the stadium for the first time in fourteen years, calling to an end his feud with Yankee owner George Steinbrenner. In the very same ballpark, of course, Berra had caught the most famous perfect game of all time, the only one ever thrown in the World Series, by Don Larsen in 1956 against the Dodgers. And most astonishingly of all, Larsen himself was not only in the ballpark, he had thrown out the ceremonial first pitch.

"I remember in the second or third inning, an Expo hitter foul-tipped a ball back and Girardi caught it and turned around," Barrett recalled for me. "He goes, 'That's the first time I've ever seen a foul tip all the way into my glove.' Usually, I guess, your glove is moving in the direction of the ball and it just goes in. He goes, 'I actually saw that ball go in my glove.' Then he said something like 'This is a special day going on here.'

"And the Yankees made some great plays," Barrett said. "Ricky Ledee came in on a ball, a line drive, and it hit him here, on the forearm, popped up, and he caught it. And Chuck Knoblauch, who'd been throwing balls all over the place that year, went into the hole, planted, and threw a strike to nip the guy, an absolute perfect bullet throw. And Girardi made a catch over by the dugout that was great.

"Anyway, about the seventh inning I looked up and I knew [Cone] was facing the minimum. That's something I do in my mind. When I was young, I always liked pitchers' duels, and I'd think, 'Wow, this guy is facing just three over the minimum' or 'That guy's four over the minimum.' So in the top of the seventh the leadoff guy comes up and I'm thinking, 'Hey, he's facing the minimum.' And then I looked at the board and I saw zero hits, but I couldn't remember, maybe there had been a walk and a double play. So I knew it was a no-hitter. I didn't know it was a perfect game until the ninth."

For an umpire, a perfect game is a career-marking occasion, a brush with history. (Only four umpires on the 2008 major league roster could claim they'd worked one behind the plate.) During the game, particularly in the late innings as the possibility of perfection gets closer, there's some pressure. You don't want to screw up the pitcher's shot at a genuine baseball distinction, and you kind of want to be part of it yourself; on the other hand, you don't want to be too generous and help the pitcher too much, cheapening the achievement.*

I found it touching that Barrett's recollection of an occasion nine years earlier was letter-perfect; I went back and checked his description against the box scores and the game accounts. So it was memorable for him. But that week nothing mattered on the field, which is perhaps the most poignant legacy of 1999, the things that might have but didn't matter.

"The game was over, and of course I had this elated feeling," Barrett said. "'This is a piece of history, this is cool.' I got held up a little bit at the airport that night, something with my ticket. We were going to Boston, and I missed the flight, so the guys went without me, and I got in later. So that night I was by myself, thinking about it, and I got a little nostalgic about going to games as a kid with my brother, and we'd say to each other, 'Hey, the guy's got a no-hitter going' and 'Wouldn't it be neat if it was a perfect game?'" which of course never happened. And I thought about playing Wiffle ball in the backyard and trying to get a perfect game.

"And you have to understand. There were constant phone calls going at that time. Everybody was calling everybody: 'What's the info?' 'What's going on?' So people were calling me. I heard from about twelve people that night. But nobody said congratulations. And I did have a period of feeling sorry for myself. For a few days afterwards, I was thinking, 'A perfect game. And nobody cares.'"

---

*Film of Larsen's World Series game seems to show that Babe Pinelli, who was behind the plate that day for the last time in his career, gave Larsen the last strike, a fastball that passed by the Dodger hitter, Dale Mitchell, nearly shoulder high.

CHAPTER EIGHT

Living the Dream,
Such As It Is

In the early days of the game, the umpire had far less important points to decide upon, and far more power for arbitrary decisions. Year by year, however, the revised rules of the game have lessened the opportunities for discretionary action, and transferred to the rules themselves what was formerly entirely in the hands of the umpire to decide upon.
—Henry Chadwick, 1875

Ted Barrett had had a long road to the majors, ten and a half seasons before he landed officially in the big leagues, and it was a poppy seed in his dentures that he didn't get full credit for it. After all, he had been spending his summer days on baseball fields since he entered professional baseball in the Northwest League in 1989. And at the beginning of 2008, he had completed nine seasons as an *official* major league umpire, though he had actually worked his first big league game in 1994.

He considered himself a twelve-year veteran; he had three seasons' worth of games under his belt before he was "hired," so he had twelve years on his pension, and he was twelve years along on the union salary scale. But on Major League Baseball's Web site and in other printed information, all it said was that he'd joined the staff in 1999. That's the information reporters and broadcasters habitually use, so umpires often feel as though they're being portrayed as less experienced than they are.

"They short us all the time, and it irks all of us," Barrett said.

It especially bugged him because, in the wake of 1999, he and the others who were hired during that miserable summer continued to be lumped together, stigmatized as the new guys, the younger generation. Moreover, having filled in at the big league level for five and a half seasons, he'd been thoroughly immersed in the insular culture of the older umpires, the defiance and hubris that was the thorn in baseball's side for so long, and he identified with the older generation at least as much as he did with the generally better-educated and more media-savvy, if not as colorful, younger one. As the 2008 season began, Barrett was forty-two.

At one point I asked him if he thought he could improve as an umpire, and he surprised me by answering like an aging veteran, saying he didn't think so, that the biggest challenge for him from then on was in not slipping backward.

"Anyone with ten years in the big leagues I don't think is going to get better on the field, but the concentration level is going to be what sets you apart," he said. "You're getting older, your joints hurt, your knees hurt. You put on weight, you don't move as well. You kind of lose your willingness to fight. When I came up, some of the older American League guys, that's what got them in trouble. I remember being flabbergasted: 'What are you doing? Pay attention!' The guy's looking up in the stands and they're asking him about a check swing!

"But now I can kind of see how they got to that point after so many years."

A strapping guy with the build of a college tight end (which he had been, at Cal State Hayward), Barrett was especially formidable behind the plate. In a deep crouch and squared to the pitcher, he could have been an umpire advertisement back there, broad-shouldered, lantern-jawed, a roadblock. His strike mechanic was unflashy but emphatic, out to the side, a pump with the elbow, a point with the index finger—a silent pistol shot. His strike call—"Ah-eeee," a gravelly siren with the pitch rising on the second syllable—was loud enough you could usually hear it on television.

He was a devout Christian with a master's degree in biblical studies, and by the time I met him—he spent a few days at umpire school while I was a student—he was studying for his doctorate in theology. He was married to his high school sweetheart, and they had three kids.

Every March at his home in the suburbs south of Phoenix, he threw a big barbecue for all the spring training umpires in the area, major and minor league, and their families, and on the week after every Thanksgiving, he was the host of a Christian retreat at a woodsy church camp in rural Oklahoma, part of a ministry for umpires he had established and appropriately named Calling for Christ. More than once—more than twice, even—I heard other umpires say, "If I had a son, I'd like him to be like Ted," which gives you an idea of how middle-American and mid-twentieth-century the umpire ethos is, and how solidly Ted Barrett fit into it.

But Barrett was a little more complicated than that. I got to know him pretty well, not least because unlike many of his colleagues he was willing to get to know me. We met periodically over two and a half seasons, and he was reluctant to speak candidly only when it came to pointing out the mistakes of his fellow umpires. A soft-spoken, thoughtful guy—"mature" is a good word—who nonetheless liked to ride a Harley and drink beer, he seemed genuinely engaged by the dilemma of reconciling traditional values of all kinds (in morality, in politics, in umpiring) with the contemporary world. And I found him appealingly self-aware; he could say, sincerely, that the Bible is the ultimate rulebook, then laugh at what a cornball he sounded like.

At one point I was trying to explain that over time, a fan's curiosity about umpires extended beyond the safes and outs and the balls and strikes, that people like me began to yearn for a greater, well, intimacy, with the game, and that we couldn't help being captivated by all the private conversations we saw going on during a game, both idle-seeming and purposeful, usually involving umpires. What's everybody saying? Talk about inside baseball!

Barrett knew exactly what I meant. His response was to tell a brief, self-deprecating story about a young umpire and a Hall of Fame celebrity, revealing a little of the character of both.

"I rang up Cal Ripken one time on a pitch that might have been a little outside," he said. "It was one of the first times he'd seen me. He was the baseball king, and I was the mere peasant who didn't serve him his wine on time. He looked back and he said, 'Oh, I highly doubt that.'"

During the off-season between 2007 and 2008, Barrett was at a garage sale in his neighborhood outside of Phoenix one afternoon when he saw a man he didn't know walking up and down the street. It turned out he was a representative from Major League Baseball, and he'd been asking Barrett's neighbors about him.

"I barely knew my neighbors," Barrett said, "and now this guy is knocking on their doors asking questions about us. He asked, Did we live above our means? Did we throw big parties? Did my wife wear jewelry? What kind of cars did we drive? I mean, my neighbors don't know how much money I make. How do they know if I live above my means?"

Anyone who knew Barrett would find the suspicion of him silly. But actually, the snooping was going on in umpires' hometowns all over the country. The previous summer, the basketball referee Tim Donaghy had been caught consorting with gamblers, casting a shadow over the integrity of all professional sports and suddenly making all officiating suspect. There was no evidence that any umpires were corrupt; nor was there any evidence that baseball even suspected any of its umpires of dishonesty. But in the interest of reassuring the fans—and maybe Congress, since the federal government had been growing increasingly disapproving of the management of professional sports—the commissioner's office sought to ratchet up its oversight of umpire security.

Umpires are open about the fact that they aren't angels. They admit they're fond of a dollar and whine loudly and often that baseball undervalues them. They concede there's a profession-wide mentality that takes hold of them in the minor leagues, when angling for every spare nickel becomes a way of life, and even in the big leagues, where they pay for their own lodging out of their per diem, they are wont to cut deals with Marriott or Hilton or Hyatt so they can live as luxuriously on the road in New York and Los Angeles as they can in Cincinnati or Milwaukee. After years of cutting corners in the minors, most umpires are pretty good dealmakers, expert in schmoozing reservations clerks and hotel-chain reps. They have been known to barter tickets and baseballs and autographs for bargain rates. (Though it doesn't always work out. Barrett and a fellow umpire, Lance Barksdale, tried a new and unvouched-for place in Manhattan their first trip to New York in 2008 and ended up in bunk beds in a West Side rooming house.)

There's no evidence, however, that this kind of thinking translates into the way umpires call a game, and they're pretty carefully watched in any case. They are thoroughly vetted when they are hired, and the commissioner's office has unofficial spies in every major league city, cops and other informants who will let baseball know when umpires are spotted in places frequented by known gamblers and other unsavory characters.

I asked probably a dozen major leaguers if they'd ever been approached by gamblers, and not one said he ever had, though it's true, some said, that when you go out in public, you can never be sure whom you're talking to. The guy at the hotel bar who asks what pitchers have the best stuff this year—"That Brandon Webb looks pretty good, doesn't he?"—or whether so-and-so has an undisclosed injury— "Thome's bat looks a little slow, don't you think?"—might just be a zealous fan, but might just as easily have less wholesome motives. I noticed that when umpires were in public and talking to fans they didn't know, they usually claimed not to pay attention to that stuff, which really isn't true.

Umpires were understandably miffed by the investigations into their personal lives—one investigator asked the neighbors of one umpire whether he was a member of the Ku Klux Klan—and they resisted baseball's attempt to implement deep searches into their personal finances. All of it sent the message that they were somehow weak links, and always suspect: Baseball didn't go out and investigate players, did they? And why not? Because the players get paid so much there's no incentive for them to gamble? Okay, just pay us more and you won't have to worry about us either.

"They did fire the guy who asked about the Ku Klux Klan, I'll give them that," Barrett said to me. "But you know, there was no communication with us. If Selig or somebody had come out and had a conference call with us and said, 'Listen, the media is all over us about this Donaghy thing. Can we do something? Can we do a little investigation? We'll make the results public. It'll be good for us, it'll be good for you'—we'd have been fine with that."

Baseball tries to accommodate the preferences of umpires when it comes to creating crews and coordinating travel schedules—but not all that hard. The way it works is this: The supervisors select the seventeen crew chiefs, and the crew chiefs send in their requests for three partners to the commissioner's office, where a supervisor creates the crews, trying to make sure that each chief gets at least one of his choices.

Then seventeen separate schedules are sent to the senior chief, who selects one for his crew, passes along the sixteen that are left to the next senior guy, and so on. The choices are generally made according to when the vacations fall—on any given week, two crews are on vacation, as well as three individual umpires from other crews—and how often the crew will be sent to a city near the crew chief's home. So when all the crews are formed and the schedules selected, every year there's grousing by chiefs who get stuck with umpires they don't know or don't like, and by umpires who end up having to go to, say, Baltimore, four different times and only once to Southern California, where they live.

In 2008, Barrett was set to begin the year as the number two man on Tim McClelland's crew, which opened the season on vacation, a great deal for Barrett, who would simply get to park himself at home in Arizona for another week before heading off to Los Angeles.

But then Larry Poncino, a veteran umpire who'd been hurt after being hit in the mask with a foul ball the previous season, was unable to return; he'd had to have neck vertebrae fused and went on the injured list to rest and consider his future. So baseball's umpiring office shifted Barrett to Poncino's place on Dana DeMuth's crew. There went the week at home; Barrett opened the season in Cincinnati, working with DeMuth, Doug Eddings, and Lance Barksdale. Ten days later, the crew was in New York, and I caught up with Barrett after a three-game series between the Mets and the Phillies.

"In the beginning there's a little anxiety," Barrett said when I asked him about joining a new crew. "If you don't mesh, it's going to be a long season." He'd never worked with DeMuth or Eddings before, he said, and hadn't worked with Barksdale for years, since both were in Triple A.

"Besides, we haven't had a chance to gel," Barrett said. "Lance was out on vacation the first week, then Dana was out for a week, then I'll be out next week. It'll be week five before we're all together." A Triple A umpire, James Hoye, was filling in for a month.

I wondered whether there was such a thing as crew unity, whether having a piecemeal crew affected the job they did, especially at the beginning of the season. Barrett said that working with different partners every day didn't make the umpiring worse so much as working with the same guys every day made it better.

"You do need to get into a rhythm," he said. "For the individual, spring training usually knocks the rust off, but then again, even when you go off for a week's vacation, you have to find your rhythm again. The first game of the series, I was at second and I thought Doug missed a lot of pitches, but his QuesTec score was tremendous, so I learned I can't judge, not even from second base."

I had a bit of a sneaky reason for asking about rustiness. In the final game at Shea, the Mets had won when Barrett called Jose Reyes, the Mets' speedy shortstop, safe at the plate on an impossibly close play in the bottom of the twelfth.

The Phillies manager, Charlie Manuel, had briefly argued on the field, then went in the clubhouse to watch the replay, after which he told reporters, "The guy was out. He didn't make it. Maybe Ted wanted to go home. . . . Maybe he ought to go look at it."

That kind of public comment especially irks umpires, the suggestion that they don't take their job seriously or that they don't understand that the guys who play the game do. Barrett told me he did look at the play right after the game; he had it right, he said.

It's clear, of course, that self-interest can influence one's view of a close call; I watched the replay several times and couldn't call it for sure one way or the other.

"You always look at close calls," Barrett said. "For two reasons. Number one, you hope you got it right. I mean, you don't ever want to miss a play at the plate. The other reason is, if you did miss it, you want to see if you could get a better angle next time. Why you did miss it?

"I'll give you an example. In 2004, the Cubs were playing the Expos in Montreal, and Juan Rivera—he plays for the Angels now—slid in to the plate. Paul Bako was catching for the Cubs; Maddux was pitching. And I remember I got too close to the plate. It was a ground ball to first base, and because plays at the plate are usually from outfield throws, when it's a play on the infield you have no time to adjust. Rivera slid by the plate and got his hand on it, but I was too close, the catcher was in the way, and I deduced that he didn't touch the plate, that he was so far behind it that he couldn't have. As it turned out, it was just a great slide. The Cubs won. Fortunately, it wasn't a one-run game.

"My very next plate job was in Toronto, and I had the exact same play, and this time I moved. I was able to get to third-base line extended, far enough away to get the angle, and Delgado slid in and this time he *missed* the plate and I saw it. And I remember chuckling to myself, thinking if I had done this last week, I'd have gotten the play right. I had arguments on both plays, and in Toronto it was a much better feeling knowing I had it right."

So what about Reyes in New York?

"As soon as the game was over, I went in to look at it," Barrett said. "We slowed it down frame by frame, all four of us, plus the clubhouse guy, and we agreed we got it right. When I made the call, I was ninety-nine percent certain; when I looked at the replay, I saw it was closer than I'd thought. It was one of those plays where it was so close it didn't matter what you call. We have a saying in umpiring: 'If it's a whacker, you didn't miss it.'"

As we spoke about Poncino's injury, Barrett reminded me that he had never missed a game due to injury as a professional umpire, and I reminded him that I was at the game that was his closest call.

It was in April 2006, just a couple of months after we'd met, and once again at Shea Stadium, where Barrett was behind the plate for a game between the Mets and the Washington Nationals. Pedro Martinez was on the mound for the Mets, and he was blithely wild, throwing inside all evening and irritating the Nationals, especially Jose Guillen, a burly and temperamental outfielder, whom Martinez hit twice.

After the second errant pitch glanced off his upper arm, Guillen charged the mound. The Mets' catcher, Paul Lo Duca, tried to restrain him, but Guillen was a much bigger—and much angrier—man, and it was up to Barrett to grab hold of Guillen, who still had his bat, and prevent mayhem.

It was a terrific bit of umpiring, alert, assertive, controlling, and physically forceful; Martinez never even left the mound. But what made Barrett's act especially notable was that the pitch had hit *him* after it had hit Guillen. In fact, it had rammed his throat guard back against his Adam's apple. The next inning, Barrett's throat had swelled, and Jerry Manuel, then the Mets' bench coach, pointed out to him he was bleeding. The crew chief, Rick Reed, was concerned and wanted Barrett to go to the hospital, but Barrett told him it was fine, he'd finish the game. Nonetheless, Reed found a way to overrule him.

"My throat hurt," Barrett recalled. "I had lost my voice and I was trying to call strikes. So I was told, 'The doctor's in the dugout and he just wants to look at you.' But it was a trick Rick had set up. The players were in on it. When I got into the dugout, they stood in the way."

When I spoke to Barrett two days after the incident over the phone, his voice was a little raspy and weak, and he said the doctors had told him not to talk, but he wanted to make sure I understood that he was pissed, that he and Reed had had words. His anger came through even in a whisper. (Two years later he said his singing voice, often put to use at karaoke bars, had not returned to full volume.)

"They made me come off the field, and that was baloney," Barrett said, adding that as a result, if a similar circumstance arose he wasn't likely to acknowledge being hurt.

"You never want to come off the field," he said. "I never have before, and I never want to again."

The incident was illustrative of a couple of things, one being the role of the crew chief, which is basically to be a papa bear, a part that different men play with different levels of paternalism and imperiousness. In the past, the tradition was that by the time a man ascended to crew chief, he had earned the stature of a pasha. He didn't have to handle any of the mundane umpire chores like arranging plane tickets or hotel reservations for the crew; he determined what visitors were allowed in the dressing room and was always the one who spoke for the crew to reporters. Some chiefs were known for their condescension and kingly disdain and for creating resentment among younger umpires.

The Hall of Famers Nestor Chylak and Al Barlick were like that. Jim Evans once got so fed up with Chylak that he flung his mask at him in the locker room after a game. Afterward, he and his fellow crew member Larry Barnett stopped talking to Chylak, and the silence went on for days until Chylak finally broke down and apologized. And Doug Harvey, who became dean of the National League umpires, told me a story that pretty much summed up the education of a young umpire by a chief.

"I broke in with Barlick; he was my crew chief for two years, and he was tougher on me than anybody," Harvey said. "We were in Houston one time, and it was between games of a doubleheader. And Barlick said that Aaron, Henry Aaron, had come down to first base and told him, 'The kid behind the plate told me he missed that pitch, the strike he called on me.' And I said, 'He's full of shit. I never said anything like that.' And Barlick said, 'Well, that's what Aaron told me.' And I said,

'Is that right?' Well, I walked right out the door and into the Milwaukee dressing room, and I went right over to Henry Aaron, and I said, 'Hank, Al Barlick is telling me you said I admitted I missed a pitch. Did I?' And he said, 'No, you didn't.' And I said, 'Will you come over and tell Barlick?' And he said, 'No, I won't.' And I said, 'Well, somebody's full of shit.' And I turned around and walked back and I said to Barlick, 'If this is a hanging party, then why don't we get a fuckin' rope and you guys just lynch me?'

"Now, did Aaron really tell him that? I have no idea."

That dynamic has largely cooled, though not entirely, especially among crews with older chiefs, which is partly what made Barrett bristle at Reed. But a more prominent change occurred less gradually, with the new umpire manual and its new regulations. Much of the independent authority that crew chiefs had long enjoyed was taken away from them.

"We all work the same system now," Barrett said. "But before '99, the chiefs all had different systems, and for guys like me, filling in on different crews, you had to adjust. In the American League there were eight crew chiefs and six different ways to work in the four-man system. If you're working second base and there's a runner at first, on a fly ball between the left fielder and the center fielder, on some crews the second base umpire would go out from the middle to cover that; on other crews the third-base guy would go. On Barnett's crew, they would never rotate; the plate guy would stay home no matter what. Then you go to Garcia's crew, and the plate guy would move no matter what, no matter how many outs, no matter what situation: bases loaded, first and third, nobody on. Didn't matter. Line drive in the gap, the plate guy was going. Then on other crews the plate guy would only go with a runner at first base and less than two outs. For a young guy, without a job yet, it was intimidating."

Barrett's nearly disastrous injury was a reminder, too, of how close umpires routinely come to actual calamity. It's rarely recognized that the job is dangerous, though in 2008, after a rash of serious injuries, it was clearer than ever. On April 26 in Los Angeles, Kerwin Danley was behind the plate when a 96 mph fastball thrown by Dodger pitcher Brad Penny entirely eluded the catcher, Russell Martin, and struck Danley in the mask near his jaw. Danley reacted as though a roundhouse punch had been delivered, straightening up slightly as if with a momentary understanding of events, then keeling over like a felled redwood. He lost consciousness briefly, then was carried off the field on a stretcher and missed several weeks with persistent headaches.

Danley's case was dramatic but nowhere near unique. When he went down, he became the fifth umpire on the 2008 roster to be disabled by a blow to the mask or the head, the others being Mark Carlson, Tony Randazzo, John Hirschbeck, and Poncino. A month later, almost exactly to the day, Jerry Crawford was hit in the back of the head with a bat when Carlos Lee of the Astros followed through on a swing; stunned and bloodied, Crawford was removed from the game and taken to the hospital.

It's difficult, I think, for a fan to get a sense of what being hit flush in the mask is like; it happened to me in amateur games a couple of times, and it made me feel like a cartoon character, Elmer Fudd maybe, being rapped in the forehead with a mallet, briefly stunned with a bit of a residual ringing in the ears. But those were foul balls at amateur pitching speed, slow motion compared to a big league fastball.

"When you're hit in the mask, your jaw will usually lock up," Tom Hallion told me. "It stiffens up because of the shock."

At any rate, being beaned is only the most obvious physical threat to umpires. It's remarkable that baseball never monitored umpire health or assigned any medical staff to them before the 2000 season, when it hired Mark Letendre. A garrulous man who couldn't possibly be any happier than he seemed to be when he was talking about, say, "the frontal, transverse, and sidereal planes that define the matrix of umpire movement" (he really talked like that), he had a couple of theories for why plate umpires seemed to be taking balls off the mask so often, more often than in the past.

One reason, he said, was that many catchers were now wearing the bucket mask, akin to a hockey goalie's, a plastic canister that fits over the face and has few hard angles on its surface. Some umpires have gone to a version of it as well (and more probably will, though many resist because of how warm and confining it is), but Letendre said that when a ball hits the catcher's bucket mask, it is less likely to be deflected to the side or down than the same pitch that hits a conventional mask, and more likely simply to glance off and continue on to bash the umpire.

The newly enforced high strike zone is another reason, he said, because players are now swinging at higher pitches more often, resulting in more foul balls deflected directly over the catcher.

While umpires have never exactly been known for taking care of themselves, Letendre said, it's not surprising that they get out of shape, is it?

"Baseball sticks a straw in you from day one, and it continually sucks and very rarely replenishes you," he said. "And in the officiating world, the two biggest stress relievers are food and alcohol, just like they are everywhere else. I'm doing battle against a hundred years of culture here."

Letendre has provided umpires with volumes of information about diet and exercise, and he's devised umpire-specific exercise programs—largely stretches and core-strengthening workouts aimed at how umpires move. Most major league locker rooms are now equipped with stretching mats and modest exercise equipment.

"What they are is industrial athletes," Letendre said. "Industrial athletes make athletic moves but they're not necessarily athletes. Same thing as a guy on the assembly line in Detroit."

One day I e-mailed Letendre asking for a list of injuries that umpires suffered in the 2007 season, and in about fifteen minutes he sent back twenty. In addition to the ones you would expect—muscle strains and pulls, contusions, bone bruises, heat exhaustion in full equipment on ninety-five-degree days—he mentioned a number of freak accidents that together made it pretty clear that umpiring is hazardous duty. One guy, for example, suffered a concussion and a bloody temple when a bat shattered and a shard flew into the side of his head. (Citing concern for their privacy, Letendre wouldn't say who the individuals were.)

Another guy was rightly positioned for a play at the plate, on an imaginary extension of the third-base line, and had his ankle broken when the runner slid into home plate and rolled over him.

One guy sprained his knee while racing into the outfield to make a call when he stepped on a sprinkler head that hadn't properly sunk into the turf after it was turned off.

One home plate umpire had his finger broken by a foul ball, even though he was in his proper stance, with the hand protected behind his knee; the ball hit the dirt, hopped up at an odd angle, and clipped him.

One second-base umpire found his forehead in the path of an errant throw to first base; he was taken to the hospital for stitches.

Another broken bat: This one hit home plate, bounced crazily, and hit the umpire in the knee, requiring him to be taken off the field on a stretcher.

And one umpire suffered a herniated lumbar disk as he squatted in position to call a pitch. This might sound jokey, or the result of his being overweight. But you try making an exaggerated squat 250 or 300 times in three and a half hours, thirty or thirty-five games a season. That's eight thousand or nine thousand squats in six months.

Not surprisingly, perhaps, umpires face all this risk with a glibness and gallows humor. There's a manly code among them; they're supposed to be tough. In 1999, when Wally Bell, who was thirty-four at the time, had quintuple bypass surgery, he was back on the field eleven weeks later.

"John Hirschbeck came up to my hospital room when I was waiting to go into surgery," Bell recalled for me. "I'm in bed and my neck is all marked up, and everybody is really tense. And Hirschbeck goes, 'Hey, if you check out, can I have your chest protector?'"

Visiting the umpires' locker room in St. Louis in September 2007, I asked Ed Montague for some injury stories. Montague was finishing his thirty-first full season in the big leagues and was about to become— after Bruce Froemming retired just a few weeks later—baseball's senior umpire.

"I was on a roll this year," Montague said. "I think out of my first ten plate games I got nailed in eight of them."

He laughed, then recalled two serious incidents. He was good-humored, but the stories were hair-raising.

"I missed a month and a half in '94 when I got hit by a throw during a spring training game," he said. "And I was hit in the throat before that, a ball that came that far from crushing my larynx." He held his thumb and forefinger an inch apart.

"That was the first time I was hurt real bad," he said; this was in 1980. "A foul off the bat of George Foster, and Jeff Reardon was throwing about ninety-eight miles per hour. I was in New York, and the Mets are playing the Big Red Machine. Foster just ticks the ball, and this was before we had the throat guard. I was just wearing the mask, cut off at the chin, and the ball just came straight back. And I was down, man. I couldn't speak. I'm trying to put my fingers in my mouth so I don't swallow my tongue. They carried me off on a stretcher.

"I remember I kind of blacked out a little bit, just for a bit because I remember I could still hear the crowd. The week before I'd thrown Johnny Bench out of a ball game, and Joe Torre, I'd thrown him out a couple of times that month, and I looked up, and there's Bench and there's Torre. I thought I'd died and gone to hell or something."

He didn't miss a game. "I was back on the field the next day, but I couldn't talk. You know what? You never talked about it; you just went out there."

But that wasn't always the case.

"The worst was spring training '94," Ed Montague said. "We were working three-man, and I was at the plate. LaRussa was managing the A's, and they're playing the Cubs, and so a ball is hit to left, and the third-base umpire goes out, and I go down to third to cover the bag."

Montague was in fair territory when he made the call.

"Ron Darling, the pitcher, is running, and he slides in and I call him out. And Steve Buechele, he's playing third, he comes up throwing—he's as far away as from me to you—and boom!"

The ball hit Montague flush on the forehead.

"This kid, Buechele, had a cannon, and he threw it so hard that the ball went into the stands. Everything went black." Montague's got a bit of ham in him, and he paused for just a second. "They stopped the game, and I'm laying there, and I opened my eyes. And LaRussa comes by and he says, 'Great hustle, Eddie.'"

Montague missed six weeks of the season with a concussion, and he battled recurrent vertigo for three years.

"It's never really gone away," he said. "Just the other day, looking up at the dome in Toronto? And when I look straight up at a foul pole? Good luck."

If he and his contemporaries had an advantage over older umpires, Ted Barrett said, it was that they arrived in the big leagues when instant replay on television was already established. The guys who came up in the 1970s didn't have the constant scrutiny of an electronic eye; their mistakes weren't routinely exposed in slow motion to a nation of couch potatoes. They didn't grow to maturity in the big leagues with the healthy fear of videotape bred in them.

"We came up in the technology era," Barrett said. "It didn't seem like it at the time, maybe, but it's turned out to be a good thing for us."

This particular conversation took place in New York City, in May 2008, over a Thursday lunch; that night Barrett was finishing yet another series at Shea Stadium, then heading off to Boston for three games before leaving for a week's vacation. He dodged a bullet.

It was three nights later, with the Mets having headed crosstown for an interleague series against the Yankees, that the instant replay debate flared conclusively. Umpires filched a home run from the Mets' Carlos Delgado, ruling it foul even though replays showed the ball had clearly struck the base of the left-field foul pole.

Amazingly, this was only the first of *five* miscalled long balls in the big leagues that week, the sort of confluence of events that occurs in sports sometimes and seems almost divinely inspired. By the end of the seven-day span, if God himself weren't saying, "Wake up! Take a look at this!" the sports media were. "A bad week for the men in blue" was the teaser for ESPN's *SportsCenter* on Sunday. On every talk-radio show and in every newspaper sports section, the call was renewed that umpires should avail themselves of videotape to make close calls on the field.

On vacation, Barrett hadn't heard about the Delgado call until I told him about it the next day, on the phone, and explained to him what had happened. Mike Reilly, the crew chief, who was working at third base, had called the ball fair, correctly but tentatively. The Yankees objected, and Reilly huddled just beyond shortstop with the other crew members—Alfonso Marquez, Andy Fletcher, and Bob Davidson, the home plate umpire, who arrived last and with evident decisiveness—and subsequently reversed the call. It was a rare and unhappy occurrence, the changing of a call to make it incorrect.

"Oh, shit," Barrett said, in sympathy with his colleagues; then he leaped to their defense. "You know, that foul pole in Yankee Stadium is set back three feet from the fence," he said. "Don Mattingly used to come out to the home plate conference and point it out to us. He'd say, 'You know, a ball can cross in front of the foul pole and land on the wrong side of it and still be a home run.'"

Baseball has encouraged umpires to huddle up on difficult calls—insisted on it, in fact, not the umpires' favorite dictum. In the aftermath of the 1999 reshuffling of the umpire staff, it was part of Alderson and Nelson's effort to combat the perception that umpires were arrogant, more interested in preserving their authority than in getting the calls right. But umpires felt they were just replacing one perceived reality with another, namely that they were inept. A huddle, after all, might just as well be a sign that says "oops," an advertisement for their inability to get the job done, and it couldn't help but undermine their authority on the field. What were they going to say to one another in a huddle, anyway?

I was at a game in Milwaukee in 2006 when the umpires huddled on a ball that had hit either the wall or a railing above the wall before bouncing back into play, and the next day I asked them how the discussion went. It was a vote, they said. One thought it hit the wall; two thought it hit the railing. One didn't have a good look. Hence, home run.

In the press box, instant replay had shown they were wrong.

It's widely but incorrectly assumed that umpires oppose the use of instant replay to help them with calls; in truth they're in favor of anything that makes their job easier, and most admit they would welcome help on those drives near the fence that either do or don't leave the field in fair territory. Every umpire everywhere says these are the most difficult calls they have to make.

That's long been the case with fly balls that pass either in front of or behind the foul pole. Umpires call them pole benders, and they're miserable to judge for two reasons. One is that they're almost always observed from a long distance away; the other is that it's frequently the case that the closest umpire does not have the best angle to see the path of the ball in relation to the foul pole, which means that an umpire with a better angle is not only even farther away but probably has other responsibilities on the play.

In recent years, several new ballparks have been built with shorter fences and idiosyncratic configurations, with angles and niches in the outfield fences or high walls with lines painted on them to separate a home run from a ball in play, with more seats right on the foul lines and along the tops of walls so that fans can reach into the field. So there are more problematic home run calls than ever, which might be a signal not only that home run calls are more suitably monitored on videotape than in real time, but that a calamity (in baseball terms) is waiting to happen. Home runs, after all, are often game-changing events, and no one—not the commissioner, not the players, not the umpires—wants to see a playoff or a World Series decided by a call that either undeservedly adds or illegitimately subtracts a winning run.

Besides, fixing a mistake on a home run call is relatively simple and painless. Everyone scores if the ball is eventually ruled out of the park; everyone returns to their original bases if it is eventually ruled foul. The possible complication is a ball initially ruled a home run that turns out to have stayed in the park in fair territory; then the umpires would have to place the runners according to their judgment of how far they would have advanced.

"I have no problem with it," the veteran Tim McClelland said to me when I asked if he'd object to instant replay on home run calls. "It takes the pressure *off* us."

In the National Football League, it's now routinely assumed that instant replay is a legitimate tool for the officials, an acknowledgment on the part of everyone that their job is too hard to do without it; there is no shame for the officials in their consulting the videotape when it is called for. This has a lot to do with the collective "Who cares?" that umpires gave to me when I asked about the possibility that replay would be added to the game. (On August 28, 2008, it was. From then on, umpires were permitted to go to the videotape, as it were, to determine the proper call on potential home run balls. It seems to have been, initially at least, a successful experiment. Replays were invoked seven times during the remainder of the season. Five calls on balls that were initially called home runs were upheld.*)

"Ten to fifteen years ago, the technology of the month was that big overhead camera," Fieldin Culbreth said. "Then there was slow-motion replay, then QuesTec and the strike zone they put up on the TV screen. But you know what? Every step along the way, technology has ended up befriending the umpires. It just ends up proving how good a job we actually do."

---

*On the other two, the umpires ruled that the balls remained in play, but replay showed they were, in fact, home runs. In both cases the umpires explained afterward that they were being cautious and making conscious use of their new tool. Reasonably but not entirely certain to begin with that the balls were home runs, they signaled play to continue, knowing they'd be able to check the replay. This was solid reasoning, and in fact, a paradigm for good umpiring: If they'd initially allowed the balls to be home runs and turned out to be wrong, they'd have to send the batter and all the runners back on to the field and place them according to their best guess of what would have happened had the play continued without interruption. By allowing the play to conclude on the field, they avoided such an artificiality, and even though replay dictated the calls be changed and the home runs awarded, the remedy allowed the game to proceed without a taint.

After all, most umpires say, they have been doing impossible work for a long time; adding instant replay would only be baseball admitting as much—a good thing, especially if it is the umpires themselves who get to view the videotape. (One suggestion floating around was that a fifth umpire—a replay official who sits in the press box—be added to each crew. That was rejected, of course. Too expensive. Instead, all games are monitored by an umpire supervisor at major league head-quarters in New York, and the replay feeds are provided from there.)

"Jeez, are you kidding? Bring it on," Chris Guccione said when I asked if he favored using replay on problematic home run calls. Just a week or so earlier Gooch had been the first-base umpire at Yankee Sta-dium when a drive by Alex Rodriguez had banged off the painted yel-low facade of a staircase over the right-field fence and ricocheted like a bullet back onto the outfield grass. It was Guccione's call, but he was backed by the rest of the crew. They called it a double. Replays showed it wasn't even close, that the ball had cleared the fence by ten feet.

"I kicked it big-time," Guccione told me, adding he'd been on the field and seen a ball hit in batting practice that day carom off the same staircase, so that when A-Rod's drive headed in that direction he was aware of the possibility that the ball would hit it. But from the distance he had to call it from, and at the speed the ball was traveling, he just couldn't see what happened; nor could any of his crewmates.

"You got instant replay on television, you got the Internet, you got the announcers in the booth, you got the scoreboard replaying it for the fans," Guccione said. "Everybody in the world knows what hap-pened on that play except the four guys on the field who are supposed to see it. Does that make any sense to you?"

A day or so after the Delgado mistake at Yankee Stadium, I con-tacted Mike Port, baseball's vice president in charge of umpiring. Port, who succeeded Alderson after the 2005 season, was, like Alderson, a refugee from team management. He'd been the general manager of the California Angels from 1984 to 1991, and he worked for the Boston Red Sox, eventually as vice president of baseball operations from 1996 to 2005.

But, unlike Alderson, he was a bit of a turncoat. Having gotten a close look at the world of umpires, he'd become their ardent defender. In his new job, he told me, it was his duty to give an umpiring report at the annual general managers' meetings, and when he heard the predictable litany of complaints, he'd say the umpiring was better than ever, but that television technology was, too, and that it had brought to light what had never been visible before. And inevitably that would lead someone to say that that was an argument for figuring out a way to replace umpires altogether.

"And I always want to say, 'In that case, why do we need general managers?'" he said.

I first met Port at umpire school when he was still fresh in his job and he'd come down to learn something about the craft of the men he was supposed to supervise; one day he stood in the batter's box with a bat as I called balls and strikes. Since then, he'd come full circle; he said to me several times he had had no idea what a difficult job umpiring is and how well the guys on his staff do it. When I asked Port what baseball does in a situation like the Delgado missed call, he responded with a lengthy e-mail:

"Certainly we try to evaluate all that went right, as well as what might have gone wrong. To wit: Why is the foul pole two colors, black near the bottom and yellow the rest of the way? As shown on ESPN, why does the foul pole appear out of line with the foul line? Did either of the aforementioned have any effect on the call?

"From the umpires' standpoint: How strongly did Mike Reilly feel about his decision? Did he indeed lose the ball? Why wasn't the consultation longer? It seemed to conclude just before Bob Davidson joined the group. What did Bob Davidson see that convinced him so firmly?

"We'll be reviewing all this on our weekly supervisor conference call.

"On the positive side: Mike was correct. Beyond that, the crew was not averse to doing everything within their capability to get the call right."

Port added a few choice comments about the ESPN announcers for the game, who, he pointed out correctly, made more mistakes than the umpires did. And he concluded:

"Overall, with respect to the call, the Mets handled it the right way, by scoring 11 runs to overcome the adversities the game presents, as opposed to the tired refrain 'the umpire's call cost us the game.' I have an understandable bias showing, but the game remains in the hands of the players."

* * *

Mike Port's stewardship of the umpires was more sympathetic than that of Alderson and Nelson, and the umpires liked his honest admiration of them and his willingness to defend them, even though they feared he didn't have the clout with Commissioner Selig or his executive vice president of baseball operations, Jimmie Lee Solomon, that his predecessors did. He probably didn't. In terms of shifting the umpires from their own independent track to one laid out by baseball, Alderson and Nelson had done the heavy lifting, and Port was there to maintain things as smoothly as possible.

By 2008, a little perspective was possible on Alderson and Nelson, and while memories of their post-'99 regime were still grating, they had clearly accomplished some things. If you asked most major league umpires about Alderson and Nelson, they'd tell you, maybe a little grudgingly, that they weren't so terrible.

The strike zone did get tighter, but it probably needed to get tighter. With the dismantling of the American and National League offices, their dual umpire cultures lost their anchors, and the damaging resentments they caused were slowly dissolving. The central control of the umpires had allowed baseball's administration to defend its umpiring staff more avidly to the public and the press; and despite the fact that criticism of umpires remained regular and often vehement, the public image was indisputably improved from what it had been at the end of the 1990s. With Mark Letendre's attention, umpires were getting better medical care, and baseball had also created a central umpire Web site, where information could be shared—about which teams were feuding, for example, and were likely to exchange beanballs—and where film clips of close or controversial calls could be reviewed.

Perhaps for the first time in nearly half a century, there was relative peace between the union and the owners. In 2005, a collective bargaining agreement was reached with nary a whimper from either side, though partly this was because the umpires swallowed some of their demands to make an agreement that would bring Hallion, Hickox, and Davidson back into the fold. Aside from Jerry Crawford, by 2008 all the other holdouts—the umpires who had been loyal to the old union—had given in and joined the new one. And even Bruce Froemming, who retired in 2007, had agreed to go to work for the enemy, joining the commissioner's umpire supervisory staff.

Ted Barrett's career was balanced perfectly on the pivot of 1999, and his temperature was worth taking. He hadn't entirely shaken off the travails of that year and held, too, to some of the old tenets of umpiring that allowed umpires some leeway on the field, that gave them some flexibility in exerting their control of the game. He recalled his evolution from a pre-'99 to a post-'99 umpire. His attitude distinguished him from a strictly old-school umpire like Jerry Crawford, who responded, when I asked how the strike zone had changed, by shrugging and saying it hadn't.

"I will not give in and say the strike zone was any different, or at least my strike zone was any different, than it was in 1977, when I had my first full year," Crawford said. "Any umpire worth his salt would probably say the same thing."

Well, Barrett didn't.

"The strike zone has definitely changed," Barrett said. "I'm not going to say it's good or bad, but my zone has changed drastically. I called a wide zone, no question; I saw an old clip on ESPN the other night, and I called a strike on Miguel Tejada that was way off the plate, and I went, 'Whoa! Was that really my zone?' I used to have a lot of pitches, three and four inches outside, that I'd call strikes. And with QuesTec, Frank Pulli, he'd look at my games, and he'd say, 'I'm worried about those five- and six-inchers.'

"The thing is, I'd always had positive feedback, even from catchers and hitters, so the first couple of years"—after the implementation of QuesTec, he meant—"I didn't know how serious they were. I brought it in maybe a little bit. And Pulli would say to me, 'You gotta bring it in, you gotta bring it in,' and I'd say, 'Yeah, yeah,' and Pulli'd say, 'Ted, I'm not kidding.'

"Then it became difficult. But you know, once you learn to umpire the machine zone, it's easier. My outside zone used to be a few inches off the plate and it was undefined. Now I know; at this point I'm looking strictly on the plate, and sometimes I'm two inches off."

Barrett's ambivalence pertained to Alderson and Nelson's other moves as well, though as with the strike zone, you could read between the lines and recognize that he didn't disapprove, say, of making sure all umpires were held to more rigorous physical standards.

The commissioner wanted a younger, more athletic roster of umpires, and umpires were especially sensitive about the issue of aging. Of course, they all wanted to be able to work as long as they were able, wanted to earn their substantial salaries as long as they could. But umpires who were sticking around the game for thirty or thirty-five years were working beyond their best days and blocking the path for younger umpires waiting their turns in the minors. Senior umpires clogging the system also made the problem of diversity on the major league staff—or more accurately, the lack of it—more difficult to solve.

"They took almost all the choices away from crew chiefs," Barrett said. "And that was mostly a message to the older guys. Guys that couldn't run well had found ways to do things so they didn't have to move, and that was a Ralph Nelson thing: Everybody's going to have to have the same responsibilities. Everyone is going to have to move. You couldn't help thinking, though, they were trying, on purpose, to send a message to some of the older guys, like a Bruce Froemming or an Eric Gregg. Guys who couldn't run, they were trying to expose that a little bit."

In addition to focusing on the strike zone, Alderson had another hobbyhorse: the length of games. He wanted them shorter. In 2000, a major league game averaged just about three hours, a few minutes more in the American League, with the designated hitter, than in the National. The reasons were easy to locate.

Spurred by strategists such as Billy Beane, the general manager of the Oakland A's, who was lionized in the Michael Lewis book *Moneyball,* and the legendary statistician Bill James, both of whom were advocates of the on-base percentage as an indicator of player value, hitting coaches had returned to the old tenet "A walk is as good as a hit" and the old advice "Wait him out." Hitters had become more discriminating, taking more pitches, trying to increase the pitch count of starting pitchers to force them out of the game and make the opposition use the weaker arms in the bull pen.

Of course, television advertising increased, which added length to games as well, and with all the extra waiting around, players got in the habit of lollygagging on their way from the on-deck circle to the batter's box. It's not certain that fans actually noticed or cared, but the press somehow did, and perhaps the most crucial occurrence was an acerbic story by the *Sports Illustrated* columnist Rick Reilly, who applied a stopwatch during the telecast of a three-hour-and-fifteen-minute playoff game in 2000 between Oakland and the Yankees and wrote that the time the ball actually spent in play was twelve minutes and twenty-two seconds. Reilly concluded that he'd never watch another ball game on television again, something that had to send a chill through baseball's administrators and their broadcasting partners.

The commissioner's office had a number of suggestions to remedy this, including pressuring the teams' front offices to urge their players and managers and coaches to concentrate on not taking their sweet time to do every damn thing on the ball field. But the umpires were held most accountable.

Alderson instituted a statistic for plate umpires known as pace of game; it was calculated by taking the total length of the game, deducting the time allotted for television advertising between innings, then dividing the result by the total number of pitches. (For locally televised games, the commercial time between innings was standardized at 2:05. For national games, it was 2:25; and in the postseason it went up to 2:55.)

The pace of game, which thus more or less corresponded to the average number of seconds per pitch, was provided to each plate umpire after every game, along with his QuesTec score, and it became part of the total-performance evaluations that were used to determine All-Star and postseason assignments. The target was 26.4 seconds per pitch, which corresponded to an average nine-inning game length in the neighborhood of 2:45.

The thing is, there wasn't a whole lot umpires could do that they weren't ordinarily doing. The next time a ball is fouled off into the stands down either line, for example, instead of watching the ball, watch the plate umpire and the catcher; you'll see a practiced and efficient ballet. The ump will reach into his ball bag before the batted ball has gone out of play; the catcher, usually without turning around, will reach over his shoulder with his gloved hand and turn the glove upward like a dish, and the umpire will place a new ball in it like an egg in a nest. By the time the foul ball lands in the grandstand, the fresh one is already on its way back to the pitcher.

Beyond that, there aren't many time-saving tools in an umpire's repertoire. He can tell players to move faster on their way to the plate from the on-deck circle; he can try to enforce the edict that says a pitching coach has to trot, not walk, to the mound to talk to his pitcher; he can wait not quite as long for a mound conference to break up before going out to call an end to it. But if the players are determined to take their time, the game is going to last a long time. One afternoon in the dressing room in St. Louis, the day after he and his crew worked a fourteen-inning game, Bill Miller showed me the pace-of-game statistics from around the major leagues the night before.

"We went four twenty-five," he said. "Jerry Layne saw 440 pitches, and his pace of game is 27. But here's New York and Boston, and they're always notoriously slow. They went three hours and ten minutes, but they only had 252 pitches. The pace of game was 33.8. That's 33.8 seconds it took for every pitch! You going to blame the umpires for that?"

Alderson insisted on an on-field regimen in which the second-base umpire, who held a stopwatch, flicked it on after the third out of an inning and, with forty-five or fifty seconds left to go before the end of the allotted between-innings time, raised his hand to signal the plate umpire, who would then signal the pitcher that he was down to one more warm-up and tell the leadoff batter to move to the box.

"The pace-of-game stuff drove me crazy at first," Ted Barrett said. "We got a lot of shit about it from Alderson. That's pretty much gone now, but they used to post all our scores, and it became a competition. I thought, 'I'm not going to signal the pitcher and the batter, that's just bull.' At the time I was working with McClelland, and he kept telling me, 'You got to do this.' And I'd say, 'Why?' And he'd say, 'You got to show them you're doing what they want.' And I said, 'I'm not going to do this just for some guy watching me in the stands. It's just a show and I'm not going to do it.' But eventually I gave in and started doing it, and you know what? It's really not just a show. It does kind of keep the game moving. Between innings, I used to do the old-umpire-school thing, stand on the baseline on the other side of the team coming to bat. Now I actually stand on the side of the team that's hitting, close to the on-deck circle, so after I signal the pitcher, I can turn around and say to the batter, 'Time to go. Let's go.'"

Actually, over a few seasons, the average length of games did come down to about 2:45, but whether the umpires had a lot to do with it is impossible to figure; so is whether the difference mattered to anyone. Standing around the batting cage one day in spring training, Ozzie

Guillen, the irrepressible manager of the Chicago White Sox, offered his summation of the pace-of-game initiative:

"Media is the one complaining about how long the game is. I never hear no fucking fans complain how long the game is. I never hear a manager complain. The fucking media want to get the fuck out of there quick, so they're worried, man, 'This game's long!'"

In any case, on August 18, 2006, the Yankees and the Red Sox still managed to play a nine-inning game lasting 4:45, the longest in history.

"Nobody is blameless," Ted Barrett said about the 1999 mess and its aftermath.

I asked him if it was finally over, and he said no; it certainly wasn't over for Larry McCoy, Jim Evans, Mark Johnson, Ken Kaiser, and Dale Ford, the umpires who lost almost everything. He worried that a generational schism was opening, with older umpires accusing the younger ones of being too accommodating of baseball and of not supporting a tough union, and the younger ones believing the older umpires' outlandish demands and implacability had brought about the 1999 mess to begin with.

And Barrett worried that too many of his colleagues would forget about 1999 long before they finished living with its consequences: "There're guys who said they didn't do anything wrong, and they did. There are guys who were saying one thing and doing another. I like Jerry Crawford and Ed Montague, but they made promises to the five guys who are still out there that they didn't keep. They jumped up and down at meetings and said, 'Those guys lost their jobs and we won't rest until they get their jobs back and their kids can go to college.' But we're not doing anything for them now. I stood up at the last meeting and I said, 'Notice how those five are all old American League guys?'

"And the new representation, they're already yelling about the next contract: 'They don't do enough of this. They don't do enough of that.' And I'm thinking, 'You gotta be kidding me.'

"We're the best umpires in the world, and we've got some who are just rockheads. We are so stupid we're going to walk right back into it. I wouldn't put it past us."

CHAPTER NINE

Strapping It On

I never missed one here.
—Bill Klem,
   pointing to his heart

I remember once in high school the umpire called me out at third base
when I was sure I was safe. I got so mad I took out my glass eye,
handed it to him, and said, "Try this."

—Peter Falk

You can't hide on a ball field. Every fan knows this; it's part of the
deliciously cruel and fateful nature of baseball that if you want to
take part and not just watch, there's no escaping your karma in the narrative of the game. If the right fielder has a weak throwing arm, at some
point he'll have to gun down a runner at the plate to keep a winning run
off the board. If the cleanup hitter can't help lunging at a slow curve, the
pitcher coming in from the bull pen to face him with the bases loaded
will have a good one. If the catcher is especially slow afoot, in a tight
game he'll be the base runner trying to score from third on a fly to left
with one out in the eighth.

And if the umpire has never seen a big league fastball . . . ?

Well, that was the thought that kept me up the night before I made
my major league debut. After spending more than a year carrying a
visa in the land of umpires, I remained, of course, a rank amateur,
someone who'd never called a game beyond the high school or amateur
adult level.

But during spring training 2007, I arranged to go behind the plate for a three-inning intrasquad game at the San Francisco Giants' spring training stadium in Scottsdale, Arizona. What I kept thinking, tossing and turning the night before, was "What if I can't see the ball? What if, literally, it's too fast for me to follow?" I was fifty-three years old and my eyesight wasn't much better than serviceable; I didn't like to drive at night. I figured a major league pitcher could throw the ball some 20 to 25 percent faster than the high school kids and older amateurs I'd practiced on, meaning that instead of traveling at 75 mph, the pitches I'd be examining would be moving at 90 or 95, and it would take approximately .43 seconds for a pitch to reach the plate from the pitcher's hand instead of .55 seconds. Those twelve-hundredths of a second might be the difference between my being able to follow the path of the ball and merely knowing it had been thrown and caught. The added speed meant an average pitch would spend a mere .011 seconds (give or take a few ten-thousandths) passing through the strike zone instead of .013 seconds. Would I miss those extra two-thousandths of a second when I was trying to determine whether a fastball had nipped the corner?

Lying in bed in my motel, I found myself giggling at the hoariest umpire apocrypha, the tale told about an ump overmatched by Smoky Joe Wood or Walter Johnson or Bob Feller or Sandy Koufax or Nolan Ryan or Roger Clemens—some fireballer, anyway. After the second or third time the umpire fails to call a perfectly good pitch a strike, the story goes, the skeptical catcher turns around and says, "Where the hell was that pitch?" To which the umpire responds, "It sounded outside."

But that was only one of the things that kept me awake. For umpires, working the plate is like an experience in italics; it has an aura that elevates it. On any crew, the plate umpire is the king for a day, wearing not only a mask and a chest protector but an invisible robe and crown. It's an enterprise that has its own mythology and argot. To an umpire, if you're behind the plate, you've "got the stick"—that is, you're in control of the game, or at least manning its controls, like a pilot in the cockpit. And whoever has the stick is doing "a plate job" or, more popularly, "strapping it on."

So for me home plate in a major league stadium loomed as a hallowed destination, a more fearsome place than any I'd encountered before in baseball. Every risk that I'd come to accept at the slower speeds of amateur ball suddenly seemed intensely more serious and more threatening. I worried about a foul ball finding its way between my mask and chest protector and splitting my Adam's apple, or careening off my elbow and shattering a bone, or nipping at a fingertip and tearing off a nail, or hitting me flush in the mask and causing a concussion, or landing square on the inside of my biceps and leaving me with a blue-and-orange bruise that would take weeks to heal.

I worried about a meaty catcher leaping up from his crouch to chase down a foul pop behind the plate and simply running me over.

I worried about a close play at the plate, with a two-hundred-pound base runner colliding in a cloud of dust with the catcher, tumbling into me and knocking me silly.

I worried about the pitcher and the catcher meeting the manager on the mound and lingering there long enough so I'd have to interrupt them and encourage them to conclude their business, only to have the manager tell me to fuck off or, worse, ignore me.

I worried about losing track of the count, the umpire's equivalent of forgetting the alphabet. It's amazing how easy that is to do, especially when you have so much else to worry about.

And I worried that the moment my judgement was questioned, I'd lose whatever confidence and dignity I'd walked onto the field with.

Funny, but I didn't much worry about the judgments themselves. You call 'em as you see 'em, the saying goes. Say what you see. As anyone in authority can tell you, the moment of decision is the easy part.

If I'd learned anything in the year I'd spent among umpires, it was that umpiring is a test of nerve and perseverance under any circumstances, even for the guys who've been doing it every day for years.

This is not so much because it's difficult to get the calls right, though that can be difficult enough, but because umpiring has no forgiveness built into it, a condition that stands in considerable relief from the game's other human endeavors. Baseball is, after all, a sport that has a fetish about failure. That the best hitters succeed a mere third of the time is familiar enough to be a cliché. It's also true that twenty-three pitchers in the Hall of Fame each managed to lose more than two hundred games, and that Connie Mack, the most prolific manager in major league history, had a sub-.500 winning percentage. But for umpires, screwing up is simply ruin. Only the umpire is expected to consistently subdue the challenges of the game.

Professional umpires have an adage they repeat as reliably as captured soldiers will recite their name, rank, and serial number: "We have to start out perfect and improve from there." This reflects a martyrdom and self-aggrandizement that is part of the professional umpire's pose, but it isn't entirely wrong or even misleading. No one on the field is watched more closely for the minutest departure from flawlessness. You get everything right—everything!—or you suffer for it. It's that simple. And of course, even if you get everything right, that's no shield against the arrows of scorn that shower down upon the umpire in his work space.

Vigilance, in other words, is both all and not enough. The task requires you to be acutely aware of all that is happening in the ballpark and to be on high alert for things that *might* happen. It's a brutal kind of readiness, which is why tension headaches are a routine umpire complaint, and why anxiety, even at the highest level, is an accepted hazard of the profession. Virtually all umpires speak about games as being survival tests, and their conventional wisdom is that the best moment of the day is the final out. As I tried to sleep, I tried to think like an umpire and keep in mind that, after all, it was only three innings, it was only spring training, it was only an intrasquad game, and it would soon be over.

I'd been in umpire dressing rooms dozens of times, but never to dress. Umpires wear enough stuff, especially plate umpires, that putting it all on is something of a ritual, and it takes some time, and some practice especially if you're not doing it every day. I had to learn, for example, that shin guards aren't interchangeable; there's a left and a right one, the straps properly fastened on the outside of each leg so the clasps can't catch on each other and trip you up. And before I went to umpire school the previous January, I hadn't even worn a protective cup in thirty years. Now I was preparing to step out on a major league field wearing not only the cup and a pair of hand-me-down shin guards with rusty fastening clasps, but steel-toed plate shoes, a bulletproof-vest-like chest protector (a Jim Evans discard), and a padded mask that I could, at long last, flip up without my hat coming off.

I'd forgotten to bring the long johns that plate umpires wear under their trousers, even in the hottest weather, to absorb sweat, to pad the lower leg against the shin guards, and to keep the shin guards from sliding around as well. One of my partners, Jeff Macias, who'd be graduating that season from Double A to Triple A, gave me an old pair of his, and my other partner, Scott Higgins, donated a plate brush. For some reason, I couldn't find mine. Happily I located my ball-and-strike indicator without a problem.

Higgins, a former Triple A umpire with more than two hundred games as a big league fill-in, had given up the chase for a full-time major league job a few years earlier. Later, he'd go on to umpire professional baseball in Taiwan, but at this point he was a bartender at Baer's Den, a hole-in-the-wall bar in nearby Tempe that was probably the best-known umpire hangout in the country. There are umpire bars in every major league city (and many minor league ones), places where umpires go when they're in town, like Foley's, down the street from Madison Square Garden in Manhattan, or the Missouri Grill in downtown St. Louis, but the Phoenix area is unusual because dozens of umpires, major league and minor league, live there. Twelve major league teams hold spring training camps within an hour's drive of one another, so umpires can stay home and work for six weeks in February and March, a boon for men who have to spend most of the next six months on the road. (A lot of umpires live in Florida, too, for the same reason.) And Baer's Den, where the signatures of dozens of current and former umpires are scratched on the wall, was a gathering place, a place to drop in to.

Higgins, who was in his late thirties, was a big guy, tall, hulking, and fleshy, and I came to think of him as something of an umpire paradigm in terms of temperament: He was wary, a tad haughty, not especially talkative or terribly welcoming if you weren't a fraternity brother. I'd first met him a year earlier at Baer's Den, and he'd shaken my hand as if I were ill and contagious; I was surprised when Macias, who was in charge of all umpire assignments for "B games," as the unofficial spring training contests are known, told me that Higgins had agreed to partner up with us—with me, I mean. Of course, unlike me, he'd be getting paid.

Higgins wasn't unfriendly in the locker room, just a little chilly, though he did give a bit of a snort when I borrowed his plate brush. He also teased me about my shirt, a generic, dark blue umpire jersey that I pulled from the bottom of my bag, badly in need of an iron.

"Who lent you the shirt?" he said.

Actually, at the tail end of February, the weather in the desert was sunny but brisk, and I'd wanted to wear long sleeves because I was already nervous and didn't want another reason to be shivering out there, but Macias and Higgins made it clear that that would make me a wuss. We walked out of the dressing room and stood in the dugout while the baselines and batter's boxes were limed, and I watched players doing their halfhearted final stretches and wind sprints in the outfield.

I scanned the figures out there for the two Barrys. One was Barry Bonds, of course, the slugger then on the verge of breaking Henry Aaron's career home run record while also under the shadow of accusations that he'd used illegal steroids to enhance his performance and lied to a grand jury about it. Bonds is a notoriously unpredictable personality, occasionally charming and chatty, just as often surly and forbidding. I'd interviewed him a couple of times in previous years and seen both sides. It was amusing to visit the Giants' clubhouse and watch the press corps deal with his presence, everyone remaining a respectful distance from his locker as though an invisible force field surrounded it, but keeping an ear cocked in his direction in case he cleared his throat and said something.

The first time we talked, I screwed up my courage, crossed the no-man's-land, and said, "I'm new here, so I don't know that I'm not supposed to talk to you," which made him laugh, and we had a good chat about Bruce Froemming. Bonds recalled that when he was a young player with Pittsburgh, he had argued with the home plate umpire after being called out on strikes, and that Froemming, the crew chief who was working at first base, walked all the way out into the outfield between innings to warn him about showing up an umpire like that.

But the next day when I said hello to Bonds, he showed no recognition and sneered at me, which is the image that popped up in my mind in the dugout while waiting for the game to begin. I revisited the previous night's fantasy of my calling him out on strikes on a close pitch and then having to face down a steroid-fueled rage. In the dressing room, Higgins had fed my edginess with a well-aimed tweak: "Barry doesn't like called strikes," he'd said to me casually, mischievously.

I was also looking for Barry Zito, the free-agent pitcher the Giants had signed to a seven-year, $126 million contract in the off-season. Zito's best pitch is a curveball that breaks both sharply and deeply, tracing a humped arc on the way to the plate whose concluding, downsloped path is often described as twelve-to-six, referring to the poles of a clockface. I'd spoken to Zito briefly at the All-Star game the previous summer, and we'd discussed changes in the strike zone, especially those brought on by QuesTec. This new, higher strike was a good thing for him, Zito told me, because of his curveball, which he could now drop into the strike zone from above a hitter's shoulders. In my motel room, both curious and uncertain, I had also thought about getting a look at the famous pitch from close range.

For an umpire, calling breaking balls is an acquired skill; their paths to the plate are more deviant and unpredictable than those of fastballs, and they cut through (or around) the strike zone at varying speeds and counterintuitive angles that are difficult to anticipate and trace. That's why it generally takes a mature hitter to be able to hit a curveball; you have to see a lot of them before you can begin to grow familiar with all the ways it might move. The same is true for an umpire; I'd seen only amateur breaking pitches, and I'd been deceived, occasionally, even by them.

Naturally, neither Bonds nor Zito was on the field or in the lineup. My first amateur misjudgment of the day was that they would be; they probably weren't even in the ballpark. For my debut, mostly it was hopeful younger players whose names I didn't know and who were competing for the entry-level spots on the major league roster, the bull pen and utility-player roles.

This did nothing, or less than nothing, to cure my nerves, and I can only apologize for the reporting on the players that, in my jitteriness, I failed to do. For the most part I have no idea who they actually were. I remember only three. Two were the catchers—Justin Knoedler and Todd Jennings—whose names, stitched on the backs of their jerseys, were literally under my nose on every pitch. The third was Tomas de la Rosa, who, in the final inning, struck out looking on a close pitch, maybe even a questionable pitch (it was a curve), and gave me a sour look on his way back to the dugout. I didn't know it at the time, but he was a journeyman shortstop, a twenty-nine-year-old who'd once been in the Expos' system and who had played forty-nine games overall in the big leagues, with a career batting average of .289 and two home runs. Higgins knew him from his umpiring days, which I discovered after the game when he congratulated me for having called an actual major leaguer out on strikes, then deadpanned that he hoped I hadn't hurt the poor guy's chances to make the team.

I did have one opportunity to be starstruck. The ball boy for the game, that is, the guy who supplied me with baseballs at the start of each half-inning, was Dave Righetti, the Giants' pitching coach. Righetti was a former star for the Yankees and one of a small number of pitchers in baseball history to succeed both as a starter and a closer.

In the 1980s, Righetti had been a favorite player of mine, a lefty like me, and near my age. (Actually he was five years younger.) He also saved my life once, sort of. Early in the summer of 1983, a woman I wanted to marry left me, and I went into a kind of panic I'd never experienced before, with the sort of intense emotional ache that is made worse by foolishness and immaturity.

On July 4, Righetti pitched a no-hitter at Yankee Stadium against the Red Sox, the first Yankee no-hitter of my baseball-cognizant life—when Don Larsen threw his perfect game in the World Series, I wasn't yet three—and the suspense of it as the innings mounted was fortuitously transporting, perhaps the only thing capable of yanking me out of my inner-directed misery. I watched it all on television, alone in my shabby apartment on the Upper West Side of Manhattan, chain-smoking menthol cigarettes, and when the game was over—Righetti struck out Wade Boggs to end it, Boggs waving awkwardly at a breaking pitch on the outside corner—I realized I hadn't been thinking about the girl. The future suddenly seemed possible after all.

This all ran quickly through my head when Righetti walked out to home plate with a sack of baseballs. I didn't mention any of it to him, I'm happy to report. Instead, when he asked me how many balls I wanted, four or five, I said five, if I could fit them all in my ball bag, my first authoritative decision as a plate umpire on a major league diamond.

In truth, though I hadn't been behind the plate before, this was my second workday on a major league field. Earlier in the week, Macias had arranged for us to team up on the bases at Diablo Stadium in Tempe, for a Los Angeles Angels of Anaheim intrasquad game. Jake Uhlenhopp, a Triple A guy I didn't know, had the stick, and he and Macias sent me out to third base, where Chone Figgins, a valuable and versatile major leaguer—among other significant accomplishments, he had stolen more than a hundred bases over the previous two seasons—was smoothing the infield dirt with his toe. A couple of the Angels' coaches knew what I was up to—one of them shouted to us, as we stood at home plate with the manager, Mike Scioscia, before the game, "Who's writing the book and how can I get in it?"—but I don't think the players did. Figgins looked up as I walked by and simply registered an unfamiliar face. He put out his hand.

"I'm Chone," he said (pronouncing it Shawn). "How you doin'?"

There's nothing like casual acceptance as a legitimate member of a group to make you feel like a fraud, and of course I *was* a fraud, so Figgins's greeting, his pure expression of goodwill, instead of being reassuring, made the sweat turn to icicles on the back of my neck. I had an urge to confess—"Hey, I'm not really an umpire, you know"—which I fortunately suppressed. My mind went back to umpire school, to one of Jim Evans's sayings: "Umpiring is role-playing!" After Figgins shook my hand and resumed taking warm-up grounders, I put my education to its first work and pretended I belonged exactly where I was standing, behind third base along the foul line, doing exactly what I was doing, waiting with my arms folded in a businesslike fashion for the first pitch.

Umpires call third base the rocking chair, the idea being that nothing much happens over there, and that working third is kind of like a day off after you work the plate. (Umpiring crews generally change positions game by game, rotating clockwise around the bases.) But this is misleading. For one thing, you can never tell when a game will pivot around plays at third base or fair-foul calls along the left-field line; some games it just seems that everything of consequence happens on that side of the field. For another thing, even on a sleepy day at third, maybe especially on a sleepy day at third, the required vigilance is that much more forcefully intense; if you have to make only one call all day, after all, it would be calamitous—not to mention humiliating—if you weren't ready for it.

Beyond all that, I faced some unusual circumstances in this game. Ordinarily, major league games are umpired by four men, each with the responsibility for a base, but this day there were only three of us, which is what Macias and Uhlenhopp were used to because the three-man system is regularly in place in the higher minor leagues. But I had been trained only in the two-man system, so not only didn't I have the luxury of concentrating only on third, I also didn't have the comfort of being familiar with my responsibilities.

The three-man system, with a host of if-then options for the base umpires in every situation, is the most complex and counterintuitive of all the different umpiring curricula. Before the game, Macias simplified things for me a bit, giving me, in two broad strokes, what I most needed to know. First, with no one on base, I'd be responsible for running into the outfield on any ball hit in the air from dead center to the left-field line, largely to rule whether a ball was fairly caught. (In a real game, the third-base umpire has responsibility for some outfield fly balls even when there are base runners.) Second, with a man on first, or men on first and second, or with the bases loaded, I'd be positioned inside the infield, behind the pitcher and to one side of the mound or the other, with responsibility for stolen-base attempts, force plays, and tag plays at second and third.

It's hard to explain what it feels like taking your position for the first time as an umpire on a big league diamond, but psychologically speaking, I think it akin to what it must be like commanding an army on the battlefield for the first time, or ascending to the throne after the king dies; you survey the field, and it seems to stretch on forever, and it occurs to you that this is your territory, your domain, that you're supposed to assert dominion over it and that you don't have a clue of the appropriate method or demeanor for doing so.

The intimidation factor was both real and curious. I've been in National Football League locker rooms, where every visitor is subject to the sapling-among-sequoias effect, but that wasn't the case here. Like all professional athletes, baseball players often seem solider than nonathletes (I was about to say normal people), as though their flesh, muscle, and bone have been compacted within their frames like cars at the dump, but the frames themselves are, well, ordinary-size. Figgins, for example, was four inches shorter and thirty-five pounds lighter than I am, not to mention twenty-four years younger, but as I watched him effortlessly fielding grounders and flipping the ball, with the snap of a wrist, over to first, I had a moment of self-awareness: I'm a bigger-than-average guy, six feet one and about 190, but my mind's eye often perceives me as smaller than that, especially in situations where physical prowess reigns. I couldn't help but intuit that Figgins, with his athletic strength and grace, saw himself as bigger than his frame; he simply evinced the sort of confidence in his physique and physical skills that allows the gladiator to be at home in the arena. To be next to someone like that is kind of awe-inspiring; to be in the midst of many people like that, as though the arena were its own planet, is discomforting.

I followed the arc of one of Figgins's throws to first, a clothesline in the wind bending this way and that, and the distance the throw covered seemed enormous. The first baseman was so far away I saw him as a miniature, as though through the wrong end of a telescope, and my ally Macias, who was lined up behind him, seemed beyond shouting distance. Watching the outfielders making their pregame long tosses, the infielders doing their slide steps to retrieve practice grounders, and the pitcher—John Lackey, an All-Star—warming up, I felt as though I were standing next to the world and not in it, that it was a busy place indeed, and managing to turn powerfully on its axis without the least notice or need of me.

Umpires will cite a variety of differences in the way the game is played in the major leagues and the minor leagues, but not always the same ones. The control of the pitchers is one you hear a lot; the discipline of the hitters is another. But one thing they all agree on is that at the top level the game simply moves faster.

For me, this was self-evident; I hadn't worked any games where the pitchers threw the ball so hard or the hitters hit such vicious line drives or the base runners galloped from station to station like cheetahs, and these physical attributes alone, which were clear to me from the top of the first inning on—after Lackey's first fastball, after the first line drive that whistled over my head, after the first stolen-base attempt that had me scrambling late into position—were enough to ratchet up my concentration to headache level.

But when umpires talk about the speed of the game, that stuff isn't exactly, or only, what they're talking about. You can, after all, find minor league pitchers, even high schoolers occasionally, who throw 90 mph, or hitters with mammoth power and runners with the foot speed of Olympians.

What major leaguers do faster on a ball field than anyone else, however, is think and react. Their powers of anticipation approach clairvoyance; it often seems that a fielder has read the ball off the bat from a moment before it was hit. Their initial movements in the direction of making a play are not only instantaneous, but forceful and sure. As the umpire Tim Tschida told *Sports Illustrated*: "Middle infielders get to more balls up the middle that minor leaguers would never get to—and not only get to them, but turn them into double plays."

Then there is a skill that might be called ball-handling, that is, the dexterity with which a player receives the ball off the bat and does something with it—slings it across the diamond, shovels it to a base-covering teammate, pins a tag on a runner. As a fan, I never appreciated this sufficiently. From a distance it's hard to perceive gradations of quickness, and even play-by-play analysts, who are always talking about quick hands and quick wrists, couldn't prepare me for what I learned from my day with the Angels. A major league shortstop or second baseman can transform the ball from an incoming missile into a useful defensive tool with a niftiness that is almost alchemical, as if he hadn't touched the ball at all but simply allowed it to pass through him with its course properly and drastically altered. What I suddenly understood in the first inning is that an umpire positioned within the infield is a unique witness to this phenomenon—and is also in danger of being a victim of it.

When the game began, I took my position on the third-base line in short left field. (You're supposed to line up fifteen feet behind the third baseman, so you're as close to the potential infield action as you can be without risking getting in the way of the fielder.) The first hitter popped out to short, and I stood and watched the play, signaling the out (unnecessarily—you're taught to leave the obvious alone). No harm done, but actually when the ball went up, I should have run into the infield behind the pitcher to be prepared should the shortstop drop the ball and the runner attempt to reach second. The tag play there would have been my call.

The next batter singled in the hole between short and third, and this time I did react properly, heading away from the ball and into the infield. When the throw came into second base, the runner simply retreated to first, and I stayed where I was, behind the pitcher, just to the third-base side of the mound. That's because I was responsible for whatever might happen to the runner from first on his way to second, whether he was trying to steal, being forced on a grounder, rounding the bag on a base hit, or anything else. On the first pitch, the runner did, in fact, steal, and I had my first indication of what a major league arm can do; the catcher's throw whizzed by my head as I turned to face the play at second. I had a startling pang of fear—yikes!—as I recognized that the trajectory of the throw was straighter and lower (not much higher than eye level) than any other catcher's peg I'd ever viewed this closely. That was enough for me to be too slow to witness the play properly; I was still pivoting, my feet not yet set, my eyes moving, as the runner—I wish I could tell you who it was—slid in.

Fortunately, the throw was clearly late, and my safe call required nothing more than a perfunctory mechanic, an easy spread of my arms just to let everybody know that what seemed to be the result of the play was, in fact, the result. By most calculations, in other words, I'd gotten the play right, except that as an umpire I knew I'd screwed it up, and so did my colleagues; on top of being late, Macias told me I'd lined up on the wrong side of the pitcher, that I'd been out of position, that if I'd lined up on the first-base side of the mound rather than the third-base side, I'd have ended up with a far better angle on the play.

The next batter walked, and with two men on, my immediate responsibilities doubled, since plays at both second and third were now equally likely. This is where I learned that trying to think ahead of the play is crucial for an umpire, especially in the major leagues, where the players are so lightning quick in their physical movements that you can't let them have a mental edge on you as well.

The batter hit a ground ball to the right of the shortstop, not fully in the hole but perhaps three steps to the shortstop's right. I did what I'd been taught, stepping up with my right foot and pivoting 180 degrees so I was facing the ball. As the shortstop made the play, I assumed he'd throw to third for the force because he was moving in that direction anyway; it was the easy out. So I cheated in that direction—a turn toward third and a step or two—only to be caught going the wrong way when in the merest instant of transition the shortstop not only gloved the ball but slung it back toward second, the first stage of a double play. Recognizing my mistake, I put on the brakes—and slipped and fell flat on my ass on the infield sod, which hadn't yet dried from its pregame watering.

Seated, I saw that the force at second was tight but not arguable, and that the throw went on to first, where the play was a banger, the foot on the bag and the throw in the glove landing within milliseconds of each other. Macias, smiling and enthusiastic, rang up the batter with an emphatic punch-out. Double play.

Self-consciously I picked myself up. Nobody noticed. Or at least nobody said anything.

Of course, a lot of what goes on in a regular season game doesn't go on in a spring training intrasquad game. For one thing, there aren't any fans in the stands, so you don't get the sizzle that a partisan crowd brings with it. For another, the games don't count; that is, they don't count in the standings, so the stakes are reduced by a rather significant order of magnitude, and that makes the game feel more like, well, a game, and not the matter of life and death that it can become, say, during a pennant race. The Angels didn't even keep score that day, I don't think. (Maybe they did, and I didn't have enough attention in my attention span to notice.) A different pitcher came in from the bullpen each half inning, and by the sixth, even Dino Ebel, the team's third-base coach, with whom I'd been exchanging pleasantries, was surprised that anybody was left and that the game was still going. They ended up playing eight, and Ebel was scratching his head with a they-never-tell-me-anything look on his face.

Further, a number of the players on the field were big league regulars, and they didn't have the pressure of earning a spot on the roster, so the mood was pretty easygoing. Between half-innings, the team ran bunt drills, not so much for the bunting practice, but so the fielding team could practice coordinating the necessary teamwork for making plays to the proper base. One of the closest calls I had all day was on one of these drills, when, with men on first and second, the throw from the catcher, who had fielded the bunt, went to third but it was wide, pulling the third baseman's foot off the bag. Still, the throw was to the runner's side, and the runner didn't slide, so when the ball hit the fielder's glove, the runner's shoulder was right there, colliding with the glove and ball an instant before his foot sneaked in to the bag. I ruled he was out, making a short, downward punching motion with my right fist. "He's out," I said as loudly and gutturally as I could. It came out more like "Eee-yah"—and though in a real game I might have expected an explosion of temper, instead a handful of players just laughed, pointing at the runner as if he were getting a deserved comeuppance.

Okay, so my experience may have been major league umpiring lite, the players' skills on display without the extra engine of competitive intensity. But with all the things I was trying to keep straight in my mind, it helped that I didn't have to worry about tilting the competitive balance with an incompetent call or giving the game away unfairly. However, in the middle of the game, Howie Kendrick, the Angels' starting second baseman, was on first with two out, and as the pitcher delivered, he took off for second. He's fast, but the throw from the catcher was true. The play was close, very close, and Kendrick made one of those incredibly graceful and athletic slides in which the runner seems to stand up even as he lunges feet first into the bag, in one motion sliding and getting set to take off again. It's a smug, presumptuous-looking thing to do—I'm in here easy, it seems to say. But an instant before Kendrick reached the bag, the shortstop's glove snipped his toe, and I saw it.

I called him out, emphatically if awkwardly, I admit, pumping my right fist but stepping forward with my right foot, so I looked like what people mean when they say someone throws like a girl. Kendrick scowled and jerked his head up and away from me, whipping the helmet off his head in the same motion—he didn't throw it, just yanked it off in frustration—and the notion hit me instantly: *Now* he's competing. Weirdly, I almost said something: What, you think you were in? But that impulse, so much a part of my character, passed instantly, and I reverted to the role of an umpire, a role I'd been taught. I simply turned on my heel and walked away.

There was a lesson in this for me, though, namely the difference between calling plays and umpiring. Just having to be in the right place at the right time was intimidating enough, and I was surprised at the energy, both physical and mental, that I had to spend just to keep up. Staying aware of your precise location on the field and knowing where everyone else is as well; keeping in mind the situation and the possibilities for action, both likely and not so likely, these things are energy-sapping. At one point, with a man on second, I was so intently focusing on the pitcher in his stretch and the possibility of a balk that I barely moved when he whirled and fired a pickoff throw back over my head.

The most complicated play of the day happened in midgame with men on second and third. The batter knocked a bouncer down the third-base line, and the third baseman, a hustling young player named Robb Quinlan, came in to intercept it in front of the bag so he could throw home. The ball hit the heel of his glove, however, and deflected high in the air into foul territory toward the dugout.

I was lined up behind third, and my first responsibility was fair or foul—I called it fair—and my second responsibility was to follow the ball to see if it went into the dugout and thus out of bounds. I forgot to do this, however; I was focusing instead on the runner from second coming into third, making sure he touched the bag as he rounded it.

Quinlan, in the meantime, intercepted the ball just before it went into the dugout—I didn't actually see this, but Macias fortunately did. I did see Quinlan leap in the air so he didn't fall down the dugout steps and fling the ball home. The throw was too late to get the lead runner, but the catcher whipped the ball back to third, where the shortstop was covering, to try to get the following runner, who had made his turn, as he headed back to the bag.

I wasn't sure where I was supposed to be to make the call: Should I move into fair territory? Foul territory? Stay on the line? Instinctively, I stayed just foul and got as close as I could to the bag, peering at the tag through a maze of legs, including those of the coach, Ebel, who had snuck right up on the action. The runner beat the ball—I spread my palms and called safe—but then the ball squirted away behind the bag, right at me, and I had to scramble out of the way, into fair territory, as the shortstop went after it.

The runner got to his feet and started for the plate again, took a few steps, then changed his mind. By this time the pitcher had come over to cover third, and the shortstop threw it to him, so there was yet another call to make at third, but this time I was on the infield dirt, looking at the throw from the opposite angle. Safe again.

Did I do everything right? I don't know. Macias said to me afterward that you should generally try to be in foul territory—you get a better look at swipe tags that way—but you also have to use your instincts and adjust to the unexpected plays and unusual angles that the game throws at you. I got the calls right, so my instincts were at least satisfactory, but when the next batter whistled a line drive past my ear down the third-base line, I was still thinking about the previous play. Not only was I nearly beaned, but I forgot to pivot to make the fair-foul call. Good thing Uhlenhopp, the home plate umpire, was on the case. When I looked up, he was doing my job for me, straddling the line a few steps in front of the plate, his hands in the air above his head.

"Foul," he said, in a booming voice, and though he wasn't looking at me, I imagined he was and took it as a terrible reproof. It occurred to me right then that alertness might not be a state you can will yourself into, that it might well be a gift, like a strong throwing arm, and that I simply don't have it in me to be as alert as a major league umpire has to be.

With a ball bag full of balls with Dave Righetti's fingerprints on them, I settled into my stance behind the catcher, Justin Knoedler, while the first of many pitchers—he was wearing number 62, so according to the Giants' press guide it was a young Dominican right-hander, Kelyn Acosta—was still throwing warm-ups. I was immediately relieved. The pitches were startling in their speed and movement, but the ball was visible; its path left its mark on my mind.

This is crucial for an umpire, or at least it was crucial for me. From the first week of umpire school you are taught to take your time when you're calling balls and strikes, to follow the ball all the way into the catcher's glove before even beginning to render a decision. Many umpires—not all, but many—speak about calling pitches as considered judgments, as though pros and cons were involved, and many (again, not all) say they try to replay the pitch in their minds—"run the tape" is a phrase I've heard more than one say—before committing to a call. The patience and rhythm applied to calling pitches is known as timing.

"Take it slow," Higgins had reminded me before he lumbered out to first base. "It's all about timing. Don't feel like you have to be in a hurry back there."

With the game set to begin, Knoedler threw the last warm-up pitch down to second, and as the infielders whipped the ball around and the batter, who was right-handed, stepped in, I should have walked around and brushed off the plate, but didn't. I forgot. So Knoedler simply brushed off the plate with his glove. I held up my right hand, flat palm facing out at Acosta, to keep him from rushing the hitter, who was digging himself a couple of footholds in the box, then flexed my wrist and pointed at the mound.

"Play!" I said. (Contrary to popular myth, umpires don't say, "Play ball!" Why everyone thinks they do, I don't know.)

All this should be absolutely ritualistic. From the first week of umpire school, your plate procedure to start an inning is drummed into you. You stand beside the plate with your mask under your arm. You warn the pitcher when he has one more warm-up pitch. You stride aggressively out in front of the plate, bend over with your butt to center field, and with a flourish of the wrist brush the plate clean of infield dirt. Then you stand and turn, stride back around the plate, your eyes toward the field and on the pitcher. You fix your mask in place over your face; you hold your palm up to the pitcher, letting him know it's you, only you, who starts the game, and then you do it, you tell him, "Play!" And you glare out at him and take your stance.

The purpose of all this is to establish a base of authority, a metronomic pace, a stable floor for the events of the inning to unfold upon. When you do it right, the game opens with the rhythm you've created and seems to join a momentous tale already in progress, the everydayness of baseball, like a stream joining a river. When you don't—when you forget, for instance, to brush off the plate—the start of the game has a hiccupping quality, an awkwardness that often communicates itself into the opening moments. It isn't damaging to the game, necessarily, but it feels artless and is therefore disheartening.

Actually, I had trouble with my stance, too, a comic sort of trouble suited to a Chaplin pantomime. Properly, I positioned myself in the slot. My feet were wide for balance, my left foot slightly forward, right toes aligned with my left heel. And I tucked my right hand just behind my right knee and crooked my left elbow so the forearm and a lightly curled fist lay across my belly, protecting the softness there just below where my chest protector left off. Then a moment of uncertainty set in. Shouldn't my arms be the other way around? I could never remember which arm was supposed to be protecting the belly, the one on the hitter's side or the one away from the hitter. So I quickly switched them, a test, then switched them back, as if instead of calling balls and strikes I was sending semaphore. (If you watch major league umpires, it turns out it doesn't matter much.)

Finally, with my arms still, I was standing easily, straight, until Acosta rocked back and the delivery was imminent; then I bent my knees and lowered my bottom, crouching with my back erect so my chin was even with the top of Knoedler's head, and locked my shoulders in direct perpendicularity to the line between the rubber and the plate. I felt both ready and crippled by anticipation.

I didn't know what to expect, but probably I should have. This time of year, before the real competition began, the pitchers weren't yet so concerned with finely painting the corners as they were with waking up their stuff and corralling it, getting their pitches both to move and find the plate. Throwing strikes was on the agenda, and the hitters came up looking for them, coiled and predisposed to swing. The first pitch was a fastball with a tail like a comet—my first impression of a major league pitch was that you could actually see the path, as though it left skywriting in its wake—headed outside but fading inexorably back to the middle of the plate. I would probably have called it a strike if the hitter hadn't swung and laced it into left field for a hit.

The second guy also swung at the first pitch; he singled to center. And the third guy also swung at the first pitch, doubling to the gap in right center. So men were on second and third, a run was in, and I hadn't called a pitch yet.

"I guess we don't need you," Knoedler said to me, over his shoulder.

If you watch baseball a lot, you know that each umpire has his own style in calling pitches. Each gestures differently. Some indicate a strike with a brusque slash of an upright forearm, the fist rattling quickly like the clapper of a bell. Others point emphatically to the side. Still others chop their forearms forward and at an angle. Every now and then you'll even see a guy using two hands, one imitating the other like an underscore or a reflection. This is about personality and vanity, and it matters to umpires; they want their own signature mechanics. Most minor league umpires can identify major leaguers by their strike mechanics alone, and in the minors much time is spent in experimentation. Once, in a minor league locker room, I heard the following conversation:

Umpire 1: "I noticed you going to the side today."

Umpire 2: "Yeah, I thought I'd try it. How'd it look?"

Umpire 1: "Okay, I guess. A little faggoty."

Umpire 2: "Yeah? I was afraid of that."

So, I was curious about my own mechanic. I wasn't sure what it would be. I couldn't even remember what my signals looked like in my amateur games the previous September, or what my strike call sounded like. The first pitch I had to call was on the fourth batter; the pitch was way outside, so it was easy. You call a ball basically by not calling a strike; you stay in your crouch and you can even stay silent, though if it's sort of close you might grunt, almost under your breath, "Ball!" or, as it sometimes comes out, "Hawh!"—so the catcher and the batter know the call right away.

Finally, I had to call a strike, a fastball right across the plate, thigh high, the no-argument pitch that umpires call a cockshot. The batter was taking, apparently. I followed the ball with my eyes into the catcher's glove—you never move your head, just your eyes—raised up out of my crouch, and kind of watched and listened as I was making the call. I can't really tell you how these elements of style came about. For lack of a better word, they were natural.

Here's what I learned: that my strike mechanic has two elements to it, a downward slash in front of me, toward the catcher, brief and deliberate like a hitch in a hitter's swing, followed by a sharp single blow with a fist, like a rap on a door, with the forearm held vertical from the elbow. Out of my mouth came a long, loud, guttural cry—"Raaaaahhhhhy!"

I was okay with it all. It felt personal, mine. It didn't seem to me I was copying anyone. It didn't make me feel awkward or self-conscious. And as far as I could tell—from behind my mask I cast a look around—nobody laughed.

The first breaking ball I saw gave me a flashback. About a year earlier, I had first asked a major league umpire what it was like to be behind the plate, a witness to major league stuff. I was walking in New York's Little Italy with Tim Timmons, who joined the major league roster in 2001; we'd just had lunch and I told him that like most baseball fans I was curious about what the best pitchers' pitches looked like as they approached home plate. The example I used was Mariano Rivera, the Yankee relief pitcher whose main pitch, basically his only pitch, is a cut fastball that nobody can seem to hit even though they know it's coming. What's it like to watch Rivera's stuff come at you? I asked, and Timmons stopped on the street and gestured, his right hand moving straight toward me, then suddenly shifting onto a whole other path. "It's like being in traffic and watching a car change lanes without signaling," he said.

This turned out to be a splendid foreshadowing of my experience, even though the pitchers I observed weren't anywhere near as accomplished as Rivera. It's hard to overemphasize this for a fan who has never gotten so close to home plate: The movement on major league pitches is so abrupt and severe that the ball almost seems to be mechanically wrenched across space. Timmons's automotive imagery was useful: Some of the breaking pitches I saw couldn't possibly dive and swoop the way they did, I thought, unless a driver, a little man behind a steering wheel, were embedded in the ball.

Then, too, the pitches are hugely various. The recipe for breaking stuff calls for such fine seasoning that every pitch seems to have its own sly wrinkle, and one curveball that sweeps horizontally across the front of the plate is followed by another that, on its way past the inside corner, makes a mere flirtatious dip at the back edge. This is one reason the strike zone ends up as such a negotiation. The paths of pitches don't so much pass through the strike zone as you think you know it; they teach it to you by drawing and redrawing its boundaries.

Finally, there is the element of deception, that is, how pitchers change speeds and spot their pitches in different locations, how they try to set hitters up, seduce them into looking for one type of pitch in one part of the strike zone, then surprise them with another pitch elsewhere.

Lip service is frequently paid to this by television analysts; attentive fans understand the concept of a pitcher's altering the plane of a hitter's vision. Nonetheless, it's remarkable to see it carried out just a couple of feet in front of you. I hadn't umpired before for any pitcher with nearly enough control to effectively deceive a hitter. Teenagers and adult amateurs tend to use the plate as a general target; it doesn't get any more refined than that. But in the first inning in Scottsdale, a young pitcher threw two biting curveballs to a left-handed hitter, who swung above them both, missing them badly as the pitches clipped the inside corner at the knees. The next pitch was a fastball, high in the strike zone on the outside corner—or at least near it. Guarding against, and probably anticipating, another curveball, the hitter didn't have a chance. I didn't either. Not only had the pitcher conditioned the hitter where to look for the ball, he'd done it to me, too, and I was surprised enough by the fastball that I had to move my head, instead of just my eyes, to watch it— a definite taboo. I'd never have called it convincingly, one way or the other; fortunately, the hitter managed just to foul it off, barely ticking it with a desperate flick of his wrists.

This is a good time to interject something in general about ballplayers' wrists, and in particular how strong they need to be to effect the last snap of a swing, the part that propels the bat across the plane of the plate, that supplies its vicious purpose. From my umpire's crouch behind the plate, this couldn't have been more evident, and it may well have been my first revelation of the day. When the first hitter of the game swung at the first pitch, it was as though he had snatched the ball, saved it with his bat at the last possible instant from being swallowed up by the catcher's glove, and slung it into the outfield on a line. From that moment on, I noted each hitter's wrists as he stepped into the batter's box and took a few practice swings, and when I compared them with my own each time I held up my right forearm to call a strike, suddenly it was obvious: A professional ballplayer's wrists—thicker, more sinewy and athletic than those of the rest of us, at least an order of magnitude more powerful than the norm—are as defining a characteristic of a breed as stripes on a tiger. They are essential in allowing them to do what other people can't, namely hit a baseball thrown by a major league pitcher, a skill that Ted Williams famously called the single most difficult thing to do in sports.

All this is not to say that I was intimidated back there; that's not it, exactly. Dazzled is closer to it, and deeply impressed. For the first inning and a half or so, I wasn't doing much but marveling at what I was seeing. A few pitches missed the plate by plenty, but most skipped by with a seeming wink at me, teasing at the edges of the plate and, pitch to pitch, shifting the angle of their approach. I did my best and may have missed a few close pitches, but my calls, if not entirely deft and incisive, were accurate enough that the game pretty much resembled baseball.

Over the whole three innings, I blew only one pitch egregiously, an off-speed pitch, a breaking ball from a left-handed pitcher to a right-handed batter. Though its path had it headed for the middle of the plate, midchest high—a meatball, it appeared—it dived at the last moment, like a pelican after a fish, and nearly hit the batter in the rear foot. The catcher's glove had to turn upward to make the catch, and I lost my timing. The speed of the pitch fooled me, and I started to rise up before it landed. The instant I called, "Strike," I knew I'd blown it. The dugout erupted with plaintive yapping, and the hitter yanked his neck around to glare at me. Unfortunately, the hitter was Knoedler, who had been a friendly presence behind the plate up till then. Eventually he walked, but when he came back out the next inning with his catcher's gear on, our pleasantries were done.

*   *   *

Near the end of the first half-inning when, with a right-handed hitter at the plate, I took my stance in the slot, and just before the pitch was delivered, Knoedler moved, shifting his position from the inside to the outside edge of the plate, establishing a sharply distinct new target for the pitcher with his glove. The last-second shift is meant to confuse or deceive the hitter, to keep him guessing about where the catcher is expecting the pitch, and also, when there are runners on base, to keep them from relaying the catcher's position to the hitter. But it's often a problem for the umpire. Sometimes, the catcher moves right in front of you, into your line of vision; in this case, though, he moved completely away, which left me in a position I hadn't anticipated: facing down a fastball with nothing but sixty feet six inches of space between me and it. I believe I actually gulped.

But instead of a calamity, what happened was an object lesson. First, I didn't throw my hands up in front of my face in a panic (another image featured in my motel nightmare); I didn't even flinch, which made a huge, confidence-boosting impression on me: *I'm not a flincher!*

Second, the ball hit the target, which made me, well, not exactly grateful, but cognizant of how satisfying, even exciting, it is when a pitcher does what he's supposed to do. It makes you want to reward it. Umpires at the major league level read the catcher's glove—it tells you where to look for a pitch—and this is one reason, I suddenly understood, that when a pitcher hits the corner but misses the catcher's glove (especially if the catcher has to make a sudden movement to make the catch), the pitch is often called a ball.

Indeed, umpires are quite sensitive to the catcher's glove. They don't like it when a catcher stabs at the ball, or when a catcher doesn't regularly get his glove set in receiving a pitch; when the glove is moving—for example, if it is sliding outside as a pitch approaches the outside corner—the path of the pitch through the hitting zone is that much more obscure.

Umpires get offended when a catcher, trying to "help" an umpire make a call, holds his glove in place for an extra beat after the pitch arrives—a practice known as "sticking it"—ostensibly to prove the pitch was a strike. Then there's the catcher's practice of "pulling" pitches, that is, catching a pitch that's a little outside and yanking the glove an inch or two toward the corner. Umpires aren't especially sympathetic to that, but they don't mind it so much because they feel it's basically the catcher telling them the pitch was off the plate. If a catcher pulls a pitch, generally he loses any chance of the umpire calling it a strike.

On the other hand, umpires admire a catcher who "frames" a pitch gently and naturally, receiving the ball rather than snatching it and showing it to the umpire with a subtle emphasis. "He gives you a good look" is, about a catcher, high umpire praise.

All of this became evident to me in the first inning of my game, light-bulb after lightbulb going off in my head as I began to recognize the nuances of calling pitches. Don't get me wrong: I couldn't cope with the nuances well. I simply understood that nuances exist. But that was pretty thrilling. When I had to call my first strike three to end the bottom of the first, I did so with relish. The curveball came in to a left-handed hitter, broke across the plate belt high, and he didn't swing. The catcher, Jennings, gave me a good look. The ball nestled in his glove like a toddler snuggling in under the covers. It wasn't close. The batter knew it. Jennings knew it. The pitcher knew it. I didn't have a doubt.

Unanimity around the plate is a glorious thing. I pumped my right fist forward, then made a fist with my left, pulling back hard as though on an enormous trigger.

"Rahhhhhhhhy!" I said, and the batter turned and walked away. This was just great. I almost laughed out loud.

In a regular game, I'd have had responsibilities other than calling balls and strikes. When runners are on base and the umpires rotate on a hit to the outfield, for instance, the home plate umpire must hustle down to third. Before the game, however, Higgins and Macias both told me not to worry about that stuff; they'd do what needed to be done. I would have to make fair-foul calls along the baselines in the infield, and of course a play at the plate would be mine, too. But they didn't want me worrying about running anywhere or wondering whether I ought to be somewhere else.

Still, you can't hide on a baseball field.

One of the things I'd had a flash of worry over the night before was dealing with check swings, those times when the hitter begins to bring his bat around, then tries to stop, and it's your job to determine whether he succeeded. It's always a dicey call—so much so that if the plate umpire says the batter didn't swing, the catcher is permitted to have the home plate umpire ask a base umpire to confirm the call or overrule it—and it's especially touchy with two strikes on the hitter.

The call often results in a dispute because no one really knows at what point a check swing becomes a strike. The rulebook has no guideline, and check swings are notorious among umpires for needing personal interpretation, sort of the way pornography was for Potter Stewart, the Supreme Court justice who famously declared in 1964 that though he wasn't about to try to define what constituted obscene material, he knew it when he saw it.

In the bottom of the second inning, with one out and two strikes on the hitter, the pitcher threw a high fastball near the outside edge, and the hitter, overanxious about protecting the plate, began his swing, then struggled to hold up. I watched as he tried to keep his wrists from breaking, but he couldn't quite, and the bat head swept across the whole plane of the plate before he drew it back. It was a swing, all right (I was pretty sure), which would have been strike three, of course, but then the unanticipated complication arose: He'd either ticked the ball with his bat—or not—and the catcher hadn't held on to it.

Now, there are some fouls like this that call themselves. In the instant before the ball hits the catcher's glove, your ear somehow registers the tiny tick, or your eye makes note of the minute redirection in the path of the ball. This wasn't one of those, alas. If the ball had ticked the bat, it was a bare brush; if its path had been altered, it was so minuscule a change that the only visual clue was the catcher's miss—circumstantial evidence.

I froze. Did I actually see the ball fouled or hear it? Was I making it up? I reran the tape in my head and still wasn't sure, but in the end decided that my uncertainty was a reason to make the call. Why would I even be wondering about this if I didn't have reason to suspect that the bat had touched the ball?

This sounds inept, I know, amateurish, and I guess it was, but, jeez, this stuff happens fast. And I hadn't made a mistake. Not yet, anyway. Then I did.

I gave the wrong signal. I stood up and with my arms high slapped the fingertips of one hand off the fingertips of the other, mimicking a ball ticking off a bat. It's the signal you're supposed to use to indicate a foul tip, which, contrary to the popular usage of the term, is not simply a ball that ticks off a bat. A foul tip is specifically defined in the rules as a foul ball that goes directly from the bat into the catcher's glove, meaning the result of the pitch is the same as if the hitter had swung and missed. As an umpire, the only reason you signal the tip is to let everyone know you saw the ball hit the bat, so there is no dispute about that.

The problem for me was that the catcher didn't catch it—i.e., the ball didn't go directly into his glove—so this was not a foul tip but a simple foul ball. The signal for that is very different. You raise both hands above your head and out in front of you—sort of a cross between Stop! and Touchdown!—and call out "Foul!" so everyone, especially the catcher and the hitter, who are likely to have their backs to you, is aware that the ball is dead.

Of course, not only is the signal different, so are the repercussions. If I'd properly called foul, the action would simply have stopped, the hitter would have stepped back into the box, and the pitcher would have gotten ready to deliver the next pitch.

Instead a whole different reality began to unfold. Because he hadn't heard me say anything—nor did he see me make the (improper) foul-tip signal—the hitter assumed there had been no foul, that he had missed the pitch and that the catcher had simply dropped a third strike, which would allow him to take off for first. Which is what he did.

Assuming the same thing, the catcher, meanwhile, located the ball that had dribbled away toward the on-deck circle, scuttled over to it, picked it up, and fired to first to make the putout, whereupon the first baseman started whipping the ball around the infield, the ritual that pro teams engage in when an out is made on the infield with no one on base.

In the meantime, I was standing behind the plate, watching in dumb horror, having recognized, after a delay, what I should have done moments earlier but remaining at a loss as to what I should do now.

During the previous year, I'd had umpires explain to me over and over and in a variety of different ways that they don't work in a context of absolutes. It's impossible, they'd told me, to be 100 percent certain on every call. At times, maybe not every day, but often enough, you don't get a good look at a play and you just don't know what to call.

So you bolster your judgments with whatever clues are available. You use common sense to make the game run smoothly, to minimize disputes. You use experience, your knowledge of the game and how well or badly it is being played, to help you with close calls.

To wit, when Tomas de la Rosa came to the plate, and I called him out on strikes, I wasn't certain the final pitch had caught the corner. But I knew de la Rosa had been outmaneuvered. The pitch had fooled him. He'd mistimed its speed, stepped too soon, and robbed himself of the balance he needed to swing. This was the pitcher's good work, de la Rosa's failure. The pitch was close. The call could've gone either way. But de la Rosa didn't deserve the benefit of the doubt, and the pitcher did. I recognized all this in the moment. But what made the call easy was that when the ball went past him, de la Rosa turned to me with a plaintive, hopeful, guilty look of worry. That assured his fate—strike three! I knew there wouldn't be an argument.

This was good umpiring. It was authoritative, and if you learn one thing as an umpire, it's that you can't go about your business as if you are anything other than sure.

Which brings me back to the foul ball.

Higgins saved my bacon. In the past he had been an instructor at umpire school, so he was experienced at spotting the kinds of mistakes that inexperienced umpires make. When he saw me signaling foul tip instead of foul ball, he knew instantly what I'd *meant* to do. He was positioned along the right-field line, about fifteen feet behind the first baseman, and when the throw came to first, he realized he'd given me enough time to step in and undo the damage myself and I hadn't done it. He stalked in toward the infield, throwing his hands above his head.

"Time!" he called as the infielders tossed the ball around the infield. "The ball was foul."

Then he pointed at the hitter, who was just reaching first and preparing to return to the dugout. "You! Back to bat."

And that was it. The infielders looked momentarily perplexed, but they shrugged and trotted back to their positions. The ball found its way back to the pitcher. Higgins lumbered back behind first. Everything was repaired, evidently, except my ego. Jennings, who was the catcher, walked past me as he got set to squat behind the plate again.

"That was foul?" he said. "I didn't hear you call it foul."

That's when I proved I wasn't an umpire.

"My mistake," I said. "Sorry."

CHAPTER TEN

THE BRAILLE WATCH

You're standing out there, it seems like forever, and you get to a point
where you don't care how long it takes. When it's done, it's done. But
you're thinking, "Please don't let something happen where they can
blame it on the umpire."

—DON DENKINGER, March 2006

The 2007 World Series was the first for Mike Everitt, who had been in the major leagues for nine years and pro ball for twenty. He was forty-three, a solid baseball citizen who had earned this honor, who had every right to feel proud and maybe a little puffed up, and whom no one would blame for being a little nervous. Indeed, when he took the field for game one between the Red Sox and the Colorado Rockies at Fenway Park in Boston, he had butterflies, a kind of anxiety, the sense, both pleasurable and awing, that he'd reached a goal, the pinnacle of his profession.

It had been a long couple of weeks for him. He'd had trouble tamping down the anticipation he'd been feeling since he finished his first-round playoff series and Mike Port, baseball's vice president in charge of umpiring, called to tell him he'd gotten the World Series assignment.

"It has been a gamut of emotions," Everitt said. "First I was extremely excited and then very quickly after that extremely nervous. I started thinking, 'Oh my God, when did I work the plate last?'"

In the first round, Everitt had been on one of the crews for the National League divisional playoffs; the Arizona Diamondbacks beat the Chicago Cubs in three games, and he had worked third, second, and first.

"My first round was a sweep, so I didn't work the plate," he said, "and I had to go back to the calendar. September twenty-eighth was my last plate game, and all of a sudden I'm thinking, 'Goodness, I've got game five of the World Series. We've got such a long break in between, and I've never gone that deep into a season before.' I mean, usually by now I'm well into a transition into being a husband and father again."

Among the umpires I'd gotten to know, Everitt struck me as proto-typical, both physically and temperamentally. He was good-looking in a nondescript middle-American way, round-faced, large, and athletic, but not muscular or burly. Like most umpires, he carried himself with an understated grace. He was a religious man—"These are prayerful times," he said, as a way of describing what it was like to be in his first World Series—and a family man, with a son and a daughter who were with him, along with his wife and her sister, for the Series, and who were responsible for his getting up early enough for a Sunday-morning interview after a long Saturday-night game. He was politically conservative (his profile on the Major League Baseball Web site mentioned his avid Republicanism) and had a sentimental streak. He wore uniform number 57, he told me, to honor his late father, whose prize possession had been a 1957 Chevy truck he'd kept in mint condition since he'd bought it as a teenager.

We'd spoken a few times before, just casually, and he'd been polite, uninformative, not terribly interested in revealing any fraternity secrets. So I was surprised he agreed to meet during the World Series, and even more surprised at his chattiness and candor. We were at a hotel in Denver, between games three and four. It was the morning of October 28—exactly a month since he'd worked the plate, which he was scheduled to do again the following night. (He never did. Later that day, with Everitt working at first, the Red Sox completed their sweep of the Rockies.) By this time, some of the apprehension he'd felt before the Series had worn off, but the memory of it was still fresh.

"After I got the call, a lot of veteran umpires gave me advice," Everitt said, "and one of the things a lot of them said to me was 'You have to just treat the games like any other games.' They said, 'Now, it's impossible to do that, but you don't want to just get caught up in the atmosphere because you won't be able to umpire like you know how to umpire, like how you've been taught to umpire.' And it's true, the first pitch, the flashes of bulbs—it was just incredible."

For game one, Everitt had worked along the left-field line, one of the two extra umpire positions that baseball adds for postseason play, and as he entered the field from the dugout along the third-base line, his crewmate, the third-base umpire Chuck Meriwether, told him to take a second and look up at the famous left-field wall, the expansive ver-dant acreage known as the Green Monster, and the scoreboard implanted in it, an old-fashioned one that disdains computer graphics (and even electricity) and relies on actual human beings deployed inside the wall to post the numbered tiles that display the game's totals of runs, hits, and errors.

"You know that famous scoreboard at Fenway, right?" Everitt asked me. "Chuck said, 'Look up there.' He said, 'You know you're the only show in town when there's no other scores up there.'"

You might not think of umpires as nervous or prone to sentiment, and generally they don't behave that way. Everitt didn't express himself with especially dynamic feeling; that's typically umpire—the confession of vibrant emotion in a nonchalant, even toneless, mode. But though the players in the World Series often come across more like privileged millionaires than dedicated athletes who are getting their just reward; and though the World Series has become such a corporate event, so tied to artificial spectacle, advertising, and television that the games sometimes seem little more than the business meetings at the heart of an industry convention, completely stripped of the romance and emo-tion of baseball—the World Series *is* emotional, and tense and thrilling, for at least one group of participants: the umpires. This is especially so for the rookies, the guys who are getting their first taste of their chosen profession's most glaring spotlight.

"It took me several innings before I calmed down, before I felt, 'Okay, this is cool,'" Wally Bell had told me in St. Louis in 2006, the day after he'd worked his first World Series plate game, fourteen years into his big league career. As Everitt would be a year later, Bell said he'd been on edge from the moment he learned of the assignment.

"You get the call and you're thrilled," he said. "It's jubilation, but then reality sets and you're going, 'Don't let me fuck this up.'"

Ted Barrett, who got his first Series assignment in 2007, said he was rather calm until he walked out to home plate in Fenway Park for the pregame meeting with the managers. As he was shaking hands with Terry Francona of the Red Sox and Clint Hurdle of the Rockies, he said, "That was when I had my 'holy crap' moment."

And Laz Diaz, who worked the plate in game two, said the coolest moment for him was probably when Mike Lowell, the Red Sox third baseman, batted in the bottom of the second. Lowell had been a teenager, playing for the Southwest Miami Boys Club in the early 1990s, when Diaz, who had already abandoned a minor league playing career, was working as an amateur umpire there.

"The first time he came up, I said, 'Hey, Mike, from the Southwest Boys Club to this, eh?' And he said, 'Yeah, incredible.'"

But Everitt's story about the Fenway scoreboard was the most telling because it was a hand-me-down. A couple of hours after our conversation I ran into Chuck Meriwether.

Meriwether, a major league umpire since 1993, was working his second series. Coincidentally, he'd been behind the plate when the Red Sox secured their last championship in 2004, and I asked him what I'd asked Everitt: For an umpire, what's the difference between the regular season and the World Series?

He didn't hesitate: "This is what you work for. It's what you think about from the first day you step into umpire school. As you work your way up through the minor leagues, this is the goal you're trying to accomplish. This is what it's all about."

But on the field, I said. Does it feel different on the field?

"Oh, yes." He described the moment when he first recognized the difference, a moment, he said, that caused his whole career to flash in front of him. It sounded remarkably familiar.

"A few years ago, at my first World Series, I was working with Brian Gorman," Meriwether said. "And we walked on the field at Fenway, and Brian looked out at the Green Monster and the scoreboard and he said, 'You know you're the only game in town when you look up there and you don't see another score.'"

I spent two World Series, 2006 and 2007, with the umpires, and the hope was that the games would be close, that the competition would seesaw, that the Series would go seven games, that the quality of play would be polished to a high sheen, and that the umpires would be in the thick of it all.

To my chagrin, but to the great relief—and to some degree, the credit—of the umpires, none of this happened. In 2006, the St. Louis Cardinals disposed of the Detroit Tigers in five sloppily played games—Tiger pitchers alone made three throwing errors—in weather, cold and wet, more suitable for going to the movies than the ballpark. And in 2007, the Red Sox swept the Rockies with such conviction and dispatch that the Series barely achieved the tension of a lazy midweek day game in August. No drama. (The 2008 Series between the Philadelphia Phillies and the Tampa Bay Rays was pretty much a dud too.)

What emerged for me instead was the World Series as a lab experiment for observing umpire behavior under controlled conditions, because the World Series is a crucible, an enclosed and heated vessel that intensifies observable characteristics. The World Series is an interesting time to watch umpires at work—and to speak to them—not least because it's the only time the spotlight is big enough to include them, and they find themselves in it along with everybody else. Under the artificial media glare that annually drenches "the only game in town," the techniques, the decision-making, the varying styles, and to some degree the personalities of the umpires are revealed with a hyperbolic clarity that doesn't pertain during the regular season.

For example, as the crew rotates positions under the spotlight, with a different member taking the plate each night, the personal styles of umpires seem more acute and more pertinent to the game. Alfonzo Marquez's crisp, dance-step-to-the-side, finger-pointing strike mechanic gives the game a distinct rhythm, almost like an orchestra conductor. On the other hand, Wally Bell, a bearish guy who not only employs the scissors stance but is the only remaining big league umpire who takes pitches with a knee to the ground, gathers in the spectator's eye almost the way a catcher gathers in a pitched ball; his appearance and positioning seem to slow the game down, like a light anchor on a floating boat. I thought maybe this was just me, that because I was watching the umpires so intently I was projecting qualities onto them. But this wasn't so.

"In these games you definitely have a different mentality," Mike Everitt told me. "The regular season is a physical grind, but the postseason is a total mental grind. It's such a confined, concentrated experience. You know it's going to end, but the pressure is just so intense. I've found it to be a total strain. You walk off the field and you're mentally exhausted, and you might not have even had a play all night long. It's just the waiting for it."

After game one on the left-field line, Everitt spent game two at third base, where the action is usually at its most sporadic and the waiting at its most grueling. In the bottom of the fourth, he had the closest call of the night.

The game was tied, 1–1, and the Red Sox had men on first and third with two out when their shortstop, Julio Lugo, laced a sharp grounder down the third-base line, inside the line but tailing toward foul territory as it skittered through the infield like a flat stone on water. When it reached third on its second hop, it either barely clipped the airspace over the front corner of the third-base bag, or just passed in front of it. The difference between fair and foul (and thus at least a run and maybe two) was a matter of maybe an inch, and Everitt, who was positioned behind the bag, executed the call—"Foul!"—with certainty and flair even as he was avoiding getting hit, sidestepping the ball as it sped by, throwing his arms straight up in the air and then sweeping them down again and across his body toward foul territory, as though he were a linebacker shoving an oncoming blocker out of the way.

He repeated the gesture for emphasis, selling a close call at an important juncture of the game; it was a fine umpire moment, forceful, graceful, timely, and accurate. Replays showed how close the ball's path came to slicing off a millimeter of third base, and as Everitt's dance was replayed along with it, the Fox play-by-play broadcaster, Joe Buck, no friend to umpires ordinarily, was moved to declare it "a great call by Mike Everitt."

"It's one of the things you're always looking for," Everitt said, referring to a scorcher down the line. "You're looking for it, but when it happens, it happens so quickly you just react. I position myself just a little behind the third baseman. Mostly it's so if he has a diving-line-drive catch, if I have to rule catch or no catch, I'm close enough. But it's a twofold thing, it's also to keep myself in the game; if you're farther back, your depth perception comes into play, especially on a play like the one we're talking about, the Lugo play.

"I'll tell you one thing, I've never believed in that rocking-chair stuff," he went on, ticking off the possibilities that he tries to stay aware of from pitch to pitch when he's working third base. "You're thinking fair-foul calls, you're thinking check swings, you're thinking, 'Okay, two runners on, maybe there's no outs, so possible bunt.' You're looking at the runner on second, seeing if he has good speed, or even average speed, so you can anticipate when he might run on a ground ball or a wild pitch or even a steal. You're thinking about what the score is, whether they might try to hit-and-run; you're thinking, 'Okay, two men on, a ground ball to the shortstop that takes him to his right, maybe the play will come to third for a force out'; that doesn't happen much, but it did happen last night. Remember? And if you're not ready for it, it'll bite you in the ass. You're thinking about a line drive to the third baseman or shortstop, and whether he might trap it and what the base runners will do. You're constantly going over this stuff in your head, and then the pitcher throws it, and nothing happens, and you take a deep breath and do it again."

After the game, Everitt fielded a lot of calls about the Lugo play. It would have been routine during the season, just an umpire successfully executing one of his tougher everyday duties. But this was the World Series. He heard from friends. He heard from other umpires.

"Some of them said, 'Relax, you sold it,'" Everitt said. "And some of them said, 'Hey, I didn't know you could move that fast.'"

Umpires used to be chosen for the World Series largely by reputation and seniority, which is why Bill Klem once officiated in five straight Series (1911–15), and why his record of eighteen total appearances, the last in 1940, will never be broken. (No one else has more than ten.) But complaints of unfairness by the umpires and the umpires' union—postseason assignments bring more pay—finally caused baseball to employ a rotation system.

This didn't sit well with all constituencies, either, with participating clubs and the media complaining that the best umpires were too often not on the field during the season's most important games. Eventually a compromise resulted, which was implemented in 2000. Now umpires chosen for postseason assignments are still paid extra for their work ($15,000 for the Division Series and $20,000 each for the League Championship Series and the World Series in 2007), but in addition, all umpires, whether they work playoff games or not, share a bonus pool that provides them about $25,000 apiece.

Selections for postseason assignments are made one round at a time. The twenty-four Division Series umpires are announced on the next-to-last Saturday of the regular season; those twenty-four are ineligible to work the second round, the League Championship Series, so twelve additional umpires are given those assignments on the last Saturday of the season.

The six World Series umpires are gleaned from the twenty-four who worked the first round, and though only those who worked the World Series the year before are officially ineligible, an unwritten rule is that a first-time Division Series umpire will not work the World Series, that he'll have to return to the postseason again at least once to work the second round before he earns his chance to officiate in the season's ultimate games.

Major league umpires are observed even more intensely during the season than their minor league brethren—in 2008, the big leagues employed seven full-time supervisors who have had professional umpiring experience and nine trained observers with baseball, if not umpiring, backgrounds (Bill Russell, the former Dodger shortstop, was one), which means that umpires were officially being scrutinized in about half of all games—and all the postseason assignments are made largely on the basis of performance during the season.* But other factors are involved as well.

Seniority is one. The idea is to put a high-achieving crew on the field and at the same time have a mix of umpires: senior guys who have been there and done that and aren't likely to be surprised by anything or taken aback at a crucial moment, and up-and-coming umpires who deserve the honor but need the high-profile experience to complete their résumés and their seasoning. In 2007, the crew chief was Ed Montague, whose first season in the big leagues was 1976; second in seniority was Mike Reilly, a thirty-year veteran. Meriwether had just finished his fifteenth big league season, and rounding out the crew, Everitt, Barrett, and Laz Diaz had all joined the staff in 1999.

It's a pretty good system; umpires are generally satisfied with it, and according to Port, the office doesn't hear so much complaining from

---

*The performance rating is dependent on a number of factors, including QuesTec scores, situation management, missed calls, display of overall umpiring knowledge, pace of games, on-field mobility, hustle, focus, and general demeanor.

the clubs anymore, either. But it isn't perfect, and the example most often raised comes from game two of the 2005 American League Championship Series, between the Anaheim Angels and the hometown Chicago White Sox.

The score was tied, 1–1, in the bottom of the ninth, with two outs. The White Sox hitter, A. J. Pierzynski, had two strikes against him when he swung at a split-finger fastball delivered by Kelvim Escobar. He missed, evidently strike three, evidently ending the inning. But it was unclear whether the ball bounced and was quickly smothered and scooped up by the Angels' catcher, Josh Paul—which would mean Paul would have to tag Pierzynski to record the out—or whether Paul snatched it up cleanly, an instant before it hit the dirt.

The home plate umpire was Doug Eddings, who was thirty-seven years old at the time, finishing his sixth full season in the big leagues. When Pierzynski swung at the ball, Eddings signaled strike three, but then didn't signal that the batter was out, which would ordinarily seem redundant, but in this case, because it was unclear whether Paul had caught the ball cleanly, was necessary. Eddings thought the ball had hit the dirt, but he didn't make a vocal call to inform Paul and Pierzynski of the ruling, which led them to assume different things.

Paul, thinking the batter out and the inning over, rolled the ball back to the pitcher's mound. Pierzynski, thinking he needed to be tagged, took off for first and, with the ball rolling in the infield, easily made it and was allowed to remain there. After the inevitable argument, the White Sox scored the winning run on a stolen base and a double.

The problem was not the call itself. Replays were inconclusive regarding whether the ball hit the ground before it was caught, and it wouldn't have mattered to anyone what the call was had only Eddings made it clear and definitive. Because he ruled the ball had hit the ground, he either had to signal that the ball remained in play—pointing at the ground to show where the ball had hit or making a safe sign to indicate the batter was not yet put out—or at least to indicate verbally that the ball remained in play to the two players closest to him. "No catch!" he could have shouted. "No catch!"

Eddings explained afterward that he was simply making the same strike-three sign he had made for swinging strikes all game long, and his defenders said it was not up to him to do more than that. But a number of senior and retired umpires—none of whom wanted to have an opinion attributed to him because it is anathema to offer public criticism of another umpire—said that Eddings's first obligation was to avoid a mess ("preventive umpiring," in one former umpire's phrase), and that allowing the batter and the catcher to believe that different calls had been made is the very definition of losing control of a game.

No one thought Eddings an unfit umpire. But according to several colleagues, he had gotten this postseason assignment, his first in a League Championship Series, largely on the strength of excellent QuesTec scores, and that was the problem. Anybody can, with practice, master the QuesTec technology, but you can't practice experience; you can't practice foreseeing disaster. As one veteran umpire told me, if Eddings had been around a little longer, "he wouldn't have ended up in the shithouse."

It's not unusual for an umpire to spend eight or ten years in the majors before he is selected for the World Series, and for some it's much longer than that. Gary Darling served sixteen seasons before working the 2003 Series; so did Jerry Layne before being named in 2005. As of 2007, Larry Poncino, with fifteen years in the big leagues, was still waiting; so was Bill Hohn, for whom 2007 was his nineteenth season.

Why does this happen? It's hard to say exactly. The commissioner's office has to sign off on all of the postseason umpiring assignments, which means that political concerns and even personal grudges are sometimes involved. And though Major League Baseball is fond of proclaiming that its roster of umpires represents the best of the best and that all of its umpires are worthy, a pecking order clearly exists. Ed Montague, the crew chief for three World Series since 2000, was at the top of it. So was Randy Marsh, who worked four Series between 1997 and 2006, including three as crew chief, and Tim McClelland, who was named to the World Series crew in 2000, 2002, and 2006.

By the same token it was pretty evident that Darling, Layne, Poncino, and Hohn were not among Major League Baseball's gold-starred umpires; nor was Rick Reed, a twenty-five-year veteran and a crew chief who hadn't been to the World Series since 1991, largely, some umpires say, because of a vendetta against him by Sandy Alderson.

And Mike Winters, who worked the 2002 and 2006 World Series, had his postseason assignment in 2007 taken away from him after a highly publicized on-field incident during the final week of the season.

Winters was working at first base in the eighth inning of a game between the San Diego Padres and the Rockies, when a Padres outfielder, Milton Bradley, singled with two outs. Bradley was generally known as a hothead and, among umpires, as a pain in the neck, and when he reached first, he and Winters picked up a squabble that was rooted in an incident earlier in the game in which Winters told the home plate umpire, Brian Runge, that he believed Bradley had flung a bat in Runge's direction after a disputed called third strike.

In the eighth, Runge questioned Bradley about this—foolishly, really. Why not let well enough alone? Bradley angrily proclaimed his innocence, but when he reached base, he asked Winters if he had, indeed, accused him of throwing the bat, and Winters acknowledged that he had. Then, according to another umpire who was briefed on the incident in a union conference call after Winters was suspended, a fan screamed from the stands, "Hey, Winters, you suck!" And Bradley, who was taking a lead off first with his hands on his knees, looked back over his shoulder and said to Winters, "I agree with him." Winters then called Bradley "a piece of shit" (or maybe it was "a fucking piece of shit"—I've heard both versions), and Bradley went after him.

For his overly aggressive manner and disrespectful language, Winters was suspended for the last week of the regular season and lost his post-season assignment. But that might not have happened if Bud Black, the Padres' manager, hadn't raced from the dugout to intercede, grabbing Bradley from behind, which brought the whole stupid incident to a blackly comic climax. In the wrestling match with his own manager, Bradley tore a knee ligament. Baseball might have punished Winters anyway, though it doesn't seem likely. It was the bizarre injury that caught the attention of the national press and ratcheted up the outrage of writers and fans against Winters until baseball had to act.

Though no one will admit it, or at least volunteer it, the other factor that enters into the selection of World Series umpires is diversity. The ethnic imbalance in the major league umpiring corps is, well, shameful, and in recent seasons it has clearly become important to the commissioner's office to counteract the impression that baseball has been lax in dealing with it.

Sixty-four of the seventy umpires who began the 2007 season on the major league roster were white. Of the six others, one, Alfonso Marquez, was born in Mexico; one, Angel Hernandez, is from Cuba; one, Laz Diaz, was born to Cuban parents in Miami; and one, C. B. Bucknor, was born in Jamaica. Just two umpires in the major leagues, Chuck Meriwether and Kerwin Danley, are African-American, and even more startling, in the 131 years that the major leagues have employed umpires, only six blacks have been on the official roster.

Further, between 1970, when Emmett Ashford became the first black umpire to work the World Series, and 2004, when Meriwether worked the first of his two, only Eric Gregg in 1989 and Charlie Williams in 1993 appeared in the World Series, meaning that you could have watched more than three decades' worth of postseasons and only twice seen a black man in a position of on-field authority in the final week of play.

Baseball has, tacitly at least, acknowledged that this must change. Nonwhite umpires have appeared in six of the last seven World Series, and in 2007 not only did Meriwether become the first black umpire to appear twice (Angel Hernandez, who worked the 2002 and 2005 Series, broke that particular barrier for Latinos), but he and Diaz comprised the first pair of nonwhite umpires ever to be named to the World Series crew.

This went largely unnoticed, except among other umpires, more than one of whom mentioned to me the existence of "the colored slot," noting that Meriwether was returning to the Series after only three years ("though you can't really say anything about that," one umpire said to me, "because Montague is, too") and that Diaz had received his first Series assignment even though he hadn't touched the usual landmarks; he'd worked two previous Division Series but never a League Championship Series.

Diaz came to the big leagues in 1999, just as Everitt did, as one of the umpires hired to replace those who were part of the mass resignation, and he told me he didn't see any oddity in his being asked to work the World Series; he was ready and deserving, he said, which, in fact, no one disputed. Diaz is widely respected by his peers. And when I asked Meriwether why so few blacks were in the umpiring pipeline and so few in the big leagues, he shrugged and said simply that it's not an easy road for anyone, no matter what color you are.

Jimmie Lee Solomon, baseball's executive vice president, who is himself black, acknowledged that the paucity of black umpires is a problem he's determined to solve, though that won't be easy. As of the

2008 season, in terms of seniority and experience, the next several Triple A umpires in line for major league jobs were white, including at least three—Chris Guccione, Rob Drake, and James Hoye—who have worked more than five hundred games each in the big leagues. If Solomon were to promote a black umpire ahead of them, several umpires—white umpires—told me, the resentment would be fierce.

Given the importance of the games, you'd think baseball would make it as easy as possible for umpires in the World Series to do their jobs, but pretty much the opposite is true. Part of this has simply to do with the size of the event and the sense of moment with which baseball and its television partners market it. Umpires selected for the World Series discover more or less right away that it's impossible for them to observe their normal routines and perform their jobs under familiar and comfortable circumstances.

For one thing, during the season umpires are used to an almost complete separation of their home lives and work lives, but in the World Series, their families often join them—baseball encourages this—and virtually everyone reports this as a mixed blessing. It's great to share this professional highlight with their wives and children, umpires say, but making sure they're looked after and entertained is both exhausting and a distraction from the task at hand.

The umpires' dressing rooms, most of the time inner sanctums where visitors are discouraged and where not too many people actually want to visit anyway, are, during the World Series, carnivals. The umpires' room is never all that commodious to begin with, but in the postseason it's usually the weather center, where rain (or snow) is monitored by radar and discussed with groundskeepers, general managers, and officials from Major League Baseball and television. The commissioner and his entourage become presences there before the games; so do umpires' kids, occasional reporters, television techies, and representatives from sponsors. Every year, Mike Port told me, the umpires plead, essentially to no avail, to have pre- and postgame traffic in the dressing room curtailed.

"You work all your life to get here, and you want your family to be a part of it, but then it's an absolute circus," Ted Barrett told me in Denver in 2007. "You walk into the locker room and there's tons of people in there. My wife came to Boston with me, and we got in on Monday. And then my brother came down from Buffalo. I was happy to see him, but he drives down on Tuesday, and we visit with him, and there are some friends from Buffalo there, too, and by the time game two comes around on Thursday, and I walked out on the field to work first base, the biggest first-base job of my career, I was absolutely exhausted. It was terrible. I thought, 'I wouldn't let myself get this worn-out before a regular season game.'"

Oddly enough, on the field, the World Series—the postseason as a whole, actually—throws a whole new element of the job at umpires; it is often the first time in any umpire's career that he works a six-umpire system. The idea, of course, is that extra umpires make the job easier by spreading responsibilities among more pairs of eyes and specifically by having umpires in place to rule on potentially controversial fair-foul or spectator-interference calls deep in the outfield and by limiting the complicated rotations umpires ordinarily use on a four-man crew when one of them has to turn his back to the infield with men on base.

But the protocol is nonetheless unfamiliar; you have to learn it, and many umpires report a self-consciousness in the six-umpire system, an inclination to talk to themselves and tick off their responsibilities in their heads instead of reacting with an instinct honed by long experience.

During game one of the 2007 Series, for example, the first hitter for the Red Sox, Dustin Pedroia, smacked a long fly ball to left center that hit the ledge on top of the Green Monster and bounced back onto the field. Was it a home run? And whose call was it? Usually, calls involving fly balls between left center and right center are the responsibility of the second-base umpire—in this case Ted Barrett—but in the six-umpire system, the left-field-line umpire and the second-base umpire divide those responsibilities.

"It's very odd to work the lines, very odd," Mike Everitt said. "In fact, when we first got to the ballpark in Boston, we all walked the field together and looked at anything that might give us a problem. And if you're the left-field ump, you have that Green Monster, and that little ledge out there, and of course in the bottom of the first, what happens? Pedroia hits one up there. Teddy and I both went out. I didn't have the chance to look at him, it happened too fast. Luckily we had the same call."

As television revealed, both men had one arm raised, circling from the elbow, a finger of the raised hand pointed upward—the signal for a home run.

Still, unfamiliarity with the six-umpire system may have been responsible for one of the most famous missed calls in baseball history, in what came to be known (in New York and Baltimore, anyway) as the Jeffrey Maier game.

Jeffrey Maier was a twelve-year-old from Old Tappan, New Jersey, who cut school to attend the first game of the 1996 American League Championship Series at Yankee Stadium. He was seated in right field, just above the fence, when, with the Orioles ahead by a run, Derek Jeter led off the bottom of the eighth with a long fly ball. Young Jeffrey leaned over the fence and tried to gather the ball in. He fumbled it, but he indisputably interfered with a ball in play and deflected it into the stands. Replays showed conclusively that if Maier had kept his hands off the ball, it would not have gone out of the park, and that Tony Tarasco, the Oriole outfielder who was waiting at the wall with his glove upturned, would more than likely have caught it.

Spectator interference involves a large measure of umpire discretion. The umpire assigned to the right-field line, Richie Garcia, could have ruled that Tarasco would have caught the ball and declared Jeter out; or he could have ruled that the ball would have hit the wall and awarded Jeter two bases. However, he ruled no interference at all, meaning the ball was a home run, which tied the game and eventually sent it into extra innings; the Yankees won in the eleventh and went on to claim the Series.

Garcia said afterward he was focusing on Tarasco and Tarasco's glove and that he never saw Maier. (He also said that at one point after he acknowledged his mistake, he started to cry.)

"I was working right field," he told *Referee* magazine during the 1996–97 off-season. "Being aggressive, when the ball was hit, I took off. Some people say I got too close to the play. Some people say I was too close to the fence. But who's to say? I really don't know. I thought I was in pretty good position."

But Mike Everitt said the uncertainties of the six-man system kept Garcia from getting close enough.*

---

*The suggestion that Garcia was too close is puzzling; in television replays, you can see him sprinting down the right-field line as the ball is hit, and when the camera catches Tarasco with his glove up and Maier snatching the ball, it's a midrange shot and Garcia is not even in the frame.

"If you're working four-man, and you're on first or third base, your first reaction when a ball is hit deep down the line is 'Go!'" Everitt said. "So you're running, and then you stop and get set."

In the six-man system, he said, you don't necessarily have to do that, but it's still your reaction, and you can run yourself into trouble. There's no way, he said, you can get a proper view of a pole-bender if you've run under it. That's why, Everitt said, the foul-line umpires generally take positions so closely behind the first- and third-base umpires that to spectators—and television commentators—they appear redundant.*

Still, that leaves an umpire vulnerable to just the sort of play that the Pedroia fly ball represented—or that Jeffrey Maier's interference did—because if you're worried about getting too close, you run the risk of not getting close enough.

"On TV, the experts who know everything always want to know why the right-field and left-field umpires don't work deeper," Everitt said. "The reason is that you're not going to see the ball bend around the pole; you lose perspective on it. But it's a double-edged sword, because in some stadiums you've got the possibility of fan interference. That was Richie Garcia's play. In Yankee Stadium there's no way he's going to see a ball that goes near the foul pole up around the third deck, so he couldn't line up any deeper, but if he had lined up deeper to begin with, he would have seen the play."

On the field, the cacophonous and bloated presence of television, whose scrutiny of umpires is brutal enough all year long, becomes especially intense in the postseason. Networks employ additional camera angles, and microphones seem to be everywhere. Ed Montague wore one behind the plate for the opening game, but only under duress.

"You've already got QuesTec and that's a distraction," he told me. "And this is another one. I mean, I'm out there to call a ball game. I'm trying to focus on every pitch. I don't want to be thinking about a wire, or what I'm saying, or an on-off switch."

During the regular season, television broadcasts allot two minutes

*During the 2007 American League Championship Series, the former shortstop Cal Ripken, working as an analyst on TBS, made just that complaint. It was surprising to hear Ripken grouse that way, but perhaps he was remembering Richie Garcia's call in the Jeffrey Maier game; he was a member of the Oriole team that was screwed by it.

and five seconds between innings for commercial advertisers to present their wares, but in the World Series that jumps to 2:55, an extra fifty seconds that umpires have to spend standing around. This doesn't sound like much of a hardship, but umpires are the only participants in a ball game who never leave the playing field, who never get to sit down, who don't have the luxury of a nearby bathroom at regular intervals. (Every umpire has a story involving an unfortunate digestive experience.) In addition, it tends to be cold during the World Series, which is played in late October, often in Northern or high-altitude cities like Boston and Denver. As game three of the 2007 Series got under way, the temperature was forty-five degrees. It lasted four hours and nineteen minutes, the longest nine-inning game in World Series history, and by the end the temperature had dipped to thirty-three.

"That's one record I didn't want, but now that I have it, I wouldn't wish it on anyone else to break it," Barrett, the home plate umpire, told me the next morning, referring to the length of the game. "And in the middle of the game the temperature dropped pretty fast. About the seventh inning, I realized I couldn't write the lineup changes onto my lineup card. My hand was going numb."

Longer television broadcasts also mean more airtime to fill, which is often accomplished with extra replays of close calls and the accompanying commentary about the umpiring which—need it be said?—is almost always skeptical. The only real controversy in either of the two World Series I followed was precipitated by a Fox television camera that, in 2006, caught the Tigers' game-two starter, Kenny Rogers, with something brown and gluey smeared on his pitching hand at the base of his thumb. A "foreign substance," the rulebook would call it, but it looked like pine tar.

It seemed possible—if not absolutely evident—that Rogers was tapping his fingertips on the stuff and using its adhesive quality to augment his grip on the ball in the chilly, damp Detroit night. Amazing as it was that a veteran pitcher, known for his caginess on the mound, would violate one of baseball's most famous dicta in the World Series, it was even more amazing that he would do it so openly, hiding the illicit gunk in plain sight.

Ordinarily if the umpires notice something on a pitcher's hand, they'll try to resolve the issue quietly: Clean it off and let's proceed.

No sense causing a ruckus. If the opposing manager requests that the umpires examine a pitcher for anything gummy or slimy on his person, or for the presence of a thumbtack or sandpaper or anything else that might disfigure the ball, then they are more likely to do so, though they will act with discretion, and only if they believe there is probable cause. (Otherwise, managers would routinely ask for such examinations.)

In this case, the television pictures, not to mention the announcers' harping on the possibility that Rogers was cheating, largely usurped the umpires' authority. In the press box, reporters with access to the broadcast were astonished by the stain on Rogers's hand. Even fans in the stands, who had access to radios, portable televisions, and ballpark word of mouth, seemed to be aware of Rogers's transgression before the umpires were.

Eventually it was brought to their attention—perhaps by Tony LaRussa, the Cardinals' manager, who probably learned about it from a clubhouse television; perhaps by Steve Palermo, an umpire supervisor who spoke to the home plate umpire, Alfonzo Marquez, between innings—but instead of having the situation in their grasp, the umpires found it presented to them as a challenge. What were they going to do?

In fact, between innings, Marquez spoke to Rogers as he came off the mound, and the crew chief, Randy Marsh, walked over to the Cardinals' dugout and spoke to LaRussa. Only after that did Palermo have his conversation with Marquez, a lengthy one that delayed the game and clearly gave the impression that instructions were being given. The implication was that the commissioner's office, represented by Palermo, wanted to direct the umpires' actions.

In the end, the umpires did essentially nothing; Rogers emerged from the dugout in the second inning with the brown smear on his hand gone, and he pitched eight shutout innings as the Tigers prevailed, 3–1, the only game they won.

Did Rogers simply put the stuff somewhere else on his body, not so easy to detect? Or did he just not need it? Was he trying to cheat? We'll never know. Answering questions in the pressroom after the game, Rogers drew chortles of disbelief when he said it was nothing but "a clump of dirt" that he was unaware was even there until the inning was over. He also said that Marquez hadn't said a word to him about anything on his hands, that the umpire was only reminding him that he had more time than usual between innings and that he might want to slow down his warm-up pitches.

Jim Leyland, the Tiger manager, said that LaRussa had said his hitters were complaining that "the ball was acting a little funny," but that he didn't want to create a stir. Leyland himself was a bit obfuscatory.

"I'm assuming Tony wasn't sure," Leyland said. "From time to time hitters talk about the ball's acting funny. Whether you do or don't make a big deal over it is not really an issue."

LaRussa never addressed the issue publicly, though he was widely given credit for not insisting that the umpires examine Rogers and thus forcing a confrontation that might have made a cheating scandal the focus of the Series. And Palermo, the one participant in the episode who would speak at any length about it, actually added more confusion than clarity.

In the pressroom after the game he contradicted Rogers, saying that Marquez had, in fact, told the pitcher to wipe off his hand. But then in a later interview, he contradicted himself; he told me that Marquez and the other umpires didn't know anything about the substance on Rogers's hand until he himself, Palermo, informed Marquez about it in their conversation at the screen.

Palermo said he hadn't been ordered by the commissioner's office to intervene, but that as a supervisor who had been following the television coverage, he simply wanted to make sure that Marquez and the other umpires knew what everyone else in the stadium did.

"We monitor the broadcasts," Palermo said. "A television camera can get a whole lot closer to something than an umpire can, and in an unassuming manner. TV can zoom in on somebody, and now they zoom in on Kenny Rogers's hand. Well, I saw that, and I called Fonzy over, and I tell him they're picking up on all this, and there's a problem. They have monitors in the clubhouse, and there are players up there, sipping coffee, eating licorice, chewing bubble gum, whatever, reading the newspaper, and they're watching this. So now they go running down and telling the manager, 'Hey, Skip, there's something on Kenny Rogers's hand.' So everybody knows except those six guys out on the field. We don't want them getting caught and blindsided by all this. So I just informed Fonzy what was going on."

A former umpire himself, Palermo had a high public profile even before he became a sometime television analyst, owing to the circumstances of the end of his career on the field; he was shot and partially paralyzed when he and others attempted to foil a late-night mugging outside a Dallas restaurant in 1991. He had a bit of a self-important swagger to him, and his reputation among working umpires was that he considered himself the world's foremost authority; umpires respect Palermo's career and experience and resent his hubris. I spoke to several of them who were not at the World Series in 2006 and who were infuriated that Palermo inserted himself in the Rogers flap. They said he had taken advantage of Marquez's inexperience—he was working his first World Series—and should simply have let the umpires on the field do their jobs.

"I can tell you one thing, I'd never have talked to him," one veteran umpire, Derryl Cousins, said to me about Palermo's sojourn behind the screen. "I'd have let him fuckin' sit there."

Finally, Palermo did reveal a few things that were neither contradictory nor unreasonable. One was that baseball was irritated at its business partner, Fox, for exposing a potential distraction from the actual games. In this instance, for a change, the interests of the umpires and the game's administrators were coincidental, and it explains why everyone was so eager to make the Rogers problem simply go away. Palermo said he offered Marquez a path to this result.

"We play on a dirt field," Palermo told me. "And dirt's not an illegal substance. There are plausible reasons why that could be dirt on Rogers's hand." He said he told Marquez, "Observe his hand. If you see something on his hand and you detect it's not a foreign substance, just get it off, so we can go out and focus on playing baseball, as opposed to this tempest in a teapot that's brewing."

I asked Palermo if this was really a proper approach, whether the umpires, who are so proud of their role as keepers of the game's integrity, shouldn't have gone out of their way to find out whether Rogers did, in fact, flout the rules. Palermo responded that the umpires' main concern is, in many ways, the same as the players' and the managers', namely to get through the game and not have it turn into "something that isn't baseball."

Palermo said, "That's the fine line everybody has to walk." After all, he added, if you're Tony LaRussa, what does it profit you to make a stink about pine tar on a pitcher's hand? "What are you going to do that for, to boost yourself as the sage manager who detected this?"

By and large, the whole episode passed with a shrug. Rogers, LaRussa, Leyland, Fox Television, Palermo, and Major League Baseball all came out of the episode looking guilt-free and professional. In retrospect, only the umpires looked foolish and impotent. They didn't see the stuff on Rogers's hand; they didn't try to determine whether he cheated; and not only did it appear that they looked the other way, but it also appeared that they ceded their authority on the field to their employers.

Umpires who didn't work the Series were indignant—they felt like scapegoats.

"They let us look bad," one of them told me. "Business as usual."

As for the umpires who did work the 2006 Series, they were tight-lipped. When I asked Marquez what had happened in the Rogers incident, he said only, "It was no big deal. He washed his hand. End of story." None of the other umpires would comment at all.

Marquez's response was especially telling because generally he was a cooperative and loquacious guy. Of course, everyone called him Fonzy. He had joined the big league staff when he was only twenty-seven, and seven years later he was still the youngest umpire in the majors. He was fun-loving, even a little reckless. He liked motorcycles. He had a reputation for late nights; once, he told me, early in his big league career he broke his hand in a bar fight and worked in pain for weeks as he hid his injury from his supervisors. He was popular among the men on his crew, but probably owing to his youth and youthful ways, he had a few feuds going with some older umpires who never cottoned to the 1999 replacements and one or two others who disapproved of his party habits.

Still, all agreed that Marquez had the umpire gene, that he bought into the us-against-the-world credo, the circle-the-wagons umpire defensiveness; when he was around other umpires, especially senior umpires, his deference was palpable and sincere. He habitually referred to his crew chief as "Chief."

Moreover, it escaped no one that his talent was huge; whatever undisciplined wildness found its way into his social life was entirely absent on the field, where his signals were crisp, his positioning was precise, his reading of plays intuitively keen, his plate work aggressive, and his manner authoritative and confident beyond his years. Phil

Janssen told me that Marquez was the best young umpire to enter the game in a generation.

Marquez wasn't a large man, but he was formidable in an argument, not afraid to whip off his mask and go nose to nose with far more experienced baseball men. In the first inning of a Yankees–Devil Rays game in Tampa the previous month, Marquez had ejected the Rays' pitching coach, Mike Butcher, and their manager, Joe Maddon, for disputing his ball and strike calls as the Yankees poured six runs across the plate and basically ended the game shortly after it had begun. The argument had turned apoplectic when Marquez whipped off his mask and seemingly went after Maddon. It made for exciting television, but Marquez's aggressiveness seemed like a questionable umpiring tactic, as if he were pouring fuel on a fire that was already fading to ashes.

Later when I asked Marquez about it, however, he told me that Maddon and Butcher had gone beyond simply questioning his strike-zone judgment, which in itself is cause for ejection. As the argument continued, he said, they had brought up an old and sensitive issue—the accusation that umpires disdain weak clubs such as Tampa Bay was then, and that the stronger teams, especially the Yankees, always get the close calls.

"I only got mad when they questioned my integrity," Marquez said. "In a case like that you're not just defending yourself, but you're defending all umpires."

"It was Beanie Baby Day," Tim McClelland was recalling. "Back then Beanie Babies were huge, and there were fifty-five thousand people there."

McClelland was speaking in St. Louis in late October 2006. It was pouring rain outside. He was comfortable, relaxing in a hotel lobby, anticipating that game four of the World Series would be postponed, which it eventually was. McClelland had spent the first three games of the Series along the lines and at third base, and he would never get a plate game. Generally the crew chief (in 2006, it was Randy Marsh) works the opening game, dealing with the initial spectacle; then the crew rotates in order of reverse seniority, so the younger umps get their experience, and the older ones take their turns as the stakes get higher. In a seven-game series, the crew chief returns to the plate for the ultimate game. McClelland was scheduled for game six. I had asked him about games where he'd been in the spotlight, expecting to hear about World Series past—he'd been in three others—but the occasion that leaped to mind for him was David Wells's perfect game at Yankee Stadium in 1998. May 17. Beanie Babies Day.

"In the fifth inning, Marty Cordova comes up, and he says, 'I'm gonna break up this perfect game again today,'" McClelland recalled. "The day before, somebody had had a perfect game going, I don't remember who, but it was Cordova who'd gotten a base hit. That's when I looked up at the scoreboard and realized it: David had a perfect game.*

"In the seventh," McClelland went on, "Paul Molitor had a two-one count on him and a pitch came in that was just off the plate, which showed just how much command David had that day. Everybody said he had great stuff, but it wasn't his stuff; he had a curveball, a changeup, and a fastball, and he was just putting everything wherever he wanted to. So when the pitch was off the plate and I balled it for a three-one count, he brought it back in a couple of inches and put it on the plate. The next pitch I called strike two, and the next ball he swung and missed for strike three. That was about the closest he got to losing the perfect game all day.

"The point is, from about the sixth inning on, every ball I called, everyone would boo. I watch the tape now and you can see people in the stands; you can see them, no matter where the pitch was. It could have bounced, and they're going, 'Booooo.' I was thinking I wanted to keep my strikes consistent from pitch one to pitch one hundred fifty, because I didn't want to take away from what Wells was doing. You know, if I'm calling pitches four inches outside, people would say, 'I could pitch a perfect game if the umpire was calling those pitches.' But David was so good that day I knew I didn't have to worry about calling the pitch off the plate. It was fun. When the last fly ball goes out to right field, everybody sees David Wells pump his fist. Well, they don't see the home plate umpire pump his fist. I knew I was one of a select few to work a perfect game in the major leagues. That's in the top three of my plate jobs, I would think. Maybe number two of all time. Besides working my first World Series."

---

*The previous day's pitcher had been Ramiro Mendoza, and Cordova, a journeyman outfielder, had led off the fifth with a single, the Twins' first base runner.

At fifty-five, McClelland had been in the big leagues since 1983, and he had long been one of baseball's best respected umpires, always ranking high whenever players and managers were polled and earning postseason and All-Star assignments with regularity. He was also one of the game's most distinctive figures. At six feet six, 260 pounds, he was a skyscraper out on the field, with a bearish, lumbering grace and a penchant behind the plate for signaling strikes with such deliberate slowness that television announcers, who rely on the umpire's arm signals to get their ball-and-strike information, were habitually irritated with him. I asked him if he did it on purpose, a kind of subtle retaliation against one faction of umpire tormentors. He said no, but I thought he was being disingenuous; he laughed. He had a deep voice, a bass rumble.

"I'm a big man," he said. "I do everything in my life slow."

I'd met and spoken with McClelland a few times before, and I always felt something plaintive in him. His long face often seemed drawn and weary, maybe a little sad, and he had surprised me before with remarks that made me think that he saw umpiring as a burden—a worthy one to carry, but a burden nonetheless.

Yet within the fraternity, McClelland was also known as something of an egotist. He was an advocate of greater umpire sovereignty on the field and higher umpire salaries, and he generally carried himself with a presumption of stardom. More than once he corrected me for using the phrase "bad call."

"I'm not chastising you," he said. "But I get upset when people say, 'It was a bad call.' And I know you think I'm arguing semantics, but no umpire makes a bad call. He might make an incorrect call. He wasn't trying to get the call wrong; he just happened to be incorrect."

Though he was as wary of some of my questions as any other umpire—he was especially brusque and dismissive when I asked about the Kenny Rogers episode—McClelland was unusual, in that he had an awareness of umpiring's ambiguities. He seemed comfortable with conflicting descriptions of the job.

"The umpires should have one hundred percent authority on the field," he said. "We're the ones running the game, and when we go out there, it should be understood we're running the game." But when I asked him if he had an overall philosophy that governed his behavior on the field, he said he thought of a baseball game as a theatrical event.

"David Cone said this to me a long time ago," McClelland said.

Cone, who pitched for five major league teams, was known for his tenacious competitiveness on the mound and for his sagacity off it. "He said, 'We're all in this together to put on a show. So I go out there with the attitude that all of us, managers, coaches, players, umpires, we're putting on a show. We're putting on a play.'"

I'd thought before about the idea of a ball game as a play; you know, a narrative that wholly unfolds in an evening, with characters who behave well or badly, suspense that is created and resolved, a climax and resolution that are either satisfying or not. But oddly enough, I'd never conceived of the umpires as among the performers. McClelland, who was the first and only umpire I met to make the theater-baseball connection, reminded me that, of course, they are. To continue the metaphor, an umpire often ends up in the most crucial of roles, a member of the company who steps out in a crisis, one of the townspeople or the chorus, someone whose presence is familiar but not his persona, that is, until he is forced by circumstances to step forward and do something, well, dramatic.

Almost exactly a year later, McClelland did exactly that, providing an ending to the National League season that was downright literary in its resonance.

Having worked the World Series in 2006, McClelland was ineligible to do so in 2007, but he had been named crew chief for the National League Championship Series, and in a signal of his standing, he was selected to work the plate for that baseball rarity, a playoff game between teams who were tied at the end of the season. In this case, the San Diego Padres and the Colorado Rockies, after 162 games, shared the right to the National League wild-card slot in the playoffs.

Perhaps the baseball gods do have a well-developed theatrical sense, because throughout the history of the game, end-of-season tiebreakers have been memorably suspenseful and thrillingly resolved. The Bobby Thomson home run off Ralph Branca, known as "the shot heard round the world," which sent the New York Giants to the World Series instead of the Brooklyn Dodgers in 1951, ended what is probably the most famous game ever played. The Yankees' 5–4 defeat of the Boston Red Sox in 1978 to claim the American League pennant—the winning margin provided by a Bucky Dent home run—might well be next.

The 2007 game between the Padres and the Rockies was of that ilk. It came down to a perfect storm of happenstance that turned an absolutely decisive moment into an equally ambiguous one.

The game was tied after nine innings, and the teams were scoreless for the next three, but the Padres scored two runs in the top of the thirteenth to take an 8–6 lead. In the bottom of the thirteenth, the Padres sent Trevor Hoffman in to close out the victory, something he'd done more often than any other pitcher in the history of the game, so everything seemed to be anticlimactically over.

But Hoffman gave up extra-base hits to the first three Rockies hitters, the last a triple by Matt Holliday, then issued an intentional walk. With the score tied, men on first and third and none out, the next hitter, Jamey Carroll, laced a line drive to right field that was speared by the Padres' Brian Giles. Giles, not known for his throwing arm, flung the ball toward home plate on a high arc that seemed to have no shot at nailing Holliday, who had tagged up and was heading home with the winning run.

Nonetheless, the ball and Holliday arrived at just about the same time, though the throw was a smidgen short, making the Padres' catcher, Michael Barrett, attempt a short-hop snatch and sweep tag as Holliday slid in, headlong, his arms outstretched. Barrett had been blocking the plate, but as he gloved the ball, the contact with Holliday knocked it loose. Still, Barrett's foot remained planted, knocking Holliday's hand away before it touched the plate. Or maybe not.

Holliday was stunned by the collision—he was bleeding afterward—and he lay on the ground beyond home plate as Barrett sought out the ball, picked it up, and ran over to tag him. Just before he did, McClelland made the call—safe. He was, in effect, saying that he saw Holliday touch home plate before his hand was knocked away.

But it was an oddly tentative signal. McClelland had swung around, properly, to a vantage point along an imagined extension of the third-base line. But he wasn't quite stationary when he made the call, as he should have been, and he raised his arms more thoughtfully than decisively. They rose to the level of his shoulders as if lifted by slowly inflating balloons, and no repeated or forceful gesture followed, nothing to sell a close call in a crucial situation. Like everything else about this moment, it was both final and uncertain.

Amazingly, there was no argument, just a frenzy of celebration as the Rockies stormed the field in their first moments as National League wild-card champs. After the game, Michael Barrett said it didn't occur to him to question the call because it was McClelland. "I've never, ever second-guessed Tim McClelland at home plate," Barrett told a reporter for the Web site mlb.com. "And when he told me he was safe, there was no argument in my mind."

For his part, Holliday said he thought he had touched the plate, but he couldn't be sure. No television replay from any angle could do more than suggest that Holliday never reached the plate; his fingers seemed to be deflected an instant before getting there, but it was impossible to declare that with certainty. McClelland himself told the *Des Moines Register*, his hometown paper, that, yes, he had some doubts after watching the replay, but that he would make the same call again.

Did Holliday touch the plate? Perhaps this inquiry doesn't quite have the same resonance as, say, was Hamlet insane? Or does Godot exist? But in the sense that a ball game can be seen as a drama, I've come to think of it as baseball's equivalent. For one thing, it had the highest stakes attached to it, life and death in baseball terms. If Holliday had been called out, the score would have remained tied with two out, and the game might well have continued into the fourteenth inning, when the Padres would again have had a fair shot to win. The whole World Series could have been different, contested between Boston and San Diego. For another thing, there is no answer that cannot be refuted. And as in a great performance of a great play, this was a moment that resonated with discussion.

Only later, as the call and the result sank in, did questions as to what had happened begin to surface. Newspaper columnists checked in, talk radio went nuts, even local television stations far from San Diego and Denver ran the replays on their sports reports; video entries from spectators who had been all over the ballpark were posted on YouTube. Nothing settled the issue. Finally, a remarkably detailed, if somewhat biased and maybe a little bit crackpot, examination of McClelland's call, complete with video links and myriad postings, appeared on the Web at www.hollidaynevertouchedtheplate.com.

Created ostensibly by a Padres fan, it was helpful to me, but I tended to agree with the reader who posted the following response: "Maybe, someday, Oliver Stone will make a movie about this, and you can die vindicated."

The dozens and dozens of people who posted comments on the site seemed to give this one play a genuine importance. So many people cared. The result raised such a hue and cry—Use instant replay!—that baseball's administration grew rather sensitive about it. When I asked Mike Port about McClelland's call, he launched into the legitimate but defensive-sounding position that even if umpires make mistakes, at dozens of moments within a game the outcome is influenced by a questionable play by a player or move by a manager. A single call is never wholly responsible for the outcome of a game.

"The San Diego team gave up two runs," Port said to me during the World Series. "The San Diego pitcher gave up a shot to right that let the runner tag; the San Diego right fielder let go a throw that could have brought rain; and the San Diego catcher didn't hold on to the ball. So you're going to blame everything on the umpire?"

Port continued, "Nobody else saw what he saw from where he saw it. If you have to go to the slow-motion replay in order to see what happened, well, you can't fault the umpire, and the replay was inconclusive, anyway. If it was a matter of going to replay, we'd still be arguing over it and we wouldn't even have had the playoffs yet, much less the World Series."

In retrospect, it did seem peculiar that McClelland waited to make his safe call until Barrett picked up the ball and started to chase Holliday down. Did that mean he saw Barrett tag Holliday in time and that he would have called Holliday out if Barrett had held on to the ball? That was the explanation I came up with; but then, in a radio interview two days later, McClelland said, yes, he had held his ruling until he could determine whether Barrett had held on to the ball, but, no, it would not have changed the call even if he had. Holliday was safe. So why did he wait? What difference did it make? Or was he just uncertain and betraying his uncertainty?

McClelland's answer was poignantly, some might say infuriatingly, elusive; the call, he said, like any other, needed to be subject to an umpiring process. Then he described the equivalent of running a replay in his mind:

"That's part of what I need to do on that play. . . . When I make a call, I need to make sure that Michael Barrett retains the ball, and so I wait to have Michael Barrett show me the ball and that he has retained possession of it. So I delay the call, I process everything that's happened, and when I saw the ball roll away, I knew that Matt was safe at the plate because Michael had not held on to the ball. . . . I want to make sure I see the whole play, process the whole play, then make a determination on whether he was out or safe."

What struck me about this answer was both McClelland's lack of defensiveness and his lack of argumentativeness. It was the statement of a man in the public eye doing a job properly in the face of terrific pressure and criticism, a guy who didn't shy away from a difficult thing simply because his job was not to, a guy owning up to his responsibility. It placed him squarely at the fulcrum of this baseball drama in a way a player or a manager is never placed there. And though I don't want to overreach—as a moral paradigm, he wasn't exactly being John Proctor or Sir Thomas More—he was accepting responsibility for a consequential event simply because it had to be done and no one else could do it. This was a statement of morality, baseball morality, anyway, and the episode does, I think, resonate as a kind of real-life narrative literature.

The radio interviewer Dan Patrick thought McClelland had blown the call—"I don't think Holliday has reached the plate yet," he said to McClelland—and he was pushing the point when he asked McClelland whether he ever beat himself up after a game.

"I can't beat myself up," McClelland said. "I saw what I saw and I called what I saw."

McClelland had mentioned his first World Series, which was 1993, Philadelphia versus Toronto. He was on the left-field line for the final game, game six, and he was the closest umpire observer when Joe Carter of the Toronto Blue Jays hit a walk-off home run off the Phillies' closer, Mitch Williams, ending the series. It was only the second Series-ending walk-off in history (the other, in 1960, was hit by Bill Mazeroski of the Pirates, topping the powerful Yankees), and like the Wells perfect game and the Colorado–San Diego playoff, one of a striking number of notable occasions in which McClelland has been a character. He's just been involved in a lot of famous games.

I don't know what you call this, the knack for being Johnny-on-the-spot. Is it a gift or a curse to be one of the few who are, when something needs to be done, fatefully elected to do it?

Some players are like this—George Brett, the great Kansas City

Royals third baseman of the 1980s, the Yankees' Derek Jeter, and David Ortiz of the Red Sox would all fall into this category—men who seem, more often than others, to be present and accountable when the game is on the line, when an ordinary circumstance is elevated to an extraordinary one, when history is about to be made. Would you call this a talent? It is true, isn't it, that memorable events seem to gather around memorable people?

For an umpire, it's a harder case to make, but I submit that this Zelig-like quality is more than mere serendipity. Here's the reasoning: Being in the spotlight is, after all, something an umpire is taught to avoid. It's held out as a fearful circumstance, and when it nonetheless happens to an umpire, the psyche reacts, and it either acknowledges a role in a spectacle or not. The next time an occasion suddenly, unexpectedly looms large, that umpire will either welcome the pressure—responsibly, I mean, not hubristically—or shy away, and in so doing exert some kind of an influence on the event itself. Of course, no one person can turn the world, or even a ball game, by the force of his will or his personality alone, and no matter what psychological inclinations an umpire has, he doesn't control his postseason assignments. But if he's not the sort of guy we're talking about, the home plate umpire in an emergent perfect game can just as easily see ball four instead of strike three on a slider that tickles the black.

This is precisely what happened on September 2, 1972, at Wrigley Field in Chicago when Milt Pappas of the Cubs retired the first twenty-six San Diego Padres and had a 2-2 count on the potential final hitter, Larry Stahl. The next two pitches were close enough to have gone either way, but Bruce Froemming called them both balls, sending Stahl to first and keeping Pappas from a career-making achievement; Pappas retired the next hitter, but he held a grudge for years. Meanwhile, Froemming, though baseball's longest-serving umpire, rarely put himself at the center of games that glow in history. He worked in eleven no-hitters, though only three others behind the plate, and the only other perfect game he witnessed—Dennis Martinez's, in 1991—he was at first base, close but no cigar.

Regarding Tim McClelland, when he called Holliday safe, he was taking on the spotlight's harshest glare, since the call decided the game then and there. Either call would have been equally defensible, and someone not prone to being where the action is might well have opted, subconsciously if not consciously, for the out call, which would have prolonged the game and taken the onus of decision off his own shoulders.

But by that time, McClelland had shown a proclivity for being in the crosshairs of baseball history. That predilection was established in his first official season, when he signaled one of the most controversial and memorable calls ever made.

The date was July 24, 1983, and the place was Yankee Stadium. With two outs in the top of the ninth inning and the Yankees leading the Kansas City Royals 4–3, George Brett hit a two-run homer off the Yankee closer, Goose Gossage. After Brett circled the bases, McClelland was approached at the plate by the Yankee manager, Billy Martin, who insisted that the umpires invoke an obscure rule, 1.10 (c), which declared that pine tar on a bat handle, which players use to enhance their grip on the bat, may not extend more than eighteen inches from the knob.

McClelland asked for the bat, laid it down along home plate, which is seventeen inches in diameter, determined that the bat was, indeed, in violation of the rule, and raised his arm, signaling that the home run was disallowed, that Brett was out, the game was over, and the Yankees had won.

What happened next was bizarre and, in retrospect, comic. An infuriated Brett stormed from the dugout waving his hands and screaming, his face contorted in lunatic protest, an image of him that has become indelible from television highlight reels. He appeared about to attack McClelland, who, with the shaggy hair and mustache fashionable in the early eighties (well, somewhat fashionable, anyway), looked dumbfounded and unprepared for the assault on his judgment, not to mention on his person.

Brett was subdued by a combination of players and umpires, summarily ejected (along with his manager, Dick Howser, and a Royals coach, Rocky Colavito), and the teams finally left the field, but the Royals protested the game. A few days later, the protest was upheld by the American League president, Lee MacPhail, on the grounds that the players should decide the game on the field and that rulebook technicalities shouldn't. Brett's violation was not in defiance of the "spirit of the rule," he said. The game, therefore, had to be resumed at a later date, beginning with two outs in the top of the ninth, the Royals leading, 5–4. This occurred on August 18, before another scheduled game between the Yankees and the Royals.

It was probably the appropriate outcome, but for the umpires was a public humbling that they didn't deserve. After all, had they ignored what the rule said and enforced its spirit, that would have created a whole other kind of outrage. After the episode, Rule 1.10 (c) was amended, with an explicit note that violating the eighteen-inch dictum would result only in the bat being removed from the game, but "shall not be grounds for declaring the batter out, or ejected from the game."

McClelland had no quarrel with the rule change; in his view, it corroborated the decision he and his partners had made on the spot, essentially acknowledging that the rule as it had previously been written required the umpires to look elsewhere in the rulebook for guidance and thus to do precisely what they had done. After all, a pitcher caught applying pine tar to the ball (and not, à la Kenny Rogers, simply with a spot of it on his hand) would have been tossed out of the game, right? What still miffed McClelland more than twenty years later, he said, was MacPhail's reversal and its reasoning. For one thing, McClelland said, it's not the role of the league president or anyone else in an office somewhere to seize the on-field decision-making from the umpires.

But second, and more specifically, McClelland said, "I can't rule on the spirit of a rule. What would have happened, do you think, if I had turned to Billy Martin and said, 'Hey, Billy, you know what? You're right. But, jeez, wasn't that something? A home run like that in the ninth inning?' Billy would have taken a pine tar bat to me."

Indeed, the entire episode was fresh in McClelland's mind, and he recalled it for me in remarkable detail.

"When Martin came out, he was very adamant. He said, 'You gotta check the bat. There's too much pine tar.' He didn't get right in my face, but he was adamant, so it was something I had to at least consider, to see if there was any credence to it. So I grabbed the bat. We didn't have a measuring stick, so I sight-lined it, using the trademark of the bat, and it was a good six or eight inches past the trademark.

"I called the crew together. Joe Brinkman, he was the crew chief, was at second base, and Nick Bremigan was on the crew, and Nick was probably the best rules umpire I've ever known"—Bremigan died of a heart attack less than six years later, at forty-three—"and we talked about it. I wanted to make sure that, one, I was interpreting the rule correctly, and, two, that we were sure there was too much pine tar. We determined we'd lay the bat across home plate, which is seventeen inches across, and we said if it's more than three or four inches beyond the width of home plate—the pine tar, that is—we'd call him out. Well, it was eight or ten inches more than home plate. So Brinkman, being the crew chief, said to me, 'Do you want me to call him out, Timmy?' And I said, 'No, I got the plate. I'll call him out.' So as everybody has seen on ESPN, I pointed the bat at Dick Howser and called Brett out. I think if I had to it over again, I wouldn't have pointed at him, I'd have called Howser out of the dugout and told him what was going on."

In fact, Howser had known. The Yankees had been in Kansas City about two weeks earlier, and their catcher, Rick Cerone, had brought the excess of pine tar on Brett's bat to the attention of the umpire Richie Garcia, who later delivered a warning to Brett.

"We found this out later," McClelland said. "Cerone had told Richie that if Brett got a hit, he should be called out for too much pine tar, and Brett didn't get a hit, but Richie went over to the dugout and, using preventive umpiring, he said, 'Hey, George, you gotta clean your bat up.' Next time Brett came up, it was down the legal limit. So everybody knew about this."

The implication, of course, is that when the Yankees noticed in New York that the pine tar on Brett's bat had crept back toward the trademark, they felt they had a secret weapon and were simply waiting for an appropriate moment to use it. Brett's apparently game-winning home run was obviously it.

I asked McClelland what was going through his mind when Brett came tearing out of the dugout looking intent on mayhem.

"He's screaming, he's saying, 'That's bullshit!' and 'That's not right! You can't do that!' but I wasn't thinking anything, really," McClelland said. "George didn't want to hit me or run into me or anything. If you look at the tape, right at the end he kind of veers off, and the guys kind of grab him."

At that point, the oddities began to mount, as the Royals tried to commandeer the evidence. Gaylord Perry, a Hall of Fame pitcher notorious for his illegal spitball, twisted the bat out of McClelland's hands and tossed it to Colavito.

"And Colavito kind of raised it above his head like he's going to hit me," McClelland said. "And I'm going, 'Whoa! Whoa!' Then he threw it to Leon Roberts, one of the Royals players, and Roberts ran it into the dugout and up the runway toward the clubhouse, and Brinkman and myself, we ran up the runway after him. At the top of the runway, Yankee security stopped him. That's how we got the bat back."

For McClelland, that was hardly the end of it. The pine tar game was the finale of a four-game series, and the crew had the following day off. McClelland planned on spending the day at home in Iowa, and when he went to the airport to make his flight, he found the Kansas City Royals waiting at the next gate. Brett himself was on a nearby phone.

"You know, I've always said about George Brett that he is probably the best ballplayer to umpire that I've ever been around," McClelland said. "He was funny, loved to play the game, loved to joke around with umpires. He almost seemed like a friend to umpires. Except for this one experience. Anyway, he was just hanging up. And he looked at me, and I said, 'George, are you really mad?' And he said, 'Hell, yes, Timmy, I'm mad, that's fucking bullshit you calling me out,' and I said, 'All right, all right, never mind.' And I walked to the gate and went home."

The media, naturally, went crazy, with a dip in interest after a day or two followed by another tidal wave after MacPhail made his ruling that Thursday. The timing was perfect; the following day was McClelland's plate game, and not only that, he and his crew were in Detroit, where, in delicious serendipity, who was visiting the Tigers? The Kansas City Royals. When Brett came up in the first inning, McClelland, seeking to defuse any tension, asked Brett if he was going to do anything with his bat, if he wanted it checked, or if he was going to just lay it down on home plate to measure the pine tar.

"And George said, 'Know what, Tim? I'm really tired of it, aren't you?' and I said, 'Absolutely, thank you very much.' He just got in the box and we played the game."

This might well have been the end of the tale, or at least McClelland's involvement in it, but as with any good story that has a complex plot, this one had a coda, a final twist. The Yankees were enraged at MacPhail's decision, and on August 18, they protested by subtly mocking the legitimacy of the resumed game. Jerry Mumphrey, who'd been in center field for the Yankees for the original game, had since been traded to Houston, and in his place, Billy Martin sent out Ron Guidry, a pitcher. Then, before the Yankee pitcher—George Frazier, not Gossage—threw a pitch, Billy Martin had him make appeal plays at both first and second base, claiming Brett had missed the bags on his way around the bases. The four umpires on the field that day were not the same ones who had worked the original game, and Martin made the point that they could not know whether Brett had touched the bags. A brilliant ploy, really.

But McClelland's crew, which had stuck it to the Royals a month earlier, this time fixed the Yanks. Somehow, the major league umpire supervisor, Dick Butler, either had gotten wind of Martin's plan or else, knowing Martin's devilish turn of mind, simply outstrategized him. Before the resumed game, Butler circulated among the four umpires from the original game an affidavit affirming that Brett had touched all four bases on his home run trot.

"Dick had all of us sign it," McClelland said. "It was stamped and sealed."

When the appeals were denied and Martin came out of the dugout, asking how the umpires could know Brett hit the bases if they weren't even there, the second base umpire that day, Davy Phillips, pulled the envelope with the signed affidavit out of his pocket and presented it to Martin, who was rightfully astonished. The moment was recounted in Phillips's 2004 book, *Center Field on Fire*.

"An affi-fucking-what?" Martin said.

Twelve minutes and four quick outs later, the pine tar game was history.

The pride of major league umpires generally has a good measure of ego stirred up in it, and they are forever complaining about the credit they never get. It didn't escape their notice or their resentment, for example, that they were omitted from the official 2007 World Series program.

But one of umpiring's deeper and more interesting contradictions has always been that the attention the umpires feel deprived of and can't help wanting is also anathema to them and constitutes their biggest worry. Working in the spotlight, having to do their jobs with the largest possible audience in games that have genuine consequence, at least in terms of the attention that is paid to their outcomes, is an anxiety-making pressure that affects even the lions of the profession. Fay Vincent, the former commissioner, named one veteran umpire during his tenure who he said had to be replaced at the World Series because he had a nervous breakdown, and another who wept and apologized to the commissioner after performing poorly.*

Umpires all remember the Jeffrey Maier game and the plight of Richie Garcia, but that, at least, was only the playoffs. Then there was Larry Barnett, who was viciously booed for twenty-five years in Boston, where fans blamed him for turning the 1975 World Series against the Red Sox. Barnett had a stellar career on the field, lasting more than three decades, and he subsequently worked as a major league supervisor. But years from now, the headline on his obituary is most likely to mention the controversy stemming from one call and the enmity it earned him—even though he was right.

The game that made Barnett infamous took place in Riverfront Stadium in Cincinnati. The World Series was tied, 1–1, and in game three the Red Sox appeared poised to seize momentum after a two-run homer by Dwight Evans in the ninth inning gave them a scintillating reprieve, evening the score at 5–5. It was still tied in the bottom of the tenth, however, when the Reds' leadoff hitter, Cesar Geronimo, singled to center. The next hitter, Ed Armbrister, squared to bunt, laid the ball down directly in front of the plate, and trying to avoid running into the Red Sox catcher, Carlton Fisk, who had leaped into the field to make the play, essentially stood still in the vicinity of the plate and ended up getting in Fisk's way, anyhow. Fisk's throw to second, attempting to force the runner, went into center field; Geronimo went to third and eventually scored the winning run, ostensibly the turning point in the Reds' seven-game Series victory.

Barnett, thirty years old, and in the seventh year of a thirty-one-year major league career, was working his first World Series plate game, and the call that thereafter made his very name poison to Red Sox Nation was actually no call at all. He judged that Armbrister was not guilty of interfering with Fisk; he allowed the play simply to proceed and its result subsequently to stand.

---

*I've chosen not to name them because the accusations would be reputation-sullying and are impossible to verify. Confronted with Vincent's comment, the first said it was simply untrue, that his reason for opting out of the Series had nothing to do with nerves. He'd come down with a legitimate physical illness, he said, an explanation that one other umpire independently confirmed. The umpire whom Vincent said had wept is now dead.

"It was down the first-base line, just a hair," Barnett recalled for me, sitting in his Ohio living room more than three decades later. "They just collided. I felt that the guy had as much right to go to first base as the other guy had to catch the ball. And he didn't whack him or anything like that. It was just a bump, and Fisk was able to pick up the ball and throw it."

If Fisk had simply made a good throw, Barnett added, the issue would never have gone any further.

Though some fans will never believe it, Barnett's call was the right one because tangles between the hitter and the catcher around the plate have always been treated differently from collisions elsewhere on the bases. In this case, neither player gained or lost an advantage from what was inadvertent contact.*

Watching the play now, it actually seems pretty clear. Armbrister stopped a mere step or two into his run to first and even ducked his head a bit, evidently trying to steer clear of Fisk, and though they nudged each other, Fisk easily snatched the ball out of the air in his bare hand and had an unobstructed throw to second.

The commissioner, Bowie Kuhn, speaking after the final game of the Series, Barnett recalled, told him he'd been "one thousand percent right" and said that had he been behind the plate, he would have made exactly the same call. And the final vindication came in 2007, when *Referee* magazine cited it as one of the eighteen greatest calls in the history of sports officiating.

But in spite of being right, Barnett—who, oddly enough, twenty-one years later was behind the plate during the Jeffrey Maier game—was excoriated on television by the NBC broadcasters Curt Gowdy and Tony Kubek, and in the weeks following the series the controversy persisted furiously enough that Kuhn agreed to look into how umpires were chosen for the World Series, a betrayal that Barnett never forgot. Meanwhile, he lived through death threats delivered against himself, his wife, and his young daughter.

"It was a living hell," said Barnett matter-of-factly. "We got letters,

---

*Such a situation was eventually codified in the rulebook, which now declares that unintentional interference in front of home plate is no interference at all: "When the catcher and the batter-runner have contact when the catcher is fielding the ball, there is generally no violation and nothing should be called."

from Boston, from all over. They just said they were going to kill us. They were threatening to take our daughter and put a gun in her mouth and blow her head off."

The immediate danger eventually subsided, though when his crew opened the 1976 season in Baltimore, where the Orioles were hosting the Red Sox, he registered in a separate hotel from the other umpires under a false name. Only after six or seven years did he and Carlton Fisk speak to each other again, Barnett said, but they eventually resumed what had been a professional friendship, and when Fisk caught his last game for the Chicago White Sox in 1993, Barnett was behind the plate.

"Carlton shook my hand, and he said, 'Hey, it's been a good run for both of us,'" Barnett said.

Barnett, who was sixty-one when I met him, was a bearish, white-haired man with an expansive manner, and in his retirement he came across as a kind of small-town American that as a city dweller you tend to forget is still around and thriving. He and his wife, Sharon, lived about a mile and a half from the house he was raised in, near a park with a Little League field that is named for him, and down the road through a few miles of cornfields from the Whirlpool factory that has been the leading local employer for decades. He described himself as happy, grateful to baseball for a career and a life that gave him more than he could have hoped for, which made his even-tempered recollection of the 1975 Series and its aftermath that much more poignant, as if having had his family's safety threatened and suffering years of abuse were normal professional hardships of the sort that any citizen of the world might face.

"Yeah, that was a tough time," he said. "It's your first World Series, and you're thinking to yourself, 'Maybe we'd all have been better off if I had been making dryers up at Whirlpool in Marion.' I had always wanted to be a state trooper, and at that time I thought, 'God, maybe I should have done that.' But we got through it."

I asked Barnett how long the animosity in Boston continued.

"Never went away," he said. "I remember I was working a game in Boston, had to be the early nineties, and they were getting beat by the Angels, like eighteen to nothing in the eighth inning, and a man and his son, a little boy that was with him, he stood up and he was screaming at me, saying it was all my fault, and using all kinds of profanity, and I remember thinking, 'Well, that's a great thing to teach your son, sir.'"

At the end of our discussion, Barnett, a genial man, became conciliatory, sort of. He said it got easier for him, that by the end of his career in 1999, he almost came to enjoy the boos, that he felt as if he'd made his mark on the city. Boston was a great sports city, he said, a place "where I always believed they could get thirty thousand people in Kenmore Square to watch two guys shooting marbles." He laughed. "If you really want to have fun, and you want to see what an umpire's life is all about, go into a bar in Boston and tell 'em that you're me. Tell 'em, 'I'm Larry Barnett. I'm here to have a drink.'"

For umpires the most fearsome ghost of World Series past, even more than Barnett's, is that of Don Denkinger, whom St. Louis Cardinal fans still think cost them the 1985 Series when he badly missed a call at first base in the ninth inning of game six.

Like Barnett, Denkinger had a thirty-one-year career, and like Barnett, he was a reliable umpire's umpire, popular with his colleagues, counted upon by baseball's administrators to work in the highest-profile situations. He worked three other World Series, in addition to 1985, and four All-Star games. Denkinger's story has an arc similar to Barnett's: a traumatic event that has to be lived with, excruciating in its immediate aftermath, growing less intense over time, with an uneasy peace in the end. The difference, of course, is that Denkinger actually erred, indisputably and, to many, inexplicably, because as replays showed, the play wasn't all that close.

During spring training in 2006, I met Denkinger, sixty-nine at the time, a burly man with leathery skin, a flattop haircut, and a gravelly voice, at his home in the Arizona desert, and he did, in fact, have an explanation for the miscall. It wasn't an excuse or even a rationalization, but in retrospect he had been able to piece together what he'd done wrong.

As in a good Hollywood baseball story, the crucial play occurred in the bottom of the ninth. It was the sixth game of the 1985 World Series, and the St. Louis Cardinals, who were ahead in games, 3–2, appeared ready to close out their cross-state rivals, the Kansas City Royals. The score was 1–0 when a Kansas City pinch hitter, Jorge Orta, who was leading off, swung at a pitch that was high and off the plate and chopped it toward first.

Orta was speedy, and his hustle forced the Cardinal first baseman, Jack Clark, moving to his right and in, away from the bag, to adjust his throw at the last instant; an underhanded flip wouldn't get there in time. So with a snap of his wrist he slung the ball across his body to the pitcher, Todd Worrell, who had raced over to cover first base.

From his starting position on the line about fifteen feet beyond Clark, Denkinger had floated into foul territory and in toward the bag. By the time the ball arrived, he had gotten within a few feet of the play, but he was still moving. As the ball arrived, he was behind Worrell, almost directly in line with the throw, and his eyes were cast slightly downward—evidently he was watching for the touch of the runner's foot on the bag—but his momentum took him a couple more steps, to the home plate side of first, before he could stop. He gestured twice—Safe! Safe!—pointed at the bag, and gave the sweeping, hands-flat mechanic a third time: Safe!

But Orta was clearly not safe. For his final step he had made a desperate leap toward the bag, and he seemed to hang in the air, as if waiting for the ball to arrive and Worrell to catch it, and he was out by a long half-stride. You couldn't even call it a banger. The Cardinals' volatile manager, Whitey Herzog, and an adamant Worrell argued, but to no avail. Orta stayed where he was. Man on first, none out, instead of one out, none on. The Royals would score two runs, winning the game, tying the Series, and disheartening the Cardinals, who lost the deciding game the next day, 11–0.

"I didn't know I missed it when I called it," Denkinger told me, describing a scenario that was business as usual. "Whitey came out, and he said, 'You missed that call!' and I just said, 'No, I don't think so,' and Worrell's saying, 'My foot was on the bag! My foot was on the bag!' And I said, 'I didn't say your foot wasn't on the bag, I just said he was safe.' I didn't think any more of it. After the game was over, I headed into the umpires' room, and Peter Ueberroth, our commissioner, was standing out in front of it, and it wasn't unusual for him to be there. And so I said to Peter, 'Did I get that play right?' He said, 'I don't think so, Don, I think you missed it.'

"And it's just a terrible, sinking feeling that you get. Peter was the first one I saw that I could trust, you know? And I was devastated. We were supposed to go to some kind of cocktail party afterwards, but when I came out of there, my wife just looked at me and knew damn well we weren't going anywhere but back to the hotel, and we didn't do anything that night. Didn't watch TV. Didn't read the newspapers. And I mean, I was the crew chief; I had the plate the next night. You know? Seventh game. I've got the plate."

So what had happened? I asked Denkinger to take me through the play from his perspective, moment by moment.

"Well, Clark had to come in some to field the ball," he began. "And I don't know if he had trouble getting it out of his glove"—on the taped replay it appears Clark either reaches twice for the ball in his glove or has to readjust his grip on it—"or just because he had to run in, but the play didn't develop like I thought it should have, where you get a ball hit to the first baseman, and he flips it to the pitcher, and you have a footrace to the bag. That was the position I was in—to call that play, because that's what's going to happen ninety to ninety-five percent of the time.

"So I was in foul territory, on the outfield side of first base, and I was getting really close to the bag. And Clark has to throw the ball, and he can't underhand it because it's not going to get there in time, so he throws it, and by that time, I don't have a footrace anymore. Now I have a sound play."

He was referring to a situation that frequently occurs at first base, in which the umpire cannot keep both the base and the ball in his line of vision, so he watches for the runner's foot on the bag and listens for the sound of the ball in the fielder's glove.

"But there isn't any sound," Denkinger said. "Not in the sixth game of the World Series when fifty thousand people are screaming and yelling at the top of their lungs."

It was striking to me that at probably the most notorious moment of umpiring in the history of baseball, the techniques being invoked were those I'd been introduced to, and that I'd practiced, from the beginning of my instruction—reading the angle of the throw, finding the proper position by getting close to a play but not too close, and especially the sound play. Back at school, Jim Evans had demonstrated the usefulness of an umpire's ears by staging a banger at first base and having a student umpire make the call while wearing a blindfold; you had to distinguish between the sound of the runner's foot hitting the bag and the ball hitting the fielder's glove.

It was also striking that all his training and all his experience couldn't inoculate Denkinger against a fateful combination of tiny forces—the AstroTurf in Kansas City, which made Orta's bouncer bounce just a little higher; Clark's double-clutch at the ball in his glove, to name two—that contrived to make him see what wasn't there. I again had the thought that the instantaneous decision-making that defines an umpire's responsibility is the sort of challenge that most of us, in our personal as well as our professional lives, shy away from. And no wonder. Where would most of us be without the assumed prerogative to sleep on it, to think it over, to take a minute and mull the options? Most of us have the luxury of acknowledging and even embracing ambiguity. An umpire doesn't.

"So I just did what I could do," Denkinger said. "I looked up, I saw Worrell catch the ball, looked down, and saw the runner's foot was on the bag, and I called him safe. The amount of time it took me to do that was enough to permit him to be safe. I blame myself for not having good position. I was in too close; I couldn't get everything in my view, and when I realized what was happening, I couldn't get back far enough. Still, I thought I had it right."

Denkinger didn't lose the Series for the Cardinals, of course. Even after the missed call in the ninth inning, the Cardinals screwed things up on their own. Clark misplayed a foul pop-up he should have caught, and the hitter, with a new life, delivered a base hit. The tying and winning runs moved into scoring position as a result of a passed ball. Then the whole team folded up like an umbrella in game seven.

But that didn't stop the blame from settling on the umpire. In the fifth inning of game seven, with the Royals, already ahead 5–0, they poured six more runs across the plate with two outs and the Cardinals lost their cool. A relief pitcher, Joaquin Andujar, angrily threw his hands in the air and shouted in at Denkinger, and Denkinger, thinking to himself, "Shit, we're not going to do this," removed his mask and started for the mound, intending to warn Andujar that one more outburst and he'd be thrown out.

"And I was intercepted by Whitey," Denkinger said, "and I just told him, 'I'm going to shut him up and keep his hands out of the air, or he's gone,' and Whitey says, 'Let me talk to him,' but then he stops and goes,

'But let me tell you one thing. If you had gotten that play right last night, we wouldn't have to be here tonight.' And I said, 'If you guys were hitting better than .122, we wouldn't have to be here tonight, either.'"

The argument didn't cease there, and Herzog was ejected shortly thereafter, but in a measure of how bizarre the circumstances had become, Denkinger agreed to let Herzog proceed to the mound—after the ejection—to calm Andujar down. The calm didn't last.

"So I get back behind the plate, and Joaquin throws another pitch, and it's about that far outside," Denkinger said, holding his hands six or eight inches apart, "and I said, 'Ball three,' and I look out there, and goddammit he's got his hands in the air again, so I said, 'Get your ass out of here. Go with your friend Whitey.' And he comes in from the mound and bumps me, and he's putting on a real show."

Even viewed on videotape from a distance of two decades, Andujar's temper tantrum was extraordinarily acute, fueled by the frustration of looming defeat and the proximity of a man he could blame it on.

"Finally, they bring in Bob Forsch to pitch," Denkinger said. "Now, at this point, Bob Forsch is forty-two years old, I think"—actually he was thirty-five—"and he's a starting pitcher, and it takes him twenty minutes to warm up, and all that time, we're just standing there, and I'm getting beat to hell on national television and there's not a thing I can do about it."

But even then, Denkinger said, he didn't understand what was in store for him. The morning after the game, a Monday, he drove back to his home in Iowa from Kansas City.

"I had some controversy; no big deal," he said. "The game was over, you know? I wasn't thinking any more about it. But I get to the top of the street that I live on, where you have to turn off a fairly busy road, and I turn left and there's a cop car sitting there, closing off the street. And I pulled up and he said, 'You can't come down here,' and I said, 'What do you mean? I live down here.' And he said, 'Oh, Don, there've been a lot of threats that they were going to burn your house down.'"

Two disc jockeys in St. Louis had given out Denkinger's address and phone number, encouraging listeners to harass him.

"I had three daughters who had come to the first half of the Series, and then my mother-in-law had taken them home because they had to get back to school," Denkinger said. "They'd had calls that they were going to burn the house down. They had calls that they were never going to see their father again. It just got real ugly. And then the letters started coming, over two hundred of them."

Finally, the media did Denkinger a good turn. There had been so much uproar over the sixth-game call that *Sports Illustrated* visited him at home in January 1986 and published a long feature on his ordeal, which turned public opinion in his favor and produced another stream of mail, this time largely favorable. When the season resumed, he heard about the famous missed call from vocal fans. "Rain delays were the worst," he said. "All those leather lungs who would come down into the front row with something to say." But that was one guy who ran a construction company in St. Louis continued to write to him with regular, seemingly benign, disparagement.

Then two years later, in 1988, a postcard arrived in the mail saying, "I know what you do. I know where you go. And when I point my .357 Magnum at you, it'll blow you away."

Denkinger called Major League Baseball's security department, which brought in the FBI. They located the postcard writer—it was his persistent correspondent, the builder, who'd apparently been struck by a particularly virulent paroxysm of hatred—and brought his harassment campaign to a close with the suggestion, according to Denkinger, that "one more letter, one more phone call, and we'll be down here to arrest you."

From then on, Denkinger had to face only the memory of his call, which would be easier to do if he weren't reminded of it every time an umpire made an arguable call in the postseason. Just a few months before our conversation, Doug Eddings had had his unfortunate moment in the 2005 American League playoffs, and Denkinger was number one on the speed dial of seemingly every sports reporter in the country.

"The phone started ringing at six a.m.," he said. "By that afternoon it was crazy. I went out and called my wife, and she answered the phone, 'Don Denkinger's secretary!'"

Denkinger called a lot of the reporters back; he also called Eddings, who complained to him about all the attention his single call was getting. I asked Denkinger if he told Eddings that the experience would be character-building for him, and Denkinger laughed.

"I don't think it'll make a lot of difference for him," he said. "Life goes on. I had a pretty good career. I had an excellent career. I made one mistake. And nobody wants to talk to me about anything else. They don't want to talk about all the World Series and all the championships and all the final games I worked in the playoffs."

We did, actually, talk about some of those. Denkinger, like Tim McClelland, seems to have had in him whatever it is that attracts the notorious event. He was behind the plate in the 1978 playoff game between the Red Sox and the Yankees at Fenway Park, the one decided by Bucky Dent's home run.

He was behind the plate again in the final game of the 1991 World Series, the greatest Series ever played, according to a 2003 ranking by ESPN, in which the Minnesota Twins edged the Atlanta Braves. The seventh game, a thrilling pitcher's duel between Minnesota's Jack Morris and the Braves' John Smoltz, went scoreless into extra innings and was finally decided on a one-out single by a journeyman player, Gene Larkin, in the bottom of the tenth.

"It's added pressure, a tight game like that, extra innings, just like working a no-hitter, and of course it's the seventh game of the World Series," Denkinger said.

I asked him if he could talk a little more about what that kind of pressure is like, and he broke into a big smile to tell a story. When Larkin came to the plate, he recalled, the Twins had a man on third, Dan Gladden. The Atlanta manager, Bobby Cox, had gone out to talk to his pitcher—by that time it was a reliever, Alejandro Pena—and had gathered his infielders on the mound as well, to discuss strategy. Eventually they brought the outfield in shallow, guarding against the line drive over the infield that would ordinarily be a hit, but giving up the possibility of catching a long fly ball, since the runner would score on a caught fly ball, anyway.

"So Cox is walking back, and we're just standing there at the plate, and I turned to Gene and I said, 'Hey, Gene, if he keeps bringing all those outfielders in, even you could hit one over their heads.' And he never says a word. Like I wasn't even there. I didn't know what his problem was; I had talked to him before. And then he steps up and hits one over the left fielder's head. And the Series is over and I go home.

"Then you know, every year in the winter, they always bring the winning team into the White House, the Rose Garden, for a ceremony. And I went. And we're in a holding room, and all the Twins are there and their wives, and the umpires and our wives, and I'm standing at one point next to Gene Larkin, and I say to him, 'Do you hear well?' He said, 'Yeah. Why?' I said, 'You didn't hear what I said to you at home plate in the seventh game?' He said, 'I heard exactly what you said. Matter of fact I went home and told my wife.' And he turns to his wife and says, 'Tell Don what he said to me.' And she did, she said, 'If they keep bringing the outfielders in, even you could hit it over their heads.' So I said to him, 'Well, why the hell didn't you say something?' He said, 'I couldn't.' He said, 'I couldn't talk.' He said, 'My mouth was so dry, there was no saliva there, there was nothing I could say.' And I said to him, 'That's pressure.' I said, 'That's what it's all about.'"

Telling the story seemed to put Denkinger in an expansive mood, and he returned to the infamous call from the 1985 Series, adding a chapter he'd not spoken of before.

The latest episode had happened in just the past few months, after the 2005 World Series. Whitey Herzog, who still lived in St. Louis, had invited Denkinger to speak at a charity dinner that would honor the twentieth anniversary of his National League championship team. And Denkinger, maybe surprisingly, did. He was received warmly, he said, by all the attendees at the dinner, including the old Cardinal players. After he'd spoken, Herzog joined him at the microphone and presented him a gift, ostensibly for his appearance at the dinner. Denkinger opened it onstage.

A Braille watch.

My meeting with Denkinger had come about serendipitously, early in my travels. I'd recently finished umpire school, and I'd spent a couple of weeks in Florida, umpiring my first games and arranging and conducting a few haphazard interviews. Then I drove across the country to Phoenix for spring training in Arizona, where I knew I'd find the greatest concentration of umpires in any one place at any one time. I was in the umpires' locker room before a game at Hohokam Stadium, the Chicago Cubs' spring training facility in Mesa, when Denkinger popped in to pay his respects to the crew, and he invited me to his home the next day.

At the time, I thought it was a pretty good interview, not memorable but useful. I had already known a great deal about the 1985 call; what I'd wanted was to hear it all in Denkinger's voice, and he'd obliged me nicely. But like a lot of umpires, he talked about his career and about the profession in a practiced, generalized, and not especially revealing way.

I hadn't yet figured out that this disinclination toward self-scrutiny was a widely shared umpire trait, that all the years of cleanly dividing their perceptions—between balls and strikes, fairs and fouls, safes and outs—leave umpires with a ruling indifference to ambiguity. It isn't that they see everything in black and white. Rather, if something isn't black and white, it doesn't seem to spark their curiosity. They're not probers. They tend to accept seeming contradictions. No need to explain. It is what it is.

By his example, Denkinger was the first to teach me that. But as time went on, he came to seem emblematic to me in many other ways as well. The more umpires I talked to, the more I thought about Denkinger—about his career, about his solid service, about his perseverance and day-to-day excellence which were undermined in a moment by a high hop and a disadvantageous line of sight—the more it seemed to me that Denkinger, really, is the umpire's umpire. His name had come up often, unbidden, probably more than anyone else's, and at the 2007 World Series, he seemed to be almost a palpable presence, acknowledged by the older umpires and the younger ones.

When I asked Ed Montague, who was working his fifth Series, what it was like to get on the field in October—did the thrill of it wane after a while?—he responded, "This is the main event, man. You've got everybody in the world watching, millions and millions of people. Now, when you get out there, you don't think about that, you don't hear the crowds—well, you do, they're pretty loud. But you're just focused on getting everything right, every pitch right, every play right. You just pray that—we call it a gorilla running around the field—you just pray that it doesn't get you and you don't end up like Don."

And when I asked Ted Barrett, in his first Series, a similar question, he sounded similar notes:

"There are all these milestones you have as an umpire. You go from working your first big league game to working tough games in September, and then you work the first round of the playoffs and the second round, and I've had such a foundation that I felt this was just the next step, not a quantum leap. So I've had this calm about me. But I know I can go out to right field tonight and have something bad happen, and it wipes out all I've done. That's the nervous part. And that's kind of why all six umpires, we're kind of all hoping for a sweep. It's not that we don't want to be out there and work, but it's like, 'Let's get out of here before the monkey jumps on our back.' We're all one play away from being Don Denkinger."

The name Denkinger coming out of his mouth spurred a memory for him. Ten years after the infamous call, Barrett worked with Denkinger for the first time.

"I had a play in Seattle, I remember it like it was yesterday," Barrett said. "It was my second year, 1995, and I was still pretty green. We were at the Kingdome, and Rich Amaral was leading off first, and he gets picked off. And B. J. Surhoff, who's playing first, makes a terrible tag; Amaral was safe and I called him out. I knew right there and then that I missed it. And Piniella came out"—Lou Piniella was the manager of the Seattle Mariners then—"and Lou would always wait for the crowd to watch the play on the monitor, wait for their reaction, and now they're all booing, so he knows I missed it. And he's putting on a little bit of a show, and Don came over and got in his way. Anyway, after the game I'm walking off, and I said to him, 'Yeah, that's a bad feeling, knowing you kicked a play,' and Don says, 'Hey, kid, try screwing one up in the World Series.' It hit me right there. The stakes are high out here."

For the World Series umpires, Denkinger's ghost seemed to be hovering nearby even when not being explicitly invoked. In their conversations at the World Series, their sentiments could be described as resigned or wary or even disappointed; some emotion or tone in almost all of them put a governor on the joy they might otherwise be feeling at the pinnacle of their careers.

When I asked Montague, for example, how the game had changed in the time he'd been in the big leagues, he said the main difference was that it was now administered with an eye on the bottom line, that the game on the field had become a mere product, played solely for the benefit of the club owners. For the umpires this meant that they felt more unwelcome in the game, on the field and off, than ever.

"If they could get in our heads, stand in our shoes, maybe things would be different," he said, referring to Commissioner Bud Selig and his two chief assistants, Jimmie Lee Solomon and Bob DuPuy. "But they're not interested. I mean, gee whiz, put us in the World Series yearbook. It's such a small thing, such an easy thing. Give us a little recognition and then forget about us, that's fine. When Peter was in, and

Bart and Fay"—Montague was referring to Ueberroth, Giamatti, and Vincent—"they made us feel like we were part of the baseball family. Now it's like they're mad we're out there."

When I asked Mike Everitt what was the one moment he'd remember from his first World Series, he said it was a conversation he'd had with a fan, just before the first game got under way as he stood along the left-field line in Fenway Park.

"The guy said, 'So how long did it take you to get here?'" Everitt recalled, immediately lost in a story. "And I told him nine years, and he said, 'How many years in the minors?' And I told him I started in A ball in 1987. And he said, 'I bet the best times were in the minor leagues.' And I said to him, 'That couldn't be a more accurate statement, sir.'"

Then Everitt turned to me to explain. "We were making less money, traveling by car, working two-man instead of four-man, and certainly not staying in nice Hyatts like this one. How could that be more fun? Because the pressure wasn't as great. You didn't even know what pressure was. You just knew you had a six-hundred-mile trip that day to go and work another game. But you were driving towards your dream."

Major leagues umpires are driven and aggressive men, goal-oriented and highly competitive, which is why it's so odd—poignant and odd—that they've chosen a profession in which literally they can't win and figuratively they don't, in which not only does disappointment always threaten but triumph is almost always bland. Listening to Everitt, I had to wonder when he'd begun to understand this, when any umpire does, and what does he then make of a professional life where at any time the agony of defeat is, in Ted Barrett's words, just one play away, and where the closest you get to the thrill of victory is getting to the end—of an inning, of a game, even of a career—without ruin.

I umpired my last games in the spring of 2007. For me the joy in umpiring just couldn't make the responsibility worth it. You hold the game in your hands, and even if it's a crummy game, an inconsequential game, you can still gum it up for the players, give them an experience that is less than baseball. Not to be too earnest about this, but that's really what umpires mean when they talk about upholding the integrity of the game, not just making sure that an individual contest is played fairly and by the rules but guarding the game itself—the Game—against diminishment.

It's my belief that this is what big league umpires are doing when they speak about "the right way to play the game" and enforce the rules in ways that seem, well, interpretative. The nature of baseball is elusive enough that the rules themselves are always being tweaked and altered to adjust to new exigencies; there is no better example than the implementation of instant replay. But between the time that a rule ceases to be effective and the time it is changed, the umpires are the ones who must navigate the game through the undelineated straits. This is what happened with the strike zone. In the 1990s, during an era when home runs markedly shifted the balance of the game, the umpires, reading both the trend and the clamor of the teams on the field, gradually, collectively, instinctively—and for the most part, I think, responsibly—temporarily adjusted the definition of a ball and a strike until the administration of the game took notice and made official changes.

The argument of those who wish to bring greater electronic scrutiny to baseball and someday eliminate umpires altogether is that the players shouldn't be penalized and competition shouldn't suffer because of the frailties and inconsistencies of nonparticipants. But I would argue that umpires, ingrained in baseball from its origins, *are* participants, that their judgments—sincere, immediate, and imperfect—are embedded in the game as deeply as any other form of seeming whimsy that defies the players' control. No one screams when a gust of wind blows a pop-up away from a catcher or turns a fly ball into a lucky home run. No one objects when a ground ball hits a pebble and hops over the shortstop's glove. No one objects when a swarm of bugs distracts a pitcher or a hitter. Indeed, you can easily make the case that when baseball has acted to offset unforseeable events like these—with artificial surfaces and indoor stadiums—the results warped the game more than any stroke of weather, sudden entomological gathering, or any groundskeeping oversight.

To my mind, the judgment of umpires belongs in the same category. It's usually predictable, but occasionally not, and when it isn't, the players—and fans—have to adjust. So what? It makes the game more complicated, more suspenseful, more human.

"This umpiring crew has had a rough World Series," Joe Buck, the Fox broadcaster, said on the air during the first inning of game four of the 2008 Series between Philadelphia and Tampa Bay. "And you don't want to say that, you don't want to pick on umpires, but here it is again."

Buck had just watched the replay of a rundown play between third and home; Jimmy Rollins, the Phillies' shortstop, had dived back into third base, and umpire Tim Welke had called him safe. The replay showed, however, that Evan Longoria, the Rays' third baseman, had tagged Rollins on the rear end before his hand reached the bag. Rollins should have been called out. This followed a disputed balk call—actually, Welke had declined to call a balk on the successful pickoff of a Rays' runner—in game one; a missed hit batsman call, by Kerwin Danley, in the ninth inning of game two that cost the Phillies a crucial base runner; and in game three, an incorrect safe call at first base by Tom Hallion that helped the Rays rally for two runs.

Of course, Buck's disclaimer, "you don't want to pick on umpires," was disingenuous; that's precisely what he wished to do. But he could only do it after the electronic replay slowed the play down and isolated a freeze frame of the moment that Longoria's glove nestled against Rollins's ass.

Why is it so easy to forget that before television replays existed, baseball got along just fine without the after-the-fact proof that an umpire was right or wrong? It's worth pointing out that the 2008 World Series was poorly played in general; in particular, if the Rays' pitcher, Andy Sonnanstine, had made the proper throw to second to start a double play instead of attempting to catch Rollins between third and home, Welke's contested call wouldn't have been made at all.

It's also worth pointing out that the more closely you scrutinize any endeavor, the more imperfect you're going to discover it to be. As a journalist I've always strained to get the facts right, and often bolted upright in the middle of the night when the stray thought of a name whose spelling had gone unchecked crossed my nearly asleep mind. But it happens that you err on small things or even not so small things when you're concentrating on bigger ones. That doesn't make the journalistic enterprise worthless (perhaps I should say horseshit). Close examiners of this text will likely find mistakes in it; I hope not more than a few and I hope they don't dismiss the book and the things it gets right because of it. I don't think they should.

In any case, the umpires couldn't possibly screw things up as badly as baseball does routinely. After the four uncertain calls during the 2008 World Series, Mike Port felt compelled to offer a defense of the crew. During the season, he said, the six men—Danley, Hallion, Welke,

Fieldin Culbreth, Jeff Kellogg, and Tim Tschida—had been observed by supervisors a total of 420 games and had missed only seven calls.

"The point being, things find you on the biggest stage," Port said.

Well, that might be the point; it also might be the point that they got nervous and choked. To my mind, though, it shouldn't matter; that calls made with integrity, right or wrong, have always been part of the game. And in any case, the 2008 World Series will not be remembered for umpires' calls but for the commissioner's.

Game five, which turned out to be the finale, began on a Monday night in Philadelphia with the temperature in the low forties and rain threatening. By the second inning it was raining, by the bottom of the third raining hard, and by the bottom of the fourth a steady downpour was drenching the stadium and the wind was so harsh that Jimmy Rollins had to chase a pop fly all over the infield before having it glance off his glove. The conditions were unplayable, but the teams were playing anyway, and when the game passed through the top of the fifth with the hometown Phillies ahead and then became an official game, it looked as though the teams would have to play nine full innings in a near-hurricane. The other option was unpalatable, that the game be called and the World Series possibly decided by a rain-shortened contest. Only a run scored by Tampa Bay in the top of the sixth, evening the score, allowed the game to be safely interrupted, and shortly thereafter suspended—resumed and played to its conclusion two days later.

Throughout the rainstorm, the Fox news cameras frequently found and lingered on the umpires being pelted by the rain, hands on their knees, water beading on their jackets and dripping from the bills of their caps, as if to ask: Why don't they do something? But in fact, though the rulebook gives umpires the authority to bring teams off the field and cover the infield with a tarp, in this case they were being directed by the commissioner, Bud Selig. ("I can tell you from experience," one veteran umpire told me, "that when it starts to rain during the World Series, the commissioner and his guys, they go into panic mode.")

I was watching the game on television, amazed the umpires would let the game continue under circumstances that essentially ruined it as a legitimate contest. The players looked tentative and miserable; base runners were slipping, throws were squirting from fielders' hands. You wondered about the dangers of a pitcher losing his grip on a 95 mph fastball with a batter at the plate squinting through raindrops.

"There's no way that game should have gone as far as it did," one umpire who didn't work the game told me, an opinion echoed by a handful of others (though one said he wasn't sure, that "it always looks worse on TV"). The prevailing opinion was the game should either never have been started, or that it should have been called before the fifth and replayed in its entirety.

In the fourth inning, I called Mike Port, and much to my surprise he picked up the phone.

"Mike, what's going on?" I said. "Why are they letting it go?"

"I don't know," he said. "We're not in the loop. It's all the commissioner."

Later I'd learn that twice, between innings, Selig consulted with umpires about the condition of the field and he was told that it was draining well and the puddling on the infield was bearable. So he let the game proceed. He was thinking of the economic and logistical concerns of postponing, he explained afterward, the complications that would result for the fans and the teams. Chances are he was also thinking of Fox, which stood to lose its highly rated night of programming on Tuesday night if it had to broadcast a make-up game.

In sum, the umpires were prevented from exercising the judgment they're trained to exercise, their authority taken away from them on the ultimate stage. The result was that the World Series was decided by a game begun on a Monday and finished on a Wednesday, begun in one set of weather conditions and concluded in another, begun with the pitchers in one state of rest and readiness and concluded with the pitchers in a different state.

A baseball game warped out of all recognition, but not by the umpires.

The final game of my career—ha!—was an adult-league game in a Long Island suburb. It was a still night with a dim haze hovering above the field. The players were pretty good, especially one of the pitchers, who threw hard with good movement and good enough control to spot the ball in the strike zone now and then. His team was well ahead in the fifth inning and, with a man on first and two out, threatening to score again.

I was behind the plate. When the batter swung and lined the ball toward the left-field corner, I leaped out from behind the catcher and straddled the third-base line and immediately knew I was in trouble. As in many community ball fields, the lights were insufficient. About halfway out to the fence, the ball disappeared in the haze and I lost it completely. I didn't see it land; I didn't see it roll. The last I knew the ball was in the air, well in fair territory, but like a lot of hard-hit balls pulled by right-handed hitters, hooking with a sharp grace toward the line.

I guessed. With a 50 percent chance, I called it fair and got it woefully, haplessly, disastrously wrong. A spectator told me later I'd missed it by about thirty feet, but in any case, I knew right away, from the nature of the argument—the hysterical disbelief of the team in the field, their honest expression that I must be kidding or stupid—that I'd blown it. (A hint for umpires: In such a case, when you really don't know, call it foul. That way, if you're wrong, you've caused less damage.)

I asked my partner if he'd seen it, but he'd been too far away, in the infield, on the right-field side of second base, to help. So I did the only thing I could do. I stuck to my call. I let the players vent their anger longer than I ordinarily would. After a while, I told them: "Okay, okay, I understand you don't like the call. I get the point," which inflamed them further. "It's not that we don't like it; it's that you're wrong," one guy kept saying, trying to force me to admit my mistake.

But the point I was making was that whether I was wrong or not was irrelevant; I'm in charge, I was saying. My only other alternative, of course, would be to change the call, which would have engendered a whole other high-voltage dispute with the other team and, worse, would have made every call from then on a matter of debate. So I put up with the disdain of one side and the quiet delight of the other for the rest of the game. And even though the score ended up 11–1, some of the guys on the losing team made a point of following me to my car to let me know once again what a mess I'd made of their evening of recreation.

That was enough for me. Baseball, I know, needs people who can not only make snap decisions but live with them, something most people will do only when there's no other choice. Come to think of it, the world in general needs people who accept responsibility so easily and so readily. We should be thankful for them.

Afterword

December 2009

Are umpires obsolete?

If you paid attention to big league baseball in 2009, the question had to cross your mind, if only because talk radio hosts, newspaper columnists, play-by-play analysts, and bloggers burned so much verbal gas discussing the shortcomings of the major league umpiring roster. This, actually, wasn't anything new. But in recent years the usual complaints about umpires—that they were haughty and confrontational, that they were too old, too fat or otherwise out of shape, and that baseball lacked a system to hold them accountable for their mistakes—generally flared up only when a few closely spaced calls were exposed as inaccurate by instant replay cameras on national telecasts. With the occasional exception of a player or manager flying off the handle about a plate umpire's strike zone, rarely did anyone assail the umpires on matters of general competence. That is, it has always been pretty much a given that they were getting the great majority of the calls right.

In 2009, however, it was this fundamental assumption that was called into question. And for the first time, it seemed to me, the idea that baseball might be better off without the umpires gained a traction it hadn't had before.

This had to do with the acceptance by fans of the electronic improvements (so-called) introduced to the officiating of other sports, namely tennis and football. It also had to do with the genuine improvements made in television technology and the crisp, superslow-motion, irrefutable video evidence offered on a play-by-play basis, so that you could be sitting on the couch at home with a tub of popcorn on your lap and have a better view than the umpire on the field of a banger at the plate—the second time around, anyway.

Critics seized on a few highly publicized situations that were rebroadcast again and again on ESPN and elsewhere, and the idea that big league umpires are inadequate to their professional task began to take hold. In June, for example, in the seventh inning of a tie game between the Atlanta Braves and the Boston Red Sox at Fenway Park, home plate umpire Bill Hohn appeared to miss a called strike three against the Red Sox J. D. Drew, who singled in the go-ahead run on the next pitch. In the brouhaha that followed, Hohn ejected the Braves' manager Bobby Cox, Braves pitcher Eric O'Flaherty, and Braves third baseman Chipper Jones.

In early July a third-base umpire, Marty Foster, called the Yankees' Derek Jeter out as he slid into third headfirst, though whether the third baseman actually made the tag was in dispute; Jeter argued and, as he told the media afterward, Foster told him the tag was irrelevant, that the ball had beaten him to the bag.

Later that month, a wild game between the Oakland A's and the Minnesota Twins ended at 14–13 when the Twins' Michael Cuddyer attempted to score from second on a wild pitch and was called out by umpire Mike Muchlinski, although Cuddyer had clearly slid across the plate in advance of the tag by the A's pitcher, Michael Wuertz. And in September, again in Fenway Park, the Los Angeles Angels' closer Brian Fuentes appeared to have struck out Red Sox hitter Nick Green twice—once on a swinging strike, once on a called strike—an out that would have ended the game, but Reed ruled first that Green had checked his swing and called the second pitch a ball. Green walked, prolonging an inning in which the Red Sox eventually won the game. As the umpires left the field—in Fenway, they must exit through the visiting team's dugout—the Angels' coaching staff reportedly berated them. Reed later acknowledged that the final pitch to Green "very well could have been a strike." The incident led to published accusations by players that umpires are intimidated by the home crowd at Fenway and that late-game calls there routinely go against the visiting teams.

In the aftermath of these and other events, the tenor of the complaining about umpires went from generic—"Umpires stink!"—to specific: "*These* umpires stink!" All season long, for example, Mike

Francesa, the influential talk show host on WFAN in New York City, argued that this group of big league umpires was the worst he could recall; indeed, he made discrediting the current crop of umpires a personal cause, a persistently bloviated disdain not unlike that of Lou Dobbs on the subject of illegal immigrants. Mike Vaccaro, a columnist for the *New York Post*, summed up the opinion of many in the press box when he wrote in October, under the headline "Ump to No Good": "Now, baseball faces a conundrum because, let's be very honest about this, while just about everything attached to the sport—from the players themselves to the equipment used to the high-definition broadcasts—is far better, and far more sophisticated than ever, there is one aspect of the game that has gotten worse over the years. And that's the umpiring."

Francesa, Vaccaro, and the many other umpire critics may have intuitively picked up on something that was statistically true. According to Major League Baseball, which has umpire observers at about half of all games, the umps had a down year; the rate of incorrect calls in observed games was about 20 percent higher in 2009 than it was in 2008. But it's also true that the official roster of sixty-eight big league umpires was almost exactly the same as it had been the previous year. Only one umpire, Larry Poncino, retired after 2008, and he was replaced by a highly experienced Triple A umpire, Chris Guccione, who as a fill-in over the past several years had logged more than one thousand major league games. So did the umpires suddenly get collectively worse? Did the game suddenly get faster and more complex, beyond the skills of experienced men? Or maybe the better theory is that a few guys just had an off year, bringing down the average.

One possible reason for the statistical downturn is injuries. The major league umpire roster is a skeleton crew; that is, the fifteen major league games that are played most days between April and September require sixty umpires. But because umpires are entitled, by their union contract, to four weeks vacation per week during the season—272 weeks total—that means about ten umpires per week are on vacation, which means that on any given week the major league roster is at least two umpires short of the number necessary to officiate every game.

Any injury, illness, or family emergency affecting a working umpire adds to the absentee rate. And in 2009 many veteran umpires got hurt. Ed Montague, John Hirschbeck, Jerry Crawford, Kerwin Danley, Tim Welke, Rick Reed, and Ed Hickox all had extended absences, and at one point ten of seventeen crew chiefs were not on the field. Alfonso Marquez missed the entire season with a back injury, perhaps because the previous year he led major league umpires in number of pitches seen behind the plate; that is, he had to squat more than eleven thousand times.

So minor league fill-in umpires (like Mike Muchlinski) were more prevalent than usual on big league diamonds in 2009. But even so, that's a shaky explanation for a bad year in umpiring. Most Triple A umpires have six, eight, or even ten years of experience in professional ball; most of them know the major league players because the players were once in the minor leagues themselves. Players and umpires grow up together. They get separated after Triple A because a talented player is irresistible to major league teams, but an umpire hits the ceiling and can only ascend to the big leagues if there's a retirement. They can make the calls, in other words. By general consensus in baseball, what separates Triple A umpires from big leaguers is not positioning or judgment, but big league experience and what comes with it—the confidence, the emotional wherewithal, the guts to run a ball game at the highest and most highly scrutinized professional level. It isn't that fill-in umpires make more mistakes than the regulars—they don't run the games as crisply.

Anyway, this all became irrelevant in the postseason, when a rash of embarrassing errors in the opening rounds of the playoffs by veteran umpires created more outrage about baseball officiating than at any time in more than a decade. Actually, the gaffes began the day after the season ended, in the one-game playoff for the American League Central division title between the Detroit Tigers and the Minnesota Twins. With the bases loaded in the twelfth inning of a thrilling game that was eventually won by the Twins, Brandon Inge of the Tigers had his jersey snicked by a pitch and should rightfully have been given first base, forcing in a run. But home plate umpire Randy Marsh ruled the ball didn't hit Inge or his jersey and kept Inge, who subsequently grounded into a force play, at the plate.

From then on, the missed calls came almost daily. In game one of the American League Division Series between the Red Sox and the Angels,

C. B. Bucknor missed two calls at first base, ruling on one that as Kevin Youkilis, the first baseman, made a sweep tag, his glove missed the batter-runner, Howie Kendrick; as replays showed, Bucknor was wrong. A few innings later, on another ball hit by Kendrick, Bucknor ruled that Youkilis didn't touch first base in time for the out; once again, replay caught Bucknor in an error.

In game two of the ALDS, between the Yankees and the Minnesota Twins, a ninth inning drive down the left field line that bounced into the stands for a seeming ground rule double by the Twins' Joe Mauer was called foul by the left field line umpire Phil Cuzzi. Cuzzi was in perfect position to make the call. Replays showed he was straddling the line and focused on the landing of the ball, but he inexplicably missed it; the ball was fair by several inches.

In game three of the National League Divisional Series between the Philadelphia Phillies and the Colorado Rockies, Chase Utley of the Phils continued running to first after he fouled a ball off his leg, and neither the home plate umpire, Jerry Meals, nor any other umpire, spotted the foul ball and Utley was safe. The play moved a runner to third with one out, allowing the subsequent hitter, Ryan Howard, to drive in the winning run with a sacrifice fly. (There was also a question about Ron Kulpa's call at first; the throw was wide and pulled the Rockies' first baseman, Todd Helton, off the bag. Kulpa called Utley safe, but many felt that replay indicated Helton had managed to keep his foot on the bag long enough. For the record, even after viewing the replay, I sided with Kulpa.)

Perhaps the most egregious errors occurred in game four of the American League Championship Series between the Yankees and the Angels. First, in the fourth inning Nick Swisher of the Yankees was picked off second by the Angels' pitcher Scott Kazmir, but Dale Scott, the second base umpire, called him safe. A few moments later, Swisher tagged up and scored on a sacrifice fly to center, but the Angels appealed the play, saying Swisher left third too soon, and their appeal was upheld by third base umpire Tim McClelland. Replays clearly indicated, however, that Swisher had waited until center fielder Torii Hunter caught the fly ball before he set sail for home.

The following inning was even more bizarre, especially for McClelland. A peculiar rundown play ended up with two Yankees, Jorge Posada and Robinson Cano, in the vicinity of third base, but neither standing on it. The Angels' catcher, Mike Napoli, tagged them both, but McClelland astonishingly ruled only Posada out. Fortunately for McClelland, the Yankees won the game in a rout, 10–1, but in a postgame press conference, he appeared stricken. He said he thought Cano had been standing on the base and that he was sure, until he saw the replay after the game, that he was right about Swisher. Initially, I suspected that McClelland had upheld the Angels' appeal on Swisher as a sly correction of Dale Scott's call at second; after all, Swisher shouldn't have been at third base to begin with. But watching him bravely facing reporters after the game, I knew otherwise.

"In my heart," he said, he thought Swisher left too early. The comment was much ridiculed—"Next time use your eyes," Mike Francesa said—though he was only using traditional umpire argot, echoing the great umpire Bill Klem who once declared, pointing to his heart, "I never missed one here."

There were other errors as well, and by the time the World Series began, the umpires' poor performance had become nationally attention getting. Buster Olney, the ESPN analyst, called for the immediate expansion of the major leagues' use of instant replay to officiate games. ABC included a segment about the umpires on its evening network news telecast, *World News Tonight*. *USA Today* published a front page feature under the headline: "Do Umpires Need Help?" Bucknor and Cuzzi, each in line to work their first World Series, were denied the assignment by Major League Baseball, evidently responding to the pressure. This was a painful decision for baseball; not only was it embarrassing on the face of it, but without Bucknor, who was born in Jamaica, the World Series crew was entirely white, something baseball has sought to avoid in recent years.

The mistakes were especially problematic for umpires because they were especially galling for fans. They were judgment calls, yes, but such terrible judgments! Cuzzi's gaffe and McClelland's two, in particular, were so egregious that many fans rightfully felt that anyone could have done a better job on those calls than the guys who made them. They were, in fact, inexplicable. Cuzzi seemed to be looking right at the ball as it landed. And McClelland, who is one of the most respected umpires in the game, was lazily out of position on the appeal play; he was standing too close to third base. You learn in umpire school to back away from the bag on a possible tag-up and align yourself with the bag and the fielder, so you can embrace both the base runner's foot and the fielder's glove in your line of vision.

The missed tag play was even more baffling. Umpires will tell you they are more likely to err when the players screw up, and it's certainly true that Posada and Cano were guilty of doofus-like baserunning when neither of them chose to stand on third base and essentially waited to be tagged. So it's possible that McClelland allowed himself to think that Cano was on the bag because any attentive player would have been on it. But, jeez, open your eyes! In umpire lingo, the term for such an obvious mistake is "brain cramp."

It was also crucial that the errors were easily correctable. Reversing the calls, if such a thing were allowed, would have been simple. Place Mauer on second. Allow Swisher to score. Call Cano out. Easy. No guesswork. No disruption of the flow of the game. And thus were the arguments for the expansion of instant replay as an officiating tool ignited.

In August 2008, spurred by a rash of missed calls involving drives to the outfield wall or over the foul pole, baseball instituted the umpires' use of instant replay on a very limited basis. The umps were allowed to view replays to decide "boundary" calls, that is, batted balls that might be home runs or might not be—because they hit below the marked home run line on the outfield wall; or passed over the fence to the foul side of the foul pole; or were interfered with by fans while still on the field of play.

In some respects this was long overdue, and much to my surprise, umpires welcomed it. They had been saying for years that these were their most difficult calls, largely because they had to be made from such a long distance away, but also because in recent years many new ballparks had been built with wildly asymmetrical outfields, nooks and crannies in the fences, eccentric ground rules governing home runs, and seating for fans along the walls that made it easy for them to reach into the playing field with batted balls. Electronic scoreboards would then routinely replay the ball, leaving everyone in the ballpark with a better idea of what happened on the play than the men who were supposed to call it.

The same inequity is behind the logic to implement replay on an array of other calls—like the ones that were missed in the playoffs. Television now provides nearly everybody in the universe—including managers and players, who watch replays on clubhouse sets—with a second (and third and fourth) look at any close play on the field, leaving the umpires out of the loop and, all too often after a mistaken call, wallowing in the ignominy of a television close-up, the clucking disapproval of broadcasters like Tim McCarver and Joe Buck, and the boos and catcalls of fifty thousand stadium fans. Why not rescue them and restore the accuracy of the calls all at once?

A number of methods have been suggested to accomplish this. A replay official could be posted in the broadcast booth and assigned to review each questionable play—or perhaps each play of a certain type, like bangers on the bases. When he spotted a missed call, he would communicate with the home plate umpire, or maybe the crew chief, through an earpiece, and the call could be instantaneously reversed.

Or else each manager would be allowed a specified number of challenges to umpires' calls per game, say two or three. (Perhaps they could even be supplied with those cute little red beanbags that NFL coaches toss out on the field.) A challenge would be signaled by the crew chief to the broadcast booth, where the play would be readjudicated by the fifth umpire.

Bud Selig, the baseball commissioner, has opposed the expansion of instant replay thus far on the grounds that he doesn't want to prolong games that have already grown too long for his liking and that he doesn't want the so-called flow of the game to be disturbed. As many people have pointed out, this reasoning is hooey; such solutions as the ones described above aren't exactly complicated, and they would certainly be no more time-consuming than the arguments over calls that routinely take place now and would ostensibly no longer arise.

I don't much care for Selig or the way he runs the game; under his supervision, Major League Baseball, with the players, the owners, and their television partners making obscene amounts of money and milking the fans at every ballpark in the country, has become as loathsome a business enterprise as Goldman Sachs. But in this case, I think Selig's reticence is appropriate, even if his reasons for it are dopey. (Of course, this is being written in November, just after the conclusion of the World Series, and by the time it is published, he may have changed his mind altogether.)

What Selig may not be able to explain but may feel in his bones—or maybe, like an umpire, in his heart—is that each incursion into the umpires' authority is a substantial alteration in the fundaments of the game. It's worth remembering that umpires have been part of baseball as long as there has been baseball, and that they are woven into the very structure of the game. Over the past 134 years, since the inauguration of the National League, umpires have been on the field for every professional contest, hundreds of thousands of games in the majors and the minors, and I'd venture to say there have been two or three missed calls in every one of them. The idea that this is suddenly a problem, that the system is flawed or broken, strains logic.

Of course, the problem is not the umpiring system, or the current crop of major league umpires. The problem is that technology has now let fans, in the ballpark and at home, in on what the people on the field already knew: that the umpires' calls are essentially approximations of actual results. It's almost always the case that the approximations are precise enough to satisfy the players, to keep the players persuaded that the game is being decided by their own skills and their own actions. Even when they feel gypped or unjustly penalized, the players will usually tell you that a bad call doesn't decide the game, that it's just another obstacle that has to be overcome on the way to victory.

The fans, the broadcasters, and the media have not been so easily convinced. Their argument for expanding instant replay, usually made with exasperated indignation at what seems a silly, terrible, and unnecessary injustice, is that if a missed call can be made correct, it might as well be made correct. Why live with an inaccuracy if we don't have to?

There are a number of good answers to that. One is that if the idea is to eliminate bad calls, then an expansion of replay, no matter how it is deployed, is only a partial solution. Some inaccurate calls will still be left to stand and others will be reversible, only at the cost of more guesswork; let's say, for example, that with two men on, the batter laces one down the right field line, the ball lands just fair and bounds into the corner, but the umpire calls it foul. The runners return to their bases and the batter to the plate. When the call is challenged and reversed, where do you put the runners?

Okay, so you make certain types of calls challengeable and others not, the way it is in football: that reduces the number of mistakes, perhaps, but at the cost of an electronic invasion on the favorite pastime of Luddites, a weird technocratic interference in the least technocratic of sports. Baseball doesn't even have a clock, for crying out loud. Besides, the elimination of some errors by umpires would inevitably create a next level of expectation. The mistakes that remain would eventually cry out for correction.

This slippery slope is real. I have no doubt—do you?—that technology alone can umpire a ball game, if not already then certainly with a little dedicated work. Tennis has shown us that the foul lines can be electronically monitored to adjudicate fair and foul calls. A few critically placed sensors—on the base bags, in the players' shoes and gloves—could eliminate the uncertainty over bangers on the bases. Even balls and strikes can be called by a machine; the people who made the machines that tracked pitches for the World Series broadcasts on Fox say their calls are accurate to within half an inch—interesting, if true—which is better than the umpires would claim for themselves.

Those who argue for the expansion of replay often say they don't want to rid the game of umpires, that they don't want machines calling balls and strikes; still, they are essentially urging that we nudge umpires off the field one responsibility at a time. And I wonder if it ever occurs to them what baseball loses by the active, enforced minimization of such a crucial element of the game. The skill of the umpires is certainly worth preserving, even if most fans don't understand it. The game the umpires play within the game—to be in optimal position play after play; to keep the game rolling at its briskest possible pace; to keep hostilities to a minimum, and to walk off the field without the monkey on their backs—is a drama all its own. It's not as interesting as the main story line of competing opponents, but like a good subplot, it deepens that primary drama; the main story would be less interesting without it.

Why would any fan—perhaps I should say any thoughtful fan—forego the pleasures of watching the relationship between the players and the umpires, the managers and the umpires? The yapping from the dugout and the umpires' struggle to maintain equanimity; the negotiation among the pitcher, the catcher, the hitters, and the umpire over the precise dimensions of the strike zone; the plate umpire's decision to grant or not to grant time-out when a hitter asks for one; the umpires' exhortations of a dawdling pitcher to step up his pace; the umpire's attempt to read the mind of a pitcher who has just thrown a beanball to determine if it was intentional; and, of course, the nose-to-nose, spit-flying, finger-poking, cap-brim-beaking screamfests that entertainingly break out on a field when the authority of the umpires and the competitive nature of the athletes combust: these are deep-seated elements of baseball, psychologically fascinating and dramatically complex.

Neither I—nor, happily, Bud Selig—wants to shave away these aspects of the game. And even if you're a dunderheaded-enough fan not to care about such things, do you really want to do without the pleasure of screaming at the umpire yourself? Each time you take away the power of an umpire to make and uphold a decision, you give yourself less of a reason to treat him as a scapegoat. Yes, I've gotten to know the umpires, and I like a lot of them, but as a Yankee fan it still makes me nuts when the guy behind the plate starts squeezing Andy Pettitte. Jeez, who wants to go to a ball game and pat the umpires on the head?

The idea that instant replay or some electronic improvement is necessary is an outgrowth of the attitude that umpires are baseball's necessary evil, that they're only on the field because no other adequate system for running a ball game has come along. It's the same attitude that holds that umpires are baseball appendages, attachments, not part of the main body of the sport, and the same attitude that holds that being an umpire is about as much of a craft as being a toll booth operator.

What I'm proposing is an attitude adjustment. Let's assume, for the moment, that umpires are integral to the structure of baseball, which, in fact, they have been for a century and a half. Let's assume they are not an evil but a positive good, that they not only do a pretty good job under adverse conditions but that they add something immeasurable to the game. Let's assume that they are not a problem to be solved but an asset to be maximized. Let's assume Major League Baseball didn't feel ashamed of the umpires but proud of them, and that the umpires were worth their support. What would that be like?

One thing that would happen, as former commissioner Fay Vincent suggested in an op-ed piece in the *New York Times* during the playoffs, is that Major League Baseball would invest in umpire development. They'd recruit talented umpires from high school and college leagues; they'd coordinate with the private academies that handle introductory umpire training now and create a unified program; they'd work with the minor leagues to oversee umpire development in Single A and Double A ball, and they would make this introductory period of professional life less arduous by increasing the compensation and improving the benefits and perquisites of young umpires.

On the big league level, the idea that umpires' responsibilities should be handed off to machines who can handle them better would be replaced with the idea that it's worthwhile to have human beings upholding the integrity of the game on the field. Rather than implementing methods to limit the scope of umpires' performance, baseball would implement strategies to improve their performance.

One of those strategies should be the establishment of a system of competition and accountability among umpires. The image and reputation of umpires is indisputably damaged when veterans like McClelland and Marsh screw up so glaringly in the public eye, and the disdain for them is only enhanced because to the average fan (and the average sportswriter) there don't seem to be serious repercussions for poor umpire performance. Marvelous television technology and not so marvelous umpiring have created a public relations disaster for baseball. *Something* should be done, no?

But if technology can monitor the umpires for the purpose of reversing their calls, it can certainly monitor them in order to measure the quality of their work. That is, why not use instant replay to observe every umpire call electronically, and then keep records of each umpire's accuracy and make the results public?

Umpires won't like this; they'll say it is one more thing that holds them up for ridicule. But to rank umpires statistically according to a number of categories—say, overall percentage of correct calls, percentage of force plays called correctly, percentage of tag plays called correctly, number of balks called, number of ejections—would be to treat them exactly the way the players are treated and make them answerable on the playing field for their successes and failures. Let the announcers point out that Tim McClelland had a down year in tag plays or that Phil Cuzzi missed more than his share of fair/foul calls; let the fans read in the newspaper that, say, Tom Hallion has the lowest overall percentage of accurate calls among big league umpires so far this season. Let the umps hear about this from the stands during the games the same way A-Rod hears about it every time he whiffs with a runner on third.

Like the players, who are benched or sent to the minor leagues for continued lackluster performance, umpires should be held accountable in a more consequential way as well. This is a long-standing issue in umpire-dom; the lifetime tenure (more or less) that big league umpires enjoy is a reward for their endurance of the rigors of minor league life, but it undoubtedly creates resentments. The players resent it because they think umpires are unmotivated to keep their skills sharp. The owners resent it because it means most umpires are long-serving and thus on a pay scale that rewards seniority. The minor league umpires resent it because it makes it almost impossible for them to reach their professional goals. And the fans resent it because they see the same umpires on the field year after year with no assurance that they are the best the game has to offer.

It's a no-brainer that adjusting the current system, with its close-to-permanent umpiring roster, would solve a lot of problems. But rejigger-ing the rules for promoting umpires to the big leagues and reconfiguring the major league umpire roster are things neither the umpires' union nor the major league owners would likely agree to.* But here's how it could work.

First, increase the number of major league umpires by twelve, to a total of eighty, with the additional dozen unassigned to a crew but des-ignated as fill-ins for umpires who are injured or on vacation. In other words, take a dozen of the minor league umpires who are currently working as fill-ins and grant them status as major leaguers, increasing their pay and benefits. Much of the time they will be working in the big leagues, but when their services are not called for, they would be assigned to Triple A games.

Second, use the statistical information described above to rank umpires' performances, and at regular intervals—each year, perhaps, or

*One underreported fact during the playoffs was that at the time, negotiations were taking place for a new five-year contract between Major League Baseball and the umpires' union, the World Umpires Association. The previous collective bargain-ing agreement expired on December 31, but as this epilogue was being written, in mid-November, the talks were still going on and very little information about them was available. One person with knowledge of the talks—he would speak only with-out attribution—said some modification on the tenure issue had been discussed (I assume, without confirmation, that it was a length-of-service cap) but that no major change was expected.

twice a year—reassign the twelve lowest-ranking umpires to fill-in status and reconfigure the umpiring crews accordingly. Provisions could be added to further penalize poor-performing umpires, even dismissing them if, say, they remained in the bottom twelve for three consecutive seasons.

Now, umpires will tell you that there is more to the job than simply getting the calls right, that experience counts in important ways—in things like keeping brushback wars from exploding into brawls, for example—and that you can't measure authority and the ability to run a game with statistics. This is true, and it might be perfectly appropriate for baseball's umpiring office to mitigate the numbers in some cases to account for an individual's intangible qualities. But once again, the players are a model here. Jason Varitek may be a clubhouse leader for the Red Sox, and a first-rate field general behind the plate, but he's going to lose the starting catcher's job to Victor Martinez in 2010 because he's hit over .250 only once in the past four seasons.

Such a system would open up more opportunities for younger umpires to join the major league fold. (Some of these jobs would go to minority umpires, addressing another issue that baseball, rightly, has on its agenda.) It would create motivation for senior umpires to stay in shape and keep their skills polished, and establish the kind of competition among umpires that belongs at the top level of professional sports. It would assure fans that baseball is working to reduce the number of missed calls by assuring that the hottest umpires—that is, those having the best seasons—are the ones on the field. And as a result, it would, I believe, reduce the number of missed calls without intruding on the game with artificial intelligence and without undermining the colorful and valuable tradition that the umpires represent.

In the many discussions I've had about instant replay with those who are in favor of expanding its use, one thing I hear frequently is that the umpires are in favor of it, that they don't relish standing out on the field being lambasted for missing a call that everyone else in the world has had the chance to see from four or five different angles in slow motion. That argument is irrelevant. The umpires' job is to make the calls; they should do their job. I prefer to cite the players, most of whom aren't in favor of expanded instant replay because they like the game the way it is, with the umpires' best judgments being just one of many factors that affect the game—the weather is another one, so is the amount of foul territory in a given ballpark—that the players have no control over. Listen to Torii Hunter, the splendid Angels' center-fielder who is one of baseball's most thoughtful players:

"This is the way it's been forever," Hunter told ABC News during the umpire-error-plagued playoffs. "Why would we change it? Human error is good sometimes. Trust me."

ACKNOWLEDGMENTS

The entire 2006 staff of the Jim Evans Academy of Professional Umpiring deserves my thanks for putting up with a journalistic intrusion on their professional lives. Of the roster—Chris Bakke, Lance Barrett, Craig Barron, Tyler Bolick, Fran Burke, Tom Clarke, Tim Daub, Shaun Francis, John Gelatt, Takashi Hirabayashi, Chris Hubler, Darren Hyman, Jason Klein, Clint Lawson, Mark Lollo, Mark Mauro, Roberto Medina, Dick Nelson, Masaki Nonaka, Brent Persinger, Brad Purdom, D. J. Reyburn, Andy Russell, Aaron Stewart, and Garrett Wilson—some are still umpiring in the minor leagues, but most aren't. They were all unfailingly helpful, however, even when they were yelling at me.

To the many umpires and baseball officials who shared their stories and opinions with me, I extend my thanks and the hope they recognize themselves in the text. Several umpires, former and current, in the major leagues and the minor leagues, who spent time with me but are not mentioned on the previous pages, should know that their contributions were substantial and necessary and that I'm grateful to them: Ramon Armendariz, Brett Cavins, Marvin Hudson, Cris Jones, Jerry Layne, Jim Reynolds, and Rich Rieker.

Mike Port, Major League Baseball's vice president in charge of umpiring; Tom Leppard, director of umpire administration; and Cathy Davis, senior coordinator, handled many, many requests from me with patience and frequent, if not complete, accommodation.

Away from baseball, I had ample assistance as well. Dan Prosterman, an able young scholar, provided valuable historical research. My editor, Colin Harrison, was a reliable source of advice, tempered enthusiasm, and lunch. Oh, yeah, he also made some good suggestions about the manuscript I turned in. His assistant, Jessica Manners, handled the necessary business of being a pest on matters of book production in such a pleasant and professional way that I barely minded. An anonymous but impressively diligent copy editor launched a ferocious assault on my penchant for passive verb constructions; he or she reduced the number of awkward sentences herein by a significant percentage. My agent, Amanda Urban, a master prodder, not to mention an unflinching truth-teller, knew uncannily when to bug me and when to leave me alone.

Several friends—Rick Woodward, Chris Calhoun, Amy Handelsman, Allen Steinberg, Avery Corman, and the late, alas, Walter Clark—read portions of the manuscript, offering astute (and sometimes even helpful) observations. My old pals Bill Joseph, Glenn Shambroom, and Bob Ball deserve thanks as well for no other reason than that they're my old pals.

I'm grateful to my employers at the *New York Times*, who agreed to hold a job open for me while I worked on the book, and then held to the bargain after I extended my absence beyond what I'd anticipated. And credit (or blame) goes to Jane Karr, the editor who sent me to umpire school in the first place, unwittingly setting in motion the whole business.

I'd also like to remember Lisa del Casale, who did a stranger a good turn; and (sigh) Coco, who kept the keyboard warm.

Thank you, Roie. You were there through it all.

And I'd be especially remiss if I didn't thank Steve Jones and the Knickerbocker Bar and Grill, where comradeship and solace were never in short supply.